D1239210

Praise for *Not for Turning*

"[A] lively and accessible insider's account." —*Financial Times* (UK)

"It is refreshing . . . Harris is like a long-faithful courtier freed by a monarch's death to speak the truth about them."
—*The Guardian* (UK)

"No-holds-barred, well-written . . . contains the most authoritative account of her life after leaving office . . . a dramatic account."
—*The Times* (London)

"Readable and well-informed . . . detailed and fascinating."
—*The Spectator* (UK)

"A pacy and entertaining book . . . well-sourced and packed with anecdotes. A first-rate potted history." —*Express* (UK)

"[Harris is] shrewd and sympathetic enough to do full justice to [Thatcher] as a politician and as a person." —*Standpoint* (UK)

"Insightful and very readable. Its strength lies in its personal approach." —*Catholic Herald* (UK)

"Irresistible reading . . . the brilliance of Harris's gift for narrative has not deserted him." —*The Times Literary Supplement* (UK)

NOT FOR TURNING

The Life of Margaret Thatcher

Robin Harris

Thomas Dunne Books
St. Martin's Press
New York

THOMAS DUNNE BOOKS.
An imprint of St. Martin's Press.

www.thomasdunnebooks.com
www.stmartins.com

Library of Congress Cataloging-in-Publication Data

Harris, Robin, 1952–
    Not for turning : the life of Margaret Thatcher / Robin Harris.—1st U.S. edition.
       p. cm
    "First published in Great Britain by Bantam Press, an imprint of Transworld
    Publishers"—T.p. verso
    Includes bibliographical references and index.
    ISBN 978-1-250-04715-1 (hardcover)
    ISBN 978-1-4668-4751-4 (e-book)
1. Thatcher, Margaret. 2. Prime ministers—Great Britain—Biography. 3. Great Britain—
Politics and government—1979–1997. 4. Conservative Party (Great Britain)—Biography.
5. Women prime ministers—Great Britain—Biography. I. Title.
    DA591.T47H395 2013
    941.085'8092—dc23
    [B]

                                                                    2013023171

First published in Great Britain by Bantam Press, an imprint of Transworld Publishers

First U.S. Edition: September 2013

10   9   8   7   6   5   4   3   2   1

CONTENTS

CONTENTS

ACKNOWLEDGEMENTS

Many people have contributed to this book over the years, some eagerly, others unwittingly, a few anonymously. It involves much of my life as well as Margaret Thatcher's, and it should be stressed that the judgements are, therefore, in more than the merely conventional sense, uniquely mine. I wish, however, to express my special gratitude for their assistance to Andrew Dunlop, Sir Bernard Ingham, Professor Tim Congdon, Cynthia Crawford, Rupert Darwall, Lord Forsyth of Drumlean, Lord Lamont of Lerwick, Lord Powell of Bayswater, Professor Patrick Minford, Patrick Rock, Peter Schaad, Julian Seymour, Sir Stephen Sherbourne, Lord Wakeham of Maldon and John Whittingdale MP. Mark Worthington, director of Lady Thatcher's office, was immensely helpful, not least in reading and correcting several chapters. Like everyone writing on this subject, I am also indebted to the Margaret Thatcher Foundation, which has made accessible so much of the Churchill College Thatcher archive on-line and on CD-ROM. (Naturally, I saw the bulk of this material earlier when assisting Lady Thatcher with her memoirs, but recollections need refreshing.) Finally, I thank Eddie Bell, my agent, for his consistent encouragement, and Doug Young and his team at Transworld, for their expert advice.

NOT FOR TURNING

PREFACE

A number of biographies of Margaret Thatcher appeared during her lifetime. A further, 'authorized', two-volume work is expected. So why another? Any new account of Margaret Thatcher's life must seek to fulfil one or more of three possible objectives. It might, of course, seek, by scouring sources for more material at home and abroad and contacting even more of the remaining actors or confidants than have so far spoken, to provide a still fuller treatment. The present book, although it contains new insights and makes use of some new material, does not, by and large, seek to do that. Alternatively, a fresh biography could concentrate on the significance of the subject's life, judged in the light of events unknown at an earlier stage. Then again, such a study might seek to give a personally informed view – an inside story, as it were – of the person and her intentions: one which, for reasons of delicacy and discretion, would have been inappropriate during the subject's own lifetime. The present book does try to achieve these last two objectives. Indeed, my purpose throughout has been simple. It has been to describe what Margaret Thatcher was like, to explain what she was trying to do and why, and to assess the consequences.

I understood and agreed with Mrs Thatcher's aims from the time she became Tory leader. It was why I joined the staff of the Conservative Research Department in March 1978 and stayed in various political capacities as part of her team until her downfall, which I was happy to make mine too, in November 1990. From the early 1980s I was a political adviser, first in the Treasury and then in the Home Office. From the mid-1980s, when (overriding some opposition) she appointed me Director of the Research Department, I got to know Mrs Thatcher not only as a politician but also as a person, largely through writing speeches for her. In the last two years of her premiership we became close: she trusted me. After she left office, and during times when she experienced great frustration and some depression, punctuated by the occasional triumph and accompanied by the exertion of influence for good on more occasions than her critics would concede, we became friends, at least in so far as giants and pygmies can amicably associate. That, and the fact that I was closely involved in the writing of her memoirs, was why I was not appointed her official biographer, a decision for which I am now grateful. To give an exhaustive account of all that she said and did would be an oppressive task. And I could not pretend to make my account a fully detached one. As it is, I can tell her story in my own way, stressing what I think is essential while trying to clear up misunderstandings. This I have done. I have not, however, felt it necessary to strive for what would conventionally be regarded as 'balance'. I have tried to be objective. But I have not felt compelled to give equal weight to arguably equal things. Similarly, there is proportionately greater consideration of the later than the earlier period – partly because I was more closely involved in those later years, and partly because there is more that is fresh to say.

Margaret Thatcher knew that I was going to write this book and she welcomed it, as the following letter she sent me shows:

22nd November 2005

Dear Robin,

Thank you for your letter informing me of your plans to write a book about my life and all that we achieved during those exciting years at Number 10. The news was neither unexpected nor is it unwelcome.

I can think of no one better placed than you to tackle the subject. Your advice and assistance with my own memoirs was invaluable. Over the years, both during my time as Prime Minister and since, you played an important role in shaping not only my own thinking but that of the Conservative Party. As a key figure in Central Office during the 1980s you knew the struggles we endured in turning our beliefs into policy, often in the face of severe opposition. And because we have spoken about it so often, you also know, better than anyone else, what I wanted our reforms to achieve for the people of Britain.

I know that you will be your normal honest and frank self but I also know that you will understand and sympathise with the policy decisions which had to be made in the 1980s if the economy, and indeed the country, were to be saved from the terminal decline into which they had fallen.

I am sure that your book will make fascinating and challenging reading – I only regret that I will not have the chance to read it myself!

Yours ever
Margaret T.

Dr Robin Harris

Yet she would not have liked everything here. Some parts would have provoked annoyance, though I believe she would have conceded that the comment was fair. It is, anyway, as near the truth as I can offer, and it is the truth that ultimately matters. If she had overcome her exasperation at some judgements – I can almost hear her exclaiming 'No!', 'Oh no!', 'You can't say that!' – I like to think that she would have recognized the portrait and even accepted the analysis. It redounds, after all, to her credit. If this is, as I hope, the reality, warts and all, the reader will discern remarkably few warts. Though it is difficult to convey to those who knew only her public image, and though she was a cruel and dangerous enemy, Margaret Thatcher was both very lovable and greatly loved. Much more important, however, is that she was the only great British Prime Minister of modern times, and looks likely to retain the distinction for some while yet.

NOT FOR TURNING

1

THE IMPACT OF GRANTHAM

More perhaps than any other British Prime Minister, Margaret Thatcher was made what she was by her upbringing; and she knew it.[1] She never forgot her origins or early life; even the oldest scars remained painfully sensitive. Television viewers were astonished in 1985 to witness the strongest Prime Minister of modern times burst into tears on recalling the day in 1952 when her father, Alderman Alfred Roberts, was voted off Grantham Council by the dominant Labour group. From the time that Margaret Thatcher became leader of the Conservative Party, and even more frequently as Prime Minister, she would in similar interviews recount episodes of her childhood and draw lessons from them.[2] Years later, when she set about writing her memoirs, at a time when her previously razor-sharp faculties were starting to dull, it was her home and school life in Grantham that she recollected best – far more clearly than the tumultuous events of her own rise to power. And even in her early eighties, when her short-term memory had largely gone, she would still reminisce with pleasure about the great occasions in the Grantham of her youth: about the Belvoir Hunt gathering on Boxing Day outside Grantham's town hall, the cheering crowds and the mulled wine to keep out the chill; or about the excitement of the annual March funfair with its odd shows and the 'barkers' who announced them.

Of course, to say that the experience of Margaret Thatcher's early years formed her outlook is not to say that the formation was simple, let alone to deny that in her later accounts she blotted out some aspects of that experience and embroidered others. In truth, she was resolutely determined to relive her memories only from a distance. At the deepest level of her being, she may have reacted against her upbringing more than she reflected it. Certainly, she rarely returned to Grantham once she had had the chance to leave: she had escaped; and in her heart she knew it and rejoiced in it. The fact remains that to understand Margaret Thatcher it is first necessary to grasp the nature of Margaret Roberts.

Margaret Hilda Roberts was born in the flat above her father's grocery store at 1 North Parade on 13 October 1925. She was christened three months later at Finkin Street Methodist Church. Her father, Alf Roberts, was tall, blond and blue-eyed and had a certain presence, especially as he grew older. Born poor, he was a self-made man. His family, which originally hailed from Wales, had for several generations been employed in the shoe business in Northamptonshire. Alf was born in Ringstead and for a time worked in a humble capacity at Oundle public school. Intellectually precocious, he had once wanted to become a teacher, but his family could not raise the money to keep him long enough at school. So he had had to take jobs where he could find them. Yet he was certainly fortunate in another respect. No coward and a red-blooded patriot, when the First World War arrived he tried many times to join up. But his poor health – he had a weak chest and bad eyesight – prevented his fighting and possibly dying, as his younger brother did, on the killing fields of Flanders. He survived, and eventually he prospered. Indeed, by the time of Margaret's birth Alf was already on his way up in the world. By 1919 he had managed to save enough money to buy his own grocery shop. He later purchased a further shop in Huntingtower Road, on the other side of town. He then proceeded to acquire the newsagent's next door to the first shop in North Parade and expanded his grocer's business into it. He had needed a mortgage to start off. But he was always extremely industrious and very thrifty. His wife, Margaret's mother, Beatrice (or 'Beatie'), who unlike Alf's family was born and bred in Grantham, shared the same outlook. She had started off life as a seamstress and had built up her own modestly successful business.

Alf and Beatie were married in 1917 and Margaret's elder sister, Muriel, was born in 1921. The four years that separated the two daughters was perhaps one reason why, despite Margaret's public protestations, they were never close. Their photographs as little girls already reveal, however, something of their differences in character. Margaret has a sweet smile, beautiful hair, flashing blue eyes. Muriel too is attractive, but in a solider, homelier manner. The physical contrast would sharpen as the years passed – particularly when Margaret decided, almost certainly to please Denis and perhaps in imitation of his first wife whom she physically resembled, that she would cease to be a brunette and become a blonde. The contrasts in character between the sisters also mirrored their parents' expectations. Margaret was from an early age destined by them for university; Muriel never. Muriel would train as a physiotherapist in a hospital in Birmingham, during the early war years when the bombs were falling. Margaret was musical, Muriel was not, and this was another disadvantage for the elder sibling, because both parents were very fond of music: Alf had a fine bass voice and Beatie played the piano. Margaret would turn out to be ambitious, intellectually curious, desirous of self-improvement, always anxious to be appreciated, ever keen to make an impact, certainly not above manipulative use of her very real charms. Muriel was quite simply more normal – in her outlook, her aspirations, her capacities, her limits and her achievements. She was the kind of girl who longs to settle down; and she did so, as Muriel Cullen, happily married to a Norfolk farmer. Margaret Thatcher, by contrast, was incapable of settling anywhere. For her, marriage would be a place of departure, not a destination. The same restlessness helped make her Prime Minister, and a great one.

Muriel was closer to her mother. By contrast, and it is perhaps the best-known fact about Margaret's early life, the younger daughter was her father's favourite, and he hers. Perhaps Alf had wanted a son. Certainly, the kind of attention he devoted to her and the values and ambitions he inculcated in her would suggest so. Much has been made by commentators – particularly the practitioners of psychobabble – of Margaret's attitude towards Beatie.[3] They draw attention to the daughter's refusal to say anything notable about her mother at all. Yet the assumption that this wall of near-silence concealed hostility, resentment or even coldness seems wide of the mark. Margaret Thatcher would never be very interested in people's personalities as such, only in their actions – and specifically those of their actions that directly concerned her. When it came to psychology, on the individual level at least, she was profoundly unimaginative, and this applied in respect of her family just as much as it did in respect of her colleagues and even her friends. The truth is that when she was asked what she thought of Beatie, she simply did not know, for the very good reason that the two had no common tastes or interests, at least beyond Alf Roberts's welfare. It has also been suggested that Beatie starved her younger daughter of affection and that this explains Margaret's apparent chill.[4] But there is no evidence that this is so, nor did Margaret's later private conversation ever hint at such a thing. It is, indeed, most unlikely. Beatie was a kind and sweet-natured person, with a strong sense of duty to her husband and both her daughters.

In writing her memoirs Margaret Thatcher went out of her way, admittedly after some hard editorial prodding, to describe the housewifely skills, notably sewing, cleaning, decorating and (with questionable success) cooking, which she learned from her mother. But nothing more was forthcoming, for good or ill. There was certainly no falling out between mother and daughter. When Beatie was taken seriously ill in 1960 while staying with the Cullens, Denis and Margaret promptly drove her back to Grantham for the necessary, though unsuccessful, operation. Margaret did not dislike her mother. Rather, she always pitied her. Beatie's life seemed to her daughter an example of everything she intended in later life to avoid. 'Drudgery' was the word that most often came to her lips to describe it; 'poor mother' she murmured in unguarded moments, whenever the subject was raised. If pressed, she would even express surprise at the idea that such a life as her mother had lived might actually be satisfying. This tells more about the daughter than the mother; but it is not suggestive of a dark secret. In any case, near the end of her life, Margaret Thatcher seems to have felt a touch of remorse. Coming across her mother's old prayer book when rummaging through some family papers, she wrote a little note inside recording her sorrow that she hadn't thanked Beatie enough for all she had done for her.

Margaret's parents, particularly her father, had grown up knowing real hardship. But the Roberts family during her own childhood were never poor. Her father's shops served a wide range of customers, affluent and not so affluent, but he always took pride in the quality of his produce. Margaret would emphasize, certainly echoing her father, that his was a rather superior kind of shop – though the accuracy of this claim has been contested.[5] But whatever the range of goods, the grocery business was a full-time affair. The family, including Margaret when she was old enough, regularly helped out, especially during school holidays. She remembered weighing out the produce sold in the shop with her mother and sister, taking in orders, accompanying her father on deliveries. The store in North Parade was open from early morning till late into the evening: indeed, as a post office, its lengthy opening hours were officially stipulated. Apparently to ensure that business never faltered, the two parents always took separate holidays, though usually in the same place, Skegness. Beatie would take the children to the beach. For Alf, it was the place to play his favourite bowls. But probably Alf had another reason to holiday on his own, namely the understandable wish to mix with his own sex in a more relaxed and less strait-laced environment.

At least the Robertses' long working hours and application to their business brought real enough financial rewards. By the time Margaret was born, the family was already part of Grantham's modest but self-confident lower-to-middle middle class; and Alf's political and public accomplishments and connections from this point on fully reflected the fact. From 1927 he was a member of the Council, until being voted off as Alderman a quarter of a century later. For twenty of those years he was Chairman of the Finance Committee, where his prime concern was to keep down the rates. This was not always easy or even possible. But perhaps most difficult of all for this devout but realistic local politician was the challenge of combining his own allegiance to Methodist traditions and principles with the desire of youngsters, and during the war of off-duty servicemen, for some amusement on Sundays. At home, particularly while Margaret's grandmother was alive, the Robertses practised strict sabbatarianism. Beatie rose early on Sunday morning to do one of her big weekly bakes, but this does not seem to have counted as 'work'. And naturally all frivolity was discouraged. Margaret was not allowed to go for a swim on a Sunday. Even snakes-and-ladders and cards were banned. Not everyone wanted to live like this – hence Alf's dilemma. Many years later Margaret remembered clearly and with approval how he had helped the Council reach a compromise. The cinemas opened; the parks, though, remained closed. Presumably, the Sunday cinema-goers were deemed already lost, while at least the would-be park visitors could be nudged back towards propriety. Margaret Thatcher herself retained in later life no sabbatarian instincts whatsoever. She worked as much on Sundays as she did on weekdays. And restrictions on trade were, in her view, no more acceptable then than at any other time. It was one of the many ways in which she sloughed off her Methodist past.

Alf Roberts always stood for the Council as an Independent in the ratepayers' interest. During his years as a councillor party politics increasingly intruded, as they did elsewhere, but he still kept to his old label. He had, in fact, begun as a Liberal, Margaret remembered hearing; but for as long as she had known her father, he was a Conservative Party man, like most other 'non-party-political' Grantham councillors. By the twenties the Liberal Party had simply become too collectivist for its traditional business supporters. It was a point that Alf himself would make in 1949 when he spoke beside his daughter (for the first and last time) at her adoption meeting as the Conservative candidate for Dartford.

Margaret Thatcher always recognized how much her attitudes, and her father's, reflected liberalism, in its old-fashioned sense of free-market individualism, rather than traditional paternalistic Toryism. But one should not exaggerate the degree to which the spirit of enterprise which she would later exalt was appreciated at home. There it was effort, not risk, that was prized. Alf even regarded investment in the Stock Exchange as a form of gambling and so unacceptable. Some of these attitudes remained with his daughter, despite her intellectual commitment to capitalism. In a remarkable address at the City Church of St Lawrence Jewry in 1981 she would claim that work was a 'virtue', not just a factor of production.[6] And to the end of her life she always regarded the production of physically useful objects more highly than the provision of services like entertainment. She remained, in this sense too, a chip off the paternal block.

Another aspect of her father's civic involvement which made a lasting impact upon Margaret was his connection with voluntary, charitable organizations, above all the Rotary Club. In later life she would at the slightest mention of volunteering be inclined to launch off into an encomium of Rotary, with its motto of 'Service Above Self'. Rotary certainly did good work in providing help for the poor and unfortunate of Grantham. Every Christmas 150 food parcels were prepared in Alf's shop for distribution to the less well off, for which the Rotary paid. (More discreetly, Beatie would always bake a little extra at home so that those who were sick or faced hardship could be helped, and Margaret would be sent out to deliver the cakes and buns, tactfully saying that her mother had 'a little extra' that week.) It was also a badge of honour in the Robertses' eyes that the Rotary Club had been banned in Nazi Germany. Despite this, it is still odd that Rotary's activities should have so gripped Margaret's imagination, since she herself could never have joined, for its members were all men. But then, from an early age she just assumed that men did the serious work; and, as a serious girl, she came to see herself as what in many respects she was: an honorary man.

Though blest with some fine buildings, notably the Guildhall and the church of St Wulfram's, Grantham was (and is) a somewhat dreary town in the East Midlands, itself one of the more dreary regions of England. But Margaret grew up in an age when civic pride was still strong. She instinctively grasped the importance of the community into which one was born, which shaped one's beliefs and focused one's loyalties. This was the reality of what a later age would term 'civil society'. Grantham had emerged as a market town for the surrounding Lincolnshire farms. There was still a market. But Grantham's main modern advantage was its good communications, by road, canal and (from the mid-nineteenth century) rail. These had brought with them heavy industry: an ironworks, a carriage works, a brewery. Aveling Barford made steamrollers, R. H. Neal made cranes. The principal employers were in engineering and, during the war, munitions. The town as a whole was never poor. Margaret remembered seeing evidence of the effects of the Depression, the long dole queues and the pockets of poverty. But Grantham was not the industrial North, where a town's or region's workforce was likely to be concentrated on one or two employers. Margaret Roberts's heart did not perhaps bleed easily, at least for collective ills; but then, it had no reason to bleed in Grantham. This fact has some political importance.

Margaret Thatcher thus never acquired from real or imagined

experience of the Depression any of the social guilt that affected Tory grandees, let alone the rage that activated socialist radicals. Instead, what struck her, at least in retrospect, was the way in which the poor kept up their self-respect, and those with the money to do so helped out, quietly and through voluntary cooperation. Grantham would in this way become the model for her social politics.

This instinctive belief in the values of community, which balanced the harsher philosophy of self-help to which she also subscribed, was in truth what lay behind her much distorted remark in an interview with *Woman's Own* magazine in 1987 about there being 'no such thing as society'.[7] 'Society' in Mrs Thatcher's analysis turns out, and must always turn out, to be other people – individuals, families, groups – who take responsibility and put their hands in their own pockets.

It should be added that she followed the same principle in her personal behaviour. She could be extremely personally generous, even a soft touch, the chequebook opened and alarming quantities of noughts written down before anyone could stop her. The beneficiaries ranged from family members to staff who had money problems to anyone collecting for a good or apparently good cause. From the time she entered Number Ten until control of her expenditure was effectively removed from her in her old age, she had a special charitable account on which she could draw for important donations. The fund was set up by her invaluable assistant 'Crawfie' – who will figure elsewhere in these pages – under circumstances that are themselves revealing.* As Prime Minister, Mrs Thatcher found herself extremely short of cash. Her personal bank account was often in the red. But she insisted on giving. So various rich friends clubbed together to establish a fund to help her do so. And the fact that Crawfie administered it ensured

---

* Mrs Cynthia Crawford, known to Mrs Thatcher and her entourage as 'Crawfie', became her dresser in 1978. She remained with Mrs Thatcher throughout her time in Downing Street and into retirement, acting as her personal assistant, companion, confidante and faithful friend.

some control over her more whimsical impulses of generosity.

All that said, Margaret Thatcher could also on occasion be absurdly mean, usually about small sums and particularly when she suspected wastefulness. And she never quite trusted anyone, even those she had known for years, not to short-change her in some trivial regard, though at a deeper level she knew she was well served by those around her – as, indeed, she was.

The broader outlook which she gained from her experience of growing up in Grantham, and above all from her father's influence, can probably best be summed up as responsible individualism – which is also, one should add, the principle that underlay her later statement that there was 'no such thing as society'. The responsibility and the individuality were not opposites but intimately connected. Duty was understood as falling on specific individuals and directed at other specific individuals. It was not collective. Indeed, those of her father's sayings that she remembered most vividly reflected his (and later her) scorn for following the crowd. 'Don't do something just because every one else does' was the central theme. Think for yourself. Rely on yourself. Believe in yourself. Never accept that anything is impossible. Strive harder than any one else. And make no excuses. From the time she went to school to the time she left Downing Street, people were astonished at Margaret's unrelenting drive to impose her will, to attain her goals, to succeed. She learned this from her father, though she was fortunate enough to possess in herself the qualities required to put it into practice.

Given her father's position and the fact that he enjoyed a healthy income, the remarkable aspect of Margaret Roberts's early life is that the family's circumstances were not merely modest but grim. This was deliberate. Her father's proud motto was 'never waste a minute' and he did not intend that anyone around him should waste one either. The fact that they lived in uncomfortably constricted accommodation can perhaps be explained by the need to be 'over the shop', ready to supply the demands of customers and, of course, to watch the premises. At a pinch, the fact that Beatie was an expert seamstress might go far to explain the girls' dependence on home-made clothes. Even continued reliance on an outside lavatory was not at the time unusual. But the failure to install running hot water surely was. So was the meagreness and dullness of fare – even before, it should be noted, the rigours of wartime rationing. Alf Roberts prided himself on selling quality produce; but the quality was enjoyed by his customers, not by his family.

Margaret Thatcher's own later eating habits reflected this experience. She had a hearty appetite, which she indulged more when she ceased to be Prime Minister. But whenever food was served, and regardless of its expense or rarity if she was being entertained, it was all immediately hoovered up as quickly as possible. This was partly because, in office, she regarded eating as an inconvenient obstacle to speech; and she always had a lot to say. Her aides would sometimes remark on her ability even to talk while eating, without risk of indelicacy. Her preferred tastes in food and drink were always plain and unsophisticated. Once she married Denis Thatcher, who had a horror of any meat that was not overcooked, she acquired that taste too. She was not impractical, in the way that Denis always was. (He could not mend a fuse and could barely change a light bulb.) But, unlike her mother, she would never be a good cook – despite the cleverly staged business of public shopping and her well-known determination to give Denis his breakfast. She could follow a recipe, for example to make a birthday cake for the children. She could construct a menu and even serve a low-key dinner party. But that was, even as a young woman, about the limit of her abilities. She was just not very interested in food.

Later, as Prime Minister, she all but gave up on cooking altogether. The shepherd's pie she would bring out of the deep freeze at Downing Street had always been cooked by a secretary, not by her. Her friend Hector Laing sent around boil-in-the-bag meals.[8] Denis was known to complain that he didn't know whether at Number Ten he would come back to 'a hot meal, a cold meal or no meal', though this did not induce him to cook himself. When Margaret retired, Marks and Spencer's pre-prepared food counters were the main source of supplies for dinner. When she was away, she worried about what he would eat. She even enquired about meals on wheels, until she was told this was hardly appropriate. In any case, she need not have bothered. Denis invariably found some-one to take him out to a club.

Margaret Thatcher's lifelong frugality had its origins in Grantham. Conspicuous consumption was frowned upon. One of the most deadly insults was that someone 'lived up to the hilt', i.e. spent everything they earned and more. Among Methodists there was a kind of com-petition to avoid waste. In an early example of recycling, even the cottons used to tack up hems were re-used.[9] Mrs Thatcher later applied the same philosophy in her approach to the public purse, to a sometimes impractical extent. She used to do most of her work as Prime Minister in her study in a high-backed chair, and over the years her feet wore a hole in the carpet. But she refused to have a new one and had a patch inserted, before eventually conceding that the shabbiness was unacceptable and reluctantly accepting a replacement.

Alf Roberts was clearly extremely mean; and undoubtedly this trait was exaggerated by his and the family's harsh brand of religion. As Margaret Thatcher would say, in what must be considered an understatement, her family life was 'rather puritan'.[10]

The Robertses were Methodists. But Methodism in Grantham came in different shapes and sizes. The Roberts family were Wesleyans; closer, therefore, in spirit to Anglicanism than to wider Nonconformity. Margaret Thatcher would in later years seek to refute the suggestion that she came from a community of killjoys by emphasizing the social life which centred on Finkin Street Church. And it is certainly true that these Methodists met for sewing evenings, tea parties, fêtes and jumble sales. They entertained at each other's homes (without alcohol, naturally; cherry brandy and sherry arrived in the Roberts household only when Alf became Mayor in 1945). They also enjoyed music: not just hymns but the occasional oratorio. Margaret, like her parents, had a good voice. She also played the piano at home and in Sunday school and would regret not having taken her lessons further – she began at the age of five but stopped when she was fifteen. But, when all this is taken into account, and as she herself in unguarded moments admitted, there was in the Roberts household simply an excess of religion and a dearth of fun. She had to attend church four times on a Sunday, and when she suggested that perhaps she might like to go for a walk instead, as other children did, her father denounced the very thought of it – this too was the collectivist heresy. And anything like self-indulgence was anathema.

There is no evidence that Margaret was consumed by a desire to throw over the traces. She was always a serious girl. It was widely remarked of Mrs Thatcher in her adult life that she had no sense of humour. That is not completely true. She could enjoy a joke, but unless it was obvious it had to be explained to her. She had a certain dry wit and a capacity for repartee and even mimicry. She liked on occasion to imitate the upper-class accents of men she thought feeble. She was also, at least in the later years, good at sending herself up. But she distrusted frivolity and thought prolonged bouts of humour a distraction: she would cut them short by telling people to get back to serious matters.

The recollections in her memoirs and in earlier interviews of the *douceur de vivre* she experienced on visits to the cinema or an occasional musical should not be taken altogether at face value. Such events were rare in Margaret's life. Moreover, she was never a dreamer, whether at the Odeon or in Downing Street. That said, as the years went by and she grew into her teens, it must have been increasingly galling to be forced to go to church so often, to live at such close quarters with the family in such spartan conditions, to be prevented from doing the things that most contemporaries did – for example, to attend the occasional dance or private party where alcoholic drink might be served. That is surely why the prospect of Oxford, rather than nearby Nottingham University, and then of a career in London, not the East Midlands, would prove so attractive. It is why she so quickly and so thoroughly cut herself off from Grantham and most of those she had known there – including even, finally, her father.

The break did not immediately follow her leaving home. She would return during university vacations. Alf, for his part, campaigned and even spoke for Margaret when she was a candidate for the Dartford constituency in 1950. But her parents disapproved of Denis, a divorcee; relations cooled after her marriage, and Margaret Thatcher's children barely knew their grandparents. After Beatie died, Alf quickly remarried. Margaret had little or no contact with her new stepmother. But the estrangement went further than that. Alf remained proud of his daughter's political success and was listening to her on the radio when he died. Significantly, though, he left her nothing in his will. The old magic had vanished long before. She had outgrown him, and she had outgrown Grantham. Only memories remained.

Much the same can be said of the religious atmosphere in which she had been raised. The impact of Methodism upon her was certainly deep, but not perhaps in the way that might have been expected. For example, it did not leave her an obviously spiritual person, though she was extremely moral. She would always show a marked interest in religion, but more in its social and political aspects than for its own sake. Her failure to talk of God or the after-life in a personal way was surprising for a Christian of her background, and seemed to go beyond traditional English reserve. She did not seem to feel any obligation to forgive. In a sense, this was refreshing, because she did not profess to be better than she was. And in practice she did not hold grudges to the extent that many other politicians did. But she would state as a matter of fact that she did not forgive, for example, Michael Heseltine for what he had done to her. The contrast between this attitude and the fact that she was not, by and large, a bitter person, given all the adversities she faced during her career, suggests that she had really just misunderstood the concept of forgiveness itself, believing that it involved feelings rather than intentions. If so, that indicates how little Christian doctrine she absorbed for one who grew up in such a strikingly devout household.

She was not, in truth, very interested in the content of religious doctrine at all. This at least made her much more tolerant of other religious faiths and denominations than she might have been. For example, she harboured none of the anti-Catholic prejudice that has sometimes unjustly been ascribed to her. She greatly admired Pope John Paul II, and she was enthusiastic about Pope Benedict XVI. In 2009 she made a visit to Rome with Paul Johnson and Charles Moore as a guest of Charles and Carla Powell and an audience with Pope Benedict was arranged. Unfortunately, one of the party blabbed prematurely and its 'private' aspects were truncated by protocol-obsessed Vatican staff. But she found she liked the new pontiff. She also spent a short while kneeling in prayer at the grave of John Paul II, leaving a wreath of white roses and a House of Lords note-card on which she inscribed 'Pope John Paul II – a Man of Faith and Courage'.[11]

In fact, she always treated the clergy with great respect – despite political disagreements with most of the leading Anglican figures, who sorely tested her. The Church of England document *Faith in the City*, published in 1985, was probably the most damning indictment of her policies that her opponents ever devised. By contrast, she was a devotee of Lord Jakobovits – who reciprocated her regard – and she procured for him his peerage, the first ever awarded to a Chief Rabbi. She even had a certain admiration for Islam, which many from her background and with her outlook might not have shared. As always, she treated people as individuals and tried to judge them by their actions. It never bothered her, for example, that the Bosnians, whom she courageously and outspokenly supported after she left office, were mainly Muslims.* By contrast, she felt

* See p. 385.

(and once imprudently said) that imams should have spoken out more against Islamist terrorism in the wake of 9/11.*

Grantham's Methodism emphasized a personal relationship with Christ and it offered a set of moral rules by which to live. But it was not at all intellectual. That did not mean that the preachers were ignorant or their sermons empty; far from it. Alf Roberts himself was a powerful lay preacher. His sermon notes, some of which were parsimoniously made at the back of Margaret's old exercise books, reveal hints of the rhetorical capacity for which he was locally famous. But with these men charisma was always more in evidence than doctrine – which is not surprising, since they had no formal, systematic theological training.

An interesting demonstration of this disregard for systematic theology is provided by a publication called *Bibby's Annual* which was given to Margaret by her parents and was a favourite of hers, particularly for its improving verses. Some of these she continued to recite many years later – such as:

> One ship drives East, and another West,
> By the self-same gale that blows;
> 'Tis the set of the sail, and not the gale,
> That determines the way she goes.

The conclusion is clear: we make our own lives out of the circumstances that prevail; circumstances do not make us. But while the message of effort and self-help is worthy enough, the theology of *Bibby's Annual* is a mish-mash of Christianity, reincarnation, creationism and superstition; not surprising, perhaps, since it was produced by the bizarre Theosophist movement. Most Christians would not have let it into the house.

---

* This was in October 2001, when she was caught unawares by a *Times* reporter while attending a quite unconnected event. It should also be said that by this time her memory had started to deteriorate and she had probably forgotten that a number of imams had condemned the attacks, albeit in unconvincing terms.

More curiously, perhaps, Mrs Thatcher in later years did not know her Bible very well. She liked the language of the King James version and a copy was always at hand for potential quotation in speeches – though biblical material rarely made the final draft; she would reject it as too 'preachy' (a wholly pejorative word in her lexicon). But for someone brought up in the evangelical tradition she was rather shaky on details of scripture. Her knowledge of the Old Testament was particularly thin.

The lack of impact which Methodism had on her religious outlook helps explain how easily she later 'converted' to Anglicanism. She and Denis were married in Wesley's Chapel in City Road in London; but this was mainly because he, as a divorcee, could not then be married in an Anglican church. It was also very much on the 'high' side of Methodism, to the disapproval of her father, who gave her away. Henceforth, she was an occasionally practising Anglican. But she attended Matins rather than Eucharist, believing that she should not take communion, since she had not been confirmed in the Church of England. She and Denis liked traditional hymns, a good choir and the 1662 Prayer Book. As both grew older they attended more regularly, and their tastes became even more conservative.

The most significant effect of the religiosity of Margaret Thatcher's Grantham background was, then, not upon her spiritual beliefs but upon her political convictions – and for her, politics was always at root a matter of 'belief'. Unusually among her contemporaries in British politics, she always saw Christianity as a set of principles, virtues and attitudes which had direct relevance to political life. Margaret Thatcher's later style also reflected that of the preachers she had heard and admired as a girl. Thus she would often speak about political issues with a conviction that unnerved hesitant male colleagues.

Beyond home and church in Grantham, school too helped to form her – as it did many children from her background. Education, above all a grammar-school education, was the only way in which people from modestly situated families could hope to rise to a position from which to challenge their social superiors in the Tory Party or indeed anywhere else. That applied even more when it came to a woman mounting a challenge in a world of men.

Margaret was a hard-working and intelligent pupil, considerate and generous, perhaps a bit too eager and intense, inclined to be a know-it-all, her hand always up first in class, but not so outstanding as to inspire jealousy. She began her schooling at the age of five in Huntingtower Road County Elementary School. It was a mile's walk from home, a journey she made four times a day since the school did not serve lunch. It was here that she developed her later love of poetry, started to read Kipling and won a local poetry recital prize. Poetry would remain an interest, and her formidable memory gave her an advantage over most of her contemporaries, both now and later.

Then at the age of ten she gained a scholarship to the fee-paying Kesteven and Grantham Girls' School. Kesteven, with some 350 pupils, was not so large that it was impossible for one pupil to know most of the others – a fact Margaret always appreciated. A dislike of very large schools was one of her strongest preconceptions when she became Secretary of State for Education. The headmistress when Margaret arrived was a Miss Williams, whom she admired and liked. With her successor, Miss Gillies, relations were more difficult, mainly it seems because the new head was unsupportive of Margaret's ambition to go up to Oxford – making her one of the first of many resentful women whose egos the future Prime Minister would manage to bruise. Margaret had to learn Latin in order to get into Oxford and Kesteven did not teach it, so her father paid for lessons at the boys' grammar school. Miss Gillies thought it a waste of time and money.

The main influence upon Margaret at school was the science mistress, Miss Kay, who was instrumental in her decision to specialize in chemistry. This was an unusual choice for a girl. But Margaret already knew that she wanted to pursue a career and chemistry offered the prospect of a future job in industry. Science also enjoyed a certain prestige, at a time when the newspapers were full of technological inventions and advances. Anyway, it appealed to her turn of mind. So when she took the scholarship examination to Somerville College in December 1942 it was, indeed, to read chemistry. She narrowly failed. Being just seventeen, she stayed on at school and briefly became joint head girl. Then a vacancy at Somerville unexpectedly arose. She would duly go up to Oxford in October 1943.

Naturally, life at university would have a larger influence than her schooling upon Margaret Roberts's future. But the Second World War, which she lived through as both schoolgirl and under-graduate, had a more powerful impact on her outlook than either. She was fourteen when war broke out and twenty when it ended. She was, therefore, old enough to understand, while young enough to be highly impressionable. She was also young enough to escape serving, though if she had been determined, and been prepared to truncate her stay at university, she could have briefly done so. Many years later, her (predominantly male) detractors would suggest that it was the fact that she had experienced the war only at second hand, rather than through combat, that explained her hardline policies. They thought she lacked an appreciation of the social solidarity and idealistic internationalism which the serving wartime generation brought back home with it. Perhaps the exper-ience of war did mellow the politics of people like Willie Whitelaw, Edward Heath and Peter Carrington (though did their existing views need much mellowing?). Against that, it hardly undermined the right-wing opinions of Denis Thatcher, who was mentioned in dispatches and had a 'good war' – nor, indeed, those of the soldier–intellectual–politician Enoch Powell. The allegation is unsustainable.

The truth is, rather, that the war had the effect it did upon her, and this differed from its effect on others, because she saw it with her own eyes and not with theirs. Her already passionate patriotism, which was as much a matter of instinct as upbringing, was electrified by the experience of these years. She regarded then, and would always regard, the Second World War as a titanic struggle between Good and Evil. Even the fact that from 1941 the Allied cause was also that of the Soviet Union never shook that conviction.

The Robertses were moralists in international affairs. But whereas the famous Nonconformist Conscience inclined many of their coreligionists towards pacifism, in their case it did the opposite. Nor, unlike some other conservative-minded folk, did Alf and Margaret Roberts think in terms of who might be the 'enemy of my enemy' in the fight against communism. So they had detested Franco and fascism and, naturally, detested Hitler and Nazism even more; and they did so long before war was declared. Alf Roberts seems to have welcomed, as did most other people, the deal achieved by Chamberlain at Munich. But he was not, in a wider sense, an appeaser. He had, for example, stood out against the prevailing tide of pacifist Methodist opinion at the time of the 'Peace Ballot' in 1935. He certainly favoured the decision to go to war when it came.

The Robertses were exceptionally well informed about events. There were political refugees in Grantham. Both Margaret and Muriel also had foreign pen-friends. After the German–Austrian *Anschluss* of 1938, the father of Muriel's friend, a Jewish banker, asked Alf to take care of his daughter. Edith duly stayed with the Robertses and other Grantham families before moving to South America. The future Prime Minister vividly recalled being told by her how the Jews were forced to scrub the Vienna pavements.

Like other self-taught men, Alf Roberts considered that education did not end with the transition to adulthood, but was a lifetime's work. Margaret was his intellectual partner in this venture. He would take her to the Nottingham University Extension Lectures, held on Thursday nights, in which visiting speakers, often politicians, would address the issues of the day. But, above all, father and daughter read voraciously. There was the *Daily Telegraph* and then various journals of differing degrees of seriousness and complexity. Every week Margaret would also take out two books from the library, a 'serious' book for her and her father and some light fiction for her mother. Other books were borrowed from Alf's wide circle of acquaintances.

Much later, Margaret still remembered the titles if not the precise content of these volumes. They explain a great deal about the formation of her attitudes – rather more, indeed, than she herself ever fully recognized. Some were polemical attacks on the appeasement of Hitler, such as Robert Bruce Lockhart's *Guns or Butter* and Douglas Reed's *Insanity Fair*. *Out of the Night* by Jan Valtin (pen-name for the communist Richard Krebs) described in unsavoury detail the treatment of communists by the Nazis. Herbert Agar's *A Time for Greatness* saw the rise of Hitler as proof of an inner failure of Western civilization. In preparing her memoirs, Margaret Thatcher grudgingly acknowledged that much of this material shared a left-wing frame of analysis. But what never seems to have occurred to her is the degree to which, despite her patriotism and her Conservative politics, her own thinking was affected by this early reading. Anyone who wishes to understand her later suspicion of the German 'character' and her habit in conversation of denouncing 'fascism' and 'Nazism' more spontaneously and emotionally than 'communism' must begin with the attitudes she imbibed in the thirties and forties.

What she never swallowed, however, was the argument advanced by the left with such effect during and after the war that appeasement was all the fault of the 'Guilty Men' on the right of British politics. Margaret Roberts's first involvement in campaigning for the Conservative Party took the form of folding leaflets promoting the merits of the Conservative candidate Sir Victor Warrender in the general election of 1935 – the election in respect of which Stanley Baldwin was later attacked for failing to come clean about the need for rearmament. She herself, as a political realist, acquitted Baldwin. She agreed with his judgement – expressed with 'appalling frankness' to the Commons in 1936 – that the mood in the country was so resolutely pacifist at the time that an excess of honesty would have installed a Labour Government even more strongly opposed to rearmament.[12]

Four years later, Margaret listened with her family to Neville Chamberlain's announcement that Britain was at war with Germany. It was, she recalled, the only time that the family missed going to morning church. (There were, of course, three other occasions left in the day.) She had no strong feelings about Chamberlain. But she was soon entirely, and permanently, in thrall to Winston Churchill. Churchill's wartime broadcasts shaped her view of what political leadership was about. For her, Churchill was the embodiment of British fighting spirit, indeed of all the quintessentially British virtues. The veneration she nurtured as a young girl for the great war leader was nothing remarkable. But what was extraordinary, and sometimes a little embarrassing, was that she never grew out of it. As a young would-be politician she was to be heard referring to him as 'Winston', a habit which she always continued, despite the fact that it opened her up to ridicule. This quasi-familiarity did not reflect any sense that she should be ranked as his political equal – far from it. Even during the Falklands War, she never tried to adopt a Churchillian manner. In her speeches as Prime Minister she refrained from quoting him, for fear that she might be thought to be bracketing herself with her hero. In private conversation, too, she flatly rejected any comparison between his achievement and hers. She simply regarded Churchill as the greatest of the greats.

There was, though, more to the war in Grantham than listening to Churchill's broadcasts or reading the news about far-away events. The town was a major focus for enemy bombing: not only was it home to a munitions factory (the British Manufacturing and Research Company, or 'B Marcs' as the Robertses called it), but its location at the junction of the Northern Railway Line and the Great North Road made it an obvious target. The railway ran close to the

Robertses' house, which certainly did not make for quiet nights when the Luftwaffe were abroad. Several bombs fell near North Parade. In all, there were more than twenty raids on Grantham, and seventy-eight local people were killed. Alf was out most nights on air-raid duty. He would not allow his insatiably curious daughter to go and see the worst of the resultant damage. But she knew very well what was happening. Her own evenings were often spent huddled under the solid sitting-room table for protection from the bombs, while she swotted for her exams. Once during daylight she had to run for cover when a German aircraft came over.

By the time that Margaret left Grantham for Oxford in the autumn of 1943 the worst threat to Britain had, in fact, receded. At about this time, and in a moment of doubt after some bad news, she asked her father what the outcome of the conflict would be. He told her that the Allies would certainly win, but how and when were still unclear. Unclear too, he might have added, was the domestic political impact of victory. How would the Conservatives be viewed? As the authors of appeasement, or of victory? As strong leaders in difficult times, or a block on progress? One pointer had already been provided by Grantham's by-election in 1942, occasioned by Victor Warrender's elevation to the Lords. It was not encouraging. To the Robertses' astonishment, the seat had been won by an Independent, Denis Kendall, the manager of B Marcs. It suggested that not even the aura of Churchill was proof against Tory unpopularity.

2

INTO POLITICS

Margaret Roberts can have known little about Oxford when she arrived there in the autumn of 1943. She had visited briefly for her interviews. But she had no real idea of what to expect. None of her family had gone to Oxford, or to Cambridge for that matter. Moreover, the university she now encountered was quite unlike that which flourished in peacetime. There were, above all, far fewer men.

Initially, at least, Oxford life was thoroughly uncongenial. Margaret Roberts had hardly spent more than a few nights away from home. One week-long trip to London to stay with the Revd Skinner and his family, temporary exiles from Grantham, had been her only contact with city life. (In her early eighties she still vividly remembered her first experience of London: 'All those people!' – 'That never ending noise!') Oxford was different again, but no less alien than the metropolis. And so, for all her desire to get away from Grantham, she was soon thoroughly homesick. The college itself did not, it seems, offer much support. It was a cold, austere place – still colder and more austere in the war years; and many of those she encountered seem to have been prigs. Miss

Roberts was regarded as a bore, and worse still a Tory bore. She was ridiculous and quite incomprehensible to those at ease with the prevailing self-satisfied, socialistic atmosphere.[1] The fact that Margaret Thatcher was in later years prepared to make great efforts to raise money for Somerville, despite this unpleasant experience, shows how little she held grudges.

Margaret's chemistry tutor at Somerville, Dorothy Hodgkin, was herself left-wing; but her judgement was fairer. She thought Miss Roberts extremely competent though basically uninspired. This is understandable. Hodgkin was brilliant in her field, a future Nobel Prize winner, whereas Margaret Roberts was clearly nothing like as good as that. To her credit, though, Hodgkin was helpful in practical matters. Margaret was grateful to her tutor for obtaining for her various grants, though in later years she did not like to admit that she had needed them. The truth is that without such help she would have been in some financial difficulty, even though she was extremely frugal. When she needed a bicycle, she taught at Grantham to raise the money to buy one. She tried smoking, but quickly gave up cigarettes and with the money she saved bought *The Times* instead. She received little help from home. Her mother sent cakes, but her father, true to his principles and his prejudices, does not seem to have sent much money.

Dorothy Hodgkin rated Miss Roberts sufficiently highly to supervise her work in her last year, when she tried – but, through no fault of her own, failed – to plot out the structure of the protein Gramicidin B. Margaret went on to receive a solid second-class degree. If she had not been ill during her finals perhaps she might even have scraped a first.

But by now her attitude to her studies had changed. She was clear in her mind that although the degree was important in order to get a job in industry, chemistry itself was not the road she wanted in the longer term to follow. The law seemed much more attractive. During one university vacation she had visited the local Grantham Quarter Sessions with her father and been excited by what she saw of the courts. Father and daughter had later lunched with the Recorder, Norman Winning KC, to whom Margaret explained her predicament – she was reading chemistry, but she was now much more interested in law. He explained that one did not necessarily preclude the other. It was possible to complete her current chemistry degree and then do the Bar exams, studying in the evening and at weekends. He had, it turned out, done much the same himself. The thought of the hard work required never bothered the Robertses. When circumstances permitted, Margaret would elect to do just that.

Given the notable lack of camaraderie she found at Somerville, it was fortunate that she still had the social circle provided by her religion. On Sundays she attended the Wesley Memorial Church, and she was a regular participant in the study groups and other events laid on for undergraduates. Oxford Methodism was a less repressive and more intelligent faith than she had encountered at home, and she seems to have appreciated that. She also read works by the Anglican C. S. Lewis, liking his practical, realistic approach to religion, and especially his classic, *Mere Christianity*.

Along with other women undergraduates, Margaret did her bit for the war effort by serving in the Carfax forces canteen. In her spare time, she sang in the Bach Choir, which performed more than just Bach. She went to tea parties, and sometimes, in the last two years of her time in Oxford, to parties which served more than tea. Since by this time she was sharing lodgings with two other girls in Walton Street, rather than living in college, she was better able to appreciate the social life of a reviving Oxford. She went out to dances – she proved an excellent ballroom dancer. If there were, it seems, no boyfriends in the usual sense of the term, let alone any sexual liaisons, there were certainly men friends – and not surprisingly, for she was by now, though slightly plump, undeniably pretty.

But, beyond work, the main focus of her life at university was, from the very start, Conservative politics. This was a matter not only of convictions but also of constraints; for Margaret Roberts, as a woman, was excluded from membership of the Oxford Union, where so many of the next generation of politicians, and even the occasional statesman, traditionally cut their teeth. It is an interesting question whether she would have shone in the Union. On the face of it, the answer is 'no', and she certainly expressed that view many years later, suggesting that the frivolity would not have suited her. But she probably underrated herself. She was soon to show that she was a lively, forceful debater. And there was, and is, more to Union debates than jokes. In her memoirs, Mrs Thatcher mentions a number of future political figures whose paths crossed hers, including Tony Benn, a fellow Nonconformist.[2] But only with Conservatives did she have any regular dealings. She knew William Rees-Mogg slightly. But her main Tory friend was Edward Boyle. They were personally close, or at least she felt close to him; but socially and politically they were worlds apart. The gap would widen even further as the years went by – he a guilt-ridden, liberal-minded, sophisticated upper-class Tory, she a gritty and unapologetic right-wing radical. When Mrs Thatcher succeeded Boyle as Shadow Education Secretary some twenty years later, it was the passing of a baton from one kind of Conservative to another. (Only after Mrs Thatcher left office, and indeed public life, would the upper-class liberal Tories enjoy a revival of their fortunes, in the form of David Cameron and his fellow Old Etonians.)

The Oxford University Conservative Association (OUCA) was thus Margaret Roberts's political forum and focus. She became a member as soon as she arrived at Somerville. Unlike many undergraduates, more anxious to hear important speakers than to proselytize their convictions, she joined none of the other political clubs. At that time OUCA, reflecting both the national suspension of party politics and the Conservative Party's standing, was in a poor state; but when politics resurfaced with the end of the war, there were more opportunities to make a mark. It must also have helped Margaret Roberts's prospects that in 1945 another woman, Rachel Willink, the daughter of a Government minister, became OUCA's first woman President.

Naturally, that year's political activity concentrated on the general election. During termtime Margaret campaigned for Quintin Hogg, the sitting Conservative MP for Oxford; at the end of term she returned to Grantham, where a much tougher fight was under way, the Conservative candidate Squadron Leader Worth seeking to oust Denis Kendall, whose earlier by-election victory had so shocked the Robertses.

In later years it would be difficult to disentangle Margaret Thatcher's mature from her undeveloped views, and, like any senior politician, she preferred to think that she had always been consistent. But the earliest record of her opinions, which dates from this period in Grantham, provides valuable evidence that even now there was a distinctive 'Thatcher' core to Miss Roberts. She was selected as a warm-up speaker for the candidate at public meetings, a distinction in itself. The report shows that she called for Germany to be disarmed and punished. She proclaimed that the British Empire, with its unique international role, must never be dismembered. And she said that only Churchill could be entrusted with the nation's foreign policy. In changed circumstances – with Germany ascendant, the Empire relinquished and Churchill dead – she would reprise such solidly right-wing views.

But in 1945 the country disagreed. Although Hogg was returned in Oxford, the Tories nationally were routed, Kendall won again in Grantham and Churchill was out of Downing Street. Margaret had not been expecting this. She was genuinely surprised and dismayed to find that opinion among those she thought she knew had shifted so strongly against the party. So when she returned to Oxford, she fully shared the widespread sentiment among the younger generation of Conservatives – one with which the party would again become familiar after 1997 – that something fundamental had to change if the Tories were to be fit for office again. That is the political message of an OUCA report which she now helped prepare.

In March 1946, and on the back of this report, Margaret was

elected OUCA Treasurer. In the same month she attended her first Conservative conference, as Oxford's representative to the Federation of University Conservative and Unionist Associations, meeting in London. Indeed, she made a speech, emphasizing the need for the party to drop its upper-class image and to bring in more people from working-class backgrounds – again, very much what everyone else was saying. The only intriguing element of Thatcher-style individualism was her characteristic observation that, although this was the age of the common man, people should not 'forget the need for the uncommon man'. This is an echo of a sermon by the Revd Skinner, which she had heard during the war, in which he told his congregation how, from the time of Christ to the present day, it was upon the few that the destiny of the many depended. The contemporary reference was to the 'few' of the Battle of Britain. But it was a thought to which Margaret Thatcher would return repeatedly during her career.

Margaret was elected President of OUCA for Michaelmas term 1946. She had already gained a reputation as an excellent organizer and the result was a meetings card full of top-rate speakers – senior Tory politicians were now also freer to come, having lost office. Lord Dunglass (Alec Douglas-Home), Robert Boothby, David Maxwell-Fyfe, Peter Thorneycroft and the star of the day, Anthony Eden, spoke at the different functions she arranged. Rubbing shoulders with the great figures of the Tory Party on such occasions may seem to outsiders what would nowadays be called 'networking'. But there is no evidence that it worked in that way for Margaret Roberts, or, indeed, for anyone else. Senior politicians whom she met at this time never recalled her later from this era. What it did, though, was almost as useful. It gave her a sense that she was part of a powerful and numerous Tory tribe, and the self-confidence that sprang from that.

The same can be said of attendance at her first national party conference, in Blackpool that October. Margaret greatly relished the atmosphere she discovered there. Indeed, throughout her political life, she loved the conference and felt closer to the grass-roots activists of the party than did most senior politicians. Such Tory populism was one of the ways in which she would assert her leadership against her colleagues, who for the most part regarded the annual conferences as a bore, a joke or, on occasion, a threat to their careers.

On coming down from Oxford her first and pressing task was to earn a living. In the future that might mean a legal career; for the moment, though, a job in industry was the obvious target. After several unsuccessful interviews, in which there was probably some misogynistic prejudice at work, she was finally taken on by BX Plastics to work in the company's research and development section, and she took lodgings in Colchester.

As always, it was with the local Tories that she preferred to mix. Unlike most Young Conservatives of the day, she preferred political discussion and campaigning to socializing. She had, indeed, already decided to try to become a Conservative MP. Precisely how and when she did so is now obscure, not least because she later gave a number of different versions. In fact, on some occasions after becoming party leader, doubtless keen to dispel the idea that she was an ambitious plotter, she gave the impression that she had never made any such conscious choice at all.[3] But this is clearly wrong. There was a particular moment, even if it cannot now with certainty be pinpointed. It was apparently after a party back home during the vacation in her last year at university that someone remarked to her, as she was holding forth on some political topic, that what she obviously wanted was to go into Parliament. The monologue stopped, because suddenly she knew that this was indeed exactly what she wanted. The year (1947) at least is clear and of some significance. As Mrs Thatcher emphasized in discussion much later, it would have been impossible for her to think about becoming an MP until the parliamentary salary was greatly increased by Labour after the 1945 election. Before then, she could simply not have afforded it – unless she had married a wealthy man to support her. And though this is, in fact, what occurred, Margaret Roberts was no gold-digger. She had expected to fight for political success within her own resources.

Margaret Thatcher was always superstitious. She had 'lucky pearls' and she even paid attention to fortune-tellers.[4] She certainly believed in the importance of luck in politics and, despite some bad luck towards the end of her career, she always thought of herself as lucky. Certainly, she was lucky now. In October 1948 she attended the party conference at Llandudno as a representative of the Oxford University Graduate Conservative Association. An Oxford friend, John Grant, who was also present, happened to strike up a conversation with the chairman of Dartford Conservative Association, John Miller. Dartford was in search of a candidate and Grant suggested Margaret Roberts. Miller was initially unenthusiastic. Dartford was a safe Labour seat, industrial, hardly the place for a young woman just down from Oxford. But Miss Roberts was asked to meet Miller, his wife Phee and a Mrs Fletcher, Chairman of the Dartford Women's Committee, over lunch on the pier. Margaret worked her magic. The Millers would become close friends, John Miller the first of many older men to become her devoted patron–mentor. In December she was accordingly invited to come for a preliminary interview at Dartford. She was then shortlisted, becoming one of five hopefuls to address a meeting of the Executive Committee in the Bull Hotel, Dartford, on 31 January 1949. And she won. Never having thought that such an opportunity would arise so soon, she was not yet on the list of candidates approved by Conservative Central Office. But no one was minded to make difficulties. Indeed, the Tory women's chairman, Miss Marjorie Maxse, was henceforth a strong supporter.[5] CCO even involved itself in trying to find Margaret Roberts a job somewhere more convenient for the constituency, though in the end it was her own efforts that resulted in her being taken on by J. Lyons, the food manufacturer, in Hammersmith.

There were some residual doubts about whether a 24-year-old

woman was really the right person to fight the seat. So the adoption meeting held in Erith on 28 February in front of the association members was rather more than the formality it should have been. But her supporters rallied round. Speaking beforehand, John Miller commended Margaret as 'brilliant' and (a significant phrase) 'sincere about her faith'. Alf Roberts was also present, and spoke at the end about how the old-fashioned Liberalism with which he had grown up had now been overtaken by Conservatism. But his daughter was the only star; she shone; and she was endorsed as prospective candidate, with just one vote against.

What Margaret said that evening was already distinctive, at least in tone. She began with an attack on the failure of three and a half years of socialism to deliver material rewards. She urged the Government to do 'what any good housewife would do' by examining their accounts. She put her faith in tax cuts to boost production and (more dubiously) to lower prices. She spoke of the need to renew links with the Empire 'to fight the economic war' (a reference to the doomed Imperial Preference tariff system). Good housekeeping. Tax cuts. Patriotism and links with the English-speaking world. It might not have been very sophisticated, and was certainly not unique at the time, but from today's political perspective this is quite clearly recognizable as proto-Thatcherism.

Indeed, Margaret Roberts's time in Dartford reveals a good deal of her future style and provides some insights into the grounds for her future success. But clearly what drew so much local and sometimes national – in one case even international – media interest to her were her sex, her age and her looks (in that order). She was repeatedly trumpeted as the youngest woman candidate in the 1950 general election, and the style of reports of her doings and sayings would seem today embarrassingly sexist. Margaret, now and later, was adept at exploiting her femininity. But it is clear that she was already much more than just 'another woman' – as she proceeded to show by the energy, coolness, pluck and ingenuity she put into her restless, relentless campaigning.

Within a few months of selection she was living in Dartford in rented accommodation. This was more convenient for politics. But it also meant that each morning she had to leave the house at daybreak, travel by bus, train and then bus again to Hammersmith, and do a full day's work before coming back in the evening by the same tedious route for more work in the constituency. There was a great deal to do in a short time to bring what had been a sleepy and decaying Tory organization into shape, and she was always at the centre of it.

Once the general election was finally declared for 23 February 1950 the pressure became even more intense. Most unusually for a Tory woman, she took her campaigning on to the factory floor. She pulled beer in working men's clubs – whose rules would ordinarily not have let her in at all. She also held public meetings with invited speakers. Here she was in her element. The heckling, at least that part of it aimed at her, was good-humoured, and she gave as good as she got. She debated with the sitting Labour MP Norman Dodds, with whom she struck up a warm personal rapport: she would get on well with a particular sort of no-nonsense socialist right to the end of her political career. Indeed, her regard for people like Dodds, Charlie Pannel (whom she met now, and whom she would later pair in the House) and some MPs on the far left such as Eric Heffer and Dennis Skinner, was an odd and frequently overlooked aspect of her character. Even when, in the 1980s, the Labour Party had moved to a position which most Tories considered beyond the pale, she refused to suggest in anything she said that patriotism and socialism were incompatible. The seeds of that view were sown in Dartford.

The result of the election contest in the Dartford constituency was a foregone conclusion, as Margaret must have understood all along. The Conservatives just failed to oust Labour nationally, while she cut Dodds's majority at Dartford by 6,000. Unfortunately, the narrowness of the national result meant that a further early general election was also inevitable, and as a matter of honour she could not now abandon Dartford in search of a more winnable seat. The second election in October 1951 returned the Conservatives and Churchill to power with a majority of thirteen seats, and Margaret clipped a further 1,000 votes off Dodds.

Apart from proving her credentials as a campaigner – an achievement duly noted by Central Office – Margaret's time in Dartford allowed her to take several other steps decisive for her future. The first, already mentioned, was in the formulation of her political views. The speeches she delivered echoed and enlarged upon the themes of her adoption address. So she made repeated calls for reductions in taxation and better husbanding of financial resources. Large numbers of figures, derived almost certainly from party briefings, were made explicable by homely allusions. There were warnings of national bankruptcy if current excessive expenditure programmes continued. To the Tory women of Erith she inveighed against the socialist economic planner's 'pigeon hole mentality', treating human beings as mere units of account. To the Young Conservatives of Orpington she advocated a 'fifth freedom' to be added to the famous four freedoms embodied in the Atlantic Charter – namely, the 'freedom for everyone to use their talents and develop their ideas'. In the same speech appeared another *idée fixe* of the future, namely a damning denunciation of the deceit implied by the socialist concept of 'public ownership' of industry. She pointed out that it was government, not the nation, which really controlled the 'nationalized' industries, adding in language she would use as Prime Minister that 'Conservatives want power more widely diffused through private ownership'. To the Tory women of Bexley she asserted that 'personal responsibility is the key note of the future'.

There was plenty of anti-communism in her speeches too, particularly in the run-up to the 1951 campaign. The war in Korea was under way and the so-called 'domino theory' of communist aggression in Asia in vogue. She had no hesitation in linking international to national dangers, warning that 'if we have another five years of Socialist government . . . this country will be nearer Communist than Socialist'.

The second matter on which Margaret had taken a decisive step by the end of her spell in Dartford was in her relations with the opposite sex. By now John Miller was not her only affectionate male protector. Another was the neighbouring Tory MP Sir Alfred Bossom. Bossom was a brilliant architect, a rich and powerful man, and – in her eyes if not necessarily his – something of a father figure. It was at his grand house in Carlton Gardens that Margaret Thatcher's wedding reception would, in due course, be celebrated.

A neighbouring candidate, at Bexley Heath, was Edward Heath, with whom no very warm relations were likely. Margaret spoke in his constituency, and after he won his seat in 1950 he proved help-ful in finding her some senior politicians to speak in Dartford. So one must not pre-date the future deep hostility between them. They were, after all, both outsiders in Tory Party terms. They both tried to fit in socially, as their speaking voices showed: Margaret quickly lost her Lincolnshire accent and adopted a tone that the uncharitable described as posh, while Heath, from a still more humble background, adapted his vowels in strangulated imitation of upper-class Home Counties English to the point that listening to him became uniquely excruciating. But they were already completely different sorts of people, in both character and experience. He had served in the war with distinction and had come back a dedicated internationalist. She had not served, but was already an unashamed nationalist. He accepted received wisdom, while she mistrusted it. He was the technocrat, she the radical. Their views would always have made them opponents, though it was their characters, particularly his character, that would make them enemies.

The most important male acquaintance that Margaret made in Dartford was, however, Denis Thatcher. Denis (known always by his wife in later years as 'DT') had been invited to a dinner arranged by some local worthies in honour of the new candidate, Miss

Roberts, after her first adoption meeting. It was here that he first met Margaret and, since it was very late and he lived in London, he drove her to Liverpool Street station afterwards, whence she caught the last train to Colchester. His family paint business, the Atlas Preservative Company, was situated in Erith, within the constituency, and he was a leading member of the Conservative Association, with strong views, though without personal political ambitions. Denis was on the rebound from an unhappy wartime marriage with a woman who looked remarkably like Margaret Roberts. There was a ten-year age difference between him and his future wife. But he was lonely, and she was an attractive, intelligent girl who had always preferred the company of older men. In some ways, and although he was far from good-looking, he was within limits a 'catch': he had a certain dash, he drove fast cars, he knew the world. Most importantly, he was wealthy, and so would be able to support her in her political ambitions. Margaret would hardly have been human if this had not affected her decision. On the other hand, no one then or since has suggested that she simply married him for his money. She could probably have done just as well elsewhere, though perhaps not so soon, and she had not envisaged marrying early. There is, in fact, no evidence that she had considered marrying at all. She had had, as far as is known, no romantic friendships with men, and by nature she was neither obviously wifely nor deeply maternal. For his part, Denis was none too keen to rush into another marriage after a first that had ended so painfully and so recently.

Two years were to pass before they were married; years in which friendship slowly became courtship, as an un-showy kind of love matured sufficiently to overcome their mutual hesitations. They saw more of each other. Denis, for the first and last time, helped Margaret in the constituency. She moved to London before the October 1951 election, renting a flat in Pimlico not too far from his own in Chelsea. They went out to dinner and the theatre. News of their engagement was leaked by the Conservative Party just before election day, apparently without the couple's knowledge. They were married that December at Wesley's Chapel. She wore a sapphire blue velvet dress and a hat with an ostrich feather in it. A well-known photograph, turned into a fine painting, shows the bride looking happy, beautiful and quite provocative. She later explained the choice of cloth as due to its being very cold at the time. But was the colour an obscurely tactful acknowledgement that this was Denis's second marriage, a fact of which a number present at the ceremony, not least her family, will have disapproved? Or did politics come into it even then?

After a honeymoon which incorporated some business as well – their holiday in Madeira sandwiched between trips to Lisbon and Paris – Margaret moved into Denis's Chelsea flat in Swan Court, Flood Street. She also gave up her job, but not to engulf herself in domestic duties: at once she began studying law with a view to the Bar exams.

The relationship between Denis and Margaret Thatcher would remain free from the scandals that more often than not surround those at the top of politics. The media, though, need something to report about such a *ménage*, and, aside from the peccadilloes of the Thatcher children, it was upon Denis that they mainly focused. How much, though, did he correspond to the *Private Eye* 'Dear Bill' image of crude, inebriated, hen-pecked dimwit? Only to a very limited extent, is the honest answer. Denis's language was occasionally coarse, his prejudices were extreme, his directness was sometimes an embarrassment. He did drink heavily, with no obvious effect, and in his later years he seemed to live almost entirely on a diet of gin and cigarettes. Yet he was by no means subservient to his wife, and neither was he a fool. He was well read, a devotee of biographies, political and military: he had a sizeable account at Hatchards bookshop in Piccadilly. Above all, though, he was shrewd and cunning, whereas to the end Margaret retained an endearing and sometimes alarming trait of ingenuousness. He knew what was expected of him and he was socially useful to his wife. He could, for example, exert an (affected) old-world charm with women and adopt a (more genuine) jovial matiness with men that often helped break ice which his more serious spouse could not by herself have cracked. He was particularly useful in helping her understand businessmen and their priorities, broadening her horizons beyond her original limited perspective based on the experience and priorities of the small shopkeeper. His main strength lay, though, in his ability to judge character. Whereas she could be dazzled or flattered or charmed, and was capable of making some serious misjudgements about people, he was more earthy and more distrustful. He was particularly suspicious of those who claimed to be personally loyal while politically opposed, a category which by the end of the 1980s would include a large contingent within her Government. In this he was proved right.

Above all, in these early years Denis's money was enormously important to his wife's success. Without it, she would probably have had to wait a good deal longer before entering Parliament, and she would have been strapped for cash when she had done so. She did not deny the fact; she was not in the slightest bit ashamed of it; and she never ceased to be grateful to Denis for the opportunity he gave her. She knew precisely what she owed him.

They were, all in all, an extraordinarily effective partnership. He complemented her strengths and also made up for her deficiencies. He was a warm and protective presence just when she most needed it. But the popular image of Denis as the long-suffering, self-sacrificing spouse of a difficult, domineering harridan of a wife is very far wide of the mark. She did not domineer; indeed, usually, and often surprisingly meekly, she deferred. She did not begrudge him his friendships, let alone intrude on his hobbies, above all his passionate attachment to sport. She kept house. She entertained. She was a good wife. And Denis was generally a good husband, though his saintliness has been exaggerated by some hagiographers.

Despite the early security he provided, Denis got at least as much out of the marriage as Margaret did, and he brought to it some weaknesses. Even materially, he was by no means an unqualified asset, at least in the longer term. He was not, in fact, a particularly good businessman: he had inherited shares in a family firm which he managed, and he was lucky enough to sell his interest on terms that gave him a large pay-off and a good salary to boot. But it is significant that he left a very modest legacy at his death. This was because, throughout his life, and despite his training as an accountant and his eagle-eyed scrutiny of the Stock Exchange, he was a poor investor. Once his wife had become Prime Minister, and even after her retirement, it was Denis who lived off her and not vice versa. He matched Alf Roberts in his dislike of spending his own money. More generally, while (in contrast to certain of his successors) he did not raise eyebrows about exploiting his position, he certainly made the most of it. He was a celebrity exclusively because of whom he had married.

Denis expected his new wife to do everything in the home, which in the early 1950s was perhaps not unusual. But his unwillingness to help bring up the children was, even then: it smacked of Edwardian or even Victorian assumptions. Margaret was, in his view, home-maker and mother, and his role was to earn and, when not working, to pursue his own interests. So it was entirely in character that when Mark and Carol were born in August 1953 by Caesarian section, DT should be away watching cricket. Although accounts differ, it is difficult to believe that he did not know that the birth was imminent. Nor did he intend to have his life disrupted by the twins when they and their mother came home. He accordingly acquired the lease of the adjoining flat, and the children lived there with a nanny.

Of the two children, Carol Thatcher has for many years been the public favourite. Her down-to-earth, robust and cheerful personality is widely and favourably contrasted with that of her brother. Mark is widely portrayed as the classic black sheep, a devious and discreditable weakling who causes trouble wherever he goes. The reality in both cases is more complex, and is in any case relevant here only in so far as it relates to Margaret Thatcher's own life story. It is not easy to say whether Mrs Thatcher was the more affected by her daughter's remoteness – and finally insensitivity – or her son's scandals.*

The notion that her two offspring's difficulties all stemmed from her own failings as a mother, although she herself privately seemed to accept it, is also one that should be challenged. If she spoilt Mark as a child, it was because he was often ill and unhappy. If she seemed to ignore Carol, it was because her daughter was less obviously needy – except, in later life, financially, when her mother's generosity was enormous. And what about Denis? It is the role of the father, not the mother, the power of paternal example rather than of maternal love, which is usually decisive in how a son matures. It is very difficult for a son to grow up in the shadow of a powerful parent, as the cases of Randolph Churchill and many others show. Mark's problems, so widely discussed, are commonly attributed to his mother's guilty over-compensation for her absence; they could arguably be blamed in greater measure on the other parent. Then again, the assumption that children are always the psychological victims of their parents, rather than vice versa, should not pass unchallenged either. Another equally valid way of looking at the tangled web of Thatcher family relationships is that Margaret Thatcher deserves credit for coping with the real or imagined problems of two difficult children at the same time as pursuing a successful political career and, later, running the country's affairs. This took strength of character.

In some respects, Denis lacked that strength. Like many physically brave and superficially bluff men, he was also emotionally and psychologically fragile. In 1964 he had some kind of breakdown and spent a whole year away from home, apparently travelling in Africa. (He had family and commercial ties there and visited the continent every summer: but this was much more than a business trip.) Margaret, by contrast, never cracked – whatever the pressure.

* For Carol's published comments about her mother, see p. 429.

She was the stoic, he was the tearful one. She was inclined to fight, he wanted to yield. Of course, it is sometimes more painful to experience suffering by proxy than in person, and this is what Denis had to do, particularly in his wife's difficult final days in office. He loved her and he felt for her. Yet the temperamental contrast between the two Thatcher spouses is real enough. Some of the occasions on which this was manifest are well documented, though no proper account seems to be taken of them. For instance, Denis apparently suggested she should 'pack it up' when the 'Thatcher Milk Snatcher' campaign was at its height.[6] He definitely opposed her taking the huge risk involved in challenging Heath for the party leadership.[7] He was involved in her considering resignation in 1981 at the height of the Government's early public expenditure crisis.[8] And he certainly pressed her to pull out of the second ballot to retain her leadership in 1990.[9] Even the many anecdotal accounts of how Denis would periodically intervene to tell her to go to bed, portrayed as affectionate common sense, reinforce the impression. The subliminal message from her husband was always that she should commit herself less comprehensively to the task in hand. On occasion, that was good advice. She worked too hard and for excessively long hours. She underrated the effect tiredness had on the quality of her decisions. But, then, this consuming drive to master a subject was often all that stood between success and defeat. At crucial moments everything depended on her, and only her. It is not always a kindness to urge less effort.

If ever proof were needed of the driving force of Margaret Thatcher's ambition it can be found during this early period. It was while she was in hospital recovering from giving birth that she decided to send in the application papers and fee for the Bar exams. As she admits in her memoirs, she feared that otherwise she might be tempted to become merely a full-time housewife and mother.[10] It is an honest yet astonishing, not to say shameless, confession. She was determined that domesticity should not entrap her, as she felt it had entrapped her mother and so many other women.

But even the law was only a means to an end, and that end was a parliamentary seat. She simply could not resist the lure of politics. In June 1952 she told John Hare, the Party Vice-Chairman for Candidates, that she wanted to have her name placed on the candidates' list once more. Given her commitments as a married woman, it was agreed – probably at his urging – that she should consider only seats in or around London. Despite that, she applied for Canterbury; she did not make the shortlist.

The arrival in August the following year of the twins put paid to all such plans – for the moment. In reply to a tactful letter from Hare suggesting that motherhood might mean a suspension of politics, she wrote back: 'I think I had better not consider a candidature *for at least six months*' (emphasis added). Six months is an astonishingly short time to commit to bonding with two newborn children. The statement revealed her priorities – although, in the event, she would have to wait much longer than that.

One reason for delay was the need to concentrate on the law. She had thought of trying to go into patent law, hoping to make use of her scientific knowledge, but this proved a dead end. So she plumped for tax law instead. In this area, her head for figures and her clarity of thought would certainly be at a premium. Nor is there any shortage of work for tax lawyers, any more than for accountants. In fact, she would barely practise at all, working as a barrister for just two years. But the training she received was useful. To have a legal education and to know about tax provided her with skills in two areas of great importance to the modern MP.

In the course of her pupillage, she went through four sets of chambers. This was partly because she was badly let down by the head of her tax chambers, who seems to have succumbed to male prejudice. But on the way through she made some valuable contacts. The Bar, then as since, was a traditional forcing-house for would-be Tory politicians, and she made the acquaintance of future colleagues including Anthony Barber, Patrick Jenkin, Airey Neave and Michael Havers. Through the very active Inns of Court

Conservative Association, of whose executive she became a member, she encountered Geoffrey Howe. Howe was already making a distinctive political contribution, and was joint author of the influential pamphlet *A Giant's Strength* which advocated the radical reform of trade unions – a challenge which Harold Wilson ducked, which Ted Heath accepted and fumbled, and which Mrs Thatcher would triumphantly meet and overcome.

Meanwhile, she continued to press her claims to a winnable constituency. In December 1954 she heard that Orpington, adjoining her old stamping-ground of Dartford, needed a candidate and applied. She was placed on the shortlist and interviewed, but was not selected. Momentarily discouraged, she wrote to Hare to withdraw her name from the list, claiming that her thoughts were all now focused on her legal career and that she could not think about a seat 'for many years'. During the 1955 general election she spoke on behalf of other candidates, including Ted Heath in his constituency. But otherwise she had to sit it out, which she did not at all enjoy.

Nationally, the outcome of the 1955 poll was a solid majority for Anthony Eden. In February 1956 she wrote to Central Office asking to be put back on the candidates' list. There was no problem. In Donald Kaberry, now Vice-Chairman for Candidates, she found another of those benevolent male mentors who so often smoothed her early progress. The difficulty, rather, was in trying to persuade Tories in the constituencies that as not only a woman but a young mother with two toddlers she was in any sense a suitable candidate.

Many years later, Mrs Thatcher as Prime Minister would probably have seen the critics' point. In her younger days, however, she thought differently. In fact, she was now in professional, if not social (let alone sexual), terms a feminist. Her thinking is clearly revealed by an article she had written in 1952 entitled 'Wake up, Women!':

> I hope that we shall see more and more women combining
> marriage and a career. Prejudice against this dual role is not

confined to men. Far too often, I regret to say it comes from our own sex. But the happy management of home and career IS being achieved . . . [I]t is possible to carry on working, taking a short leave of absence when families arrive, and returning later. In this way gifts and talents that would otherwise be wasted are developed to the benefit of the community.

She concluded on a more political and, indeed, more self-interested note:

If we are to have a better representation in Parliament, the women of England must fight harder for it. Should a woman arise equal to the task, I say let her have an equal chance with the men for the leading Cabinet posts. Why not a woman Chancellor – or Foreign Secretary?[11]

When questioned about how she could combine a political career with dutiful motherhood, she would answer by describing how carefully she managed her time. In 1954 she wrote in another magazine, in a tone which must have been even more grating to non-working women then than now:

When I returned to [legal] studies I was constantly asked 'How do you find the time?' The answer seems to be a perpetual mystery to the woman who doesn't go out to work and quite simple to those of us who do. There are 24 hours in every day: the people who ask this question seem to be amazed at how much can be packed into them; I am astonished at how little some people seem to do. The answer is this – you can achieve as much in a day as you set out to achieve if you think ahead and get everything well organised.[12]

There is no doubt that Mrs Thatcher was, indeed, formidably well organized and that her energy allowed her to perform multifarious tasks with great efficiency. But she could also afford a reliable nanny to supervise the children when she was not present. Clearly, this was not an option for most mothers, who had to work in order to supplement their husbands' income.

Mrs Thatcher's views, one should add, evolved over time, though they never achieved any great coherence on the question of how to balance a woman's right to fulfil her talents with her duties as a mother. So, as Prime Minister, she refused to accept her Chancellor Nigel Lawson's proposals for fully transferable tax allowances between spouses, which she saw as penalizing working mothers.[13] Yet she also refused to support his successor John Major's desire for subsidized child care.[14] She upheld the right of women to work, to attain the highest positions, to succeed in a man's world, and she wanted nothing done to prevent that. At the same time, she disliked 'child minding on the state' and believed, indeed, that it was socially harmful for children to be brought up by carers rather than their mothers. She still remembered when writing her memoirs how appalled she had been, on a visit to Leningrad in 1969, to see children being taken off by their mothers at daybreak to state-run crèches. She never resolved in her mind or in her policies the tension between these two – equally real and equally conservative – priorities.

The political problem of how to provide opportunity for talented women, while ensuring family life was protected, was also on the minds of the Tory selection committees she faced now at the start of her career. It is easy to write off the criticism she faced as mere prejudice. Sometimes it was. But there were serious questions at issue. Most practically, how could she perform her role as a wife and mother while also playing a full part in the House of Commons, which in those days sat late into the night and whose committees often met in the morning too? Her answers failed to convince.

Then Finchley, a seat in North London, was advertised. Perhaps an urban middle-class audience might be more open-minded? She did not know the area well, but she quickly did all she could to find out about it. As in other London constituencies, national rather than local issues were at the forefront of politics, and she was conversant with all of those. Unfortunately, Denis was away when, on Monday, 14 July 1958, she and the other three hopefuls – all men, each accompanied by his wife – were called to address the association's executive. (Denis only learned the news of his wife's selection when he read it some days later in a discarded newspaper on a flight from South Africa to Nigeria.)

The atmosphere that evening was not helped by the well-known hostility of the sitting MP, Sir John Crowder, to the idea of having a woman succeed him. (He would continue to evince it.) Margaret Thatcher was clearly by far the most accomplished speaker, and she performed well. She also managed during questions to allay doubts about her family situation. The seat had been poorly worked and was in need of an energetic candidate to fight off what seemed a serious Liberal threat. Mrs Thatcher, as always, exuded energy. She narrowly won.

A fortnight later, with Denis now present, she consolidated her position by routing a clique of diehard opponents at a packed adoption meeting. The local press were impressed by this clever, elegant woman, dressed in black and gold and wearing a small hat, speaking without notes, 'stabbing home points with expressive hands'.[15] (Unlike Heath, she was good with her hands, though the 'stabbing' and pointing could on occasion become irritating.)

In truth, for all the party agent's worries, Finchley was a safe seat. The Liberal surge was based on the Jewish community, which had been outraged by incidents of anti-semitism at the Tory-dominated golf club. Mrs Thatcher was a quite different class of Tory, harboured not the slightest trace of anti-semitism, and quickly became close to her Jewish constituents. Indeed, they provided the backbone of her support in future years. They formed a bridge between her and not only British Jewry more widely but also the state of Israel, for which Mrs Thatcher, almost uniquely among senior Conservatives of the time, conceived a deep sympathy.

The Thatchers were on a family holiday on the Isle of Wight when the general election was called for autumn 1959. The ensuing campaign was less noisy and eventful than those earlier ones in Dartford. It was clear from the start that the Conservatives, fighting on the basis of the country's increased prosperity, would prevail. In Finchley, Mrs Thatcher campaigned, as she always did, as if it were a marginal seat, and she won it with a substantially increased majority of over 16,000. It was the first step.

3

THE GREASY POLE

With Margaret Thatcher's election, Finchley gained an extremely conscientious Member of Parliament. As she told the ever supportive and curious *Finchley Press*, she wrote almost two thousand letters to, or on behalf of, her constituents in her first ten months as an MP. Unusually, she employed a full-time secretary to help in the task.

One problem with a London seat was that although it was obviously more easily accessible than one in the far North or extreme South-West, it was also more demanding. Moreover, Mrs Thatcher did not actually live in or even very near to the constituency. The family had left Swan Court when controls on the rent were lifted, moving to a large house with a garden in Farnborough, Kent. Dormers was more convenient for Denis, and Margaret could spend her weekends painting, decorating and gardening – all of which she enjoyed. The children, who were six when Mrs Thatcher entered the House of Commons, liked living there too. For their mother, however, it was less convenient, and all her organizational skills and much of her energy were involved in trying to supervise matters at home while making a mark in Parliament. But a mark she very quickly made.

She had the good fortune to be drawn second in the Commons ballot for the introduction of Private Members' Bills. Only the first few have a chance of becoming law, so this immediately focused the parliamentary gaze upon her. As the youngest woman Member, and a new Member at that, the opportunity for at least fleeting stardom beckoned. There were, though, three accompanying risks. First, there was a great opportunity to make a fool of herself. Admittedly, many great political figures – not least Disraeli – have overcome an initial disaster, but it is still something to be avoided. Second, she would lose her chance of being inducted into the good graces of the House of Commons by an unassuming and uncontroversial maiden speech. Finally, there was the problem of choosing a topic – and it would indeed cause her problems. It would be expected to advance the party's, in this case the Government's, aims. But it could not be a large measure, because that would be to venture beyond the scope of a Private Member's Bill. As it was, any serious initiative – and Margaret Thatcher was determined from the first to be serious – would need assistance with drafting from the government machine. That meant that she had to be cooperative, at least within limits.

Various ideas attracted her. But she finally settled on a Bill to admit the press to meetings of local authorities. Some fun has been had with this choice by later commentators, who point out that as Prime Minister Mrs Thatcher strongly resisted Freedom of Information Bills, and here she was demanding that government decisions be opened up to public scrutiny. Fun or not, the critics forget the context. What caught her attention at this point was a double abuse of power, and one with its roots in municipal social-ism. Councils had been abusing their right to exclude the press when they went into committee, so as to shut down debate on how public money was spent. They had also done it in connection with a dispute in the printing industry, to support the print unions against so-called 'black-leg' (i.e. non-unionized) reporters. A notorious case had occurred in Nottingham, close to Grantham. The Conservative manifesto had highlighted the problem and promised to deal with it, but it was soon made clear to her by Henry Brooke, the Housing and Local Government Minister, that a code of practice, not legislation, was the preferred instrument for doing so. She persisted, however, and she was able to rely on strong Tory backbench and some cross-party support. So Brooke and his department reluctantly offered help.

The measure which finally reached the statute book as the Public Bodies (Admission to Meetings) Act 1960 was, in truth, a fairly inconsequential one. It had been substantially watered down and it contained loopholes sufficient to allow much of the problem to continue. But in the course of its progress Margaret Thatcher became a minor celebrity. She was supported by a House of Commons much fuller than on an ordinary Friday, because she had spent hours writing individual letters to colleagues asking their support – dashing off apposite personal notes would be a well-known Thatcher trait. All three women members of the Government, Mervyn Pike, Pat Hornsby-Smith (an old friend from Dartford days) and Edith Pitt, turned up in solidarity. Mrs Thatcher's performance showed her to be a persuasive advocate and a gifted debater. She spoke for twenty-seven minutes, barely consulting her notes. The subsequent congratulations were much more than the oily formalities usually evoked by such occasions.

But she also made an impact of a somewhat different kind on the ministers and officials who had to deal with her. She showed herself to be difficult, aggressive and opinionated. Sometimes she got her way, sometimes she capitulated. The department was, not unusually, desperate to retain good relations with the prevailing vested interests, namely the local authorities and the unions. Brooke was an old-school Tory, a practitioner of the art of the possible with a pessimistic view of the possibilities. His deputy, a certain Keith Joseph, the junior Housing Minister, was at this stage of his career no less emollient. By threatening to withhold assistance and even support, they forced her to draw some of the teeth from the measure. As a practical politician, she knew her weakness, and she conceded. To cap it all, she had to agree to conceal both the assistance received and the pressures applied when she answered for the changes introduced in committee. Despite her frustration, she kept the bargain. This was another trait that colleagues of Margaret Thatcher would come to recognize.

Mrs Thatcher's maiden speech won very favourable press coverage. But what mattered more was that she had impressed ministers and the House business managers with her acumen and her eloquence. She could not, though, have expected any early promotion. She was simply too new and too young. This probably explains why she was prepared to become a minor embarrassment over the issue of birching – on which she had already made clear her views. She was a member of the standing committee discussing Rab Butler's liberal-minded Criminal Justice Bill in 1961 and joined with other Tories to try to reinstate corporal punishment for young offenders. She spoke about her belief in giving them a 'short, sharp shock' (a phrase resurrected by another liberal-minded Tory Home Secretary, Willie Whitelaw, when she was Prime Minister). Now, as then, she doubted whether what was administered in detention centres was 'sharp' enough.

What would turn out to be her last speech as a backbencher for thirty years was made on a more politically acceptable subject, namely the economy. Speaking in the 1961 Budget debate, she concentrated on the need for better techniques for controlling public expenditure. Some time later in the summer, she learned that Pat Hornsby-Smith was planning to resign from the Government. This raised the possibility that she might be invited aboard in order to keep up the number of women – a path to promotion which Mrs Thatcher, as one who several times benefited from it, never felt remotely undignified.

As expected, that October she was summoned to see the Prime Minister and given the job which was vacant, that of parliamentary under-secretary at the Ministry of Pensions and National

Insurance. Harold Macmillan's laid-back style was the opposite to that of his new appointee and much later successor, and his initial advice stayed in her memory. She had imagined that she must rush in and start work as soon as possible. But the Prime Minister suggested instead that she go in about eleven o'clock next day, look around, sign a few letters, and then leave.

In fact, she arrived rather earlier than that to be met at the main door by the minister, John Boyd-Carpenter. He does not seem to have expected much of her, not least because she was married with a husband and young children to look after. But he quickly changed his mind. Within a short while, Mrs Thatcher's understanding of the social security system was sufficient for her to be a nuisance to officials and a formidable spokesman in the House of Commons. Her success did not stem from originality of thought. In any case, the directions of policy were broadly set before her arrival. She was, it is true, asked to examine the position of women in the system; but this was a mere curtsey to feminism, and nothing much came of it. The grind of the job was the huge load of 'case work': that is, individual cases which needed reference to a minister rather than simply rule-based decisions by officials. But Mrs Thatcher did not mind the labour at all. She was genuinely interested in people's predicaments, and though she had strong views about thriftless idlers, or the 'undeserving poor' as they had traditionally been called, she also had a strong sense of justice. It was this sense, not merely an eye for a good political issue, which caused her to champion, above and beyond her brief, the interests of widows with children. She fought to have them exempted from the 'earnings rule', that is, the requirement of those with pensions to pay tax over a certain level of income. The change was finally introduced by the succeeding Labour Government.

What made Mrs Thatcher's parliamentary performances so noteworthy, however, was her mastery of detail, and her marshalling of facts and figures within a clear framework of argument. She was also capable of summoning up, and sometimes even conveying, enthusiasm for what was, for the most part, an extremely boring subject. On the other hand, reading her speeches at this time one is undeniably struck by something less pleasant. Like many virtuoso performances, these were notable for their lack of subtlety or restraint. As a very junior member of the Government she chided, bossed and bullied, and shamelessly exhibited her abilities, in a manner which would not have been tolerated from a man, nor perhaps from a less attractive woman. The seeds of future problems as well as future promotion can be glimpsed in these debates.

In fact, while Mrs Thatcher was making a minor name for herself at Pensions, the tectonic plates of politics had begun to move. The end of the Conservative hegemony was approaching. 'Supermac' looked tired, out of date and out of touch. Once Harold Wilson became leader of the Opposition, he began successfully to taunt the Prime Minister across the Dispatch Box. The summer of 1963 also saw the Profumo affair, which made the Tory Government look corrupt and the Prime Minister himself appear a dupe. Although it was ill health that forced Macmillan to announce his immediate resignation at the start of the Conservative party conference that year, it was the Conservative Government which was truly sick; and while Macmillan quickly recovered, the Tories could not.

Mrs Thatcher's recollections of whom she wanted to succeed Macmillan and why were somewhat hazy by the time she came to record them in her memoirs. She seems not to have considered the flamboyant Quintin Hogg as a serious contender, but then – apart from Hogg himself – nor did any one much else. More surprisingly, she claimed not to have been a supporter of the obvious candidate, whom Macmillan was determined to stop, Rab Butler. Perhaps it seemed to her that Butler was too closely associated with the Party's liberal wing, and she was certainly no liberal. What is more surprising still is that she was content to see Alec Douglas-Home 'emerge' through the final (but, as it turned out, fatal) operation of the Tory high command's much criticized Magic Circle. But she had been impressed by his performance as Foreign Secretary. She read one of his speeches in Hansard and found that it echoed her own belief in the need for a strong military deterrent in the face of Soviet ambitions. In any case, he duly became Tory leader and so Prime Minister.

Margaret Thatcher always retained a soft spot for Douglas-Home, which should serve as counter-weight to the suggestion that Thatcherism can be equated with a chippy brand of meritocracy. She was in many respects an old-fashioned Conservative at heart. She liked to look up to men who were older and more experienced, particularly if they were well born and well educated. She was neither a snob nor – which must have been the greater temptation – an inverse snob. She would for ever consider that Douglas-Home had been unfairly treated by the media and point, with justice, to the recovery which the Conservatives staged during his short period as leader. She regretted the ruthless way in which he was dispatched after the defeat – in October 1964 Labour secured a majority of only four. The fact is, though, that because of how he had been appointed, without an open election, the legitimacy of his position was impaired even as Prime Minister: it was irremediably weakened once he had lost the general election.

The ensuing leadership election was the first to be openly contested. Reggie Maudling started out as favourite, with Ted Heath in a strong second place and Enoch Powell standing as a maverick outsider. Margaret initially intended to vote for Maudling. He represented the neighbouring seat of Barnet and she had got to know him as a result. They were not close; in fact, he seems always to have disliked her. But she was unaware of this, and she thought him extremely clever, which he was. He was also, however, lazy, and his reputation for laziness helped lose him the contest. For his part, Heath was no longer on terms of political friendship with Mrs Thatcher. Their paths did not often cross. Heath was thought, for no obvious reason, to be somewhat to the left of Maudling. His one great public cause, however, was Europe. While Maudling had helped create the European Free Trade Area

(EFTA), Heath was a devotee of closer integration through the European Common Market. This did not count against him for Mrs Thatcher at this stage of her career. To judge from her public statements, she fully accepted the need for Britain to join the Common Market and is on the record as pooh-poohing the danger of a loss of sovereignty as a result of doing so. When one considers that Enoch Powell too favoured British membership in the 1960s, her views become less surprising or significant.

By a nice irony, what finally determined her support for Heath rather than Maudling, to whom she had earlier promised her vote, was the intervention of Keith Joseph. The fact that Joseph was considered best placed to influence her by Heath's campaign team shows that he and Mrs Thatcher had remained close since they first collaborated over her Private Member's Bill. He now telephoned and persuaded her to support Heath with the assurance: 'Ted has a passion to get Britain right.' It was just the sort of earnest pitch that appealed to her. She followed Joseph's advice and plumped for Heath.

Having won, Heath reshuffled the portfolios and Mrs Thatcher was a beneficiary. She was moved to shadow Housing and Land, where her attacks on the Government's introduction of a Land Commission to nationalize development gains reinforced her reputation. The change was timely. She had not enjoyed shadowing Pensions in Opposition.

There had been problems of a more personal kind as well. In 1964 Denis had some kind of breakdown and disappeared for months to Africa. At the end of the year Margaret was, herself, incapacitated by pneumonia. One outcome of DT's crisis was his decision to sell the family firm. He did not make many good business decisions during his life, but this one compensated for the rest. He sold Atlas to Castrol, which a few years later merged with Burma Oil. Denis gained capital through share options and income as a board member. It was to prove a very satisfactory basis for his own prosperity and his wife's career. Home life also became simpler, if necessarily less homely, when the children went away to boarding school: first Mark and then, at her own insistence, Carol too. The Thatchers sold Dormers and bought The Mount, a mock-Tudor house in Lamberhurst near Tunbridge Wells. It was intended for use at weekends and during the recess and school holidays; while the House was sitting, the couple lived during the week in a rented flat in Westminster Gardens, within earshot of the House of Commons division bell. It was a more practical arrangement for a hardworking and increasingly senior politician.

But the party was sliding towards a much more serious defeat in the general election of 1966. Heath's policy review had not got very far. There was talk of trade union reform and, inevitably with Heath in the saddle, Europe figured largely. Mrs Thatcher loyally described the issue as a 'cornerstone of the campaign' and, adopting language she would not have tolerated in later years, argued that Europe could now 'form a block with as much power as the USA or Russia'. The outcome was quite as bad as predicted, delivering Labour a majority of ninety-eight. She herself had a healthy margin of over 9,000 in Finchley. But a full term in opposition beckoned.

In the inevitable further reshuffle of the Tory frontbench team she might have had some expectation of joining the Shadow Cabinet. Certainly others thought it possible, and her reputation was such that some already quailed at the prospect. Jim Prior recalls a discussion of whether Mrs Thatcher should become what was increasingly regarded as the statutory woman at the top table. But when he suggested her name to Heath . . .

'There was a long silence. "Yes," he said. "Willie [Whitelaw – then Chief Whip] agrees she's the most able, but he says once she's there we'll never be able to get her out." '[1]

Margaret Thatcher had no inkling of any of this. She was simply glad to be made deputy to Iain Macleod as Treasury and Economic Affairs spokesman. Macleod had specifically asked for her, and it is easy to see why. They were both sharp-witted, good debaters and very aggressive. Others might value her as a token woman; he understood that she had the makings of a formidable politician. A mutual admiration grew up between them – he even privately thought she could become party leader.[2] Their relationship might have proved significant, had it not been for Macleod's early death.

Mrs Thatcher was now fully engaged in fighting the Government's 1966 and 1967 Finance Bills. Then, as now, the Opposition Treasury team was at a great disadvantage. The Chancellor and Treasury ministers know, or should know, their proposals inside out. By contrast, the Opposition comes to them fresh and often floundering. Treasury officials are the cream of the Civil Service. The Opposition, for its part, has to rely on whatever unpaid experts it can find to help. But Macleod was an inspiring team leader, and Mrs Thatcher a formidable understudy. As at Pensions, she enjoyed demonstrating her capacity to master huge amounts of detail. She was thus, for example, able to reveal to the House that she had looked through every Finance Bill since 1946 and discovered that James Callaghan's 1966 Bill was the first not to introduce 'some social service relief or some relief in tax'. But she was not just the showy swot she had sometimes appeared as junior Pensions Minister. She had now developed into a ferocious parliamentary opponent, remorseless in deconstructing such ill-thought-out measures as that year's introduction of Selective Employment Tax (SET).[3]

During this period, the Opposition Treasury team also gained satisfaction and plaudits by exposing the absurdities inherent in the Government's pay policy. This, though, was a double-edged weapon. Macleod and Mrs Thatcher demonstrated beyond doubt that an incomes policy could not work. This in turn encouraged the pledge in the ensuing Conservative manifesto not to introduce one. That pledge would, of course, turn out to be worthless.

The October 1967 reshuffle saw Heath moving Mrs Thatcher again, this time to shadow Fuel and Power. This finally involved her promotion to the Shadow Cabinet – where Whitelaw's doleful prediction proved all too accurate.

It was now more difficult than ever to combine the life of a house-wife and mother with the demands of political and, especially, parliamentary, business. From now on, in fact, domesticity increasingly took second place to public life, until the former was almost entirely absorbed into the latter. Paid cleaners, though not cooks, stood in for the mistress of the house. The fact that the children were no longer at home helped. Denis had a more flexible life now that he had sold his business, though this did not mean that he took over the chores. At least, she lived conveniently close to work.

Mrs Thatcher spoke at that year's party conference. It was not her first platform address; she had delivered a rather pedestrian speech on local government finance in 1965, and had also spoken, to greater effect, on taxation in 1966. But her 1967 speech can be read as a textbook 'Thatcherite' assault on socialism as an economic doctrine.

Although cautious about pledging denationalization, Mrs Thatcher explained why nationalized industries could never be efficiently run – because they are accountable to no one. She exposed (once more) the bogus prospectus of nationalization as 'national ownership', when it just meant state ownership. She also placed the whole argument against state encroachment on property rights within a wider historical and philosophical context, in terms that she was to echo in speeches thirty years later: 'It is good to recall how our freedom has been gained in this country – not by great abstract campaigns but through the objections of ordinary men and women to having their money taken from them by the state ... It was their money, their wealth, which was the source of their independence against the Government. That is crucial.' She even quoted Agar's *A Time for Greatness* – 'Power over a man's support is ultimate power over his will' – surely, the only time that this left-wing tract was ever brought to the service of free-enterprise capitalism.

Margaret Thatcher's first official duty as energy spokesman was to respond to the Edmund Davies inquiry, set up to investigate the Aberfan disaster in which 144 people, including 116 children, had been killed when a slag tip collapsed on to a Welsh mining village. She was profoundly disgusted by the fact that no one at the Coal Board – let alone its chairman, the socialist magnate Lord Robens – was prepared to take personal responsibility for the catastrophe. She felt he should have resigned, though she was not authorized to say so. She poured out her scorn on the incompetence highlighted by the report.

Margaret Thatcher's brief was a not uninteresting one. The coal-mining industry was already recognized as an incubus rather than a benefit, though nobody knew what to do with it. North Sea gas was coming on stream. The future funding and development of nuclear power was an issue. Most of her time was spent, however, investigating (in vain) how to introduce private finance into electricity generation. In November 1968 she was moved again – to Transport. It was not exactly a demotion but not a promotion either, and a less stimulating brief, since the Government's own controversial measures had already reached the statute book. But she concentrated on fighting the proposal to nationalize the ports.

Mrs Thatcher was now inside the Shadow Cabinet; but she does not seem to have made much of a contribution to it. She spoke when required about her portfolios and she intervened quite frequently on a host of secondary matters, to the extent that Heath was soon tired of listening to her. What she did not do was to have, or seek to have, any sustained impact on the general direction of policy. There were several reasons for this, ones which would carry over into government. In the first place, her opinion was not wanted. She had, it is true, gained the respect of her male colleagues for her mastery of a brief and her ability to hold her own in the House of Commons. She even had some friends of sorts around the Shadow Cabinet table – notably Macleod, Joseph and Boyle. But she was simply not taken seriously as a contributor to discussion. Partly, this was because of her sex and her manner. More so, it was because she was as yet incoherent in her beliefs, her right-wing instincts still at odds with the technocratic requirements of day-to-day issues. Nor did she have behind her the support of any powerful group in the party.

Yet there was another reason whose importance analysts of Conservative politics during these years still underrate, which is the role of Enoch Powell. Powell was a powerful and polarizing figure even before the upheaval created by his Birmingham speech on immigration of 20 April 1968. Afterwards, his absence from discussion within the Shadow Cabinet was even more disruptive than had been his presence.

Now and later, Margaret Thatcher's political persona and prospects must be linked to Powell's. This might seem surprising. He was, after all, of an older generation. He was also an outstanding academic and polymath, and that even rarer beast a genuine Tory intellectual, which she was not. Like Heath he was externally cold, not particularly fond of women (apart from his wife, whom he adored), and without any high regard for Margaret Thatcher or her opinions. Later, jealousy was a factor in this; now it was merely arrogance. For her part, she had no close dealings with him. As she explains in her memoirs, by the time she joined the Shadow Cabinet, Powell was already a semi-detached member of it.[4] He took little part in discussions and had dropped the always uncongenial and unconvincing pretence of being part of a team. He had argued the case for what would shortly be described as (economic) Powellism and would much later be called Thatcherism – that is, for wages and prices set by the market not by governments, and for floating exchange rates. And he had lost. In April 1968 he was finally sacked by Heath for his immigration speech, which Heath deemed 'racist in tone and liable to exacerbate racial tensions'.

Margaret Thatcher shared many of Powell's views, though she had not first encountered them in him. She was, for example, hostile to mass immigration, and with a London seat she was well aware of the tensions it was causing. More important, she was as hostile as Powell to state intervention in the economy. She had enjoyed herself under Macleod, pulling apart the Government's pay policy. She disliked nationalization intensely. She had even begun to place some of these attitudes in a clearer intellectual context through her contact with the Institute of Economic Affairs (IEA). Again, it was Powell, though temperamentally an autodidact, who gave most coherent voice to the IEA's analysis, going well beyond anything that Margaret Thatcher understood at the time. While she was still mainly locked into attacking socialism, he was setting out the lines of an alternative. Others too looked to the IEA for ideas and guidance, notably Geoffrey Howe and Keith Joseph. Mrs Thatcher was on the fringe of this group.

Powell's ejection from the Shadow Cabinet and his launch of a one-man crusade transformed the political climate. Everything that Powell said gained a hearing. For the first time the technicalities of a floating exchange rate became a matter of fierce debate. Mrs Thatcher, like the rest of the Tory Party, was thus forcibly educated by Powell's speeches. There is no doubt that she liked what she heard, and she duly learned how to put her case in a more structured and philosophically persuasive fashion. At the same time, it became dangerous for any senior Tory to appear to be borrowing ideas from such a poisoned source. If she had embraced such views in Shadow Cabinet after Powell's dismissal, she would have been silenced and very possibly dropped.

Her sympathies, though, were clear enough. She was on his side of the broader argument. Alone among Shadow Cabinet members, it seems, she had counselled Heath, when he telephoned her, not to dismiss Powell in the first place.[5] Naturally, he took no notice. He was, in any case, informing not consulting her. When her constituency invited Powell to speak at a dinner in early 1970, she defended the invitation on grounds of freedom of speech – pointing, characteristically, to Powell's war record as a defender of liberty. But it is through her rapid intellectual formation that she responded to Powell's economic message. She was soon regarded by the IEA as one of a group of senior Tories whose heart was in the right place. In October 1969 Arthur Seldon asked Howe what he thought of her.* Prefiguring the attitude he would adopt in private during the years when he became Mrs Thatcher's political punchbag, Howe sniffily replied that he was 'not sure about Margaret', acknowledging that her 'economic prejudices' were 'sound' but complaining that she was rather 'too dogmatic', particularly on (what was by now her new brief) education.[6]

Howe was not just patronizing: he was also unfair. Although Mrs Thatcher had much to learn about the alternative free-market view and the philosophy behind it, and although (like Howe) she kept her opinions on the matter to herself when Heath was around, she had started to articulate her views. She was given the opportunity to do so when Heath himself asked her to deliver the annual Conservative Political Centre (CPC) lecture to the 1968 party conference. She knew she had been chosen because she was a woman and the assumption was that she would have some unchallenging womanly wisdom to impart. But she chose instead to speak on the subject of 'What's Wrong with Politics?' Reflecting on the uninspiring, colourless alternatives offered by Heath and Wilson, she might have been tempted to give a short and tactless answer. But instead she concentrated upon the effects that steady government intrusion, through expanding socialism, had had upon popular expectations and the resulting frustrations and resentments. It is not a particularly well-reasoned or original piece. The CPC has heard more (though also definitely less) distinguished contributions. But she did dip her toe into more turbulent waters by inserting the apparently innocuous sentence: 'We now put so much emphasis on the control of incomes that we have too little regard for the essential role of Government, which is the control of the money supply and

* Arthur Seldon, with Ralph Harris (Lord Harris of High Cross) led the IEA, almost from its foundation in 1955, for more than three decades.

the management of demand.' This, in fact, was dynamite, even though the redundant addition of the phrase 'and the management of demand', perhaps inserted by some diligent Keynesian party adviser, reduced its explosive force. The notion that the control of the money supply, not the control of prices and incomes, was the key to the control of inflation was, of course, central to Powell's economic case. It was also the core economic message of the IEA, which had just begun to popularize Milton Friedman's views – views which came to be seen as providing the classic exposition of 'monetarism'. Mrs Thatcher's analysis, like Powell's and Friedman's, thus pointed the way towards a free economy without inflation, and so towards a new basis for stability and growth.

Equally ideologically significant are the two articles which she wrote the following year for the *Daily Telegraph* to elaborate on the ideas expressed to the CPC. The first took up for the first time a theme that was to be distinctive of her approach – an attack on the idea of 'consensus' as the proper basis of politics.[7] Adopting a classical liberal, rather than a philosophically conservative, position, she pointed out that if political parties pursued more or less the same policies then the electorate was deprived of effective choice. To want, as some did (and do now), to take the big issues 'out of politics' was, she asserted, profoundly undemocratic. She was also objecting to what Keith Joseph would in later years christen the 'ratchet' effect: that is, the irreversibility of socialism. As in the CPC lecture, the style is jerky and the key ideas are not properly developed. A political curate's egg, the piece combines originality and banality in equal measure.

Much the same applies to the second *Telegraph* article.[8] Again, it starts with a classic Thatcherite attack on the notion of 'partici-pation' – defined as the idea 'that interference by Government will be acceptable if more people participate [in it]'. What would become the Thatcherite alternative to participation – giving people a stake in capitalism through ownership of property, shares and savings – is not, though, advanced. These pieces show Mrs

Thatcher's need of help from policy thinkers and writers if she was to advance her convictions more persuasively. But all three also show that some distinctive convictions already existed.

Such modestly courageous forays did Margaret Thatcher no harm. In October 1969 she was appointed Shadow Education Secretary, a significant promotion. The post had fallen vacant because of Edward Boyle's decision to retire to academia. Boyle had not at all liked the mounting pressure from grass-roots Tory opinion to oppose Labour's destruction of grammar schools; and grass-roots Tories reciprocated the dislike. By contrast, Mrs Thatcher was the ideal choice to reassure the right that the party had not given up entirely on selection by ability.

Publicly, she denied that there would be any change of policy. She told the *Yorkshire Post* in an early interview: 'I have no objection to proper comprehensive schools, they have a significant part to play. But there are a large number of grammar schools which have given a marvellous service, and I shall fight to retain them.'[9]

Initially, this meant opposing the government Bill to compel local authorities to submit schemes to go comprehensive. Such a basis for opposition sounded eminently reasonable, and it is easy to see why Mrs Thatcher and the party leadership opted for a middle way – that is, to oppose compulsion, to leave it to local councils to decide whether to reorganize, and to keep out of the debate about whether selection at eleven-plus (or selection at all) was desirable. Unfortunately, the middle way turned out to be merely the muddled way, and it soon led to embarrassment.

This was apparent when she spoke on 12 February 1970 opposing the second reading of the Education Bill. It was a poor performance, not helped perhaps by the fact that her father had died two days earlier. She sought to show, as was undoubtedly true, that universal comprehensive schooling would not guarantee equality of opportunity and that poorly planned comprehensive schools were unsatisfactory. But the fundamental problem she faced was that comprehensive schools and grammar schools could not logically, or in the long run practically, exist side by side, drawing from the same catchment area. In such circumstances the non-grammar schools were necessarily secondary moderns: that is, schools without access to the brightest pupils, who had been 'creamed off' by the grammar schools. So one was either in favour of selection and choice, or one was in favour of social engineering and planning. In her heart, Mrs Thatcher certainly favoured the first alternative, but could not admit it.

At this time only one child in three went to a comprehensive school. But the tide was flowing strongly against selection, and not just among left-leaning educationalists. Mrs Thatcher's own Barnet Council was determined to introduce a comprehensive scheme, which she and other local Conservatives opposed. Up and down the country, Tory local authorities had bought heavily into the egalitarian educational ethic. And since most of her colleagues had been to – and sent their children to – private schools, the future of the grammars was of little personal interest to them. Margaret Thatcher's children went to expensive private schools too: but she at least knew from her own experience that the chance of a good state education meant the difference between success and failure for those from modest backgrounds. Unfortunately, she was fighting a battle that was lost before it was engaged. Coping with the results of the comprehensive revolution was one of the tasks which she would have to undertake as Prime Minister, and which has plagued successive governments. If, some thirty years on, a small number of grammar schools continue to flourish, it is because the original theory of comprehensive education has been discredited – no thanks to any arguments advanced in the meantime by the Conservative Party.

In fact, the 1970 Education Bill fell when an early general election was called. A sudden shift in the polls putting Labour ahead proved too tempting for the arch-opportunist in Downing Street. It was also to prove fatal. Wilson had, in fact, little to show for his term in office. So he tried to paint the Tories as a threat – doctrinaire right-wingers with a sinister master plan for the economy. Inventing 'Selsdon Man', depicting the dull and technical Shadow Cabinet discussions at Selsdon Park at the end of January as endorsing radical change, may have seemed a brilliant tactic. But in the end it probably helped convince the public that the Conservatives had a coherent plan for government and possessed the single-mindedness to pursue it, neither of which was true.

Even judged by the rest of the aimless discussion that took place at Selsdon Park, Mrs Thatcher's contributions were undistinguished. She did not so much as attend the dinners at which her male colleagues let their hair down a little. But she did have a small but significant spat with Heath. Supported by Joseph, she urged that the party support Max Beloff's proposal for an Independent (i.e. private) University, what would become the University of Buckingham. Heath, a statist to the core, was unconvinced. He vetoed any mention of the project in the manifesto, though he felt unable to prevent Mrs Thatcher's publicly welcoming it in a speech – which she later did.

By the time the election was actually called, the Conservatives no longer expected to win it. Nor did Mrs Thatcher. The party had lost ground in the polls in May. But then some bad trade figures lifted Tory gloom. Prospects improved. The Thatchers learned of the way things were going on polling day, from early results on Denis's car radio. Margaret duly increased her majority to over 11,000 in Finchley, and the Conservatives were returned to power nationally with a majority of thirty-one seats. Britain once again had a Tory Government, and Mrs Thatcher was on course for the Cabinet.

4

MILK SNATCHER

Margaret Thatcher's appointment as Secretary of State for Education was expected, without necessarily being automatic. She had shadowed the department for eight months, and she had neither greatly distinguished nor irredeemably embarrassed herself. True, Heath had already begun to find her somewhat tiresome. But he needed a woman in his team; he knew it; and Education was seen by him and others as an ideal 'woman's' portfolio.

But was there perhaps also another reason? Mrs Thatcher and Sir Keith Joseph were probably the two Shadow Cabinet members who had become closest to the IEA/Powellite economic analysis.* The Tory election manifesto, with its explicit rejection of prices and incomes policy and of subsidies and intervention in industry, could, certainly, be read as advocating a bracing free-market philosophy. But Heath personally never subscribed to it. He was an instinctive planner, a technocrat, and beneath the veneer of consensus politics an inveterate authoritarian. At the first sign of serious trouble, he

---

* Howe too, of course, but he was malleable.

would jettison non-intervention and choose government coercion. Had Margaret Thatcher or Keith Joseph held an economic brief, he might have faced more trouble in doing so. But both were in spending departments, where, indeed, they spent with abandon. Mrs Thatcher's potential for causing trouble on economic matters, if she were allowed responsibility for them, was probably a factor in keeping her so long at Education. For her part, she would undoubtedly have liked to be moved. She seems at one time to have been considered as Europe Minister and even started to take French lessons. But the lessons did not get very far – she was not a gifted linguist – and nor did her hopes of a change in portfolio.

In any case, once the economic U-turns began in earnest she was shackled to Education, for better or worse. Cabinet unity was Heath's ultimate answer when charged with betrayal by Powell and other critics. By staying more or less silent and also staying put, Mrs Thatcher played her part in Heath's game by lending public support to the changes of policy. It was not very courageous and it was not even very honourable, but it made political sense for all concerned. It was certainly one of the reasons, alongside a measure of old-fashioned rancour, why Powell never accepted the genuineness of her later ideological conversion.

In some respects, education was by no means an ideal portfolio for Margaret Thatcher. It was outside the political mainstream. The Government's overriding objective, as its pre-election propaganda had stressed, was to reform the economy, not to devise and implement a new social policy. Moreover, education had its own special snags. In part, this was because Conservative education policy was still in so many areas intellectually confused and timid – despite the fact that a philosophically conservative approach to the subject had already been adumbrated by the authors of the so-called education *Black Papers*. These unsung and now largely forgotten innovators had begun combating the collectivist model with bravura on a range of fronts – challenging the switch to a comprehensive system, exposing a decline in standards of reading, attacking the obsession with resources, putting the case for parental choice, and even suggesting a voucher system to end the apartheid between the private and public sectors.[1] Such radicalism was neither widely understood nor regarded as sufficiently respectable to form the basis of policy. And it was certainly not championed by Margaret Thatcher.

People still express surprise at the doctrinal flabbiness Mrs Thatcher demonstrated when, as Education Secretary, she was given her first opportunity to exercise power. Although she was not unusual in this respect in Heath's Government, her behaviour was, indeed, out of character with that of the later Iron Lady. One explanation is, paradoxically, that she herself had had a relatively stress-free education at a good local grammar school. She thus came to the Education Department with certain conventionally conservative views about the importance of literacy, numeracy, discipline and parental choice and a dislike of impersonally large schools. But she had none of the interior anger, frustrations and resentments which have been the driving force of so many educational reformers and which might have caused her to strike out in a new direction.

There were, moreover, two further practical problems to set beside the prevailing, and not historically unusual, Tory philosophical funk.

The first lay in the personnel of the Department of Education and Science (DES). DES officials were far from the brightest or best in the Civil Service. But the department was a formidable fortress of egalitarianism, and the low quality of the garrison was more than made up for by its solidarity and self-righteousness. Almost to a man, DES officials regarded themselves as duty-bound to defend the comprehensive system and the ideology which underpinned it. Mrs Thatcher did not really grasp this. Or at least she did not do so until after she left the DES. She regarded the obstruction she faced as the product of inefficiency or complacency or, on occasion, personal hostility. She did not see it as systemic. She was certainly angered by it. Indeed, she was so outraged by the attitude of the Permanent Secretary, William Pile, that she complained to Number

Ten. But Heath, always more willing to listen to officials than politicians, particularly this particular politician, refused to have Pile removed.

Mrs Thatcher was, of course, half right. There was, indeed, a degree of highly personal dislike for her at the department. The officials she encountered were aghast at everything about her – her assumptions, her views, her directness, her not infrequent aggression. Unlike her Tory predecessors, above all unlike the laid-back Edward Boyle, she did not even affect the cultivated liberalism to which they were accustomed. By the end of her period the civil servants had, it is true, come to value her technical accomplishments and even to take a certain smug pleasure in her ability to fight the department's corner against the Treasury. But, as one of her biographers discovered when he interviewed them, their hostility remained fresh many years on.[2] None of this made for a pleasant atmosphere.

The other problem which confronted Mrs Thatcher as Education Secretary stemmed from the inadequate, opaque and unsatisfactory nature of the powers she wielded. The DES presided over but did not, by and large, control the education system. The most substantial powers were those wielded by local education authorities (LEAs). And the teaching unions exerted at least as much influence as central government. Pay and conditions were set through the unwieldy and allegedly independent but actually just corporatist Burnham Committee. True, the National Inspectorate monitored standards and reported to the Secretary of State, who could also commission other reports – Mrs Thatcher did so on teacher training and on primary school reading standards. The DES could also issue circulars. And, most important, it could provide or withhold funding, particularly capital expenditure. Generally, though, it was blamed for whatever went wrong and lacked the means to put anything much right. These conditions would frustrate any Secretary of State, but none more than an activist like Margaret Thatcher. She could covertly obstruct but not overtly initiate. Even her powers to prevent changes she deplored were weak. She could not effectively block, though she could try to slow, the shift towards a comprehensive system. She could not counter-attack by giving effect to radical initiatives to change what was taught in schools. Therefore, the only way to make a significant impact – and, naturally, to win political credit – was by launching new spending programmes: above all capital spending programmes, because those, at least, were less likely to be diverted into bureaucracy and misguided experimentation.

Without understanding these limitations – as well, of course, as the party's philosophical muddles, outlined above – it is impossible to explain why Margaret Thatcher's time at Education now seems so disappointing. She left office with relatively few self-doubts and a large measure of self-satisfaction. But very quickly the doubts became certainties and the satisfaction was replaced by anger. She came to feel that she had been misled, and she bitterly if privately blamed herself for allowing it. In future years, she was scathing about the DES and distrusted any proposal that emanated from it.

On her first day in the department, the new Secretary of State presented Pile with a list of some fifteen urgent action points, written on pages torn from an exercise book. This the officials found very shocking and, naturally, they took as little notice of it as seemed prudent. But there was a difficulty. Mrs Thatcher had told the press before her arrival that she would act on the first point on the list, namely withdrawal of Labour's circulars 10/65 and 10/66 – the two instruments for centrally enforced comprehensivization – and do so by the time of the first Queen's Speech of the session.*

Her promise provoked a ferocious argument both inside and outside government. The withdrawal of one circular theoretically required the issue of another, and each circular was supposed to be the object of consultation with all those concerned. Mrs Thatcher was unimpressed. When challenged, she pointed out that the

* The first required local authorities to submit plans to go comprehensive. The second backed it up by withholding funding of capital projects for councils that refused to comply.

pledge for immediate action had already been publicly made by herself and, indeed, by Heath. Moreover, what was proposed was the reversal of a coercive directive, not the imposition of a new requirement. But even when the civil servants in the department had been brought into line and the circular issued, the Opposition and the unions protested loudly. More seriously, Mrs Thatcher received a public rebuke from Number Ten. Heath was obsessed with the procedures of orderly decision-making, and for him the procedures were even more important than the decisions. So he called in her and Pile to be disciplined by himself and the head of the Civil Service, Sir William Armstrong.[3]

But he need not have worried. The only real power she possessed, one which she preferred to wield without resorting to the confetti of circulars that the previous Labour Government had issued, derived from section 13 of the 1944 Education Act. This was the power of approving and (when necessary) modifying plans by LEAs that involved the closure of, or change in the character of, schools. And even here her room for manœuvre was limited.

The country was riven by acrimonious disputes about the retention or closure of grammar schools. These quarrels sometimes pitted Conservative against Conservative, as in her own constituency when Barnet Council decided to go comprehensive. But usually the lines of division were party political. Birmingham was the scene of a particularly prolonged and bitter struggle. The Tory Council used Mrs Thatcher's change of policy to save the city's thirty-six grammar schools. But this was the exception, and the victory was only temporary. In 1972 Labour took control, not just of Birmingham but of a succession of other LEAs. The battle for selection at eleven-plus was from this point on, for all practical purposes, lost. The final figures demonstrate how little Mrs Thatcher achieved on this front. While she was at the DES, she considered 3,600 proposals and rejected just 325 of them, a mere 9 per cent. As a result the number of secondary pupils in comprehensive schools doubled. Indeed, comprehensivization advanced faster under Mrs

Thatcher than under any other Secretary of State of either party.

She herself would not have seen the issues in such black-and-white terms. She was not, after all, pledged to keep grammar schools as such. She was not even openly fighting to retain selection. Rather, she argued the merits of variety as against uniformity, and of local democracy as against central diktat. She was, above all, keen to retain 'good schools', ones demonstrably valued by parents, whether they were grammars or not. In the absence of a clear alternative to the comprehensive concept, this was a pragmatic and reasonable case which at least had some public appeal to moderate opinion.

Mrs Thatcher revealed her own still half-formed educational priorities when she was questioned two years into her time at Education by Ronald Butt of *The Times*. Her concerns were similar to those she would voice later, and more emphatically, as Prime Minister. Thus she wanted parents to take a closer interest in their children's teaching. She thought that school governors – the only non-professionals in the system – should be bolder. She called for a sharper debate about teaching methods, and she expressed serious doubts about the prevailing, fashionable 'child-centred' approach. She sympathized with the anxiety, highlighted by a critical report from the National Foundation for Educational Research, about lack of progress in standards of reading. (She even appointed a committee under Sir Alan Bullock to investigate the question, though it got nowhere.) She may have been beaten on selection at eleven-plus, but she expressed hostility to more extreme manifestations of the egalitarian comprehensive ideology, such as the 'banding and bussing' practised by the Labour-controlled Inner London Education Authority. (This involved sending cleverer children to schools in other areas, so as to preserve an 'equal' spread of ability.)[4] The interview is an earnest of good intentions, tinged with regret and frustration.

Given the unwinnable grammar-school war, it was natural that Mrs Thatcher should decide to place the emphasis on primary rather than secondary education. Here at least the doctrinal splits between progressives and conservatives were not too disabling. Moreover, there was something that Margaret Thatcher could actually 'do'. Hence her commitment to the primary school building programme, which focused on the replacement of the 5,000 or more schools built in the previous century. It was not altogether evident that better buildings would lead to better teaching, let alone more learning. But she convinced herself at the time – though she would reject the argument later – that the psychological boost to both teachers and pupils of working in bright new classrooms was worth the money.

Unfortunately, Mrs Thatcher's commitment to the large capital programme she now undertook also helped lead her into a great deal of trouble, because it prompted her agreement to Treasury cuts in the school meals and milk budgets. The Treasury had, in any case, no reason to do her any favours – even if that least sentimental of departments believed in favours. She had, after all, to Heath's great annoyance, announced at her first press conference, and without consultation, plans to go ahead with the Open University. This venture, the brainchild of Harold Wilson, seemed to her a useful investment of resources to produce more graduate teachers. The Chancellor, Macleod, had hoped to abort it, but her move prevented that and his successor, Tony Barber – Macleod died just a month after the election – had to accept the fact.

The school meals budget was accordingly cut and the price of meals rose from 9 pence to 12 pence. As Mrs Thatcher repeatedly pointed out, the previous Labour Government had raised them by more than that. Moreover, there remained a 30 per cent subsidy. Those children whose families could genuinely not afford to pay would not have to do so. There was, anyway, a perfectly good argument that those who could pay should pay; and she made it. But she was also foolish enough to try to explain how children of poor parents might be spared indignity by having money returned to them by teachers in envelopes. She would often sound particularly insensitive when she tried to be most thoughtful, and this was such an occasion. But, then, nothing she said or failed to say could have averted the abuse now heaped upon her. Parliamentary Questions became dominated by allegations, and the popular press by scare stories, of varying degrees of absurdity.

Meals were just the beginning. The left-wing Labour MP Willie Hamilton described her as 'Mrs Scrooge with the painted face'. The Shadow Education Secretary, Edward Short, declared that in Birmingham children were now 'scavenging for crusts' in pig-swill bins. But the row about school milk left school meals far behind.

It is odd to reflect, now that childhood obesity is a worry, that the proposal to end free milk for pupils under seven was considered so outrageous. Free milk could, after all, still be provided for children when recommended by a doctor on medical grounds, and schools could sell milk to anyone else if they wished. In fact, the scale and bitterness of the ensuing attacks says more about Britain in the 1970s than about the proposed change. The patronizing assumption was that the working classes still depended on government to feed their children properly.

The attacks were remorseless, personal and extremely hurtful. Short accused her of 'taking the milk away from the nation's young children' and described her Bill as 'mean, squalid and unworthy'. The *Sun* asked: 'Is Mrs Thatcher Human?' And there was not much doubt of the newspaper's answer. A speaker at the Labour party conference labelled her 'Milk Snatcher'. The insult stuck and was endlessly recycled. She was voted – again in the *Sun* – 'the most unpopular woman in Britain'. She was, as a columnist put it, 'the lady nobody loves'.

Margaret Thatcher would later describe this period of her life as a 'baptism of fire', which she hoped had made her 'stronger'.[5] It was, and it did. But she was very down while it lasted. Nor, as already mentioned, did Denis's attitude serve to bolster her resolve. Tears and a certain amount of self-pity were shown in private, and some of it reached the public as well, though without exciting any noticeable sympathy. It was the first really serious setback in her political life since she had entered the Commons. Hitherto, her youth, her looks and her femininity – as well as her brains – had ensured her an easy ride. But now her sex had suddenly become part of the problem, a basis for the taunt of heartlessness towards children.

At this juncture it was to Heath alone that Mrs Thatcher owed her political survival. Shortly after taking over at the DES she had expressed her confidence that the new Prime Minister would 'never do anything behind your back – he would never, never let you down'.[6] Perhaps she had read him correctly. He certainly did not like to be told whom to sack by the press. But then, as already noted, he also had his own good reasons for keeping her where she was. So in January 1972 she and her senior officials were very publicly invited to a seminar on education at Chequers. Number Ten subsequently briefed heavily that Mrs Thatcher had the Prime Minister's full backing. The attacks immediately eased.

She thus moved into the second and happier phase of her time at Education. The sense of crisis which had begun to surround her, and to demoralize her, subsided. The difficulties did not go away, but they became manageable. She had a breathing space, and she used it.

She now sharply backed away from a fight with student militants by suspending – which meant, in the circumstances, abandoning – plans to reform the finances of the students' unions. She had been plagued by demonstrations on the matter ever since she announced the Government's intentions in the summer of 1971. The National Union of Students (NUS), whose President Jack Straw, the future Cabinet minister, would remain for ever after on Mrs Thatcher's blacklist, was the Government's main opponent. But in this, the high point of the period of student militancy, all sorts of groups pursued their own tactics. When she went to Coventry to present the Document of Designation for the new Lanchester Polytechnic in February 1971, as part of the Government's costly expansion of the polytechnic programme, students followed her around screaming:

'Thatcher out, Tories out, fascist pig, get her f****** knickers off!' The following month she was shouted down at Enfield College of Technology in London when she tried to open a new tutorial block. In May she arrived to open the new Liverpool Polytechnic and militant students interrupted her speech by shouting slogans about school meals and milk. As this suggests, even when the proposals for reforming student union finances had been shelved there were plenty of other things to protest about. On these occasions, she saw at first hand that the huge expansion of higher and further education had done nothing to improve standards of civility. But it was the behaviour of the vice-chancellors and other university authorities, who bowed before campaigns to stifle free speech on campuses, which earned her deepest contempt.

The newspaper headlines may have all been about Mrs Thatcher's initiatives to save money – introducing museum charges (another black mark), raising the price of school meals, snatching milk – as well as protecting grammar schools and confronting students and teachers' unions; but the underlying financial realities presented a very different picture. Margaret Thatcher spent her way, if not out of trouble at least through it.

Under Mrs Thatcher, polytechnics were expanded. There was no significant reform of student grants; she publicly rejected loans. Above all, the raising of the school-leaving age to sixteen, which Labour had postponed, was now implemented, despite strong criticism from right-wing educationalists. This allowed the Conservatives to taunt Labour every time the Opposition complained of 'cuts'. Whether it made much educational sense is another question.

The high point of Mrs Thatcher's spending programmes was reached only when she had weathered the storm over school milk. Indeed, the DES spending splurge at this time can be seen as part of that general loss of nerve that affected the whole Heath Government, once the U-turns were forced upon it. On Wednesday, 6 December 1972 Mrs Thatcher duly published her White Paper entitled *A Framework for Expansion*. It was a ten-year programme involving higher public expenditure on nursery schools, secondary and special school buildings, teacher training and higher education. It would soon turn out to be completely unaffordable.

It was the expansion of nursery education that was most politically eye-catching. Previously, the approach had been to recognize the value of nursery schooling but to portray it as a social benefit to be concentrated on those poorer families deemed (by Keith Joseph among others) to be incompetent to bring up their children without extra help. It had, therefore, been funded through the Urban Programme, specifically aimed at 'deprivation'. Now something far more ambitious was envisaged. Priority was still to be given to deprived areas; but it was envisaged that 90 per cent of four-year-olds and 50 per cent of three-year-olds would eventually be covered by nursery provision. The move was widely praised, not least by the left. The *Guardian* opined that Mrs Thatcher was 'more than half way towards a respectably socialist education policy'.

The praise was welcome while it lasted, but it could not and did not last long. This was because the second phase of the Heath Government, which had been marked by industrial intervention, corporatism, controls, and monetary and fiscal indiscipline, was about to come to a juddering halt in the face of economic reality. The abrupt suspension of Mrs Thatcher's plans for 'expansion' and expenditure was just one of the consequences. In December 1973 Tony Barber announced a round of spending cuts. The DES bore less than its proportionate share of the stringency, and most of the department's cuts fell on capital spending. This was, naturally, embarrassing for a minister who had made so much of school building, but capital is always easier to cut than current, because it does not directly involve pay and jobs. Despite that, by the time Mrs Thatcher came to defend the reductions to the Commons, on 4 January 1974, the teachers were restive, like most of the rest of the public sector. Indeed, from now until the general election Mrs Thatcher's fate was subsumed in that of the Government as a whole, as it struggled to face down the miners' strike, to cope with the consequences of its own policy failure, and to endure an international economic crisis caused by the quadrupling of the oil price after the Arab–Israeli Yom Kippur War.

The lessons which Margaret Thatcher learned from the experience of the Heath Government were fundamental to her own later approach to governing. What Heath had got wrong Mrs Thatcher and her close colleagues and advisers were determined to get right. The contrast was quite deliberate. He would go down in history as the great practitioner of the policy U-turn. She would define herself as the lady who was 'not for turning'. Given this contrast, any biographer of Mrs Thatcher must be intrigued to discover the truth about what she thought, said and did when the fundamental mistakes of the Heath Government were being made.

In his autobiography, Heath scornfully observed that Keith Joseph and Margaret Thatcher 'always kept quiet at the time' when Cabinet discussed 'overall strategy'.[7] This is basically true, and the implied rebuke has some justice. But it is also disingenuous. When Mrs Thatcher wrote her own memoirs, some years earlier, she worried that her account might suggest that she had said almost nothing in Cabinet whereas, as she put it with a certain indignation, she had in fact 'said a lot'. Certainly Heath, who by the period in question could not bear her voice or even, except with difficulty, tolerate the sight of her, would heartily have agreed. She did, indeed, say 'a lot'. But in the end there was no point in either him or her describing her various contemporary observations, because they were unmemorable, peripheral or strictly education-oriented, and simply not relevant to the general direction of policy.

In any case, Cabinet was not the forum in which such discussions were had and decisions made. All governments limit discussion to tighter groups than full Cabinet or the wider committees, whenever highly sensitive issues are concerned. As Prime Minister, Margaret

Thatcher would do this herself. But Heath was more secretive and cliquey. He had an even more highly developed sense than she did of who (to adopt one of her famous phrases) was 'one of us'.* Certainly, neither Margaret Thatcher nor Keith Joseph ever figured in the category of Heath's first person plural. They were just not consulted in advance about the main shifts in policy. The more serious charge is different: it is that they did not then protest about them.

Again, though, it is important to understand the prevailing atmosphere. Although the U-turn would become almost synonymous with Edward Heath's premiership, it must not be taken to imply any personal flexibility. Heath cracked but he could not bend, and while he talked about consensus he never practised it. So Cabinet ministers faced an unpleasant choice. They were bound either to do his bidding unreservedly, or else to abandon hope of a political future. Few politicians, and certainly not Mrs Thatcher (with her ambitions, her departmental headaches and her lack of intellectual self-confidence), would risk dissent in such circumstances.

One should also add a further explanatory and mitigating factor. There was not, in fact, one single U-turn: there were several. Admittedly, one deviation was connected to another. But it was possible to take different attitudes to each, and this is what Margaret Thatcher did. She did not, for example, consider the nationalization of Rolls-Royce in February 1971 – roundly condemned as a U-turn by Powell – as constituting one at all. She was persuaded that the nation's security interest required that Britain retain its own aircraft engine capability and that the Government's taking ownership of the company was the only way to achieve that in the time available. Denis's observations about Rolls-Royce's

---

* This is, of course, the title of the readable biography by Hugo Young: *One of Us: A Biography of Margaret Thatcher* (London: Macmillan, 1989). I should add in parenthesis that I never heard her use the phrase and have some doubts about its authenticity (cf. Young, *One of Us*, p. vii). I did hear it from Keith Joseph, who asked me in 1980, when I wanted him to write a letter of introduction for use in the United States, 'Are you one of us?' I indignantly declared that I was, and he signed it. Perhaps she borrowed the expression from him.

faulty accounting practices confirmed her feeling that the management had brought the problems on itself, and perhaps that made
the pill easier to swallow. Moreover, at this time the ambitious, and
as it turned out unworkable, Industrial Relations Act was being
introduced. She had, therefore, good reason to feel that the wider
economic strategy was still on course.

The following year, however, was dominated by reversals of policy
that no one could deny, conceal or finesse. The most important
factor in all of them was the inexorable rise of unemployment,
which reached the politically sensitive figure of one million in
January 1972. The headline unemployment figure was still seen by
most of the media, by the Opposition and by the older generation
of Conservative MPs as the single most important gauge of whether
economic policy was working. Heath fully subscribed to this view.
By contrast, Mrs Thatcher did not, either now or later. She was
well aware of the political difficulties which unemployment created,
and she understood at a human level how debilitating being out of
work could be. But she was not sentimental about it; she did not
believe that government could directly control it; and she certainly
did not think that economic policy should be driven by it.

Matters were not helped by the fact that at the time the figure
was reached Britain's coal miners were out on strike. It was the first
and most serious of Heath's strikes, more economically damaging
than that of 1973–4. Moreover, the Government had made no
proper provisions for facing it. The degree of complacency exhibited still looks quite extraordinary. If ever there was a time when
Heath's political and administrative incompetence was exposed it
was now. For a while there seemed no cause for alarm. But on 10
February, out of the blue, John Davies announced to Cabinet that
power cuts were inevitable and that large parts of industry were
about to close down. Maudling was then passed a note from the
Chief Constable of Birmingham saying that he had had to ask
the West Midlands Gas Board's Saltley coke depot to close, because
the police could not resist the miners' mass picket. The episode

would come to mark the greatest triumph of violent trade unionism against the police and the rule of law. Margaret Thatcher would later efface its memory at the 'battle' of Orgreave.* But not yet.

Now the only course available was surrender. This took the form of the appointment of a court of inquiry under the High Court judge Lord Wilberforce, which compliantly recommended a huge pay increase. Even that, though, did not immediately pacify the National Union of Mineworkers. Heath hurried to make extra concessions, and so a settlement was reached – for now. The negotiations, including the final climbdown, had, for once, come before Cabinet. Mrs Thatcher, therefore, knew all that was happening and registered no dissent. The reality of defeat was too obvious. But she was certainly angry and under no illusion about the seriousness of what had transpired. In a revealing remark to her Conservative association she noted that the general public would have to pay for the Wilberforce settlement through extra taxes and higher prices. Strikes by monopoly groups like the miners, she added, were 'not strikes against the Government [but] . . . strikes against the people'.[8] That is the cry of a frustrated hawk. She knew that the Government had suffered a humiliation and she did not confuse it, as some of her colleagues did, with the opportunity for a 'new start'.

Shortly after conceding the miners' demands, the Government also signalled a further change in its industrial policy, so as to buy off another group of strikers. Bailing out Upper Clyde Shipbuilders was, in a way, even more humiliating and more dangerous, because the Clydeside strike was openly led by communists. The Government's tactic of standing firm just long enough for the militants to rally moderate support, and then of conceding when the militants upped the stakes, provided a signal throughout Britain's industrial workforce that the far left were best placed to deliver results. It was a classic recipe for extremist advance. As a result, by the end of February 1972 the economic strategy of the

* See p. 231.

Heath Government was in shreds. It remained only for the Industrial Relations Act to be discredited, when the imprisonment of dock workers in July resulted in serious unrest and the effective suspension of the Act, to bring about the complete abandonment of the policy. Arguably, this in itself hardly rates as a U-turn – the Act never having been seriously applied. Moreover, from March 1972, two other U-turns altogether dwarfed it.

Margaret Thatcher was not, as it happened, in Cabinet on Monday, 20 March when the Budget and the accompanying Industry White Paper were discussed. Both had been prepared by Heath within a tight circle of close colleagues and officials. Even the Chancellor was peripheral to the process. The Budget introduced a massive reflation – intended as a 'dash for growth' – through tax cuts and, above all, public spending increases. At the same time, the White Paper signalled a policy of wholesale industrial intervention and selective subsidy. Margaret Thatcher may not have grasped all the pros and cons of the Budget's fiscal stance; and, as a spending minister, she may even have been pleased with its implications for her department. But as a passionate believer that business must fend for itself and that market disciplines were preferable to state subsidy, she must have felt the new industrial strategy stick in her throat. In conversations many years later, she vividly recalled her dismay. But neither she nor Joseph resigned.

The Government's failure either to control its borrowing and spending or to check the rate of monetary growth had the inevitable effect of stoking inflation. This in turn propelled Heath and his colleagues towards the final U-turn, the one that sank them: statutory control of wages. 'Stage One' of the pay policy was introduced in November 1972. It was followed by two more 'Stages', until in November 1973 the miners' overtime ban began the process which led to the Government's defeat at the following February's general election.

Even more than industrial intervention, the statutory control of pay, prices and dividends was anathema to Mrs Thatcher. This profound hostility was not simply a result of what she had absorbed from the IEA. It reflected her visceral dislike of state interference in decisions that people had the right and responsibility to make for themselves. This, moreover, unlike the arcana of monetary policy, was ground she really understood, because of her work with Iain Macleod in fighting the earlier Labour Government's (much less comprehensive) pay policy. She later recalled her exasperation at the complexity and inflexibility of the formulae that Heath's policy applied. She argued her corner, though always about particulars rather than the general principle, both in Cabinet and in the sub-committee chaired by Terence Higgins, the responsible Treasury minister. In public, though, she lent the policy full support: it had been 'absolutely necessary', she defiantly declared, in order to stop large and unjustified pay awards pushing up inflation.[9] Perhaps at times she even believed this. Or perhaps, like most Conservatives inside and outside Parliament, she just felt that in what seemed the apocalyptic battle against trade union militancy and the far left it was necessary to stand firm – however flawed the policy one was defending. As the Government moved into the final phase of its doomed existence, this bunker mentality became ever more prevalent. Paradoxically, it gave Heath a still freer hand.

Edward Heath had, by his own lack of strategic vision, created the crisis in which the Government discovered itself by the end of 1973. But it was his tactical failures that finished them. First, he did nothing to ensure that the country was any better able to withstand a miners' strike in 1974 than it had been in 1972. No serious thought had been given as to how to extend endurance, except to declare a three-day working week in order to limit energy consumption. Second, he tried to deal with the crisis by means of the instrument with which he always felt most at home, a commission. But commissions are uncontrollable. A leak from the Relativities Board on 21 February suggesting that the miners' claim could have been accommodated within Stage Three of the incomes policy threw the Tory election campaign into a disarray from which it never recovered. Finally, he called the general election at the wrong time. Of course, on one analysis, he need not have called it at all, because it was how the miners voted, not how the public voted, that mattered in the dispute. But if he were resolved to go to the country, he certainly had to do it in time to capitalize upon public anger with the strikers. If emotions subsided, attention would shift to the Government's own sorry record and its lack of fresh proposals.

Reluctant to face the electorate, convinced to the end that some new concession or initiative would see him through, Heath called the election too late. On this, at least, Mrs Thatcher, who was now furious with the unions and longing for a showdown, did openly disagree with the Prime Minister. When asked in to see him with John Davies and a few others, she spoke her mind: she urged him to call an election for 7 February, the earliest feasible occasion. But he decided to go on until the overtime ban turned into a full-blown strike. The election would take place on Thursday 28 February.

Until the leak of the Relativities Board memorandum, Mrs Thatcher was optimistic about the result. Polarizing the electorate on the issue selected by Heath, 'Who governs Britain?', may, in fact, have somewhat reduced the scale of the election defeat which the Conservative Party now suffered. Mrs Thatcher's majority fell from 11,000 to 6,000, affected by an adverse boundary change. Nationally, although the Government secured a small majority of the popular vote, it lost thirty-three parliamentary seats, ending up with 296 against Labour's 301. Heath remained in denial for a few more days, desperately seeking a coalition with the Liberals and reporting back to an increasingly listless and hopeless Cabinet on his discussions. In the end, when Jeremy Thorpe, the Liberal leader, turned Heath down, Margaret Thatcher was relieved it was over.

The DES gave her a good send-off. Some officials even thought she had been, despite her quirks and prejudices, an effective minister. But doubtless the farewell party was all the more cheerful because they knew Labour were back.

Judged by the criteria according to which she herself would judge others, Margaret Thatcher's role in the Heath Government between 1970 and 1974 was undistinguished. Yet there was another side to her performance, one without which she would never have become party leader, let alone Prime Minister. She had shown qualities which her parliamentary colleagues had noticed. She was not just master of her brief. She also gave as good as she ever got in the bear-pit of the House of Commons. For example, when the left-wing Labour MP Eric Heffer recalled how he had delivered meat to one public school (Haileybury) and still considered private education a waste of time, she shot back: 'So what? My father used to serve in the tuck shop at Oundle, but he didn't come out with a chip on his shoulder.' Nor was the toughness a pose. She had courage, and she showed it under attack. She may have been tainted by Heath's mistakes: but, then, who in the upper ranks of the Tory Party was not? Her combination of wishful thinking, keeping her head down, exasperation and eventually anger exactly mirrored the reaction of the average Tory backbencher during these years. She was on his wavelength.

On top of all that, she was undoubtedly a significant public figure, one with style, brains and grit. Her unhappy spell at the DES was, therefore, the unlikely springboard for her future leadership.

5

TAKING COMMAND

Within a year of the February 1974 general election, Margaret Thatcher was leader of the Conservative Party. There is nowadays a tendency to diminish the significance of that revolution. It should be resisted. It is true that many of those whose support handed control of the party over to her were unaware of the full significance of their actions. Certainly, few at the time foresaw how far-reaching the ensuing changes would be. But a revolution, in all but the bloodiest sense, it certainly was. It represented a complete up-ending of prevailing assumptions. It marked a total defeat for the existing party hierarchy. It was the work of a very few bold men – and one bold woman – who risked all, and won.*

Most revolutions seem predictable after the event. But this one, even now, seems less predictable than most. Had the incumbent leader been someone other than Edward Heath, it would have been easy to envisage his voluntarily stepping aside for someone else, at least for

---

* The suggestion by John Campbell that Mrs Thatcher would have been forgiven and allowed to occupy high office under Heath reveals that the author has little understanding of the unremitting bitterness which characterized, now and later, the relations between the Heath and Thatcher camps: Campbell, *Margaret Thatcher*, vol. 1: *The Grocer's Daughter* (London: Jonathan Cape, 2000), p. 284.

someone of similar views and outlook. But Heath was not like that. He was, it is true, deeply shaken by the outcome of the February election, which he had always expected to win. But even after his rejection by the electorate he never for a moment doubted that he was uniquely equipped to lead both the Conservative Party and the country.

Losing three elections in four would have finished the leader of almost any democratic party in any country. It would even have finished the leader of the quasi-democratic Tory Party of the preceding era, when leaders emerged – and were duly dispatched – by the ruthless power-brokers of the Magic Circle. Yet Heath would not budge. Political assassination, not honourable retirement, was the only way to be rid of him. But no one, as yet, dared wield the knife.

As a woman, and one with relatively little experience and no strong faction in her support, Margaret Thatcher seemed a frail opponent to set up against Heath, with all the power of the Conservative organization and its social and financial establishment behind him. But as perceptions changed, so did her prospects. When in the heat of battle she turned out not to be frail at all – when, indeed, she showed that her single greatest quality was courage – she suddenly acquired the status of a heroine for the Tory men who had for so long skulked, grumbled and plotted but failed to strike. Today's revisionists who try to reduce the drama of the contest by pointing to the lack of explicitly radical pledges made by her at the time, or even in the immediate aftermath, seriously miss the point. More than any general election she fought, the leadership election that propelled Margaret Thatcher to the head of the Tory Party was a raw and ruthless struggle rarely matched in British politics.

Margaret Thatcher would claim that, in the wake of the February 1974 election defeat, she had wept. But if she did – and the notion may have been merely part of a campaign to appear softer and more feminine – those tears quickly dried.* She must have known that

---

* Interview with the *Daily Mail*, 9 March 1974. The contrived nature of her remarks is also suggested by the out-of-character observation: 'I hate hats, don't you?'

she needed the party to lose office if she was to rise much further in it. She had, after all, reached a level of seniority beyond which anything she brought to the leader in terms of ability, or even her role as the token top woman, was outweighed by the fact that she was a threat. By now Heath certainly knew she was hostile to his leadership, though he did not realize how ambitious, let alone how dangerous, she was.

In the circumstances, his decision to appoint her as Shadow Environment Secretary made sense. It was not one of the top posts whose tenure traditionally qualified a politician as leadership material. It kept her out of the powerful economic policy-making circle, where future challenges from the free-market right, to which she belonged, were likely to coalesce. But it was exactly the role in which she could excel, because of her numeracy, energy and presentational flair. The somewhat misleadingly entitled environment portfolio had a high political profile because it included housing and local government (more specifically, the rates).* These were both areas in which Heath and his advisers were convinced that they could come up with popular policies to win back middle-class support, without embarking on a fundamental reconsideration of economic strategy.

Never during her political career did Margaret Thatcher display more professionalism, and indeed more cynicism, than between the two 1974 elections. By and large, she disliked the policies which she found herself advocating. She disliked even more the way in which they were forced upon her. She can hardly, either, have been unaware of the scorn which they provoked among the very free-market commentators whose analysis she respected. But she persisted: she took ownership of the policies; she argued for them with brio; and

---

* Aside from the rate support grant (from central government, i.e. the taxpayer), local government received its income from business and domestic rates. The latter were levied on households on the basis of the (highly artificial) deemed rental value of the property. Each year councils set a poundage for the rate, and from time to time properties were subject to nationwide revaluations. The domestic rate system was always unpopular.

by doing so she established her reputation as a front-line Tory politician with a claim on the party leadership.

Mrs Thatcher was at once set to work by Heath on ways to lower the cost of mortgages and rate bills. Specific proposals were ostensibly to be worked out by two policy groups. There was a high-powered one on housing, consisting of Hugh Rossi (a housing expert, friend and parliamentary neighbour of hers), Michael Latham (who was close to the building industry), John Stanley (her future parliamentary private secretary) and Nigel Lawson (a financial journalist, at this stage a 'sound money' man and already thought bound to go far if his arrogance did not get in the way). It met regularly and worked effectively. A somewhat less high-powered and less frequently consulted group looked at local government finance. But the main decisions were taken, as were all strategic decisions for the October 1974 election, by the coterie around Heath – among whom was Peter Walker, the strongest early advocate of more or less giving away council houses to the occupants.

Mrs Thatcher was at this stage unconvinced by Walker's ideas. Her middle-class prejudices, as she admits in her memoirs, made her unduly wary of offering over-generous terms to council tenants.[1] She worried that those who had made sacrifices to buy their homes in the newly built private estates while mortgage rates soared, enjoying no assistance whatever from the Government, would resent the new policy. But she allowed herself to be convinced and later became a great enthusiast for the 'right to buy' – which would, indeed, become synonymous with the Thatcher capital-owning revolution of the 1980s.* The October 1974 manifesto did not go as far as she eventually would, but it went a long way all the same. It promised the right to buy, at a third off market value, for tenants of council houses who had occupied them for three or more years. She was also happy enough for the present with the proposal to offer help with the mortgage deposits

* See pp. 244–5.

of first-time buyers. (Once leader, she would ensure that this proposal, unlike the sale of council houses, was quietly forgotten.)

It was the plan for a government subsidy (via tax relief to the building societies) to keep down mortgage interest rates that was most controversial and – along with the domestic rates – caused Mrs Thatcher most grief. It was not that she was other than highly enthusiastic about promoting home ownership. In her eyes, owning one's home was a sure sign of the middle-class values in which she believed and which she wished to propagate. Nor was the idea itself new. It was the distinctly un-bourgeois Anthony Eden who had first made popular the Tory slogan of a 'property owning democracy'. The specific policy of subsidizing building societies to keep down the interest rates they charged to borrowers was, unfortunately, not new either. It had been part of the Heath Government's self-destructive approach of controlling prices while simultaneously stoking inflation. What was now proposed was that the policy be systematized by cutting the so-called composite rate of tax that the societies paid.

Even the idea of keeping the mortgage rate down by government intervention did not in itself worry her. Interviewed by the journalist (and monetarist) Peter Jay for the *Weekend World* television programme, she displayed no unease about the economic distortion involved. She argued that since there was currently a glut of houses on the market her proposals would not drive up prices.[2] What did make her uneasy was, rather, the cost to the Treasury of the open-ended subsidy – that is, the threat to her favourite concept of 'good housekeeping'. Prudence with public funds was something that Heath had long since ceased to consider important. So tension between leader and Environment spokesman was inevitable.

On Thursday, 1 August 1974, she found herself summoned to Heath's house in Wilton Street and pressured by him, Walker and Robert Carr to name a specific figure above which the mortgage rate would not be allowed to rise. Reluctantly, she agreed to the formula 'below 10 per cent'. (It currently stood at 11 per cent.) But the pressure continued. While she was travelling by car to Tonbridge on Wednesday, 28 August to record a party political broadcast she was 'bleeped' with a message to ring in. She found herself speaking first to Willie Whitelaw and then to Heath himself. They had decided that she must be still more specific. After some argument, it was agreed that the figure would be 9.5 per cent. This she duly announced in the PPB in a polished performance punctuated by supporting MPs (one fictional) and various artificial representatives of vox populi.

The way in which opposition policy on the domestic rates was created was still more bizarre and irresponsible. A rate revaluation in 1973 had pushed the issue to the forefront of debate, and a combination of high inflation and local government overspending then made it even more topical. In a speech to the Conservative party candidates' conference on 10 August Mrs Thatcher promised to transfer the cost of teachers' salaries – the lion's share of LEA spending – for the following year to central government. This was a half-baked proposal. As was exhaustively discussed towards the end of Mrs Thatcher's time as Prime Minister, simply shifting expenditure from local to central government does not in itself cut local tax bills – unless central government borrows or puts up its own taxes. All that was said on 10 August about long-term reform was that 'the system of local government finance must be changed so that it reflects the ability of people to pay'. This formula concealed the fact that the party had no settled ideas on the matter. Mrs Thatcher herself was attracted by a locally variable petrol tax. The honest answer would have been simply to promise a review, accompanied by enunciation of some broad principles. But honesty was not an obvious feature of Tory policy-making at this time.

The rates question thus joined the mortgage question as the subject of repeated testy telephone conversations between Mrs Thatcher, trying to escape the London summer in Lamberhurst, and Heath and his circle, striving to come up with attractive policies back in London. On 16 August she was treated to another pummelling on her policy area in Wilton Street from Heath, Whitelaw and Prior, who wanted her to announce that rates would be abolished 'by the end of the next Parliament'. She argued against the move; she lost; and again she took up the new policy and defended it with bravura. She published the full housing and rates proposals at a press conference on Wednesday, 28 August, when the press was desperate for something to report. The clever timing and the stylish presentation ensured much favourable press coverage, of which the Conservatives were otherwise enjoying little.

From now until election day, Margaret Thatcher was one of the leading figures in the Conservative campaign. She was the main performer in the party election broadcast of Friday, 27 September. On the same day she and Francis Pym (agriculture spokesman) were the main speakers at the morning press conference chaired by Whitelaw. She then showed her mettle as a tactical opportunist by gaining Heath's permission – ironically, given their past argument – to harden up the pledge on mortgages, promising that the 9.5 per cent mortgage would be introduced 'by Christmas'. This prompted the desired headlines, including 'Santa Thatcher'. In fact, by now it was she who was keenest on specific pledges and Heath who was backing away from them.

Throughout her career, one of Mrs Thatcher's political strengths, though it was also an analytical weakness, was the ability to divide her views and conduct into neat, and perfectly sealed, compartments. Like a professional actor who may have tantrums about his lines at rehearsal but delivers them with conviction in performance, she too was the ultimate professional politician. But even this analogy fails to catch just how closely her behaviour now bordered the politically schizophrenic. She was in the front rank of Heath's Shadow Cabinet, advocating economically profligate policies, while at the same time behind the scenes she was working with Keith Joseph to forge a revolution that would destroy Heath's leadership and set the party in a new direction.

There is no evidence that Joseph asked any of his other colleagues to join him at the Centre for Policy Studies (or CPS, as it was invariably called) – not even Geoffrey Howe, whose free-market credentials might have appeared excellent. But he did ask Margaret Thatcher. At the end of May 1974 she duly became Vice-Chairman of the Centre.

But when did she decide that such a radical alternative was necessary? When did she 'convert'? The answer is that, at one level, she did not. She was simply not the type. Rather, she was reverting to earlier views which, for a variety of reasons – lack of intellectual self-confidence, ignorance, prudence, self-interest – she had suppressed. Margaret Thatcher's attitude to the arguments of Hayek, Friedman and the other free-market sages whose words she read (or reread) now was respectful but also utilitarian. Their insights provided her not so much with enlightenment (as they did the cerebral Joseph) as with the arguments, ultimately the instruments, she needed to achieve the political goals that she felt increasingly called to fulfil.

At the CPS Mrs Thatcher was still at this stage very much Joseph's junior partner. She took notes, she listened, and though she produced the occasional short paper on education or social security, she brought little except her moral support and political weight to the task in hand. But, then, what was this task?

Joseph, who was more capable of slipperiness than some have supposed, gained Heath's agreement to set up the CPS on what can only be called a false prospectus. Its purpose was allegedly to engage in comparative studies of the economic systems of other, more successful, countries, and to draw lessons for Britain. It was, as such, part of the wider, roving policy role which he had been given by Heath as a consolation prize for the Shadow Chancellorship, which he was refused. But Joseph's installation of Alfred Sherman as the Centre's director ensured that it would serve a very different purpose.

Sherman would in later years exaggerate his own role and minimize everyone else's – including Joseph's and Margaret Thatcher's – in the creation of the Thatcher Revolution. But at this stage, and indeed throughout the Tory period in opposition, he was central to the project. With the zeal of the convert from communism, he lectured and bullied Joseph into setting a new ideological and policy agenda. He was brutal, caustic and often personally insulting to his master, who seemed to relish the humiliation. Sherman's relations with Margaret Thatcher were more respectful. Doubtless sensing that she was made of sterner stuff than Joseph, he minded his manners and she, who had no side, was anyway thick-skinned, and wanted to learn as fast as she could, treated his ideas with respect. ('Remember, I have no toes!' she would reassure those who disagreed with her – though Sherman needed no such reassurance.) The CPS was especially dangerous to Heath because its tentacles reached into the world of intellectuals and opinion-formers – much further than did the Conservative Party. Indeed, it brought together many who had never been, and some who never would be, Conservatives at all. The aim was to defeat what Hayek, in his dedication to *The Road to Serfdom*, had described as the 'socialists of all parties'. And no one fitted more neatly into that category than Edward Heath.

The irreverent, combative, dissident atmosphere of the Centre brought out the best in Margaret Thatcher. It allowed her to do what she had not yet done: she was at last able to work through the connection between her political instincts and her political position. From now on, recognizing the value of what she had once lacked and now found, she would insist upon relating everything back to principles. It is not too much to say that this highly intelligent woman only began to think once she joined her fate to Keith Joseph's at the CPS.

The work of re-educating the party and country, though, was left to Joseph, who decided to conduct it through a series of speeches, with Sherman as his principal draftsman. Quite how long the series would have gone on, had not disaster struck, is unclear. The first speech was made at Upminster on 22 June 1974. It set the tone for, and summarized the themes of, those that were to come. Its explosiveness derived from Joseph's repeated assertion that the problems of British industry stemmed not only from the actions of the Labour Government, which by then had been in power for just four months, but from 'thirty years of socialistic fashions'. He noted that the Conservative Party had been in power for half that time and had not reversed the socialism it had inherited – the 'ratchet effect'. The next in the series was delivered in Leith on 8 August and concentrated on the deleterious effect of inflation upon business. When the leadership learned that Joseph intended to deliver a further, still more uncomfortable, analysis at Preston on 5 September, all too close to the likely general election date, a mixture of rage and panic set in.

Joseph circulated his drafts widely. He needed reassurance that his reasoning was sound, and it was natural that Mrs Thatcher should be asked to comment. So before Preston he sent her an early draft, which she read with admiration and agreement. It began with a sobering description of the effect of high inflation on Britain's economy and society (which was not too controversial) and then (far more problematically) proceeded to describe the causes of inflation. These came down to 'the creation of new money' by government. Moreover, by stating that increases in the money supply took months or even a year or two to come through in the form of higher prices, Joseph effectively placed the blame for the current inflation rate where it truly lay – at the door of the last Conservative Government. On top of that, he downgraded the role of incomes policy, on which Heath had relied, and minimized too the importance of the headline unemployment figure, before which Heath had quailed.

Geoffrey Howe and Margaret Thatcher were now asked by Heath, who deemed them closest to Joseph and thus most likely to influence him, to try to have changes made. Apparently, the three did meet at the CPS, and Howe recalls that they secured some minor alterations.[3] But he did not know that Mrs Thatcher had already in fact signed up to it, so her compliance with the leader's wishes was feigned. On this occasion, Heath's antennae were correctly adjusted. The speech created a furore. For a while afterwards Joseph steered clear of his colleagues in the Shadow Cabinet.

Mrs Thatcher, though, was untainted by the fallout. During campaigning for the ensuing general election, which was called by Wilson for 10 October, she was, indeed, a star performer – with her sharpness, femininity and general newsworthiness – in an otherwise grey Tory firmament. But Heath's priorities once again clashed with hers. He had become convinced that his only chance of returning to power was to do so at the head of a grand coalition with Labour and the Liberals. The prospect appealed to his vanity and doubtless also to his desire to ditch the awkward right of his own party – represented by Thatcher and Joseph. How clearly she grasped this is unclear. But in any case her stubbornness, pride in the progress she had made with her policy area, and instinctive dislike of consensus politics all ensured that she was hostile to such thinking. Alerted to this and knowing that she was to appear on the politically important *Any Questions*, Heath called her in to ensure that she followed the new line. It was a tense and testy meeting, probably the worst between them. In the event, she reluctantly followed instructions. But such a relationship between the Tory leader and the Tory press pin-up was too fragile to last.

Nor did it. The Conservatives were once more soundly defeated, winning 277 seats to Labour's 319. Heath had now lost three of the four general elections he had fought as Tory leader. Only if one believed – as Heath and his circle affected to believe – that Britain faced imminent economic collapse, that is within a few months, not years, could it be argued that he should remain in place to pick up the bits.

Margaret Thatcher was by now clear that Heath had to go, though she was too canny to say so. When asked about Heath's future three days after the election, she merely replied that it was 'too soon' to speculate about it. She offered him no words of comfort,

and the same article reported that some of her supporters were saying that in the event of his departure she would be a candidate.[4] A
little later she was being touted as Joseph's unofficial campaign
manager. But when questioned, she merely laughed and said that
there was 'no obvious candidate' to take over from Heath. This time
she did offer a little condolence, noting that it 'must be very difficult for him and for everyone else to have this discussion taking
place while there [was] no vacancy'.[5] The sympathy was more
emphatic in an interview the following Sunday, perhaps because
Heath's yacht had been lost in a storm and his favourite godson
with it. She said: 'It's an agonising time for all of us in the Party. No
one really knows what to say or do. The last thing we want is to
pressure Ted.' Yet that is precisely what she proceeded to do, by
adding: 'We all feel that this present uncertainty must be resolved
before Parliament sits.'

Thus far it might be assumed that all she was doing was promoting Keith Joseph's candidature. This now subtly changed. She
began also to advance her own claims. Publication of the interview in question coincided with reports of Joseph's disastrous
Edgbaston speech (see below), but it must have been given before
then. Asked whether it was true that she was ruling herself out of
the running, her reply was clearly premeditated: 'In the long run it
isn't.' Pressed on her earlier statement – made on the eve of the
election – that it would be ten years before either the Tory Party or
the country would accept a woman leader, she answered: 'Yes, I did
feel that at one point. But I'm not sure that I do any longer. The
prejudice against women is dropping faster than I expected, and I
think a woman may succeed before that time.' Challenged further,
this time on whether she still believed that a leader should first have
occupied one of the three key Cabinet posts, Foreign Secretary,
Home Secretary or Chancellor of the Exchequer, she backed
away from that too: 'I *have* felt that. But there are notable
exceptions. Harold Wilson occupied none of those posts before
becoming Leader.'[6]

There has been little discussion of these remarks, not least because Joseph's gaffe and later withdrawal from contention overwhelmed them. But what they demonstrate, and what various mutterings about her leadership potential in the press over previous months confirm, is that Margaret Thatcher already had her eye on being leader of the party and Prime Minister. She would support Joseph while he was the front-runner. But she also envisaged a time when she would be running herself.

It came much sooner than she envisaged, because Keith Joseph now spectacularly blew his chances with a speech in Edgbaston, Birmingham, on Saturday, 19 October. The *Evening Standard* broke the embargo and took out of context the expressions which sank him. But even in context the passage was bad enough:

> The balance of our population, our human stock is threatened. A recent article in *Poverty*, published by the Child Poverty Action Group, showed that a high and rising proportion of children are born to mothers least fitted to bring children into the world and bring them up. They are born to mothers who were first pregnant in adolescence in social classes 4 and 5. Many of these girls are unmarried, many are deserted or divorced or soon will be. Some are of low intelligence, most of low educational attainment.

Joseph's wider message was that the Conservative Party needed to preoccupy itself with the remoralization of society, not merely with economics. But when in a whimsical manner he then questioned whether more use of contraception by the lower orders might be worth the inevitable risk of encouraging promiscuity, he both alienated the moralists on whom he might otherwise have counted and made himself a laughing stock into the bargain. The damage, which Heath's supporters were quick to exploit, was so great because the speech confirmed what had long been muttered, that Joseph's judgement was flawed. His subsequent explanations, elaborations and apologies also suggested that he was too sensitive to withstand the heat of conflict. It was his wife who finally decided that he should abandon his still unconfirmed plan to become party leader. But she did no more than recognize reality. Joseph could not now have won.

Mrs Thatcher was made of sterner stuff, as she had shown during the Milk Snatcher affair. She had no intention of abandoning the struggle to dislodge Heath just because Keith Joseph had destroyed himself. When Joseph came to see her in her room at the House of Commons on the afternoon of 21 November to say that he was pulling out of the race, she immediately replied: 'Look, Keith, if you're not going to stand, I will, because someone who represents our viewpoint *has* to stand.'*

News of her intention appeared in the weekend press. It was now obviously necessary that she tell Heath in person as soon as possible, so she went to see him on Monday in his room at the House. At the time the press reported that Heath, who was sitting at his desk, kept her standing, and when she told him of her intention simply remarked: 'You'll lose.' When she came to write her memoirs, she thought that both had been standing and that on hearing what she had to say he turned away and said: 'If you must.' In either case, the rudeness and contempt were palpable.[7] It was not until after the Christmas break that she publicly confirmed that she would stand. But by then the decision had become easier to act upon.

Heath managed to play his cards extremely badly. An early leadership campaign would probably have favoured him, but he refused to accept the need for one. He believed that discontent with him would abate, and he treated the executive of the 1922 Committee and its chairman Edward du Cann, who wanted a contest, as a band of unrepresentative plotters. Du Cann was certainly an enemy. But the executive's views were widely shared. Heath arrogantly questioned its legitimacy on the grounds that its members had not

* Margaret Thatcher, *The Path to Power* (London: HarperCollins, 1995), p. 266. When she later came to write her memoirs she remembered very clearly not only the occasion but the words she used.

submitted themselves to election by the new intake. But when they did, all were re-elected. His climbdown was humiliating. He now accepted that he would have to stand for re-election and set up a committee to review the procedure. The committee, chaired by Lord Home, proposed annual leadership elections. To win outright on the first ballot the front-runner would have to secure a lead of not just 15 per cent of the votes cast, but 15 per cent of the total electorate (that is, of all Tory MPs). This meant that abstentions effectively counted as votes against the incumbent leader. In fact, in this instance – unlike the case of Mrs Thatcher in 1990 – it would make no difference to the outcome.

The second factor which eventually assisted Margaret Thatcher's prospects did not start out that way at all. In an unnerving echo of the Milk Snatcher business, she was accused of 'hoarding' food, on the basis of an interview she had given to a magazine called *Pre-Retirement Choice*. It had been taped before the general election but was not published until 27 November, by which point her undeclared leadership campaign had effectively begun. She advised pensioners to follow her example of buying in food whose cost was rapidly rising – at this point, it should be remembered, inflation was approaching the peak of its spiralling rise under Labour. She either did not have a deep freeze or did not make much of use of it, because tins – of ham, tongue, salmon, mackerel, sardines – were her main recommended purchases: when she used up one tin she would, apparently, buy two more. These blameless remarks brought a firestorm of abuse upon her, during which Heath's campaign team in the House of Commons and in Conservative Central Office gleefully fanned the flames. All sorts of authorities and experts were asked by the media to comment on her remarks. Sainsbury's warned that hoarding would create shortages. A woman from the National Consumer Protection Council appealed for housewives not to follow Mrs Thatcher's 'bad example'. The National Housewives Association said her 'behaviour [was] atrocious and irresponsible'. Lord Redmayne, a former Conservative Chief

Whip who was deputy chairman of Harrods and a friend of Heath's, pompously denounced 'any sort of inducement to panic buying'. Heath himself slyly let it be known that he had asked his housekeeper to check what cans he had in store and discovered there was virtually nothing.

Mrs Thatcher was exasperated and upset. She seems to have wept a little but also declared to her friends that though her enemies had 'destroyed Keith' they were not going to destroy her. She did not hide away. She answered the accusations and, to the initial mirth but ultimate discomfiture of her critics, invited the media into her larder to reveal the contents of her stockpile, which proved extremely modest. When her enemies then planted a story that she had been seen buying up sugar, this proved a final step too far. The shop she was alleged to have visited did not exist. Within the parliamentary Conservative Party there was a good deal of disgust at the way she had been treated by Heath's men. She gained sympathy.

Given a fair fight, however, Margaret Thatcher had no need of it, as she now showed by her performances in the House of Commons. In the post-election reshuffle in November Heath had made her deputy Treasury spokesman under Robert Carr. This was a foolish decision. It was not a promotion. But it allowed her to outshine her nominal boss and to demonstrate her talents to those who would choose the next leader. There is little so dull or quickly dated in Hansard as debates about yesterday's tax law, but her speeches on the Finance Bill, first on the floor of the House and later in committee, still convey something of their original electricity. What she had done in 1966 to Selective Employment Tax she did now to Capital Transfer Tax (CTT – the revamped death duties).

Moreover, her principal victim was none other than Denis Healey, the Chancellor and the biggest bully in the Commons, before whom lesser parliamentarians shrank. Healey's record as Chancellor was already bad and would become worse. He was far from technically brilliant. But he had a ferocious manner and fearsome appearance which allowed him to bluff and bruise his way through. Not with Mrs Thatcher, though. At the second reading debate on the Finance Bill on Tuesday 17 December, before a noisy House of Commons, Mrs Thatcher eviscerated the Government's economic policy. And when Healey boorishly shouted out 'hoard the lot', she turned, taunting him and the Prime Minister with 'hoarding' houses, referring to their plush second homes. When she sat down her reputation had been transformed.

The still unresolved problem was that she did not have a proper campaign. Indeed, she had not yet confirmed publicly that she would stand. In a press interview that appeared on 25 November she had declared her willingness to do so, spoken of 'all the people asking [her] day in and day out to put [herself] forward', and even said she would challenge Heath 'if there [was] a certain amount of support'.[8] Yet when she departed to spend Christmas with her family in Kent the question was still open. The problem was Edward du Cann. He was tipped by many as a stronger candidate for the right than Mrs Thatcher. He was more politically experienced and media-savvy. Against that, he had been off the front bench for some years and his oleaginous charm was not universally admired. He would, indeed, have liked to take on Heath; but he eventually decided that he liked his City interests, and the privacy required to pursue them, rather more.

A group of some thirty or forty Du Cann supporters had been meeting from time to time and, naturally, there was contact and even overlap with those attracted by a Thatcher candidature. Airey Neave, one of the Du Cann group, had already come in to see Margaret Thatcher to discuss the outlook on several occasions. When Du Cann finally, on 15 January, told his supporters that he had decided not to stand, Neave now approached Bill Shelton and offered to run Mrs Thatcher's campaign, with Shelton as his deputy. And this is what happened. Meanwhile, Margaret Thatcher, relieved of her tactical worries – tactics never being her forte – concentrated on her performances in the House of

Commons, where the arguments on the Finance Bill had resumed.

Neave was not on the right or any other wing of the party, but he was a senior, highly respected and slightly feared backbencher – all of which helped in his role as campaign manager. He was best known for escaping from Colditz during the Second World War and he had taken part in the Nuremberg trials of Nazi war criminals. He had also stayed close to the Security Service. Heath greatly disliked him, and the feeling was mutual. Neave was not a particularly good parliamentarian. He operated best behind closed doors. In this he was the opposite of Mrs Thatcher, and thus they complemented each other. They also knew and respected one another, having shared chambers during pupillage and then having had dealings in the ordinary run of parliamentary business. It is not clear that they ever became friends. Nor did his cold and taciturn manner encourage it. But she quickly grew to trust him.

Neave and his small team – which grew larger as her prospects improved – now set about rallying and canvassing support. It was done with extraordinary thoroughness and in great secrecy. From an early stage it was clear that Margaret Thatcher could expect a substantial vote, larger than the media, let alone the Heath camp, were expecting. But the tactic throughout was to downplay her prospects, which, unlike many candidates for high office, she does not seem to have minded. Neave and his colleagues were convinced that there was a large body of MPs who were determined to have Heath out, not in order to put Mrs Thatcher in his place but in order to find a suitable replacement in the second round when the Home rules allowed other candidates to enter. On top of that, there were MPs who did not want to see Heath out at all, but who thought that he needed to be shaken up. How numerous these tactical Thatcher supporters were it is now impossible to gauge. Neave was certainly wise to assume their importance. But from the result in the second round – when MPs could, indeed, choose some one who was neither Heath nor Thatcher – it looks as if the accepted version that she won by default is rather too neat.

With the failure of the hoarding smear, Mrs Thatcher's opponents decided to focus on her prim, bourgeois, Southern image, which they predicted would spell electoral disaster outside the affluent middle classes and the Home Counties. So she was asked on television: 'Do you think perhaps North of the Wash that you'd go down quite as well as you do in the South of England?'

And she had her answer, which was no less than the truth: 'But I was born in the Midlands!'

She then continued in a strain that Heath could not match: 'I was born and brought up for the most telling years of my life in Grantham, Lincolnshire . . . All my ideas about life, about individual responsibility, about looking after your neighbour, about patriotism, about self-discipline, about law and order, were formed in a small town in the Midlands, and I've always been very thankful that I was brought up in a smaller community, so that you really felt what a community could be.'[9]

While Neave and his team waged their secret war in the Commons corridors and tea room, Margaret Thatcher was free to fight the battle in her own way. This had three elements. First, there were her performances on the Finance Bill. These continued to produce fireworks – as when she had another clash with Denis Healey on 22 January, winding up on the Finance Bill. Referring to her earlier attacks on CTT and insistence on the importance of private property, he mocked her as 'La Pasionaria of privilege'. She hit back: 'I wish I could say that the Chancellor of the Exchequer had done himself less than justice. Unfortunately, I can only say that I believe he has done himself justice. Some Chancellors are macro-economic. Other Chancellors are fiscal. This one is just plain cheap.'[10] The Tories were thrilled by such glimpses of below-the-belt aggression. They cheered, and her ratings soared.

But there was a wider audience to be won over too, and although the general public lacked a vote in the only election that (for the moment) mattered, her colleagues needed to be reassured that she could speak to the country, not just to them. Mrs Thatcher's television appearances had already benefited from the help of an inveterately cheerful, champagne-imbibing former television director, Gordon Reece. He persuaded her to lower her voice, abandon hats and emphasize her homely, ordinary side, thus exposing Heath's coldness, remoteness and inhumanity. She was a good pupil, because she had no personal pride, she respected other people's professionalism and, above all, she very much wanted to win.

The written word was also important. She was lucky to be able to rely on a talented little group of draftsmen. It was Angus Maude, previously sacked from the front bench by Heath, who wrote the article that appeared in her name in the *Daily Telegraph* – one of a series contributed by senior Tories, naturally including Heath. It confronted head-on the accusation that she was narrowly middle class: '[I]f "middle class values" include the encouragement of variety and individual choice, the provision of fair incentives and rewards for skill and hard work, the maintenance of effective barriers against the excessive power of the State and a belief in the wide distribution of individual private property, then they are certainly what I am trying to defend.'

She continued on the theme of property, which would be central in the years ahead to every explanation she gave of her policies:

> If a Tory does not believe that private property is one of the main bulwarks of individual freedom, then he had better become a socialist and have done with it. Indeed, one of the reasons for our electoral failure is that people believe too many Conservatives *have* become socialists already. Britain's progress towards socialism has been an alternation of two steps forward with a half a step back.[11]

Thus was Joseph's 'ratchet' fashioned into a weapon against Heath's record.

Finally, she had numerous private discussions with individual Tory MPs, who came in to see what she was really like. They took place in the House of Commons room of an aesthete Tory backbencher, Robin Cooke, who lubricated the occasions with first-growth claret or, occasionally, tea. On another occasion she addressed a larger group of supporters and simply spoke at length about her beliefs. Those who heard her, individually or *en masse*, were impressed. By contrast, those who came to see Heath at the dinner parties organized by his team often went away embarrassed, humiliated or resentful. Yet the Heath team still seem to have noted them down as supporters.

While the Heath camp trumpeted his prospects, Neave never ceased to play down Mrs Thatcher's. There was general acceptance – though it was stronger outside the Palace of Westminster than among MPs – that Heath would easily win. The question was whether he would win sufficiently well in the first round to avoid a second.

Superficially, Heath seemed well placed. All the Shadow Cabinet, bar Joseph, were backing him. So was the Conservative press, including the *Daily Telegraph* under the editorship of Denis's friend Bill Deedes. Lord Home also now came out for Heath, as, less surprisingly, did Maudling. The National Union – the grandees allegedly representing the constituency parties but, in those days, under the control of Central Office – declared that 70 per cent of the voluntary party backed Heath. The Thatcher camp repolled the parliamentary party. Their new figures showed Thatcher and Heath neck and neck.

On the day of the count, 4 February 1975, Margaret Thatcher was up early to cook Denis's breakfast. His car broke down, which was deemed by some a bad omen, but she was able to leave for the Commons at 9.00 a.m., remarking to the press camped on her doorstep: 'It's so close.' And she doubtless thought it would be. On arrival at Westminster her work began as usual, upstairs in the committee room where the Finance Bill debate was continuing. Meanwhile, in another committee room along the corridor a very different contest was under way, as Conservative MPs cast their votes. The ballot would close at 3.30 p.m., with the result due soon afterwards. She moved across to Neave's room to await it, while Shelton acted as her representative at the count – Tim Kitson was Heath's. The outcome was a shock, probably even to Neave and Shelton:

Margaret Thatcher 130
Edward Heath 119
Hugh Fraser 16.

Shelton told Neave, and Neave told Mrs Thatcher. It was far better than she had hoped. It was also far, far worse than the Heath camp had feared. Kitson told Heath, who was dumbfounded. After some discussion with his old friend Lord Aldington, the former Toby Lowe MP, Heath accepted the inevitable, announced his resignation, and appointed Robert Carr to stand in as temporary leader.

With the general astonishment at the result of the first round there came also a rapid and radical shift of opinion. Mrs Thatcher's prospects suddenly improved to a degree that the outside world did not immediately grasp. Nor did she. She thought that Whitelaw, who now entered the contest, would probably win, even if Neave, who understood the electoral realities, did not. Her uncertainty about the solidity of her vote accounts for her only tactical error during the campaign – that is, her publicly urging that more candidates should now stand.[12] Presumably, she imagined that they would detract from Whitelaw's vote. In fact, they posed more of a threat to her, particularly Geoffrey Howe. If Howe's campaign had ever taken off he could have drawn away some of her free-market sympathizers. But fortunately it stayed in a rut, as did James Prior's on the left and John Peyton's on the old right.

Whitelaw was, in fact, the only serious challenger, and under scrutiny his candidature looked less and less convincing. He subsequently confessed that he had disliked the whole business of campaigning, which he found disconcertingly divisive.[13] It showed.

The Thatcher campaign team's approach to getting the 139 votes required for victory in the second ballot was to adopt a stance of moderation in all things. Mrs Thatcher herself even issued a statement, to reassure doubters, that she was firmly committed to the European Common Market. But, above all, her strength of personality and conviction made Whitelaw seem woolly and out of his depth.

The two candidates now attended the Young Conservative conference in Eastbourne. The YC leadership was, and would long remain, Heathite and certainly backed Whitelaw. But it was Margaret Thatcher who took the conference itself by storm with a statement of her political creed:

> I believe we should judge people on merit and not on back-ground. I believe the person who is prepared to work hardest should get the greatest rewards and keep them after tax. That we should back the workers and not the shirkers; that it is not only permissible but praiseworthy to want to benefit your own family by your own efforts.

Afterwards, out on the promenade in front of the cameras, she and Whitelaw kissed; and, as the cameras flashed, she coyly remarked: 'Willie and I have been friends for years. I have done that to Willie many times and he to me. It was not that difficult for him to do . . .' Nor did it seem to be. Even before the final result emerged, a future partnership which would help re-unify the party – but on Margaret Thatcher's terms – had emerged.

The result itself was by now a surprise only in its decisiveness:

Margaret Thatcher 146
William Whitelaw 79
Geoffrey Howe 19
James Prior 19
John Peyton 11.

After she had heard the outcome from Neave, she went down to the Commons Grand Committee Room to meet the press. Here she gave one of those alternately cloying and abrasive performances which would become a trademark. She told her unconvinced audience that it was 'like a dream that the next name in the list after Harold Macmillan, Sir Alec Douglas-Home, Edward Heath, is Margaret Thatcher'. Then she answered a few questions at breakneck speed, discomfiting the muddled or repetitious. Visits to Central Office, where the cheers were distinctly hollow, and then to Bill Shelton's house for a victory party, where they were certainly sincere, were followed by dinner with the Chief Whip, Humphrey Atkins, and a farewell to the Finance Committee. By the time she went to bed in the early hours, it was not just her own life that had changed.

6

AN UPHILL STRUGGLE

Margaret Thatcher's achievements – and even more, perhaps, her failures – as leader of the Opposition can only be understood against the background of the crisis that affected Britain during those years. Whether she herself fully understood this is doubtful, and in a sense that is to her credit. In later years, she would frankly observe that she 'was not a very good Leader of the Opposition', before adding that she was better suited to 'getting things done', the classic job of government. Yet there was more to it than that.

Since her days at Education, Mrs Thatcher and her family had been installed in a comfortable and convenient house in Flood Street, Chelsea. She had no time to run it, of course; but now, under a constant blaze of searching media attention, she found she had no time to run the rest of her affairs either. Having prided herself on her ability to cope, she found herself overwhelmed, and she did not like it one bit. Carol has evocatively described the frenetic pace at which life was conducted in Flood Street.[1] And yet, after all the racing and pacing there was still not time to do all that Margaret Thatcher wanted – let alone do it in the measured and considered fashion which good decision-making requires.

In truth, she was very inexperienced by the standards of the time – though not those of today. She had held none of the great offices of state, nor even shadowed them. Moreover, this was an era when statesmanship, and thus leadership, was traditionally associated with foreign affairs, on which she had strong views but no proven pedigree or depth of knowledge. By contrast, she had a sure grip of domestic policy. But she still lacked a solid reputation, with the self-confidence that could bring. In practice, her inexperience was manifest in humdrum ways rather than in high policy. In matters of man management, she was, by common consent, hopeless – alternately chaotic and domineering, timid and abrasive. She was a notoriously bad chairman.

Moreover, she did not receive much help in her day-to-day tasks. Her office was theoretically under the supervision of Airey Neave, himself inclined to be easily flustered, but in practice it was run by Richard Ryder. Ryder had been recruited from the *Daily Telegraph*'s gossip column and was hardworking and loyal. But he was never close to Mrs Thatcher personally. He was nervy – and her capacity for tantrums was now at its height. Margaret Thatcher was generally good to those who worked for her, but she could be cruel, moody and unfair when the spirit took her. The men she respected were those she also feared. She did not fear Richard Ryder. With women she was less difficult. Among the secretaries who staffed the office in these years, Caroline Stevens (later Ryder) and Mrs Thatcher's constituency secretary Alison Ward (much later Wakeham) would both become friends, proving generous with time and affection when Mrs (now Lady) Thatcher was old and frail. The fact remains that the new party leader's office was ramshackle, even by the generally amateurish standards of (pre-New Labour) oppositions. The description in her memoirs of secretaries sitting on the floor opening letters, and of David Wolfson, boss of the mail-order giant GUS, being recruited to bring some kind of order to the process, catches the authentic flavour.[2]

Supporting the leader's office was the Conservative Research

ABOVE: The Roberts family. Margaret, on the far right, and her sister Muriel pose either side of their father Alfred, in his mayor's robes, and mother Beatrice.

RIGHT: Margaret (*left*) and Muriel.

BELOW: Alf Roberts's shop in North Parade, Grantham, above which Margaret was born.

LEFT: Margaret Roberts at work as a research chemist in 1950.

BELOW: With the new-born twins, Mark and Carol.

ABOVE: Wedding day, 13 December 1951.

General Election
VOTE FOR
MARGARET
THATCHER
CONSERVATIVE

TOP: Seeking the Dartford dustman's vote in the 1951 general election.

CENTRE LEFT: Campaign poster, Finchley, 1959.

CENTRE RIGHT: Speech preparation during the 1951 campaign.

LEFT: Interrupting a darts match during the 1959 campaign.

ABOVE: Finchley's MP reads a parliamentary Bill in front of Big Ben (1961).

ABOVE: With John Boyd-Carpenter on her first day as a junior minister at the Ministry of Pensions (1961).

LEFT: The Secretary of State for Education works alone in her office (1972).

LEFT: Reading lesson at a London primary school (1970).

BELOW: Sharing the Conservative party conference platform with Edward Heath, the new Prime Minister, in October 1970.

BELOW: Headlines from the *Sun* at the height of the 'Milk Snatcher' episode in 1971 (*top*); making a point, alongside Peter Carrington and Heath, at an election press conference in October 1974 (*bottom*).

If it's important to you it's important to The

THE SUN SAYS
Is Mrs Thatcher human?

Mrs THATCHER IS CANED ON SCHOOL MILK

By DAVID KEMP

RIGHT: The shape of things to come? Carrying away a portrait of Heath (1973).

LEFT: Press conference at the House of Commons after coming top in the first round of the Conservative Party leadership election on 4 February 1975.

CENTRE: Applause from Humphrey Atkins and Keith Joseph at the new leader's first party conference, October 1975.

BOTTOM: With Willie Whitelaw on the promenade at Eastbourne for the Young Conservatives' conference, 8 February 1975.

Top: Attending a Bow Group reception in 1976 with three former Tory Prime Ministers (from the left – Alec Douglas-Home, Heath and Harold Macmillan).

Above: Jim Callaghan's nemesis: the famous *Sun* headline of 11 January 1979 that condemned his complacency during the Winter of Discontent.

Right: Displaying her European credentials: campaigning for a 'Yes' vote in the 1975 referendum on Common Market membership.

TOP LEFT: Speaking at the Conservative Local Government Conference, March 1979, with the famous Saatchi and Saatchi posters in the foreground.

TOP RIGHT: Demonstrating the effect of Labour's inflation on household bills during the 1979 general election campaign.

ABOVE: Inexpertly grasping a long-suffering (and short-lived) calf during the 1979 campaign.

LEFT: Gordon Reece, the Tory publicity director, shows off the party's advertising themes to the media.

Department (CRD). This was part of the problem, and a microcosm of the whole of it. Margaret Thatcher did not start with any inbuilt suspicion of CRD. She refused to regard association with it as a black mark. She had, after all, worked well with its members in her different briefs and struck up a close relationship with Charles Bellairs, the shrewd, blind, right-winger who ran its Home Affairs Section. Yet, with a few such exceptions, CRD was opposed to the direction in which she wished to take the party and the country. It still reflected the Butskellite Toryism which had dominated the party's thinking for more than thirty years. It also shared the pragmatic, problem-solving mindset which characterizes research bodies everywhere: in such an atmosphere, ideology was out of place.

The main problem, though, was the Research Department's leadership. Mrs Thatcher had imagined that by removing as CRD chairman Ian Gilmour, a 'wet' Tory patrician, and substituting the crustily 'dry' Angus Maude, the Department could be kept loyal.* This was a typically naïve misjudgement, one of a series that would be repeated until they finally helped remove her from Number Ten. One can, of course, explain such decisions in part by the necessity of picking from a limited pool. And it does her credit, in one sense, that she was prepared to see the merits of people who did not agree with her. But for a politician to make so many mistakes in picking senior colleagues and key advisers amounts to a serious weakness. Crucially, at this point, Mrs Thatcher was persuaded to keep as its director Chris Patten, who was supported in his outlook and opinions by his deputy, Adam Ridley.† Both were affable, intelligent,

---

* The origins of the terms 'wet' and 'dry' are disputed. They were commonly used at the time, though not it seems by Mrs Thatcher herself. In her memoirs she suggests that the term 'wet' in the sense used by schoolboys to mean 'feeble', was coined by her supporters to refer to the Tory rebels and then worn by them as a badge of honour: see Margaret Thatcher, *The Downing Street Years* (London: HarperCollins, 1993), p. 51n. Ian Gow, her first PPS as Prime Minister, who had a wry wit and inventive vocabulary, may have been the author of the term. The expression 'dries' for Thatcherites was less widely used, doubtless because it was less insulting.

† Patten's political judgement may perhaps also be doubted: he gave me my first job. But, then, I gave David Cameron his.

sophisticated and articulate; unfortunately, both were also supporters
of Heath and privately contemptuous of Thatcher, Joseph and the
wider project. Patten's politics were symbolized by the Helmut
Schmidt-style cap he liked to sport, though Schmidt's views were
probably more conservative than his. It was Patten who apparently
christened Joseph 'the Mad Monk', an insult which the media took
up with relish. Ridley's contribution to Mrs Thatcher's problems
stemmed from the fact that he was the only trained economist upon
whom she could rely for speech-writing and routine briefing, and
he happened to disagree with her economics. The CRD was widely,
and probably rightly, assumed to be guilty of leaking to the press a
number of embarrassing documents whose purpose was to discredit
Joseph and the CPS and frustrate attempts to develop a more
radical approach to policy.

At Conservative Central Office, Mrs Thatcher did make decisive
changes. She ordered the sacking of Michael Wolff, the party
Director General, an out-and-out Heath man regarded as the
mastermind of the smear over food hoarding. The fact that several
of her senior Shadow Cabinet colleagues formally protested and
that Prior, in a tantrum, even refused to vote in the Opposition
lobby, shows how right she was to make the change.* The party
chairmanship, hitherto held by Whitelaw, she gave to Lord
Thorneycroft, who just happened to be Whitelaw's cousin. This
move was initially criticized, but, as it turned out, on the wrong
grounds. Thorneycroft, though old and sometimes ill with cancer,
was vigorous, a fine speaker and a fearsome personality.
Unfortunately, he had long since lost whatever ideological zeal he
had ever possessed – it was Enoch Powell who had pressed him
to resign over public spending in 1958, and Thorneycroft had
regretted listening ever since. By now he was contemptuous of

* Wolff understood what was at stake. In February 1975 he told the Thatcherite journalist
Patrick Cosgrave: 'These people want to wipe out the past. It can't be done, and it
shouldn't be done' (Patrick Cosgrave, *Thatcher: The First Term*, London, Bodley Head,
1979, p. 9).

ideas and, by extension, of idealists who got in the way of office. Power was the thing. This traditionally Conservative view, although it meant that he fitted his new role like a glove, would also contribute in opposition to paralysis of policy development, and, in government, lead to the first crisis of Mrs Thatcher's premiership.

The indispensable outside element in policy formation which Mrs Thatcher tried but ultimately failed to bring within the framework of party decision-making was, of course, the CPS. Because she did not confront either the Shadow Cabinet or the party head-on at this stage, she was forced to take her advice from those whose views she really – and rightly – valued in unofficial, semi-secret fashion. This may, paradoxically, have made her feel more important. Leaders often like to have divided counsels, because it increases their freedom of manœuvre, and she would later give every sign of enjoying this luxury: notes of private advice drawn from her handbag would prove a terrifying instrument of punishment for ill-prepared colleagues. But working in this unsystematic way was a mistake all the same, and, particularly in opposition, she paid for it.

The CPS was now, in fact, at the height of its importance. Those gathered in Wilfred Street were the originators and coordinators of the plans by which Mrs Thatcher intended to reverse Britain's fortunes, and they knew it. With the abrasive Sherman at their core, they combated with a will, if less than complete success, the propaganda from the CRD and the Cabinet wets with their own press contacts and sympathizers. More constructively, they provided an alternative framework of advice. Thus the monetarist Alan Walters focused Mrs Thatcher's mind on the real causes of inflation, though his departure to the United States in 1976 meant that he was absent at some crucial junctures. Douglas Hague, more a technician and less a polemicist, also discreetly provided economic advice: he would become for a while Mrs Thatcher's adviser at Downing Street after the 1979 election.

John Hoskyns, a businessman with strong views about how to restore Britain's economic health, was brought in by Sherman to try to impose some shape upon Mrs Thatcher's and the Shadow Cabinet's thinking. His main role came a little later in the period of opposition, as he and his colleague Norman Strauss sought to force the leadership to address the trade union problem in a series of papers for the 'Stepping Stones' process.* Hoskyns was a believer in systems, which, despite much flaunting of her scientific training, Margaret Thatcher never was. His conviction that the problems of government could be illuminated by intricate diagrams captivated Keith Joseph but left her unimpressed. She valued him none the less for his soundness and integrity and because he shared her view that change must be radical to be effective.

The ferment of activity based on the CPS at this time was, naturally, unwelcome to most of the Shadow Cabinet. Only Joseph, Howe, Maude and (intermittently) John Biffen shared the CPS analysis of what was wrong and what needed to happen to put it right. Furthermore, Howe was already hostile to Sherman personally and, indeed, to the unfashionably robust expression of views on any matter that was Sherman's trademark. Howe took as his self-imposed standard the need to convince '*Guardian* readers' of the rightness of his analysis. It implied a very different set of priorities from those of the CPS or, indeed, of Margaret Thatcher.

The surprise, now and later, is the degree to which Joseph was marginalized. He could always count on being able to gain Mrs Thatcher's attention and usually her agreement. But he dissipated and misapplied his efforts. The only major contribution he made to the public debate about economic strategy was the lecture he delivered at Stockton in 1976, which was subsequently published with an introduction by the leader under the provocative title 'Monetarism is not Enough'. It contained an important message, namely that beating inflation was only a start: cuts in public spending and taxes were also required in order to create the conditions for wealth creation. But it was not followed through and not fully grasped,

* See pp. 142–3.

even by sympathizers.* Otherwise, Joseph allowed himself to become distracted by a host of disparate subjects on which he set up conflicting and overlapping policy groups. Opinions differ as to whether the total number of these groups by the time of the election had reached the nineties or a figure well above that. Almost without exception, they proved pointless. From 1977 Joseph took the Shadow Industry portfolio, on John Biffen's withdrawal for health reasons, and after this he had even less impact. Mrs Thatcher looked on him with gratitude and undiminished affection, but not for inspiration, and she distrusted his judgement and robustness.

All this meant that an extraordinary burden of responsibility fell on her. But why, in that case, did she tie her hands further by appointing a Shadow Cabinet arrayed against her? Whitelaw was, inevitably perhaps, deputy leader, initially with a roving brief that covered devolution; later he shadowed the Home Office. His loyalty to Mrs Thatcher was personally valuable, but it came at a price. That was the watering down of the policies she wished to promote and her tolerance of vocal dissent from senior colleagues. Margaret Thatcher always remained of the opinion that this price had been worth paying. But perhaps she underrated it.

Alongside Whitelaw, as opponents of the Joseph–Thatcher free-market monetarist approach, were arrayed a group that was formidable in terms of seniority as well as numbers. Peter Carrington, like Whitelaw a patrician and less interested in the lower arts of economics than in administration and diplomacy, remained as Tory leader in the Lords. Also like Whitelaw, he soon enjoyed Mrs Thatcher's confidence and even a kind of friendship. Their closeness is sometimes ascribed to her weakness for upper-class men, and she certainly liked his style. He had a wry sense of humour, polish and a large fund of relaxed self-confidence. By contrast, she never felt any closeness to the languid Ian Gilmour,

* Sherman would rightly observe during the ferocious monetary squeeze of the early 1980s, whose impact was felt more by the private than the public sector, that the thinking of the Stockton Lecture, which he himself drafted, had never been absorbed.

from much the same background, whom for the moment she initially kept at the Home Office before moving him to Defence. Unlike Whitelaw and Carrington, Gilmour was an intellectual. He was also Patten's mentor, which gave him added influence and increased scope for mischief.

Mrs Thatcher's decision to bring Reggie Maudling into the Shadow Cabinet to cover Foreign Affairs was an unforced error. She did not know how much he already disliked her – indeed, despised would be a better word. Though largely discredited by the Poulson affair, and by character cynical and lazy, he still had sufficient knowledge of economics to cause trouble outside his brief, which he did. Presumably, she felt that she needed to find a senior figure to fill the Foreign Affairs role, where she was thought to be weak.

Whitelaw was almost certainly responsible for the surprise decision not to give Keith Joseph the post of Shadow Chancellor. Admittedly, Joseph did not ask for it: but he surely at least had a right of first refusal. Instead, as noted above, he kept his roving policy brief, and Geoffrey Howe was given the key Treasury role.

Because Howe remained at the Treasury for so long and became a successful, indeed in his way formidable, Chancellor of the Exchequer, later commentators have assumed that he was an obvious choice. But this is not so. The appointment was, as Margaret Thatcher notes in her memoirs, 'a calculated gamble'.[3] He was a curate's egg of a politician: a hawk on trade union reform, yet with a sneaking sympathy for pay controls. He was a poor speaker, easily flustered, and was to be repeatedly worsted by Denis Healey. He had an extremely high opinion of himself, and in private to his clique of friends and advisers he evinced, so far as he dared, a correspondingly low view of Mrs Thatcher. He correctly thought that he had a clearer mind and a better understanding of policy, but he confused these with the qualities of leadership, which he lacked and she possessed. Howe's autobiography is entitled *Conflict of Loyalty*. Commentators should remember that for years Mrs Thatcher stuck to him loyally, when it would have been easy, and must have been tempting, to ditch him.

She felt that she was saddled with Jim Prior as Shadow Employment Secretary for a different reason: his survival during the years of opposition and into government, despite his repeated gaffes and obvious lack of commitment to the economic strategy, was an earnest of her intent to get on with the trade unions. As with Whitelaw's appointment, the decision is understandable. But again the protection that it brought her was dearly purchased. As a result, serious strategic thinking about the union problem had to be done covertly, deniably and unsystematically, like so much else during these years.

Mrs Thatcher did, though, regard some Heath men as dispensable: Geoffrey Rippon and Peter Thomas stood down and were not recalled. Robert Carr, Nicholas Scott and Paul Channon were dropped. More significant was the disposal of Peter Walker. He could, indeed, hardly have expected to stay, though she might have blinked at the prospect of having so dangerous a foe on the back benches.

Heath himself was even more problematic. She had got herself into some difficulty by pledging to offer him a place in the Shadow Cabinet. It would have had to be a very senior one and he would certainly have proved unmanageable wherever he was put. Luckily, by the time she went to visit him at his home – the day after her success in the second ballot – he had already told the press that he would not serve. She thus felt free to offer him a Shadow Cabinet post, which he duly turned down, and then the role of leadership of the Tory 'Yes' campaign in the forthcoming referendum on European Economic Community membership, which he also unceremoniously declined. His self-destructive sulkiness was to prove a godsend.*

Had Heath been more sensible, he might have used the European issue to resurrect his fortunes and perhaps to advance his claim to be Conservative leader in a putative coalition government.

* Heath's camp (and Heath in his memoirs: *The Course of My Life*, London, Hodder & Stoughton, 1999, p. 537) subsequently maintained that he had not been offered a Shadow Cabinet job. This is certainly inaccurate, though it is true that Mrs Thatcher did not press him and was glad that he had said 'no'.

Margaret Thatcher took a back seat in the European referendum campaign, just when she was expected, as a new leader, to occupy the front one. It was a mistake. She regurgitated all the respectable lines in articles and speeches. Adopting arguments which she would later reject, she declared that for Britain to leave the Common Market would 'mean denouncing a Treaty [and] Britain does not break Treaties', adding that 'by turning our backs [on Europe] we would forfeit our right to influence what happens in the Community'.[4] She claimed that 'to come out now, with nowhere to go, would jeopardise our own and our children's future'.[5] But her performance was judged pedestrian and it coincided with a disappointing lack of aggression against Harold Wilson at Prime Minister's Questions. By the end of the campaign there was unease within the party about her leadership, which she sought to combat by promising to step up her attacks on the Government.[6]

The greater problem, however, which the European campaign itself reflected, was how to confront the crisis facing the country in a way that kept the Tory Party together. There were two possible Conservative views about what was wrong with Britain, and somehow she as leader had to straddle both of them. The first view, which was promoted by Heath and his ilk, was that Britain had been moving more or less in the right direction until hijacked by extremists who had fomented a miners' strike. The theory had the obvious attraction of exculpating the Heath Government. It also corresponded to current realities, because there was a powerful section of the Labour Party which was indeed bent on turning Britain into something approaching a communist state. If Britain was faced with such a threat, it could be argued that what was required was a coming together of moderates of all political convictions to defeat it.

The second view, which did not necessarily exclude elements of the first, was that Britain's problems were more deep-seated, and that the current crisis, real as it was, was symptomatic rather

"I don't know what effect she'll have on the enemy, but, by God, she frightens me!"

than causal. Certainly, the far left had made things worse, and its anti-British, anti-democratic activities were alarming, but there was a tide to change, not just a storm to ride. Those who argued in these terms pointed to the evidence of Britain's relative economic decline – its bad record on productivity, days lost in strikes, low profits, overmanning and lack of innovation. This was the view originally advanced by Joseph; it was now espoused and championed by Margaret Thatcher; but not even a majority of the Shadow Cabinet shared it.

What both groups could agree about was the reality of the economic crisis itself. By August 1975 inflation was running at 27 per cent: hyper-inflation seemed a real possibility. The value of sterling sank. Public borrowing ballooned. A series of Budgets, mini-Budgets and fiscal packages in 1975 and 1976 signalled that the Government's economic plans were in disarray, which further undermined the confidence of the financial markets. From July 1975, Wilson and Healey abandoned the earlier 'Social Contract' with the unions and sought to gain TUC adherence to an explicit pay policy. Naturally, Heath, Walker and others on the Tory backbenches felt vindicated, and they used this echo of their own approach to demand that Mrs Thatcher support the measures 'in the national interest'.

But she was by now convinced that such attempts to suppress the symptoms of government-created inflation did more harm than good. They eroded incentives, penalized effort, increased government's power over matters that properly belonged to the purview of private citizens, and had no long-term effect on inflation either. Under pressure from inside and outside the Shadow Cabinet, she was reluctantly prepared to accept that a short-term wage freeze might have some value. But she ruled out what she described, in a somewhat unconvincing reinterpretation of the term, as a 'statutory wages policy'.[7] It was evident that the Tory leadership was split on the issue, and this perception also undermined her self-confidence in the Commons, where her performances were often very weak. (Harold Wilson privately remarked after one such failure that she would 'never get a feel for the House' – which shows, of course, how wrong even an aficionado of the art form can be.[8])

The Government's response to its problems with the budget deficit was to put up taxes – the basic rate of income tax rose from 30 to 35 pence in the pound – rather than to rein back expenditure. On fiscal matters, at least, the Shadow Cabinet was more or less united: they all wanted lower taxes. The trouble arose when the specifics of the public expenditure reductions planned by the Tories were discussed; and the implications for unemployment were even trickier to handle. In these matters, Margaret Thatcher exhibited her instinctive caution, and indeed a certain deviousness – she had no intention of saying anything which could be taken down and used against her in the forthcoming general election. Howe had come up with a list of (fairly modest) savings that were not too painful: for example, the elimination or reduction of various subsidies and the cutting back of future nationalization plans. She repeated the list. But she was not prepared to follow him down the path of speculating how far living standards might fall in consequence, let alone join him and Joseph in predicting how much unemployment might rise.*

The breaking of a full-scale economic crisis in the summer of 1976 took the political world by surprise. In March sterling had fallen below (what seemed then) the symbolically important $2 mark; later that month Wilson suddenly resigned, to be succeeded by James Callaghan; and in April the Government lost its parliamentary majority. Uncertainty grew exponentially. In June, $5,300 million of standby credit was drawn down to boost sterling; but on 28 September Healey was humiliatingly forced to turn back at the airport, on his way to discussions with the International Monetary Fund (IMF), to deal with a new sterling crisis, as the pound plunged to $1.63. His speech to the Labour Party conference contained a tougher economic message than anything ever delivered by Mrs Thatcher or her colleagues; Callaghan's, drafted by his son-in-law Peter Jay, one of the high priests of monetarism, was tougher still.† Negotiations with the IMF continued and finally resulted in a fundamentally new policy direction. Under the terms of a Letter of Intent, and through a further mini-Budget on 15 December, Healey announced large cuts in real public expenditure – the only occasion in modern times when any British Chancellor has done so – and the adoption of targets for the money supply: in other words, the application of classic monetarism, albeit formulated in terms of domestic credit expansion rather than monetary aggregates.‡

The measures were severe and extremely effective. Although

---

* On which see Lawson's bullish view: p. 296.

† It contained the memorable lines: 'We used to think that you could just spend your way out of a recession and increase employment by cutting taxes and boosting government spending. I tell you, in all candour, that this option no longer exists, and that in so far as it ever did exist it only worked by injecting bigger doses of inflation into the economy followed by higher levels of unemployment as the next step.'

‡ George Osborne, as Chancellor, in 2010 also announced spending reductions which should result in a small real terms cut. Whether the target will be met, though, is not clear.

interest rates rose and unemployment with them, other measures of economic health soon started to tell a different story. Growth resumed, inflation fell, the public finances were stabilized, industrial profits began to recover. Monetarism was clearly seen to work. It undoubtedly helped the country that it was a Labour Government which imposed the cuts, and at the insistence of foreign bankers. But for all that, it was Margaret Thatcher who had been proved right. Indeed, the most serious cause for alarm, as a rendezvous with the electorate beckoned, was whether the IMF's medicine might prove so successful that the electorate preferred to give Labour another term.

In fact, the IMF crisis of 1976 more or less coincided with the publication by the Conservative Party of the document called *The Right Approach*. Its significance has sometimes been overrated – even by Mrs Thatcher in her memoirs.[9] It was the work of Angus Maude and Chris Patten, and as such was elegantly written. But it did not mark any serious advance in settling the future direction of policy. It made no pledges and settled no open questions, and it propounded a philosophy so uncontentious that both wings of the Conservative Party could embrace it. In fact, this was its political merit. It would also be the next best thing to a manifesto, if a snap election were called.

In the event there was no election. In February 1977 the Government was defeated on a guillotine motion on its Scotland and Wales (Devolution) Bill. But at the end of a debate on a motion of confidence, during which Mrs Thatcher made a particularly poor speech, Labour was kept in office by Liberal Party votes. What would the following month formally become the Lib–Lab pact had saved the Government.

This was demoralizing, especially for the parliamentary party. There were new rumbles about Mrs Thatcher's leadership. But outside Westminster it was a different story. She had started to make an impact, and in the long run this was more important. With the help of Gordon Reece, she was becoming an accomplished performer on television and radio. He ensured that she had plenty of exposure on programmes with a more relaxed format, like Jimmy Young's radio show, where she was less likely to become snappy and defensive. In later years, however, Reece considered that his most important role was in fostering her relationship with the print media. She received favourable treatment from the tabloid press; and it was at this time that the *Daily Mail* and the *Sun* became devotees, with a profound effect on her public image.

But it was the content of her thinking, the passion and directness of her words, which were the source of her impact. She sold well because she had something fresh and exciting to sell. It is sometimes forgotten that she was unusual at the time in being an optimist. As she declared in her first party political broadcast (PPB) as leader: 'It's been said that all that politicians are doing now is rearranging the deck chairs on the Titanic. Well, here is one who isn't.'[10] It was obviously authentic.

So was her sharp riposte to Kenneth Harris, in an interview for the *Observer*:

> *Harris*: Do you feel guilty?
> *Thatcher*: What have I got to be guilty about? What I have and what I am is the result of continuous effort and the courage to take the next step. There may be some politicians who are so conscious of being born into wealth that they are inhibited for fear they seem to be perpetuating their own privileges. I think that if a person is born to wealth, he shouldn't waste time feeling guilty about it: he should act, and use his good fortune to improve the lot of other people. One of my favourite quotations is: 'That which thy father bequeathed thee, earn it anew, if you wouldst possess it.'[11]

Her set-piece speeches also projected her beliefs, in a more philosophical framework. Their purpose was quite the opposite of the speeches which today's front-rank politicians give: it was to persuade her audiences, national and global, of the rightness of her analysis. This urgency and seriousness are what make the speeches still worth reading.[12]

The series begins with her own first party conference speech as leader. In her memoirs, Mrs Thatcher describes how it came to be written – the rejection of Patten's and Ridley's overeconomic approach, her own long if formless contributory screed, the reworking of the material with Angus Maude, and finally the importation of the playwright Ronnie Millar, whom she already knew, to polish it all up and coach her delivery.[13]

Millar would hold a special place in her affections. She enjoyed the slightly camp, showbiz quality he brought to proceedings. He made her feel like a star, which, indeed, he considered her. He also gave her good advice on style, which she took to heart and remembered precisely because it went against her natural way of working. So when she wanted to pile example upon example in order to justify some assertion, he would shake his head and say: 'Remember, dear, less is more!' Similarly, she absorbed from him his playwright's dislike of the pedestrian and predictable. 'Very fresh!' was the highest compliment he could pay to the style of a passage – and she, too, in later years, and often quite inappropriately, would exclaim the same, if she liked what she read. Unfortunately, Millar was also keen on bathing in reflected glory, and when she left the stage he started to enjoy John Major's spell in the limelight as he worked in turn on the new leader's speeches. This hurt Mrs Thatcher – and her consequent behaviour hurt Millar, as he recalls.[14] There is, though, a happier sequel, which is not untypical of her. Years later, as Millar was lying on his deathbed, stricken with cancer, he was visited by his old prima donna and comforted by her.

Margaret Thatcher was a maddening if strangely satisfying politician for whom to write. She functioned by instinct, not logic, though she could cut through others' illogicality. Certain passages she would work on herself, and indeed work to death. They usually concerned some technical matter which as likely as not would be trimmed down heavily or even discarded as the cutting, splicing and filleting of the final draft occurred, often late at night or in the early hours, as panic, anticipation and excitement fuelled her with adrenalin.

In the 1975 party conference speech one passage, spoken from the heart and received as such by her audience, is worth quoting:

> Policies and programmes should not just be a list of unrelated items. They are part of a total vision of the kind of life we want for our country and our children. Let me give you my vision: a man's right to work as he will, to spend what he earns, to own property, to have the state as servant and not as master – these are the British inheritance. They are the essence of a free country and on that freedom all our other freedoms depend.[15]

Mrs Thatcher was not to find that tone again until she became Prime Minister. Even when she gained in self-confidence and acquired new stature in the Winter of Discontent of 1978–9, the tenor was necessarily more confrontational.

A desire for confrontation was the accusation made against her as a result of the two foreign policy speeches she delivered that won her the soubriquet of the 'Iron Lady' – the first in Chelsea on 26 July 1975 and the second in Kensington on 19 January 1976. These forays did not, however, come out of the blue.

As has already been noted, Margaret Thatcher had a long-standing interest in foreign affairs, centring initially on the Empire and later increasingly on the Soviet threat. Churchill was never very far away in her thoughts. She distrusted the tendency to be weak in dealing with dictators and she was uneasy when told that the price of peace was disarmament. The Labour Government had just embarked on large defence cuts. But it was détente that caused her the gravest doubts. The question became particularly acute as the West enthusiastically took up the Soviet suggestion of an East–West summit at Helsinki. Washington saw it as an opportunity to slow the accelerating Soviet arms race and gain assurances on human rights behind the Iron Curtain. The Soviet leadership had rather different goals: in the short term, de facto endorsement of the Brezhnev doctrine – essentially, once a member of the Soviet bloc, always a member of the bloc – and in the long term a relaxation of tension in Europe, while they pursued expansion in the Third World.

Mrs Thatcher passionately wanted to speak about the issues, but she knew that she needed an expert to help her. Through John O'Sullivan of the *Daily Telegraph* (already a strong supporter) she was introduced to Robert Conquest. Conquest was a hero to anti-communists, but scornfully dismissed as a scaremongering polemicist by British Sovietologists. He had written the well-documented truth about Stalin's programmes of mass murder in his history *The Great Terror*, and not been forgiven. (In fact, he would never be forgiven – he had to find work and recognition in the United States at the Hoover Institution.)

Conquest's draft of the Chelsea speech was not seen by Reggie Maudling, who was livid when he read the press reports. In challenging whether the Soviets were serious about détente, in quoting Alexander Solzhenitsyn's attacks on the process and in drawing attention to the Russian military build-up, it had a huge impact.[16]

Conquest had departed for the United States by the time Mrs Thatcher decided to return to these themes at a speech in Kensington six months later. The draftsman this time was Robert Moss, editor of the *Economist*'s foreign report. Again, the speech rocked the diplomatic establishment, though it won praise from the press.[17] It also again infuriated Maudling. But it enraged the Soviets more. It was not their official protest that made a mark, however, but rather the foolish branding (by the military propaganda organ *Red Star*) of Mrs Thatcher as 'the Iron Lady'. Gordon Reece was delighted when he read the phrase and persuaded Mrs Thatcher to be delighted too. At a (broadcast) speech in Finchley she declared to laughter and applause: 'I stand before you tonight in my Red Star chiffon evening gown, my face softly made up and my fair hair gently waved, the Iron Lady of the Western world.'[18]

By the time of the Kensington address she had made her first visit as party leader to the United States. She was an instant success with American audiences. The British Embassy, at the urging of the Callaghan Government, implied that she was unpatriotic for criticizing Britain's economic performance. She was careful, though, to do no such thing. As she told the National Press Club in Washington, Britain still had huge potential; the national character had not changed: 'We are still the same people who have fought for freedom and won.'[19]

This theme of optimism about Britain's future – indeed, the West's future – once the damaging effect of socialist policies was reversed, also underlay the speech she gave in Zurich on 14 March 1977.[20] It was the most important economic lecture she delivered during the period of opposition, and in large part made up for her failures to explain her economic policy in the House of Commons. She worked at the draft intensively with Alfred Sherman, and it reflects well on both of them – as she concluded when she reread it many years later. Capitalism, she proclaimed, was materially and morally superior to socialism. Moreover, a 'people's capitalism', achieved through wider ownership of shares and property, would cause a 'withering away of the class struggle'. This was not inevitable – but there was a tide which 'flows away from failure . . . [I]f it is taken, the last quarter of our century can initiate a new Renaissance.' Such language had never been used by a Conservative leader, nor by the leader of any other European right-of-centre party. It marked a determination to fight socialism on the battlefield of ideas – itself a favourite Thatcher metaphor.

It was not, therefore, simple revulsion at the brutality of the hard left at home or alarm at Soviet inroads overseas which drew intellectual converts to the right under Margaret Thatcher – it was Margaret Thatcher herself. She spoke the language they understood, not least because converts helped draft it. Historians like Conquest and Hugh Thomas, journalists like Paul Johnson and Bernard Levin, former Labour politicians like Woodrow Wyatt and Brian Walden, even on the further fringes the novelist Kingsley

Amis and the poet Philip Larkin, were among the distinguished members of this group of admirers. They would not, by and large, have thought of themselves as Conservatives; indeed, their common assumption was that the Conservative Party systematically betrayed the causes it should have defended. But they found in Margaret Thatcher an unlikely heroine, a conviction politician who was determined to take risks to make a difference. She found in them the reassurance which her colleagues denied her. Slowly the political atmosphere began to change.

7

VICTORY

Near the end of the 1979 general election campaign, Callaghan confided to his adviser Bernard Donoughue: 'You know there are times, perhaps every thirty years, when there is a sea-change in politics . . . a shift in what the public wants and what it approves of. I suspect that there is now such a sea-change – and it is for Mrs Thatcher.'[1] He was proved right, but more by what Margaret Thatcher subsequently achieved than by the mere fact of her winning the election.

In any case, it did not seem like that at the time. She could very easily have lost, for the odds were in many respects stacked against her. She was unable to count on the loyalty of most of her Shadow Cabinet. Her predecessor pursued a semi-public vendetta against her. She was viewed with suspicion or at least nervousness by a large section of her party. She had been prevented, in part by recollection of what the Tories had done when last in government, in part by her timorous colleagues, and in part by an economically ill-educated public opinion, from proposing openly the course she truly favoured. And for someone whose central aim was to promote the ethic of capitalism it was intensely frustrating to find so little support forthcoming from business. Whenever the Labour Government looked like falling, and the possibility of a Conservative victory was discussed, the Stock Exchange sank like a stone – as interviewers enjoyed pointing out to her.[2] In the face of these difficulties she had to weave and tack, and rely on events to help. They finally did, but only just in time.

The mid-term message of the opinion polls, confirmed in by-election and local government election results, offered encouragement. The Tories were somewhere between nine and eighteen points ahead of Labour, depending on which polling organization one believed. But then the gap between the parties sharply narrowed or even disappeared, under circumstances to be described.[3] Suddenly, the assumptions of a Conservative landslide looked premature, Conservative MPs grew restive and the only ever semi-quiescent Shadow Cabinet became more fractious.

Fortunately, towards the end of her period in opposition, another change also occurred. There was a noticeable improvement in Mrs Thatcher's performance as leader of the Opposition. She became more confident. She looked better: she had lost half a stone to remove tubbiness and an incipient double chin. She had restyled her hair, flattening the curls, removing the parting, even allowing it to become disordered on occasion. Her voice had improved. This was not so much a matter of lowering the pitch – that she had already done. It was more a question of altering her breathing. For this she had a voice coach to help her, along with some flattering if not very effective advice from Laurence Olivier.[4] People also noticed that she spoke in less of a monotone. Meanwhile, she fought to stop herself screeching over the hubbub in the House of Commons, which became more important electorally once Prime Minister's Questions was broadcast over the radio from April 1978.

At least she could rely on noisy support from her own side in debates, even when she performed unevenly. The only major parliamentary rebellion she faced as Leader was over Rhodesia in November 1978, when 114 Tories defied the decision to abstain on renewal of sanctions. Significantly, the rebels were from the right, not the left of the party: that is, from people who were basically committed to her leadership. It was embarrassing, but no threat.

Margaret Thatcher's real difficulties stemmed from the economic upturn which reduced discontent with the Government. In these circumstances, it was necessary to advance a coherent analysis of why the fundamentals of the economy still needed reform – which a Shadow Cabinet paralysed by disagreement was unable to provide.

Nor did that other well-tried Tory expedient, drawing attention to the inroads of left-wing extremists, offer a political escape route. The threat itself was real enough. Infiltration by the far left, including Trotskyists working behind a variety of different fronts, was proceeding unhindered in Labour constituencies. In the subsequent general election, effective play was made by the Conservatives in targeted campaigns against hard left MPs. But now Mrs Thatcher found herself mocked by interviewers as implying that Callaghan was an anti-democratic revolutionary.[5] So too her 1977 party conference speech, which contained little Conservative policy and much attacking of the left, received a bad press and did nothing to halt Tory slippage in the polls.

There was no way out. If the Tories were to rebuild their position they had to return to the economy. But they were still at sixes and sevens, especially over the key issues of pay policy and the unions. At this stage, Mrs Thatcher herself was more of a radical on the first than on the second. She felt guilty, as did Joseph, about having gone along with the Heath Government's draconian statutory pay policy. But, being the sort of person she was, her guilt expressed itself in vehement expressions of resolve rather than of repentance.

This explains why she was so unhappy with the formulation contained in *The Right Approach to the Economy*. The document was drafted by David Howell but bore the policy imprint of Geoffrey Howe and Jim Prior; to these three names that of Keith Joseph was added as joint author, though he had little input. It was published in October 1978 and was supposed to square the circle between incomes policy and 'free collective bargaining'. It suggested that the German model of 'concerted action' should be applied in Britain through a strengthened National Economic Development Council (NEDC), where the two 'sides' of industry sat with the Government to discuss the economy's needs and prospects. Howe was proud of it.[6] But Mrs Thatcher's comment on the draft reads: 'We should recognize that the German talking shop works because it consists of Germans.'[7] She prevented its being adopted formally as party policy, though in practice it temporarily was. When she tried to move away from it entirely, preferring instead to stress the need for a policy for output and profits, not just (or even primarily) incomes, she was forced by her colleagues, and above all by Thorneycroft, into an ignominious retreat. The 1978 party conference was, indeed, dominated by a public dispute on incomes policy with Ted Heath. Worse, the polls showed widespread support for his view rather than hers. The outcome was a speech delivered in Paddington whose clumsy drafting and dismal tone are almost as significant as its contents:

> We Conservatives are clear where we stand. We share the deep concern of our people about inflation, which has taken place particularly under Labour. We regard its reduction as our first priority. We agree with the Government's aim: we do not agree with its methods. In particular, we do not agree with the rigid, fixed five per cent guide-line . . . Our policy on incomes was set out more than a year ago in our published paper, *The Right Approach to the Economy*. It remains our policy today.[8]

Of course, nothing came of the 'forum' once the Conservatives were elected. She made sure of that. But so also did events. What practical likelihood was there in 1979 of a corporatist consensus of the sort envisaged by Howe?

In retrospect, it is astonishing that Jim Prior was able for so long to rule out any substantial measure of trade union reform, given the views of Howe, Joseph and Maude, supported by Hoskyns. A tipping point very nearly came with the Grunwick dispute. Grunwick, a medium-sized film-processing company in North London owned by an Anglo-Indian entrepreneur, George Ward, and with an Asian staff, was in 1977 the focus of a violent industrial dispute. The normally moderate APEX trade union demanded reinstatement of staff dismissed – according to APEX – for wanting to join a union. The issue was, though, more complex than that. The National Association for Freedom (NAFF), which defended Ward, argued that the union's real aim was to enforce a closed shop upon a work-force which had no desire for union representation.* NAFF was probably right, though it was the union's tactics, not its aims, that fuelled public concern. It was an embarrassment for the Government, because at an early stage such arch-moderate ministers as Shirley Williams had appeared on the picket line. But it was also unsettling for the Tories, whose policy was to denounce the closed shop in principle, but allow it – subject to a 'conscience clause' – in practice. The issue sharply divided the Shadow Cabinet. Howe and Joseph were hawks, while Prior was so doveish as to appear perfectly content with allowing the abuse to exist unchecked. When a court of inquiry chaired by Lord Scarman produced a mealy-mouthed report that seemed to appease the union, shadow ministers adopted diametrically opposed lines. Mrs Thatcher was in America at the time and this may account for a lack of political sensitivity in the way she answered questions on the subject. But had she been back home, she would still have come down on Prior's side against Joseph. In her memoirs, Mrs Thatcher acknowledges that she was wrong.[9] Yet there is something more to be said.

The closed shop was odious to a liberal-minded Jew like Keith Joseph because it represented a blatant breach of fundamental

* The expression 'closed shop', once in everyday use in politics, has now all but passed into oblivion, like the institution itself. It refers to compulsory trade union membership, enforced in practice by an employer's refusal to employ anyone not a member of a particular union.

human rights. Margaret Thatcher did not disagree. She had, after all, been a supporter of NAFF from the beginning. But she had also been convinced by the standard criticisms of Heath's Industrial Relations Act, namely, that it did too much too fast and that it tried to use the law to achieve objectives for which legal means were inappropriate. (She would alter her view on the second point.) So she was not prepared to try to outlaw the closed shop.* She was always as much realist as idealist.

But she also understood that union militancy had found the Conservative approach wanting. Her solution was characteristic – an initiative taken without consultation, seemingly irresponsible, in fact inspired. She had been mulling over the possibilities of using a referendum on matters outside the strictly constitutional ambit ever since the European referendum campaign in 1975. In particular, she had read and reread Dicey on referendums.[10] Thus she arrived in the *Weekend World* studio on Sunday 18 September to tell Brian Walden that in the case of all-out trade union confrontation with a Conservative Government – which, however, she insisted was unlikely – she would call a referendum. The logic was far from faultless: after all, even if most people voted to back the Government, why should that force militants to abandon a damaging national strike? Nevertheless, despite confusion and dismay among her colleagues, she had struck a nerve. An opinion poll for the *Daily Express* a few days later showed that 69 per cent agreed with her.

There was also by now a more radical strategy on the table in the form of the 'Stepping Stones' operation, conceived by John Hoskyns and Norman Strauss.[11] From the summer of 1977 Hoskyns had been trying to persuade Mrs Thatcher and her colleagues that without a solution of the union problem none of the country's economic problems could be solved. His main purpose in Stepping Stones,

---

* It is worth noting that as late as the autumn of 1978 *The Right Approach to the Economy*, while it listed measures to be applied against the closed shop through a code of practice (albeit with a threat of possible legislation), did not mention the regulation of picketing or promotion of ballots.

which began with a paper to the Shadow Cabinet that led to a number of desultory discussions in three further policy groups, was to produce a communications programme aimed at convincing the public of the need for radical change. The specific policy proposals were subsidiary to that. Ironically, in practice it proved impossible to win round the Shadow Cabinet doubters, let alone the public. Hoskyns found Margaret Thatcher even more impossible than the others, for although she was largely convinced by his analysis, she refused to follow it through. But Hoskyns underrated her. She had listened and learned, and she was waiting on events.

By the beginning of 1978 the Conservatives were again in trouble. Their fortunes had declined as economic prospects improved. Pay rises now looked manageable. Interest rates were down. Inflation had fallen. A year previously, the Opposition had enjoyed a lead of 13 per cent in the polls; now they were level-pegging with the Government. The party had to revive its fortunes. Low politics had to be part of the answer. Mrs Thatcher provided some when she spoke in a television interview about the level of immigration: 'People are really rather afraid that this country might be rather swamped by people with a different culture. And, you know, the British character has done so much for democracy, for law, and done so much throughout the world, that if there is any fear that it might be swamped, people are going to react and be rather hostile to those coming in.' She then went on to 'offer a clear prospect of an end to immigration'. She denied that she would 'make [immigration] a major election issue', but she thought that the major political parties should still talk about it, so that it was not left to the (extremist) National Front to do so.[12]

Though her phrasing was clumsy, Mrs Thatcher knew exactly what she was doing. She was convinced that her instincts reflected those of the majority. She was also sincere. She had long felt that mass immigration posed a threat to Britain. She had sympathized with Powell when he was sacked for his speech on the subject in 1968. However, her views had developed since then. She no longer agreed with him, if she ever had, about the Kenyan Asians who found sanctuary in Britain in 1972. She regarded them as industrious and entrepreneurial, in fact model Thatcherites. Also, she was worried not just about race riots but also about the long-term cultural effect on Britain of mass immigration. She foresaw, albeit hazily, what would later be described as a 'clash of civilizations'.

The use of the phrase 'rather swamped' was what drew greatest condemnation from her critics; but it was the pledge to offer 'an end to immigration' that ruffled the feathers of the party bureaucracy. After much agonizing, Whitelaw came up with proposals which went some way towards the stated objective. Two of the three main elements of this programme – a register and a quota – were later quietly dropped, and only the definition of citizenship ever reached the statute book. There would be no 'end to immigration'. But the rate fell to about 50,000 a year, which was manageable. Anyway, the desired effect had been achieved. Before Mrs Thatcher spoke, the parties had been level-pegging; immediately afterwards the Tories were eleven points ahead.

Some more low politics was provided by that summer's advertising campaign, devised by the party's new agency, Saatchi and Saatchi, whose Tory account executive, Tim Bell, would quickly become a favourite of the party leader. Along with Gordon Reece, who had introduced Saatchi, and Alistair McAlpine, who as party treasurer raised the money they spent, Bell was one of the few advisers of this period who can properly be described as Margaret Thatcher's personal friends. The poster campaign with the slogan 'Labour Isn't Working' has acquired the patina of celebrity. It won a lot of publicity, particularly when it was vehemently denounced by Labour. It may perhaps have helped reverse the Tory slide in the polls. And it may thus have helped persuade Callaghan not to call the expected autumn general election (indeed, it has even been claimed, without foundation, that it was cunningly designed to do just that).[13]

Margaret Thatcher was initially hostile to 'Labour Isn't Working', and for reasons which were very typical of her, being at one level rather foolish and at another extremely wise.* She thought that you should never mention your opponent, and this obviously did.† But at a deeper level she feared – though she did not openly admit it at the time – that attacking Labour's unemployment figure (some one-and-a-half million out of work) was disingenuous. She never foresaw that unemployment would double. But she knew that it was more likely to rise than fall, as monetary discipline began to bite. Her worries were all too prescient. But she dropped her objections.

At this point, it is worth noting how unprepared the Conservatives still were for office. Four years on from the party's second disastrous defeat, the Shadow Cabinet had no coherent plan to reverse Britain's economic decline. This reflected not lack of thought, but lack of agreement.

Within the unwieldy Economic Reconstruction Group, chaired by Geoffrey Howe, some broad conclusions had indeed been reached. The party accepted the need to reduce income-tax rates, to shift from direct to indirect taxes, and to deregulate so as to encourage small businesses.[14] These themes had made their way into *The Right Approach to the Economy* and featured in Howe's speeches. By the time of the general election, secret agreement in principle had also been reached to abolish both price and exchange controls – highly controversial moves. More technically, the use of monetary targets had also been endorsed as a way of controlling inflation. That, of course, was progress.

But three gaping holes remained. The first, the failure to agree on a coherent approach to the unions, was obvious. The second, the failure to envisage how government was to manage a return to free collective bargaining, was concealed behind various forms of words.

---

* Alfred Sherman also disliked the campaign: Alfred Sherman, *Paradoxes of Power* (Exeter: Imprint Academic, 2005), p. 90.
† She also thought that you should never use a slogan where a graffito addition of the word 'not' would reverse the meaning (as in e.g. 'Guinness is [not] good for you'). Her advisers speculated that she might have daubed 'NOT' on to Labour posters in her youth and that this accounted for her concern.

The third, the failure to make realistic plans for reductions in public expenditure, was no less serious. A terror of damaging leaks had held back radical thinking on this question. Instead, in imitation of a government's public expenditure round, shadow ministers had squeezed their 'budgets' into reduced overall planning totals. This process was highly artificial and proved almost entirely useless. The planners gravely underrated the momentum of public expenditure, currently suppressed by incomes policy but shortly to be released by public sector strikes and then given a further vicious twist by the Clegg comparability exercise (see below).[15]

At this stage (1978), Margaret Thatcher was no more radical than her colleagues on public expenditure. But on trade unions she was now eager for a new approach. She had always thought that the Labour Government's policy towards the unions over pay would collapse. Promising more socialism in exchange for pay restraint – the bargain which underlay the 'Social Contract' at the start of the Parliament and the 'Concordat' at the end of it – was doomed to fail. This was because it reduced economic growth and so the scope for improved living standards, at the same time as increasing the power of unions to enforce wage demands. The clash of objectives and the resultant clash between government and organized labour was inevitable. But when would it occur?

Rank-and-file trade unionists now provided the answer. With the disappearance of the prospect of an early election, the union leaders lost the means, and in some cases the will, to impose any moderation on their members. Labour's unsustainable pay policy was battered and broken by the union power which the party itself had reinforced. These events were also a personal nemesis for Callaghan, who had based his career on appeasing the unions. His failures of nerve and judgement at this crucial juncture reflected the fact. How else to explain the damning complacency which he showed on return from that international summit in sunny Guadeloupe in January 1979? If he did not use the precise words – 'Crisis? What crisis?' – which the tabloid press attributed to him, they reflected his attitude well enough. And yet, by any reasonable standard, a crisis of huge proportions now gripped the country.

What was quickly dubbed Britain's 'Winter of Discontent' began in the militant core of the public sector. In December 1978 the health service and local authority unions rejected a 5 per cent pay deal and announced they would strike in the New Year – which they did. A bitterly hard winter added to the impact of this action. In early January the private sector caught the virus. The Transport and General Workers Union (TGWU) called out lorry drivers in pursuit of an outrageous 25 per cent increase. The combined effect was devastating. Two million workers were laid off. Essential supplies were held up by the drivers, while essential services were denied by the health and council workers. Militant shop stewards issued licences for some activity to continue. But in many cases this did not happen. The dead went unburied and cancer patients untreated. Rubbish piled up in the squares of the capital and television cameras photographed the rats that crawled over it (Saatchi and Saatchi snapped up the footage). There was no point in the Government protesting that the stories were exaggerated, which they often were. The overall impression created was indelible. In the public eye, it confirmed the transformation of a trade union movement which had for decades epitomized the struggle for social justice into a callous, selfish and overmighty agent of oppression. More important politically was how this affected the image of the Government and of the Labour Party. Ministers – above all, the Prime Minister – now appeared contemptibly impotent, utterly unable to check the disorder. Indeed, Labour itself was exposed as complicit in the chaos, for the union bosses were also Labour Party barons, alternately bankrolling and bullying to impose their terms on the party's compliant politicians.

The Conservatives and their leader were the beneficiaries of this change. Suddenly, the charge 'Labour isn't working' acquired a deeper resonance. Specifically, what had seemed to most people like Tory opportunism in undermining the Government's pay policy in

Parliament turned out to be not so opportunistic after all. The whole policy was shown to be hopelessly flawed, because the unions would ultimately do as they wished unless their power was reduced. But who could expect a Labour Government to cut them down to size? The way was finally open for Mrs Thatcher to state her alternative case for change.

Some of these impressions would gradually be effaced in the 1980s and 1990s. But not until Tony Blair created New Labour did they fully pass out of public consciousness. Mrs Thatcher herself never doubted how powerful the images and memories of that time were. Right to the end of her tenure in Downing Street she would, at the slightest provocation, demand to see the *Sun* and *Mirror* front pages of January 1979. When found – they were carefully preserved in a folder and numerous copies made – she would seize and triumphantly wave them, as if they proved that whatever difficulties the country currently faced were as nothing compared with what it endured in the Winter of Discontent. Her colleagues would quietly shake their heads and her advisers would struggle to conceal their doubts. But her instincts were not far wrong. When the British people finally forgot what happened then, the balance of advantage shifted away decisively from the Tory Party.

If there had been no Winter of Discontent in 1978–9, there would have been no shift of public opinion in favour of the Tories. So, very possibly, there would have been no Tory Government, or at best one with a small majority, which strikes would sooner or later have threatened. Margaret Thatcher was a lucky politician, and never more lucky than when the reckoning came before, not after, the election.

But she also made luck go a long way. She cunningly used the crisis to outflank Prior and his allies and make them accept a tougher policy. This was crucial in securing the victory that followed. As usual, she consulted no one. Instead, she launched herself on the public in another interview for *Weekend World*. The specific proposals she floated were less important than the tone of her remarks. The furthest she had got with her colleagues before Christmas was to have Prior accept government funding for voluntary strike ballots. He had blocked a proposal by Joseph to cut the benefits paid to strikers' families.* Now she offered a list of possible actions going beyond anything agreed with the Shadow Cabinet, including restrictions on strikes in essential services (never, in fact, implemented) and compulsory ballots before strikes (introduced, in a different form, some years later).[16]

Jim Prior's continuing – and her own past – refusal to use the law to reduce union power was thus brutally overturned. Although Prior fought back, he had already lost the argument with public opinion. Willingness to confront the unions had become a political bonus. The opinion polls confirmed it. Soon the Tories were eighteen points ahead.

The strategy had now been set. But the tactics were debatable. In particular, how far should the Opposition's tone be set by statesman-like moderation and how far by relentless radicalism? Most of Mrs Thatcher's advisers preferred the former. But her own instincts were to harry the Government and set out a clear alternative. So she did not like one bit their suggestion that she use her speech in the House of Commons on 15 January, and her party political broadcast two days later, to offer cooperation with the Government in the swift introduction of trade union reforms. But she swallowed her reservations, while making the offer on terms which she felt Callaghan could not accept. She was safe, because he could not risk a pre-election fight with the trade unions that bankrolled his party.

Callaghan was already, indeed, reliant on minority parties to shore up Labour in the House of Commons. The Liberals had withdrawn from the Lib–Lab Pact. So the Government had to offer the Scottish and Welsh Nationalists and the Ulster Unionists, or

---

* The proposed change was based on the view that unions which called strikes should compensate their members with strike pay. But it was really aimed at ending the anomaly whereby strikers could, through the benefit and tax system, be left no worse off when they were striking than working.

some combination of them, a high enough price if it was to survive. Doling out public funds for politically sensitive projects – what the Americans call 'pork barrelling' – might help, and Callaghan's Government was good at that. But only the prospect of devolution was likely to suffice. So when on 1 March referendums in Scotland and Wales were lost, the Government looked doomed.[17] And doomed it was, though the bargaining and arm-twisting continued to the last minute, when the vote of confidence was held and lost – by one vote (311 to 310).

Conservative MPs were elated and Labour deflated. But any idea that the parliamentary drama had accorded the Tories an unstoppable momentum, or even a significant advantage, was quickly dispelled. Labour set about belabouring the Conservatives in general, and Margaret Thatcher in particular, in a well-crafted, professionally competent, highly negative campaign. For their part, the Conservatives for some while did nothing very much at all, inexplicably deciding to postpone serious campaigning until the launch of the party manifesto on 11 April.

The final version of that document reflected the struggles that had occurred within the Shadow Cabinet over the previous four years, but also the fact that since the industrial chaos erupted Mrs Thatcher had greatly strengthened her position. She took a close personal interest in its contents. The first version, written in the summer of 1978, had sparked one of her explosions of vituperation. She complained that it was too long and too full of commitments, which were uncosted and distracted attention from the central themes. But she often complained about drafting when she had deeper reservations, and in this case the material on incomes policy and the unions was notably feeble. The draft was scrapped and a new, shorter and crisper, version was prepared – written again by Patten and Maude.

The 1979 Conservative manifesto is an important document for understanding the course of the next eleven years. It still reads well. And though attention is often drawn to what it did not say –

in particular to the absence of privatization pledges beyond denationalizing aerospace, shipbuilding and freight – it was in the prevailing circumstances a bold and radical document. One can easily be misled by the apparent austerity of the contents: the manifesto concentrates on just 'five tasks' and claims to eschew 'lavish promises'.*

At the core of the approach to limiting the role of government and extending that of enterprise and individuals is the promise to cut taxes: the pledge is 'to cut income tax at all levels to reward hard work, responsibility and success', and there is explicit mention of the need to cut the higher marginal rates, which at the time were 83 per cent on earned and 98 per cent on 'unearned' (i.e. investment) income. On trade unions, the analysis was that of Mrs Thatcher rather than Jim Prior, though the measures of reform were still modest. Thus the manifesto claimed that Labour had 'heaped privilege without responsibility' on the unions, making them 'distrusted and feared'. In a slightly opaque phrase, it promised to 'ensure that the protection of the law is available to those not concerned in [an industrial] dispute but who at present can suffer severely from secondary action (picketing, blacking and block-ading)'. 'Secondary' action, as here defined, thus covered with the same umbrella both the activities of pickets who were not employed at the firm being picketed – whose picketing would, in fact, be made unlawful – and businesses which were threatened with bankruptcy by union action taken to apply pressure in a separate dispute.

Another pointer to still more important changes was the promise

---

* The 'five tasks' were, in any case, quite broad and ambitious in their implications. They were: 'To restore the health of our economic and social life, by controlling inflation and striking a fair balance between the rights and duties of the trade union movement; To restore incentives so that hard work pays, success is rewarded and genuine new jobs are created in an expanding economy; To uphold Parliament and the rule of law; To support family life, by helping people become home owners, raising the standards of their children's education, and concentrating welfare services on the effective support of the old, the sick, the disabled and those who are in real need; To strengthen Britain's defences and work with our allies to protect our interests in an increasingly threatening world.'

to review the 'law on immunities'. The ultimate target here, upon which Howe and Hoskyns had already set their sights, and which Mrs Thatcher was ready to attack when circumstances allowed, was the immunity of trade union funds from legal action. If unions could be held financially responsible in the courts for their decisions, the balance would be shifted against militancy.

Outside the economic sphere, new thinking was less apparent. There were pledges of pay rises for the armed forces and the police. Immigration would be curtailed. The requirement to close grammar schools would end. But the most important pledges were in housing. Thanks to Michael Heseltine's insistence, council house tenants were offered not only the right to buy their homes, but very generous discounts for those who wished to do so – a third off the market price after three years' tenure, with a sliding scale of reductions up to a half after twenty years. This programme would do more than any other to create a property-owning democracy. Nor should the promise to free up the private rented sector of housing be forgotten. Admittedly the proposal for 'shorthold' tenure, a short, fixed-term lease without security of tenure, was a mouse. But it required courage to produce even that.

The Tory manifesto was attractive and persuasive, and so naturally the Labour Party had no intention of debating it. Instead, they attacked what they claimed was the secret manifesto behind it. The question then arose whether the Conservatives should continue to advance their own ideas or answer Labour's attacks. Mrs Thatcher's instincts were for preaching her message. But she was also cautious. She therefore tried to strike a balance between not ruling out actions which might (and in the event would) prove necessary, such as raising prescription charges and linking pension rises to prices rather than earnings, and denying other Labour accusations, such as plans to introduce charges to see a doctor, or to remove exemptions from VAT.

The biggest concession she had to make, one she and Howe struggled long and hard to avoid, was agreement to honour the recommendations of the Comparability Commission chaired by Professor Hugh Clegg. The commission had been devised by Callaghan as a means to buy off the strikers. It would lead to a huge increase in public spending that nearly blew the whole Conservative economic strategy off course. Moreover, the notion of 'comparability' – both between public and private sectors and between different pay levels throughout the economy – posed a fundamental challenge to the principles according to which Mrs Thatcher believed pay should be set, namely affordability and supply and demand. Despite that, she felt she had to yield.*

During the campaign she felt, and was, very much alone. She knew that everything depended on her. The rest of the Shadow Cabinet were largely concentrating on their own constituencies, making speeches that were not reported, and not at all anxious to be blamed for whatever might go wrong. Her loneliness was tragically increased when the INLA, an Irish Republican terrorist group, murdered Airey Neave with a bomb in the car park of the Palace of Westminster on the eve of the campaign. (Neave and she had a relationship based on mutual respect and obligation rather than personal affection; but the loss at this juncture was a body blow for all that.) Mrs Thatcher's physical isolation on the campaign trail, as she subsequently realized, was the source of wider problems. It was difficult in those days – before the mobile phone, let alone the internet – to keep in touch with the centre and to get a feel for unfolding news. Significantly, the worst breakdown in relations between the leader and Central Office occurred when she was away in Scotland – as will be described. In future election campaigns she would always insist on spending each night back in London.

The ritual of the campaign itself was well established, and

* The notion of comparability between public and private sectors had two other flaws as well: first, the private sector pays for the public sector and so the latter should always expect to be less advantageously treated than the former; and second, public sector employees, especially civil servants, enjoyed greater job security and better pension prospects than their private sector equivalents.

nobody seriously challenged it. There were morning press conferences. When she was in London Mrs Thatcher chaired them, and did so badly. She dominated her colleagues, and this was only emphasized further by her occasional embarrassing attempts to make them speak up. Towards the end of the campaign she was tired and bad-tempered, and journalists too often felt the lash of her tongue.

She would have liked to take Callaghan on in televised debate, and he, with nothing much to lose and with a substantially higher public approval rating than hers, was keen to oblige. But Reece and Thorneycroft opposed it, both of them, despite their differing estimates of her persuasive pull, agreeing that the risks were too great. The decision was understandable, for at this stage she was still an uneven media performer and Callaghan a confident one. In fact, though, he was overconfident, and by the end of the campaign his self-satisfaction had begun to let him down. When the two leaders separately faced a Granada 500 television audience in the swing seat of Bolton East just three days before the poll, she came across better, appearing more down-to-earth and attentive to people's concerns.*

Another vital element of the leader's programme consisted of visits to all the electorally important regions, offering extremely contrived 'photo-opportunities'. The most memorable, and ridiculous, of these involved Margaret Thatcher cradling a calf in the middle of a muddy field in East Anglia, while Denis warned: 'Careful, or we'll have a dead calf on our hands!' On this occasion, his gloom was justified: the calf later died. With as much vigour and relish as in her days at Dartford, she campaigned at factories, in shops, in markets and in the streets; she bought mince and joints of meat; she made (and ate) chocolates; she sampled tea; she stitched pockets; she tested electronic components; and she saw fish landed and then watched it processed. But her forte was, as always,

---

* Labour, though, won the seat.

in dealing with individuals. She listened, she did not pontificate or prevaricate, and she was especially good with women.

Finally, there were her set-piece campaign speeches at ticket-only rallies. From the beginning these were a source of tension with Thorneycroft. Mrs Thatcher's first major campaign speech in Cardiff, the site of Callaghan's own constituency, was a blockbuster. She declared in rousing language: 'If you've got a message, preach it – I am a conviction politician.' She scathingly denounced what socialism had done to Britain and pledged to reverse the national decline. Callaghan promptly claimed that she was proving herself extreme – and the blood of the Tory Party managers ran cold. Their doubts were reinforced by opinion polls that suggested Labour was catching up. Accordingly, Thorneycroft now sought to rein her in. The fear that she was too divisive, too extreme, too off-putting had now gripped Central Office. She picked up the doubts when she attended strategy meetings in London and it affected her confidence. She was starting to be visibly tense and unhappy, and on occasion lost her composure. She became aggressive when subject to hostile questioning about policy towards trade unions on the *TV Eye* programme on Monday 23 April. This strengthened still more the Tory campaign's doubts about her.

For her part, Mrs Thatcher was now relying too much on her nerves, as she was often inclined to do, and too little on her staff. At Leith her speech was barely typed when she had to deliver it, because she had spent too long fretting and rewriting. She was exhausted. Later that evening after dinner she was informed by Janet Young, an old friend and Party Vice-Chairman, that Thorneycroft had decided that Heath should appear with Mrs Thatcher on the final party election broadcast. This she regarded as a wounding gesture of no confidence. Her reaction was to erupt with such force that no one present ever forgot the occasion. She slept not a wink that night, despite Denis's attempts to calm her down, and emerged haggard and depressed the following morning.

But she finally pulled herself together. The last Sunday's

Conservative Trade Unionist rally, with celebrities and a crowd singing words adapted by Ronnie Millar, raised her spirits. Heath did not appear on the final broadcast, and it went well. She felt she had done what she could. She dared not admit that she thought she would win – she had a primitive vein of superstition in such matters – but she was inwardly confident.

The polls published on election day, Thursday 3 May, all showed a Conservative lead, varying between 2 and 8 per cent.[18] The final margin of 7 per cent – giving the Tories 339 seats to Labour's 269 and an overall majority of 43 – now looks a solid rather than spectacular victory. But at the time the swing of 5.6 per cent was the largest achieved by either party since 1945. Contrary to forecasts, there was also a healthy, if smaller (4 per cent), swing in the North and Scotland. As well as triumphing among the middle class, the Tories made particular headway among the skilled working class (those known to social analysts as the 'C2s'). Margaret Thatcher had a particular appeal to them and she thought of them as 'our people'. It was another reason why the party, despite the doubts of Central Office during the campaign and most of the Shadow Cabinet in advance of it, could not have done it without her.

It has been suggested by a recent biographer that 'Mrs Thatcher's message was muffled and in retrospect surprisingly timid'.[19] But this is misleading. The 1979 manifesto was not at all timid, given the state of public opinion. Its philosophy was original and challenging, even if the pledges were limited. Moreover, far from keeping 'Thatcherism under wraps', as the same biographer suggests, Mrs Thatcher had throughout the period in opposition deliberately demonstrated her radicalism in successive speeches and interviews:

> So what is our answer to Britain's continuing problems? It is a radical answer – for it demands that we change the fortunes of our nation and rebuild our society by firing the people of Britain with a renewed belief in their real values.[20]

Let me give you my vision: a man's right to work as he will, to spend what he earns, to own property, to have the state as servant and not as master – these are the British inheritance.[21]

The Russians are bent on world dominance . . . They put guns before butter, while we put just about everything before guns.[22]

Sometimes Britain and the free democracies of the West seem to be suffering more from a failure of nerve than from anything else.[23]

What had so often and so forcefully been said could not and would not be unsaid. During the general election campaign itself, when she was determined to be prudent, her own performances were sufficiently sharp, not to say 'shrill' (a favourite critics' word), to worry old stagers like Thorneycroft nearly to death. On top of all that, Labour's barrage of accusations ensured that the harsh reality of what Mrs Thatcher prescribed for the British sickness was understood. The nation knew, even if the Shadow Cabinet did not, that a fundamental change of direction was in store. And Margaret Thatcher's cooing on the steps of Number Ten the following day of a prayer attributed to St Francis of Assisi – 'where there is discord, may we bring harmony' – would neither efface nor even diminish that impression.[24] She had won power very largely on her own terms. She had her mandate.

8

NO U-TURNS

If Margaret Thatcher was overawed by becoming Prime Minister she never showed it. Pangs of self-doubt or fits of self-consciousness were, in any case, unknown, even incomprehensible, to her. She had, it is true, been anxious about protocol when she received her authority from the Queen, and she had then been excited by the reception from the crowd in Downing Street. But otherwise, on that first day in office, she was manifestly assured and confident – even, as it would turn out, overconfident – about the future.

Ten Downing Street was, in fact, her ideal home, not because it made her feel important but because it was so entirely dominated by the work which mattered to her. She was living, as in Grantham, 'over the shop'. She and Denis moved into the flat at the top of the building, abandoning most of their old possessions – their new accommodation was already furnished and was, anyway, far from spacious. Although Mrs Thatcher had the public rooms of Downing Street refurbished in a grand style, improving their somewhat down-at-heel appearance, the Thatchers themselves lived upstairs in great simplicity. There were no live-in staff. Denis had his study, but no secretary. There was a tiny kitchen and a restricted dining room, where Mrs Thatcher could serve breakfast or a snack and where late-night speech-writers were fed as necessary. The Prime Minister's evenings were spent poring over papers. Gone midnight, she crept into bed with Denis for a few hours' sleep – before waking to the BBC radio news and the farming programme.

Over the years, high office would have a perceptible effect on Margaret Thatcher's personality and bearing, as it always does. But at a deeper level she would remain remarkably untouched by it all. She would learn on the job, of course, but she knew already what she wanted and what she felt she had to do. Her aim was the revival of Britain, and she had very clear views as to how it must be achieved. She retained that single-minded – what her critics called simple-minded – outlook from the day she first entered Downing Street to the day she was bundled out of it. It is above all this remarkable consistency, not her sex or background, which makes her unique among modern prime ministers.

The Thatcher Government of 1979–90 was Mrs Thatcher's Government in much more than name. Her personality stamped it indelibly. This was frustrating for colleagues who drove through fundamental reforms, such as Geoffrey Howe in removing economic controls, Nigel Lawson in reforming taxes or Michael Heseltine in promoting the sale of council houses. It was annoying in a different way for the 'wet' opponents of the economic strategy, because they initially shared the blame for policies they opposed, and then had to watch the benefits come through after they had left the Government. But the widespread assumption of Mrs Thatcher's pre-eminence and omnipotence also distorts her role and encourages a misreading of events.

Margaret Thatcher was usually in a minority in her own Cabinet. Until the decisive reshuffle of September 1981 – more than two years into government – she was not able to dictate the outcome of Cabinet decisions, even in matters that concerned her very much. The criticism of her opponents confirms the fact. Jim Prior, for example, complains in his memoirs of how she relied upon smaller groups of ministers rather than on the Economic (E) Committee of the Cabinet, let alone full Cabinet, to reach decisions.[1] But this was just a reflection of her weakness.

Another aspect of that weakness was her difficult, and sometimes impossible, behaviour, which calls for some comment. She had been an unpredictable minister for civil servants to work for, and developed into a somewhat chaotic leader of the Opposition, whose chairmanship of the Shadow Cabinet left colleagues fuming. When she became Prime Minister, at last with real executive power and with more self-confidence but still facing huge opposition, these traits were exacerbated. She was always notably thoughtful towards members of her private office and, indeed, towards all the staff in Number Ten – the more menial, the greater her kindness. But she was inclined to be ferocious towards other civil servants. She was convinced that the permanent secretaries and other senior officials constituted a kind of conspiracy against the public interest. They represented everything about Britain that she believed had to be changed – the acceptance of national decline, the perpetuation of a complacent public sector, above all a worldly cynicism that artfully disguised incomprehension of the real world. She was not interested in the party political allegiances of civil servants. She was, by contrast, very interested indeed in their attitudes; and once she concluded, often on slender evidence but generally with fail-safe instinct, that they were against what she wanted, she never forgot it.

The visits she paid to different departments as Prime Minister were a nightmare for those she interviewed, though she herself generally seemed to enjoy them. One occasion, however, she did not enjoy at all. This was a dinner with all the permanent secretaries, arranged (at the suggestion of Willie Whitelaw) in order to smooth relations, but in the event achieving only a further dive in her already low view of the Civil Service management. Held at Number Ten on 6 May 1980, it was a sour occasion. The permanent secretaries were foolish enough to preplan their complaints ('morale', 'resources' and so on) and to treat her with scarcely veiled contempt. She reacted angrily and came away more resolved than ever to break down their resistance. Only towards the end of her time as Prime Minister, when a younger generation of officials, many of them recruited from her own office or the Treasury, started to run departments, did her views soften. And by then the Civil Service Department itself, which she considered the core of the problem, had been abolished.

Still more tense, however, were her relations with other Cabinet ministers. There is no doubt that, judged by the ordinary criteria of man management, or of efficiency, or even those of Christian charity, she was often at fault. Geoffrey Howe was a frequent victim. He has recorded how he had 'cause to be angry with her often ceaseless and hectoring interruptions'.[2] This is an understatement, and in his case it would get much worse. Nigel Lawson complains of her 'increasingly authoritarian' chairmanship of meetings, and her 'going round and round in circles' when she could not get her way on some point.[3] John Hoskyns' diary entries record his contemporary – and thus still more damning – views. For example, a meeting in early 1981 to discuss the state-owned loss-making car business British Leyland (BL) was rendered 'hopeless' by her behaviour, which 'demonstrates more clearly than anything previously her absolute inability to think calmly and systematically about a complicated problem'.[4] In general, he 'often found her difficult to work with. She was on a short fuse for much of the time, only partly because of the enormous pressures of the job.'[5] She was 'often bad at handling her closest colleagues'.[6]

Mrs Thatcher's bad behaviour was a weakness; but it was also a feature of her strength. The elemental force which she embodied, her power of personality and the fire of her energy, overwhelmed friend and foe alike. Now and later, she had no real sense of place. So she behaved much the same everywhere, adopting even in private discussion the same aggressive and self-justificatory stance as she would in a hostile television interview or a rowdy House of Commons. Repetition of some tangential point, as Lawson observes, was a classic device she used in order to gain time. She

"GOOD MORNING GENTLEMEN !"

was afraid that if she yielded the floor she would never be able to get it back, and that the discussion would go in the wrong direction. She had little or no confidence in the ability of even ideological soulmates to bring things to a sound conclusion. Her main fault was that she lost her sense of proportion. So she regarded every discussion, even one about minor matters, as a make-or-break confrontation. This certainly confused and upset more sensitive interlocutors, though not people like Lawson, whose ego was at least as large as her own. But those, again like Lawson, who suggest that she was just showing off, read into her behaviour too much of their own. Rather, as (in this sense) a good liberal, and adopting the reasoning of John Stuart Mill, she believed that a conflict of views would illuminate the truth, and she expected and wanted colleagues to argue their case.* But they also had to know when to stand back – that is, when something was of such importance to her that she could not yield.

* She was a liberal in her political style and economics but not her social philosophy, so she would have accepted most but not all of Mill's underlying approach in his classic *On Liberty*, which she had read.

162

An important point accepted by everyone at the time but now infrequently made, because it is highly politically incorrect, is that any explanation of her behaviour must also take into account the fact that she was a very feminine woman. Margaret Thatcher practised what is (wrongly) disparaged as 'feminine logic', though – an amusing point among those who really knew her – she prided herself on having a logical, scientifically trained mind. (She would also at times point out, to justify some impossible assertion: 'You must remember – I am a tax lawyer,' as if that ended the argument.) The feminine factor in her behaviour did not simply, or even mainly, reflect the obvious fact that she was a solitary woman in a Cabinet full of men.* In truth, that was a state of affairs that she liked and exploited to good effect, alternating between flattery and quasi-seduction at one extreme and rages and affected vulnerability at the other, to get her way in a fashion that no man could have hoped to do. Her femininity was an all-pervasive psychological fact which, if one ignored it or resented it, spelt death to fruitful collaboration. Anyone who expected her to argue a case from first principles to its conclusion, rather than mixing up principles and conclusion in her introductory remarks and then remorselessly, endlessly, repeating the mix, was likely to be disappointed. When she appeared to reason a matter through, it was an illusion – simply a rhetorical pretence or a device (like the repetition) – to gain time before some other gambit occurred to her.

Any minister who wished to engage in productive argument with Mrs Thatcher had thus to be cunning, devious, patient and yet bold, with a good sense of timing and every fact at his fingertips. He had not only to have worked out his own crisp conclusion and central argument, but also to have thought through beforehand what she would think, and even then be ready for a surprise, trap or ambush. Finally, a sense of humour helped. A smile and a joke, even if not

* Janet (Lady) Young joined the Cabinet in 1981 but left again two years later: she had little impact.

fully understood, quickly cleared the air. Mrs Thatcher was always as interested in what people felt as what they thought – another feminine trait. Grumpiness was, therefore, bad for one's prospects, and also bad for the argument one was trying to advance. After all, in retrospect she might well conclude that the case she had dismissed was right and adopt it as her own – but not if she felt aggrieved by an opponent's behaviour. If she liked you, she might even in an oblique fashion apologize when she felt she had gone too far. But those who thought they could win her respect without inspiring her affection were likely to be mistaken and to find themselves ill treated on a future, unconnected occasion. Only some men can work for a woman at all; fewer still can work for a woman like Margaret Thatcher; and probably none can do so for very long.* All of this made for a unique style of government.

One more aspect of that style should be mentioned. She shared with Ronald Reagan a useful but often (to both colleagues and critics) maddening ability to distance herself from the actions of her own Government. She was usually willing to be persuaded by a colleague on top of his brief, whose judgement she sensed or had learned she could trust. But when summing up the discussion, which she always did with scrupulous accuracy, she was very likely to end proceedings by looking the minister responsible straight in the eye and adding, albeit with a twinkle – 'And you'd better be right!'

Her frequent isolation, or at least minority status, in Cabinet meant that she had to rely heavily on the little team assembled around her in Downing Street. Hoskyns and Strauss, later joined by one or more civil servants on secondment, constituted a very small Policy Unit. Hoskyns' fundamental belief was in the need to create

---

* See the account by the one-time head of her Policy Unit, Ferdinand Mount – a mild-mannered man driven to distraction by working for her. Their relationship, unlike the one with Hoskyns, did not recover. Mount's appointment was, in truth, another of her mistakes. She (rightly) admired his prose but never stopped to consider that, first, he might not agree with her, and second, he might not very much like her. See Ferdinand Mount, *Cold Cream: My Early Life and its Mistakes* (London: Bloomsbury, 2008), pp. 343–4.

what he called 'economic stabilization', that is, a set of circumstances in which the forces of enterprise could lift Britain out of decline towards prosperity. Mrs Thatcher had only limited sympathy with this concept, and it is not clear that she ever fully understood it. Hoskyns despaired of her refusal to think things through. But she thought that he spent too much time merely thinking.

Hoskyns had been glad to be asked to head up her Policy Unit when she became Prime Minister. But there was always potential for misunderstanding. Seeing his role as strategic, he tried to keep out of speech-writing, which was Mrs Thatcher's constant preoccupation; and when he proposed 'task forces' of civil servants and experts to examine particular problems, she would exclaim: 'But *you* are my task force, John!' Knowing that he did not have the resources to come up with answers, he liked to pose questions – an approach that would always irritate her. Her highest praise was for those like David Young, who (she allegedly claimed) brought her solutions not problems.* Hoskyns was, in truth, invaluable because of his concentration on the two crucial difficulties which she and the country had to face: namely, getting the fiscal strategy right, and keeping up the pressure for trade union reform. But he did not flatter her enough and he made the mistake of ganging up on her with others – albeit for what he thought was her own good. She was very sensitive, indeed oversensitive, to this tactic and it damaged their relationship in his last months at Number Ten. In the end (spring 1982), he would abandon his role in frustration, leaving her hurt and uncomprehending. The coldness did not thaw until many years later when she asked him in to help her in preparing her memoirs, which he graciously did.

Mrs Thatcher was fortunate in her principal private secretaries. The head of the Prime Minister's private office is always a high-flyer, but some holders of the post are more congenial and effective than others. In Clive Whitmore and his successors – above all, the

* Or possibly not. David Young is not sure whether she ever said it: see Lord Young, *The Enterprise Years: A Businessman in the Cabinet* (London: Headline, 1990), p. 112. Others have since thought he said that she said it.

formidable Robin Butler – she was blest with principal private secretaries of high intellect and unstinting commitment. She earned their trust and affection, and repaid both. Charles Powell and Bernard Ingham – respectively, her smooth private secretary dealing with foreign policy and her not at all smooth press secretary – would later become friends, devotees and so much part of her personal team that the fact caused adverse comment from jealous politicians and officials.

Perhaps, though, the single most important figure around her in these years was Ian Gow, whom she appointed her parliamentary private secretary (PPS). She never had a better one, in opposition or in government. A House of Commons man, on the right of the party, he was loyal, funny, discreet and excellent at picking up gossip, which he fed back to her in the form of crisp memoranda, and on which he based cogent advice. He was also a close friend of Geoffrey Howe. Gow's departure as PPS on his appointment as Housing Minister in 1983 weakened the Prime Minister's links with backbenchers. Two years later he resigned from the Government over Ulster and thenceforward remained a backbencher. His murder in July 1990 by the IRA removed the one person who might have been able to prevent Howe's destruction of Margaret Thatcher later that year. She was fortunate indeed to have Ian Gow beside her in these difficult early days.

Having said all this, at a deeper level the public assumption that the whole Thatcher experiment was hers, and that it ultimately rose or fell with her, was accurate. Her personality, with its serious weaknesses and its dazzling strengths, not only provided the guiding inspiration for the Government's action; it also bore down on ordinary people's lives more forcefully and more deeply than that of any other peacetime Prime Minister – though it required a small war to cement the effect.

As has been observed in the previous chapter, there were plenty of straws in the wind before the election to indicate that radical change was to come. Yet the choice of Mrs Thatcher's first Cabinet hardly suggested it. This is partly because she was still hemmed in by powerful opponents, but also because she remained a poor picker of colleagues. The main feature of her choices was continuity. The key economic departments were headed by those who had previously shadowed them. But she now made John Biffen Chief Secretary to the Treasury, a post for which he was ill suited. Because of his long closeness to Enoch Powell and his record of principled opposition to incomes policy, Biffen's appointment was a source of encouragement to the right. Yet he was not tough, industrious or numerate enough to cope with the strain of reining back public expenditure. He also soon became a semi-public critic of monetarism itself.

The appointment of Christopher Soames as Lord Privy Seal with responsibility for the Civil Service was another error, and one Mrs Thatcher quickly recognized. Soames opposed her in Cabinet and mishandled the 1981 Civil Service strike, which could hardly have come at a worse time for the public finances.[7] As with Maudling's appointment as Shadow Foreign Secretary, so with Carrington's appointment as Foreign Secretary now: she felt unable to break with the Tory habit of appointing establishment figures, even when they did not support or agree with her. In all this Whitelaw encouraged her. Retaining Gilmour as Carrington's number two in the Commons and appointing the ineffectual wet Mark Carlisle at Education constituted two further mistakes. Appointing Peter Walker to Agriculture may have seemed a clever move, because he was known to be hostile to European integration and also a tenacious negotiator. But it created yet another licensed Cabinet dissenter when the economic going got tough. By contrast, Jim Prior's appointment as Employment Secretary did make a kind of sense, given Mrs Thatcher's acceptance of the strategy of only step-by-(very small)-step trade union reform. But it was to cause far more trouble than she predicted. Indeed, these three decisions – to put Biffen in charge of spending, to perpetuate a wet majority in the Cabinet, and to allow Prior his own private fiefdom at Employment – would very nearly destroy her economic strategy, and herself with it.

The new Prime Minister believed that she could exert a grip over economic policy, and she believed that she could entrust Geoffrey Howe and the Treasury with implementing it. As in opposition, she also assumed that she could rely on Joseph at Industry, Howell at Energy and John Nott at Trade to back the policy, and Willie Whitelaw, whenever necessary, to support her personally and bring along the loyal doubters with him. The dries did, indeed, ultimately prevail. But the balance of forces was very precarious, as events took their toll and fair-weather friends peeled off. Joseph proved incapable of turning off the financial tap to nationalized industries and soon lost the confidence of his colleagues and, worse still, confidence in himself. Howell stumbled into a trap laid by the National Coal Board (NCB) and the National Union of Mineworkers (NUM). And the brilliant but unpredictable Nott then dramatically defected altogether. Reliance upon Whitelaw to provide loyal but incoherent support in these circumstances was a less than glorious tactic in a Cabinet where she prided herself on winning the intellectual debate. Nor was her heavy reliance on the Treasury's judgement free of difficulties.

Because Mrs Thatcher's relations with her Chancellor and his officials were so important to the way events unfolded, it is worth examining them a little more closely. Until Alan Walters' arrival in early 1981 to act as her full-time economic adviser at Number Ten, she was for practical purposes in the hands of the Treasury when it came to setting and monitoring policy. If she wanted to question what she was told, she could only fall back on her instincts, or outside reading, or snatched discussions with private individuals.

Geoffrey Howe was a conscientious, diligent, intelligent assessor of information.* He had a high degree of intellectual integrity, which made him worry through problems until he felt he had reached the best possible solution. His strength was lateral thinking,

---

* As regards the standing Howe achieved at the Treasury, two further points should be added. First, it was in part the result of his many personal virtues. Second, the shakiness of his economics did not matter as much as might be thought, because most Treasury civil servants were not economists either. I myself came to know Geoffrey Howe and his thinking well, because I was one of the three special advisers at the Treasury who worked for him from the autumn of 1981 until shortly before the general election of 1983. He wanted me later to join him at the Foreign Office, but for reasons discussed below I declined and chose to go to the Home Office with Leon Brittan.

associating different ideas that at first sight seemed unconnected or even incompatible. In time, he achieved a large degree of personal dominance over the Treasury, whose civil servants consider themselves both the cleverest in Whitehall (which is true) and cleverer than experts outside it (which is not). But he was not an economist, so he did not question too closely the advice he was given; and his consensual methods precluded clarity of decision at a time when the practice of monetary policy was still in its early stages and had the potential to go badly awry.

It should be added that Howe was never a cipher. This mild-mannered man, who seemed the complete reverse of his forceful next-door neighbour, had in fact an extremely high view of his own abilities – above all, he liked to think that throughout his career he had been right. He was for ever reminding audiences of some obscure point he had made many years before. He liked to refer to himself as leading a 'Bow Group generation' of Tories, which no one but he had ever noticed. This quirky pride explains much of his outlook at this time and his behaviour later. For example, Howe always hankered after a policy on incomes, if not a fully fledged incomes policy, because that is what he had supported in government. (Mrs Thatcher and Joseph had supported it too, but they were temperamentally able – in Joseph's case keen – to admit later that they had been wrong.) This had, as it turned out, no practical consequences, for an incomes policy never looked a practical possibility; but it did put him intellectually at odds with the Prime Minister. On the other hand, having helped devise the Industrial Relations Act, Howe also believed in the use of law to reform trade unions: this was positively helpful to her, because it lined him up with the hawkish minority against Prior, who had set his face against change.

Howe's approach was distinctive in two other respects, where the consequences were potentially more problematic. He rejected with scorn as crude, novel and unproven the notion associated with the US economist Art Laffer that marginal tax cuts could yield substantially higher tax revenues and that they had a crucial role in accelerating economic growth.[8] And he also favoured according a role to the exchange rate that orthodox monetarists would not. This view, which was partly an echo of past practice of governments in which he had served and partly a reflection of residual Treasury thinking, was of serious political importance later, after he had left the Treasury, when the dispute over the European Exchange Rate Mechanism erupted. But it muddied the waters even now. Together, these complex inclinations meant that the advice Howe tendered to the Prime Minister reflected an outlook rather different from her own – something which she did not at the time fully appreciate. On top of that, the Treasury made some technical errors, and Geoffrey Howe did not have the knowledge, the experience or the mindset to correct them.*

The trouble began with Howe's first Budget. In other circumstances its radicalism would have been admirable. But in the prevailing conditions it caused a number of problems. The strategy it was meant to advance was clear enough. This was, in a phrase, to reverse Britain's economic decline. That ambitious task had, however, several distinct elements. The problems arose in the relationship between them and thus the relative significance attached to each.

Now and later, it would be repeated by Mrs Thatcher and others that at the heart of the strategy was the defeat of inflation. Rates of inflation higher than in other more successful economies were blamed for Britain's lower productivity levels and growth rates and for the cyclically rising rates of unemployment. By this analysis, monetary and fiscal boosts undertaken to raise output and multiply jobs resulted only in higher prices. And the terms of the trade-off worsened as the years went by. Since inflation was deemed to be a monetary phenomenon, its sustained reduction

---

* Not, of course, that I realized this at the time. But it is the privilege of historians and biographers to be right after the event. The best assessment of Howe, Lawson and Margaret Thatcher – by an economist close to the individuals, cognisant of the debate and with the technical ability to make the requisite distinctions – is that of Gordon Pepper. See Gordon T. Pepper and Michael J. Oliver, *Monetarism under Thatcher: Lessons for the Future* (Cheltenham: Edward Elgar for Institute of Economic Affairs, 2001), pp. 22–9. Pepper describes Howe as a 'political monetarist', but Mrs Thatcher as a 'genuine monetarist'. He does not consider Lawson a monetarist at all.

required control of the supply of money. This was to be achieved by altering the price of money through the level of interest rates – in those days set by the Treasury, rather than the Bank of England.

But hardly less important to the overall analysis was the role of taxation. High marginal tax rates, particularly rates of income tax, were blamed for reduced incentives to work. So cutting income tax was a priority too. Yet that was impossible without commensurate or at least substantial cuts in public expenditure. In any case, the level of public spending inherited from Labour, which the outgoing Government had planned to raise further, not only required high taxation but also resulted in a substantial budget deficit. This, if it grew too far, could – it was feared – result in a funding crisis, where the Government was unable to find purchasers of its gilt-edged stocks to finance debt and thus would be forced to print money. That in turn would set off a sterling crisis. And even if such a crisis were avoided, very high levels of government borrowing threatened to 'crowd out' other borrowers – private individuals and businesses – and so to force up interest rates, reducing economic growth. (This last worry is now regularly dismissed and Nigel Lawson, Financial Secretary at the time, claims that even then he had his doubts: but what is certainly true is that the perception of such possibilities threatened the financial confidence upon which the strategy also rested – so the Government was right to be concerned.)*

Finally, and fundamentally, there was the problem of trade union power, whose extent and abuse had led in industry to restrictive practices, overmanning, inefficiency, lack of competitiveness and declining shares of world markets. These five elements – inflation, tax, spending, deficits and the unions – all had to be tackled if economic performance was to be improved. But in what order?

In fact, the decision was made to concentrate in the first Budget and the accompanying measures on the liberalizing rather than the

---

* See Nigel Lawson, *The View from No. 11: Memoirs of a Tory Radical* (London: Bantam, 1992), p. 70. As Lawson notes, the link between interest rates and budget deficits ceased to be important – or as important – in a world of free capital movements.

controlling elements of the strategy. It is easy to see why. Having fought an election pledging income tax cuts at all levels, and having run the gauntlet of accusations that he would double VAT, it was natural that Geoffrey Howe should wish to act at once to implement the change. There was, anyway, a strong argument that the shift from direct to indirect taxes and the economically crucial cut in the top rates of income tax could only be achieved at the start of a Parliament. Yet Margaret Thatcher's hesitations at the time – and she required a good deal of persuading – now look eminently justified.

In Howe's June 1979 budget, VAT was almost doubled to 15 per cent, the top rate of income tax was reduced from 83 to an internationally competitive 60 per cent, the threshold of the Investment Income Surcharge was sharply raised, and the standard rate of income tax was cut from 33 to 30 per cent. As part of the same approach, price controls were ended, a range of industrial planning controls were lifted, and – of great long-term significance and benefit – exchange controls were abolished in two stages, the most important being that October.

The removal of exchange controls was something for which Mrs Thatcher had strongly argued in opposition. But as usual she was cautious, cross-questioning Howe about the effects before finally authorizing the policy now. She came to see it as one of the greatest economic achievements of her Government, and she was right to do so. Above all, the removal of exchange controls allowed the build-up of overseas assets when sterling was high, which would provide income for Britain when North Sea oil ran out.

Yet Margaret Thatcher's initial doubts about the Budget itself – particularly the size of the shift from direct to indirect tax – proved to be all too percipient. It resulted in a 4 per cent increase in the Retail Price Index (RPI). Strictly speaking, as a one-off boost this did not increase long-term inflation. But it made for embarrassing headlines and provided an excuse for inordinate pay demands, already racing out of control.

In other respects, too, Howe's budgetary judgement now looks mistaken. It is, of course, difficult to take all factors into account when a Budget is introduced part-way through the financial year. But the Treasury should have done its sums better, and Treasury ministers, above all Howe, should have been more prudent. They did not allow sufficiently in the forecasts for the imminent international recession caused by the soaring oil price that followed the fall of the Shah of Iran: oil prices would soon double. That recession would cut government revenues and sharply increase nationalized industry losses. Still more culpably, the Treasury did not allow sufficiently for the rapid increase in the public pay bill as a result of Clegg and other settlements based on 'comparability'. Public expenditure and the budget deficit accordingly rose much more than had been envisaged. When action was taken in the course of 1979–80, it was too little, too late. The spending ministers, most of whom were anyway opposed to the economic strategy, put up a fierce and successful resistance to further cuts. High interest rates and finally – in the 1981 Budget – higher taxes were the inevitable result. The burden of the squeeze was borne by the private sector of industry. This was precisely the scenario against which Joseph had warned in 1976 in his Stockton Lecture.*

The Treasury also made mistakes in monetary policy. A reduction of monetary growth was necessary, because the previous Labour Government had spent its last few months in office working the printing presses, hoping to enjoy the benefits of a mini-boom. But the necessary squeeze went too far. It is easy to be wise after the event. This was, after all, the first time that monetary control had been practised consistently by any British government.[9] But given the fact that senior Treasury officials – not least the Treasury's Permanent Secretary Douglas Wass – were highly sceptical about the whole business, it is odd that they demonstrated such dogmatism about the figures. Having decided that the broad money aggregate

* See pp. 122–3.

known as £(sterling)M3 was the most reliable indicator, the Treasury reacted to its wayward behaviour by relentlessly tightening the money supply, when all indicators of the real economy – the exchange rate, which rapidly rose, bankruptcies and unemployment, which increased, output, which fell – suggested that it was already very tight. Moreover, the figures for money more narrowly defined, that is money excluding credit, fell sharply.*

One of the repeated assertions in Nigel Lawson's huge and fascinating tome recounting his period at the Treasury – as Financial Secretary and later as Chancellor – is that Margaret Thatcher was constantly pressing for lower interest rates. This leitmotiv, in fact, serves Lawson as a justification for his own later mismanagement, which opened the door to monetary laxity and the return of inflation. The precise circumstances of that period will be examined later.† Suffice it to say here that if Mrs Thatcher had had the courage of her convictions and insisted at this stage on tracking narrow money, as Walters and others urged, interest rates would have fallen and the monetary squeeze would have been moderated. Of course, she herself was always pulled in two directions. On the one hand, she did not want to appear to be weakening in her determination to beat inflation. But against that, she saw what was happening to the exchange rate and the real economy. She witnessed with a sense of impotence, and without any sufficient explanation from the Treasury, a contradiction between its figures and everyone else's. This was a period during which a weaker or more sensitive – or arguably even a more open-minded – Prime Minister would have changed course. Margaret Thatcher, however, did not. She backed the Treasury's judgement. She backed Howe. She hammered on, because that was what she always did; she believed that the present

---

* This is not to say that monetary base control would have been a better long-run option. Events have since suggested otherwise. £M3 consists of notes and coins in circulation with the public, together with sterling deposits (including certificates of deposit) held by UK residents in both the public and private sectors.
† See pp. 297–304.

hardships would pave the way for recovery; and, in the end, she was proved right.

The comparison is sometimes made – and the contrast drawn – between the Thatcher economic policy and that pursued by Ronald Reagan. The debate is of continuing relevance.* At the time, Howe was very critical of the large US budget deficit that was the corollary of Reagan's 1980 tax cuts – understandably so, because upward pressure on international interest rates meant that British interest rates too had to rise. This was particularly embarrassing when in the autumn of 1981 minimum lending rate (MLR) rose two percentage points to 16 per cent, after a spring Budget designed to bring interest rates down. Mrs Thatcher was more indulgent towards Reagan, for both personal and political reasons. But in any case, the situations of Britain and the United States were in important respects different, and these differences were reflected in the respective approaches which the countries' two leaders, believing in essentially the same things, felt compelled to adopt. First, in the United States monetary policy was independently set by the Federal Reserve, whereas in Britain it was the Chancellor, having consulted the Prime Minister, who instructed the Bank on the level of interest rates. So the choice between fiscal and monetary means to stimulate or contract the economy was open to Mrs Thatcher, but not to Reagan. This advantage was more than outweighed, however, by a second difference. The sheer size of the US economy – and the fact that the dollar was the ultimate global reserve currency – meant that the US Administration would always find purchasers for its debt. The British Government enjoyed no such assurance. Third, while both Thatcher and Reagan wanted to cut public spending as well as

---

* See, for example, the article by Rupert Darwall, who criticizes the 1981 budget from a 'Lafferite' perspective: 'The Trans-Atlantic Tax Divide', *Wall Street Journal*, 22 March 2006. Laffer himself was also critical of the 1979 budget, on the somewhat unrealistic grounds that it increased taxation ('Margaret Thatcher's Tax Increase', *Wall Street Journal*, 20 August 1979). This analysis failed to recognize the huge problem which public spending growth represented. Laffer's article was so badly received that he had to cancel a speaking tour to Britain as a result.

taxes, the levers were different. At least in theory – sometimes very theoretically indeed – the British Government could both control spending and set tax rates, as long as it commanded a majority in the House of Commons. But in the United States, despite his huge power in other respects, Reagan was at the mercy of congressional spending programmes. The only way he could exert effective pressure was through implementing tax cuts, and then daring Congress to shoulder the blame for the deficit. And that is what he did – eventually with success, as the budget deficit shrank. That said, it is impossible to say definitively now whether tax cuts rather than lower interest rates would have been a better path to take in Britain in the early 1980s.

The 1980 Budget was significant in that it announced the publication of a medium-term financial strategy (MTFS). The purpose of the MTFS was twofold. First, it set out a path for monetary growth which would bring down inflation, alongside a matching path for the budget deficit – the public sector borrowing requirement (PSBR) – which would bring down interest rates. Its second purpose, however, was to affect expectations and so behaviour. It was thus intended to do what conventional economic planning and incomes policies had failed to do – namely, induce a sense of realism and responsibility. The MTFS was Nigel Lawson's brainchild, which makes it ironic that he himself, as Chancellor, would consign it to the shredder, with disastrous consequences. But perhaps it always contained within itself something of Lawson's own character, for it was too clever by half, and certainly too clever to be effective in its original form. Its second purpose – affecting expectations – was always bound to be dependent on the success of the first: that is, it would acquire credibility only if the £M3 targets themselves were met. They were not, and the PSBR target was constantly threatened by recession and overspending. In fact, to the extent that the MTFS worked at all, it did so because Margaret Thatcher was known to stand behind it. When she said that she would not reflate, and when she proclaimed, 'There is no alternative!' – so often that the phrase was shortened by some wag to 'TINA' – she was believed. But the Treasury's own figures, for good reason, were not.

In her autobiography, Mrs Thatcher writes: 'I shall never forget the weeks leading up to the 1981 budget.'[10] That is not entirely accurate. When it came to writing the account of these events for the memoirs she remembered more about the pressures than the details. Another problem was that the official documentation of the time, which she studied carefully, was almost all from the Treasury, itself suggesting just how powerful that body was in formulating economic policy. As a result, the memoirs give a truthful but not a comprehensive account of the decision-making process. Geoffrey Howe's account, too, is unsatisfactory, for a different reason: it seeks to prove that the Budget was made in the Treasury, not in Number Ten. Nigel Lawson's is also deficient, because he was not present at crucial meetings between Howe and Mrs Thatcher. The best overall account is that of John Hoskyns, which confirms and elaborates what he and Alan Walters told Mrs Thatcher as she was preparing her autobiography.[11]

In reality, the views of Number Ten and the Treasury were not fundamentally divergent. Faced with the consequences of the Cabinet's refusal to cut spending and of the Treasury's wrong economic assumptions, politicians and advisers agreed that taxes would have to rise to cover the deficit. It was Alan Walters, supported by Hoskyns and Wolfson, who was most hawkish. The Treasury seems initially to have assumed that the Prime Minister would not wear a large tax increase, especially an increase in income tax. But at a meeting at Chequers on 17 January of Howe, Joseph and Mrs Thatcher with her advisers – it was not minuted and was consequently overlooked in her own account – the impulse for drastic action came from the Number Ten team.[12] After this, discussion was a matter of tactics and arithmetic, in which the politicians – Thatcher and Howe – eventually prevailed over the advisers. The Budget cut the PSBR by £4 billion, a huge sum quite unexpected by commentators. To pay for it, income tax thresholds were not indexed for inflation (then running at 13 per cent).

But there was an underlying difference of judgement that preceded the budget discussions and affected the outcome. Mrs Thatcher had been persuaded that monetary conditions were probably too tight. She had read and been influenced by a paper from the Swiss monetary economist Jurg Niehans, commissioned by Alfred Sherman. Cutting the budget deficit was intended to allow interest rates to fall, as it reduced what government needed to borrow. But, over and above that, Mrs Thatcher and her advisers saw the Budget as part of an easing of monetary conditions. In fact, the squeeze had been moderated from the autumn of 1980. Even so, she wanted to see interest rates fall further, and this they now did – MLR was cut by 2 per cent on budget day. This was, it is true, reversed later in the year, mainly as a result of international pressures (see above). But the overall policy henceforth placed less reliance on £M3.[13]

In any case, the nuances of difference between Mrs Thatcher and Howe and their respective advisers were lost on the Budget's critics, whose howl of disapproval still echoes down the years – notably in continuing debate about the famous (or notorious) letter sent by 364 economists to *The Times*. The letter itself is a somewhat weasel-worded document, which is not surprising since the 364 would not all have signed up to something more explicit.[14] Essentially, their argument was that the worst thing policy-makers could do was to cut a budget deficit in the depth of recession, the Keynesian consensus suggesting on the contrary fiscal expansion to kick-start economic growth and create jobs, with a prices and incomes policy in reserve to control inflation. Howe, in his Budget speech, and Mrs Thatcher in her subsequent defence of the strategy, argued instead for reliance upon monetary policy to control inflation, cutting the deficit to allow interest rates to fall, and then expecting businesses and individuals to adapt successfully to the new conditions. This is, indeed, what happened. The same quarter in which the 364 put their thoughts to paper saw the economy begin to grow once more, though slowly. The recession was, in fact, at an end, though unemployment kept on rising, reaching the politically dangerous figure of three million at the start of 1982.

Those 364 economists now look rather foolish, and rightly so – though they have not necessarily suffered professionally: one is now Governor of the Bank of England. They knew that the course they were proposing had been tried repeatedly since the war and had repeatedly failed. As Professor Patrick Minford pointed out at the time, they were 'playing a dangerous and dishonest game'.[15] Their intervention was politics *tout court*, as the wording of their confrontational but unspecific final point confirmed: 'the time has come to reject monetarist policies and consider urgently which alternative offers the best hope of sustained recovery'. Whether the Budget itself caused the recovery, or whether the trough of the recession had been reached in any case, is disputable. That it did not prolong it, however, is evident. The charge which monetarist economists like Hayek or Friedman might make against it is that action should have been taken earlier to cut public spending, to break public sector monopolies and to reform trade unions. And supply-siders like Laffer disapproved of putting up marginal tax rates. But this was not the case made by the budget's critics. Had their prescription been followed, confidence in the Government's determination to bring down inflation would have been fatally undermined. As inflationary expectations resumed, interest rates would have risen, not fallen, and the painful progress businesses were making in cutting their costs and becoming more efficient would have been reversed. And if this means that the 1981 Budget must ultimately be judged more in psychological than in purely economic terms, this is not surprising. It is the kind of judgement which economically literate politicians are called upon to make. In the circumstances, Mrs Thatcher and Geoffrey Howe got it right.

Equally unsurprising was the anger of the wets inside and outside the Government. They had been taken by surprise, though not misled. They had simply not believed that the Prime Minister and the Chancellor would see it through. It is easy to understand why they had reached this complacent conclusion. A good six months before the Budget itself, the signs were that the strategy was so badly off course that only politically unthinkable action could retrieve it. The monetary and public spending and borrowing figures, the inflation and unemployment rates, made dismal reading. By the end of November, the *Economist* was speculating: 'Can Mrs Thatcher keep her present Cabinet much longer?' Geoffrey Howe was thought doomed, not least for his fumbling performance in presenting that year's Autumn Statement.[16] But, again, she stuck by him.

Above all, it was painfully evident that little progress had been made in bringing the public sector under effective discipline. BL continued to swallow up increasingly large sums of taxpayers' money. Mrs Thatcher deeply resented the blackmail. Neither she nor Nott (who was asked to examine the company's finances), nor the Treasury (which wanted to close it, knowing that somebody else would shoulder the blame), nor Joseph (who reached the point of arguing against his own department's recommendations to fund BL's corporate plan) believed that BL's volume car business was viable. If it had just been a matter of job losses – great as they would be in the politically crucial West Midlands – Margaret Thatcher would probably have said 'no' to the corporate plan. But the chairman, Sir Michael Edwardes, was involved in a high-profile game of brinkmanship with the company's trade union militants. Letting him down could have an economic cost even greater than that to the public finances: it would signal that even the strongest management could no longer manage. In the event, the workforce, recognizing what was at stake, supported the plan. So the company got its money – and another blow was delivered to the deteriorating public finances.

The three-month steel strike in early 1980 was problematic in another way, because it exposed the fundamental difficulty of non-intervention in management decisions in contexts where the Government – that is, the taxpayer – picks up the bills. Prior and Joseph were soon publicly at loggerheads. Then when Prior criticized Sir Charles Villiers, the chairman of the British Steel

Corporation (BSC), at the height of the strike, he was slapped down by Mrs Thatcher. She described Prior on television as being 'very, very sorry' for what he had said.[17] But she did not sack him and the impression of Cabinet disarray continued. The eventual settlement at BSC was widely seen as a draw. True, the country had not been brought to a halt; but the private sector had been damaged and the Government still offered no effective remedy. One beneficial consequence was that pressure increased sharply for action to tackle trade union 'blacking' of goods and businesses and to restrict union immunities. But this was only the beginning of a long struggle.

Still more damaging, though, had been the U-turn on pit closures in February 1981. This too proved how little faith could be placed in non-intervention. David Howell and the Department of Energy allowed themselves to be manœuvred by the NCB and the NUM into intervening with a vengeance, when the country was suddenly faced with a threatened miners' strike against pit closures. It turned out that there was not enough coal at the power stations to weather a strike. So Mrs Thatcher, ever prudent, overruled Howell and insisted that the NCB back down. The ensuing settlement provided the industry with even more comfortable feather-bedding in the form of guaranteed protection against imports and a new corporatist 'tripartite' arrangement that further undercut management responsibility.

In view of these setbacks, the wets could reasonably have concluded that events were moving their way. True, a certain amount of fear had been injected by a limited reshuffle the previous month. This demonstrated at one and the same time Mrs Thatcher's exasperation and the limits to which she dared give vent to it. Two ministers left the Cabinet altogether. Angus Maude had been a disappointment as Paymaster-General, in charge of Government information. Though sound and loyal, he was so inactive as to be invisible. Unfortunately, his successor in the information role, Francis Pym, would use the post actively to undermine the Government, which was worse. Pym also succeeded, as Leader of the House, the principal victim of the reshuffle, Norman St John Stevas. St John Stevas was not very interested in economics, but he was vain and a gossip, and his well-publicized comments undermined the strategy, albeit in a small way. After his dismissal he protested vigorously in a letter to Mrs Thatcher at the suggestion that he was indiscreet, and received an ambiguous reply. He would, though, have been more justified in complaining that he was a less serious offender than those who survived – Prior, Gilmour and Soames.

Pym's removal from Defence, where he had proved adept at resisting expenditure cuts, was a victory for the Treasury. But his replacement by John Nott was for other reasons unfortunate. Mrs Thatcher's thinking was that, as a former soldier and a merchant banker, Nott would have the standing and the skill to bring financial order to a department that had never known it. But he would have been better kept at Trade. He had the ability and ambition to be Chancellor and he would have been a good successor to Howe. Unfortunately, at Defence he both engaged in unsustainable expenditure cuts and yet turned into a bitter opponent of the approach in whose name they were being made. Howe was now determined to move Biffen from the Treasury, where he had already begun to behave in the 'semi-detached' manner criticized by Bernard Ingham some years later. But at Trade, which he received instead, he was ineffective: he would have been better dropped. The arrival of Leon Brittan, a friend of the Howe family and a protégé of Whitelaw, to replace him as Chief Secretary certainly helped bring discipline to the public spending round. It did not, though, please Nigel Lawson, over whose head he was promoted. Lawson protested to Mrs Thatcher and, despite the diplomatic language used in his memoirs, was also furious with Howe, for whose economics he had never had much respect. It took their future axis against Mrs Thatcher over Europe to bring them together.

The first 1981 reshuffle, then, signalled Mrs Thatcher's ability to punish; but it did not achieve a shift of balance. In February Ian Gow sent her a gloomy assessment of backbench morale.[18] So the political atmosphere on the eve of the 1981 Budget was still hostile. And the Budget measures then rendered it poisonous. Dissent had traditionally been contained in carefully coded speeches. Gilmour was a noted specialist in this. But now, in the wake of the 1981 Budget, she was beset by much bolder, albeit unattributed, briefings from Cabinet members.

To Mrs Thatcher's wet Cabinet colleagues, the inner-city riots of 1981 – in Brixton in April and in Southall, Toxteth and Moss Side in July – were a godsend. They were seen as proof that the social consequences of her economic policies were intolerable. In her own comments, public and private, then and later, Mrs Thatcher was contemptuous of this reasoning. She believed that the disorders were outbursts of criminality, opportunist, copycat and unconnected to the economic policy. She was, though, shocked by the hostility to the police she encountered on visits to affected areas. Whitelaw, as Home Secretary, was helpless and hopeless in the crisis – he wandered around shaking his head, lamenting: 'I blame the parents.' But as a way out, he persuaded her to appoint a commission of inquiry under the left-leaning judge Lord Scarman. Predictably, Scarman's report put most of the blame for what had happened on the police, and the recommendations he made for restrictions on stop-and-search, later incorporated into the Police and Criminal Evidence Act, have hampered policing ever since. But Mrs Thatcher needed Whitelaw if she was to see through her economic policy. In later years she still convinced herself that a judge's recommendations had to be respected, even Scarman's.*

June and July are often bad times in politics, as tiredness and temper are worsened by the London heat. But the late summer of 1981 was particularly fractious for Mrs Thatcher and her divided,

---

* Her weakness for Scarman had been signalled earlier when she refused to support Joseph in attacking his report on Grunwick (see above, pp. 141–2). It was, incidentally, she who insisted that the word 'distinguished' be appended to him when he is mentioned in her memoirs (see Thatcher, *The Downing Street Years*, p. 143).

frustrated and rebellious Cabinet. Despite the unpropitious circumstances, Geoffrey Howe, reasonable beyond reason, still sought Cabinet consensus. To this end, and against Mrs Thatcher's instincts, he introduced in mid-June a paper whose optimistic scenario the wets vociferously disputed. It showed that inflation was falling sharply. Output had started to rise. But with unemployment about to hit three million, the objectors had plenty of which to complain – even if no coherent alternative to offer.

The bad-tempered June discussion was, though, just a trailer for July's public expenditure Cabinet. This saw a preplanned, open revolt. Years later, Mrs Thatcher recalled the bile vented by both sides. The usual suspects found two powerful new recruits to their cause, John Biffen and John Nott. Biffen was already a sceptic, though as Chief Secretary there had been limits to which even he could argue against Treasury proposals. But it was Nott whose sharp tongue left scars on Howe and Mrs Thatcher that they would not forget. Nott's argument that the PSBR should not be regarded as a rigid target ('totem' in wet-speak), because of its unpredictability and because of the quite different components of what constituted public expenditure, was evidently not without merit. But it was also dangerous. Once the PSBR target was unpicked, control of public spending would be undermined by a plethora of special cases, leading to the collapse of the strategy. It all seemed to Mrs Thatcher, as she puts it in her memoirs, 'creative accounting'.[19] This may be unfair, but she knew – and undoubtedly Nott knew too – what was at stake. In any case, for the first – and, as it would turn out, the last – time, the Prime Minister and her Chancellor were outgunned and outargued. She left the room pledged to continue the discussion after the recess, but determined not to do so, and resolved, at long last, radically to shift the balance of the Cabinet by removing or demoting her opponents.

The final straw that summer was the manifestation of revolt from a still more dangerous quarter, one which could only signify that

Margaret Thatcher's own position was now in peril.* Pym and Thorneycroft had, under obscure circumstances, decided on a joint challenge. Thorneycroft was the driving force. But Pym would have been the main beneficiary of a policy reversal that would have involved, initially, the removal of Howe and Joseph, and in due course, almost certainly, Mrs Thatcher too.† Thorneycroft had also decided to ease out Alistair McAlpine as his deputy at Central Office, because of McAlpine's known loyalty to Mrs Thatcher – though McAlpine refused to go.‡ Pym and Thorneycroft now publicly challenged Howe's statement, based on the latest CBI survey, that the end of the recession had been reached. They claimed to foresee, in curiously similar language, little evidence or prospect of growth. Thorneycroft went further, claiming in interviews – and in allusion to the comedy series of the same name – that he shared the 'rising damp', thus publicly aligning himself with the wets. The newspaper headlines were

---

* I was myself involved in these events and it is worth explaining how. I was CRD Industry desk officer at the time. Alan Howarth, the CRD director and also Thorneycroft's PA, informed me that Thorneycroft and Pym had agreed that the latter should make a speech on the Government's 'industrial strategy'. This was intended to demonstrate the merits of interventionism, taking credit (as it was said) for the amount of public money spent. I duly saw Pym, who poured me a whisky and asked me to explain the policy to him, which I did – as one of non-intervention. Somewhat nonplussed, and without an alternative to offer, he asked me to draft such a speech. When Thorneycroft saw the result he was furious. He called me in to demand a different speech outlining a new, interventionist approach. I instead reported the matter both to Norman Tebbit, at the Department of Industry, and via Sherman to Downing Street. It was decided at the DoI that Keith Joseph, not Pym, should make the speech, which he did in the form of a long lecture to the Bow Group, restating the policy of creating a framework for industry and not intervening in its affairs, thus thwarting the Pym–Thorneycroft initiative. These events were a backwash from a wider plot, whose full details have never been fully explored but deserve to be.
† Interestingly, Mrs Thatcher was warned by Gordon Reece of a possible deputation from Thorneycroft or other senior figures telling her to step down. His political nose was always sharp – sharper than that of Hoskyns, who retails this fact, and who, unlike Tebbit, had not taken my own warnings of the Pym–Thorneycroft axis seriously: John Hoskyns, *Just in Time: Inside the Thatcher Revolution* (London: Aurum, 2000), p. 288.
‡ Alistair McAlpine also reveals that Thorneycroft had been working with Pym (and there may have been others) against her since at least the autumn of 1980: Alistair McAlpine, *Once a Jolly Bagman: Memoirs* (London: Weidenfeld & Nicolson, 1997), pp. 212, 226–7.

DRIP DRYING

dominated that August by words like 'rebellion', 'mutiny' and 'revolt'.

Margaret Thatcher's native caution was now the last remaining obstacle to clearing out the internal opposition. The main decision related to Prior. Unless he were moved from Employment, serious reform of trade union law was out of the question. In his commendably honest memoirs, he makes it clear that despite having issued a Green Paper on union immunities, despite the demands from (predominantly small) business for action, and despite sustained pressure from Number Ten, he would not have gone any further in making trade unions legally and financially liable for the consequences of their actions.[20]

By September, Mrs Thatcher had finally resolved to act. Prior overplayed his hand, publicly refusing to go to Northern Ireland, where it was planned to move him, but then backing down in face of her polite but implacable determination. He forfeited support by these tactics. He was replaced by Norman Tebbit, a tough but subtle politician, who was clear about the changes that had to be made. Prior remained a member of E Committee; but he had no knowledge of economics and now found himself without many Cabinet allies either – because of the other heads that rolled.

Out went Gilmour and Soames, the duo of aristocratic wets, both complaining loudly. Out too went Mark Carlisle, whose presence at Education had never been explicable in the first place. Thorneycroft was replaced as Party Chairman by Cecil Parkinson, a long-standing friend of Tebbit on the same wing of the party, albeit of smoother manner.* Lawson joined the Cabinet at Energy – in place of David Howell, who was demoted to Transport – with a remit to build up coal stocks to resist the inevitable miners' strike. Lady Young became Leader of the Lords and Civil Service Minister. Keith Joseph gave up Industry for Education, to be replaced by the broadly Thatcherite – and tougher – Patrick Jenkin. Joseph remained, however, on E Committee and a crucial ally on the overall economic strategy. Pym lost his government propaganda role, which was in effect now exercised by Parkinson. For the first time since becoming leader, Mrs Thatcher had a team around her which was broadly of her way of thinking. It was the only effective reshuffle she ever performed; and it was only just in time.

However, it is one thing to change the people at the top; quite another to know that those upon whose support the structure rests will rally round. The fact that they did so owed everything to Margaret Thatcher's personal role in educating opinion, in her own distinctive fashion, since she had become Prime Minister. By sheer force of personality she had come to embody the economic strategy. One can go further: it was essentially

---

* Ian Gow was dispatched to tell Thorneycroft that he was fired (McAlpine, *Once a Jolly Bagman*, p. 228).

through accepting her that the party and the country accepted it.*

How was it done? Speeches were very important. In these crucial years she relied on Hoskyns, Millar, Sherman and, more occasionally, the journalist Peter Utley, among others. Between them, inspired by the impossible dominatrix for whom they worked, the team produced some memorable lines.

The central message was stark, simple and frequently repeated: the same thought in different forms. The only way to wealth and jobs was through more effort and more efficiency, because 'the key to prosperity lies not in higher pay but in higher output'. There would be no return to the unreal world in which government stepped in to shield people from the consequences of their own irresponsibility. Above all, there would be no debauching of the currency: 'We shall not – repeat not – print money to finance excessive pay settlements.'[21]

But the single most important message was that the Thatcher Government would not change course. It would see through the task of economic reform whatever the costs – social, personal or political. In contrast to her predecessors and, indeed, successors, Mrs Thatcher gloried in her refusal to bend. Most famously, she announced with cold defiance: 'To those waiting with bated breath for that favourite media catchphrase, the "U-turn", I have only one thing to say: "You turn if you want to. The lady's not for turning." I say that not only to you, but to our friends overseas and also to those who are not our friends.'†

---

* For a discussion of this question that comes to a rather different conclusion, see Lawson, *The View from No. 11*: 'The indispensable element of the revolution which so astonished Whitehall was Margaret Thatcher herself' (p. 26); but 'Thatcherism is, I believe, a useful term . . . [but] the wrong definition is "whatever Margaret Thatcher herself at any time did or said"' (p. 64). The attempts to contrast early and late Thatcher, and Thatcher with Thatcherism, are recurrent themes in Lawson's memoirs.

† Speech to Conservative party conference, Brighton, 10 October 1980, in Thatcher, *The Collected Speeches*, p. 116. The famous line about the U-turn came from Ronnie Millar. The reference is to the play by Christopher Fry entitled *The Lady's Not for Burning*. How many people in Brighton knew that is unclear, but it didn't matter. See Ronald Millar, *A View from the Wings* (London: Weidenfeld & Nicolson, 1993), p. 287.

But not all the best lines were pre-scripted. Just as powerful, because more passionately delivered, often in scornful riposte to an unsympathetic interviewer, were the Prime Minister's enunciations of unpalatable truths. Sometimes she played matron: 'A patient who has been suffering from a serious disease for years doesn't suddenly get better – but you must have the will, the determination, the resolve to go on with the treatment until he comes through.'[22] On occasion, she reinterpreted Holy Scripture: 'No one would remember the Good Samaritan if he'd only had good intentions: he had money as well.'[23] But always she reminded the nation that when somebody gives, somebody also pays. The laws of politics could not suspend that invariable law of accountancy: 'Look! There's no such thing as government money, no such thing at all. There's taxpayers' money. And every time a politician says he's going to spend more money, he's going to take it from the taxpayer one way or another.'[24]

On the eve of the Blackpool party conference of October 1981 the *Economist* painted a portrait of a 'Prime Minister at Bay'.[25] But the attempt to force an alternative strategy of fiscal reflation on the Government was defeated. By the end of the year, the Conservatives were still third in the polls, just behind Labour and far behind the new SDP–Liberal Alliance. It was too early to say how fast the economy would recover. But one thing seemed clear. Margaret Thatcher would be judged by her strategy and not forced off it.

9

APPRENTICE DIPLOMAT

Margaret Thatcher entered Downing Street with no real experience of dealing with foreign affairs. She knew the United States, of course, and she had paid visits behind the Iron Curtain – to the Soviet Union and (twice) to Romania. From her reading, she had a reasonably well-informed understanding of the military and strategic realities of the Cold War. But of the Commonwealth and of Europe she knew little. Nor had she had any serious contact with the shapers and practitioners of policy in the Foreign Office. She had not listened to their presentations and briefings about the innumerable problems that beset Britain's international standing and jeopardized British interests. She had imbibed none of the characteristic blend of pragmatism and defeatism which permeated British diplomatic thinking. All this would in the long run turn out to be a blessing. But at the outset as she prepared to confront a range of complex and only loosely connected international problems, it left her lacking points of reference and, inevitably, lacking in self-confidence.

Most modern prime ministers take office with a surer grasp of domestic affairs than of foreign policy and then, over time, develop a preference (which may become obsessive) for the wider, politer, world stage. This shift reflects both natural and inevitable impatience with domestic criticism and appreciation of the cumulative benefits which experience yields when dealing with foreign leaders on the international circuit. In Mrs Thatcher's case, the transformation was particularly dramatic. She started with, in many respects, the mentality of a housewife–accountant; but she had graduated by the time of her departure from office into a formidable and assured world statesman.

Her future views already existed, in the form of passions and prejudices, long before she was forced to develop them. Indeed, as noted earlier, they can be glimpsed in embryo in her first recorded speeches. Yet they were to remain many years in gestation. Thus she began as a proud believer in Britain's imperial vocation. Suez and decolonization inevitably changed all that. In different circumstances, she would later choose to see the nation's post-imperial destiny as inextricably linked to that of America. Together, with the Old Commonwealth in tow, and in collaboration with as much as possible of the English-speaking world, Britain and America should project their values to entrench liberty and prosperity. Similarly, her visceral early distaste for appeasement and her unconditional admiration for Churchill's war leadership would later be reflected in her refusal to countenance compromise with aggression and her belief in the absolute primacy of strong defence. These were identifiable strands of continuity. But they look stronger now than they seemed at the time.

The truth is that despite the rhetorical forays into international affairs in opposition that earned her the title of 'Iron Lady', Mrs Thatcher had not thought about foreign policy in any sustained manner during those years. Once in power, she was altogether bereft of independent advice on the subject. Bob Conquest was in the United States and quickly frozen out by the Civil Service; and neither the CPS nor her Policy Unit was encouraged within the system to show an interest. What she had, though, were her instincts.

Mrs Thatcher's underlying attitudes to economic affairs and to foreign policy had, in reality, the same origin – her radical impatience with the prevailing mood of the post-war years. British economic decline had accompanied and accelerated British retreat from international power and responsibility. Most obviously, there was the renunciation of Empire. Margaret Thatcher was not a Monday Club Tory, opposed to decolonization as such.[1] She was never close, for example, to that group's senior spokesman, Julian Amery. But she too lamented the passing of British greatness. Her commitment to restoring the country's prosperity was always about more than raising individuals' living standards. It was, above all, the way back to British influence and power.

So it is, on the face of it, surprising that Margaret Thatcher behaved as she did when faced with the first serious international challenge that confronted her: what to do about Rhodesia. The question had been on the political agenda for years – ever since Ian Smith's white minority government in Salisbury made its unilateral declaration of Rhodesia's independence (UDI) in November 1965. Although no other major state recognized it and the UN imposed sanctions, Rhodesia initially flourished. It earned substantial foreign earnings by smuggling out its tobacco. To begin with there was little internal resistance from the black majority. The regime was covertly aided by South Africa, Portugal and Israel, while in Britain a substantial body of opinion, probably a majority of Conservative Party opinion, regarded the rebellious former colony with sympathy. Britain's retreat from Empire had left one after another African country in the hands of corrupt and chaotic black regimes, to the disadvantage of all races. Rhodesia seemed to represent the exception and in some respects even to offer a model. To the extent that Mrs Thatcher thought about the subject at all, she probably shared that feeling. But she kept quiet about her views. After all, there was no very pressing need to reach firm conclusions because there seemed no prospect of outside powers significantly influencing

Rhodesian affairs, let alone bringing down the regime. The Conservative Party in opposition, then in government, then back in opposition once again, joined in formal expressions of distaste, while sitting without much obvious discomfort on the political fence. This posture was still largely unchanged by the time Mrs Thatcher entered Downing Street. But local circumstances had, in fact, rendered it all but unsustainable.

In Rhodesia itself the so-called 'Bush War', which began as a low-key insurgency in the early 1970s, had escalated into a bloody, sustained and wearying conflict. The collapse of Portuguese control over neighbouring Mozambique in 1976 was a strategic body blow to its landlocked neighbour. Soon the guerrilla forces – Robert Mugabe's Shona ZANLA militia, backed by China, and Joshua Nkomo's Matabele ZIPRA, backed by the Soviet Union – were successfully tying down Rhodesian forces and threatening the safety and prosperity of the white farmers. South Africa's attitude also now changed, as it tried to reach an accommodation with the West. The Pretoria Government started to regard Rhodesia as an incubus and an embarrassment rather than a buffer zone. Under these pressures, Smith and his colleagues reached an 'internal settlement' with a faction of non-militant black opinion led by Bishop Abel Muzorewa. Elections were duly held in April 1979. A new majority black government, albeit with white control over security, justice and administration, thus emerged, with Muzorewa as Prime Minister. Clearly, a fundamental reappraisal of British policy was required.

Initially, Mrs Thatcher still tried to fudge. In 1978, and with the new Rhodesia/Zimbabwe internal settlement under construction, she had gone along with Shadow Foreign Secretary John Davies' preferred policy of abstaining on the renewal of sanctions. As described earlier, this had got her into difficulties with her own party.* But once the former Conservative Colonial Secretary, Lord

* See pp. 138–9.

Boyd of Merton, reported in April 1979 that the Zimbabwean elections had been fairly conducted, it was widely assumed that the incoming Government would recognize the new black majority administration.

This is certainly what Mrs Thatcher wanted to do. It was an open secret at the time, and Carrington's memoirs confirm the fact, that it was only after 'spirited discussions' – that is, heated rows – that she was persuaded that a new constitutional settlement, enjoying international, and particularly Commonwealth African, support was required.[2] When he came to give his own account, Carrington justified the approach he had pursued by the pragmatism that the Mugabe Government was then showing – albeit at the expense of the Matabele minority, subjected in the early 1980s to state-sponsored Shona genocide.* A quarter of a century later, as a corrupt Marxist tyranny left its population to starve, the Thatcher Government's policy looked more questionable. She, though, never regretted what she had done. In her memoirs, she rates the settlement a success.[3] In private discussion, she would simply assert that nothing else could have been done in the circumstances.

From Britain's viewpoint, the two most important external influences at the time were the United States and the Commonwealth. As she was later to demonstrate, Mrs Thatcher was at a pinch prepared to defy Commonwealth opinion. Moreover, any deal which the so-called 'frontline' African states – Zambia, Tanzania and Mozambique – were prepared to swallow, the rest of the Commonwealth would have to swallow too. Sheer exhaustion was pushing these black governments, particularly that of Zambia, towards a compromise. But the United States was a different matter. Jimmy Carter's reliance on black support at home would ensure that no deviation from the principle of 'no independence before black majority rule' – the principle enunciated by Harold Wilson's Government in the

---

* Carrington's self-congratulatory retrospect omits any mention of the deaths of 30,000 Matabele at the hands of Mugabe's army, unless they are to be counted among certain unspecified 'disagreeable occurrences': *Reflect on Things Past: The Memoirs of Lord Carrington* (London: Fontana, 1989), p. 305.

1960s – would receive the Administration's backing. What neither Mrs Thatcher nor the Foreign Office considered was how this could change in the event of a Republican occupying the White House, as would shortly occur. Quite what Reagan's position would have been we cannot, of course, know for sure. But it would have been significantly different from Carter's.* In any case, by the time he became President, Rhodesia had an internationally recognized Marxist government, and no attempt to overturn it would have been possible.

The process by which this transformation happened was swift. Mrs Thatcher sent Lord Harlech, the former UK ambassador to Washington, to seek the views of the frontline states and, with reluctance, to meet Mugabe and Nkomo. She now conceded that the Rhodesian constitution would have to be revised. This, though she did not know it, was fatal in the short run to Muzorewa and in the long run to Nkomo. During the transition the bishop was no match for guerrilla leaders with thousands of well-armed troops behind them. And of these two leaders, though Nkomo was the senior, Mugabe was the Shona, his tribe constituting 80 per cent of the population. Ian Smith explained these tribal realities to Carrington.[4] But neither the Foreign Secretary nor the experts on whom he relied took any notice. They were then greatly taken aback by the outcome.†

At the Lusaka Commonwealth Conference at the beginning of

---

* This is not entirely hypothetical. Henry Kissinger's proposals to Callaghan in June 1976 emphasized 'a rapid evolution toward majority rule' but also guarantees for the white minority and a moderate-led majority government – Nkomo was the favoured candidate: Henry Kissinger, *Years of Renewal* (New York: Simon & Schuster, 1999), p. 973. In fact, Reagan and his advisers understood the significance of the region to the outcome of the Cold War and were less preoccupied with European decolonization than any previous US administration. They would, at the least, have given Britain and the Muzorewa Government more time.

† Carrington, *Reflect on Things Past*, p. 303. Carrington much later claimed that Mugabe's victory was 'wholly predictable'. But there is no evidence that he at the time predicted it – or even envisaged it – and Mrs Thatcher certainly did not. See Peter Carrington, 'Did We Put a Tyrant in Power?', *The Times*, 5 April 2008.

August 1979, Mrs Thatcher scored a personal success. The photographs of her dancing with a beaming President Kenneth
Kaunda of Zambia are among the more memorable of her first year
in office.* It was not hard to persuade the Commonwealth leaders
to allow Britain to take responsibility for achieving a solution, as she
and Carrington now proposed. The ensuing Lancaster House
Conference in London, chaired by Carrington and attended by the
main parties, with black leaders dropping in to ensure their pro-
tégés were not forgotten, found Mrs Thatcher acting as
diplomat-in-chief.

She later remembered having the ascetic Mugabe, the gross
Nkomo and the diminutive Muzorewa seated together in her study
– she liked to think that they were all on a single sofa, but Nkomo's
girth must have precluded that. She thought that they all expected to
win. Perhaps they did. But only Mugabe had reason to be confident:
the only question was how large his majority would be. It was soon
clear that he did not intend to leave that to chance.

The appointment of Christopher Soames to oversee the elections
as Britain's last governor was a piece of colonial theatre, and Mrs
Thatcher thought that he filled the role with panache. The Lancaster
House Agreement provided that any party guilty of systematic
intimidation would be excluded from the election. In the areas
where Mugabe felt threatened by his rivals, especially in mixed
Shona–Matabele territory, intimidation was practised on a massive
scale. But Soames was expressly forbidden by London to rule against
Mugabe. In these circumstances, an overwhelming Mugabe-led
ZANU victory was a foregone conclusion. So Zimbabwe received its
independence in a condition no better, though admittedly not much
worse, than other former British colonies. Mrs Thatcher took credit
for the outcome. But the plaudits she received were, by and large,
from whose who did not wish her well.

---

* She liked Kaunda personally and would send him an excessively flattering letter when he
eventually left office in 1991 – after so many years spent ruining Zambia's economy. (I tried
to prevent this but failed.)

The extent to which Carrington himself fell into that category is not entirely clear. In a slightly patronizing way, he seems to have liked her, and, as has been noted, she had a fund of respect for him. But there was always the potential for trouble. Carrington's attitude to the Rhodesian question was that it had to be solved quickly, because it was a distraction from the more important tasks that a British Foreign Secretary had to perform, such as dealing with Europe.[5] That was never her view. She shared none of his enthusiasm for Europe, and it was fortunate that the principal forum for Britain's early clashes with other European states was at the level of heads of government, where she – not he – was in charge. It was still more fortunate that Carrington resigned at the start of the Falklands War. Had he, rather than Francis Pym, still been pushing the Foreign Office line, the outcome might have been very different, and much worse for her, for the Falklands and for Britain.

It was Europe which provided Mrs Thatcher with her first true foreign policy success, as confirmed both by her enhanced reputation and by subsequent events. The battle she fought to reduce Britain's contribution to the European Community budget was the first time that she imposed her distinctive style upon foreign policy. She was in her element. The issue was financial, and her grasp of the complex figuring at the heart of the dispute was matchless. The underlying principle was also, in her eyes if not those of other European leaders, remarkably simple: Britain was being unfairly treated; that unfairness must be rectified; and until it was, she would disrupt proceedings and embarrass all concerned in order to get her way.

Britain's case for a sharp reduction in net contributions was unanswerable, which was why no one was keen to provide an answer. At the time of EEC entry (on unsatisfactory terms) it had been agreed that if 'an unacceptable situation' were to arise, 'equitable solutions' would have to be found. At the time of the Labour Government's 'renegotiation' of the terms of membership in 1975, a special financial mechanism had been devised to limit the British contribution. But it had done nothing of the sort. Meanwhile,

Britain had fallen further behind the rest of Europe. It was now one of the least prosperous countries, but unless something were done it would shortly be the principal net contributor. Of course, other countries might reasonably argue that this was Britain's fault, not theirs. They were not interested in the public expenditure problems faced by the Thatcher Government. But the European partners felt no need to argue in such blunt terms. Instead, they could take shelter behind the existing system and the prevailing doctrine of the European Community. And that is why they reacted so fiercely when Margaret Thatcher started to talk about 'our money', as she did at her press conference after the deadlocked Dublin European Council of November 1979. The other leaders were outraged, not because she was pressing her case – they had already recognized that she had one by offering a 33 per cent refund – but because of her assertion that contributions to the Community's resources were the property of the contributing state rather than of the Community itself. 'Our money' as a phrase was, therefore, not merely vulgar: it, and the thinking behind it, were dangerous.

Even more dangerous, though, was the prospect that unless she received justice, Mrs Thatcher would act to withhold further British contributions. She was strongly attracted by this option. Her colleagues and her officials were definitely not. They warned that it would be ruled illegal, and it probably would have been. In the end, she chose not to proceed, partly because she could never escape her prejudice against breaking any law – even European law – and partly because the threat proved sufficient to make her opposite numbers retreat. Helmut Schmidt, on whom she concentrated her efforts and who had some respect for her, used his influence with the French to avoid forcing her hand.

The budget problem was resolved in two phases, of which the first was the more difficult. The crucial discussion came at the Luxembourg Council in April 1980. The French President, Valéry Giscard d'Estaing, was in the chair. Mrs Thatcher was offered a much reduced British contribution for two years, but no undertaking beyond that. So she refused to negotiate further and the Council broke up in recrimination. It was left to the Community foreign ministers to do better. When Carrington and Gilmour brought back the text of a new deal in May, she at first stubbornly refused to accept it. But after an acrimonious row, her objections were eventually overcome.* It was now a three-year package and involved a rebate of two-thirds of the gross British contribution.

It was not until the second phase of the negotiations, in 1983–4, that an enduring settlement was reached. By now, the main personnel had changed. François Mitterrand had taken the place of Giscard and Helmut Kohl that of Schmidt, and Geoffrey Howe was Foreign Secretary in place of Carrington. But Mrs Thatcher's objectives had not changed, and nor had her tactics. She wanted at least as much as she had obtained earlier, and she insisted that the settlement be permanent. A chaotic Athens Council in December 1983 provided her with an opportunity to demonstrate intransigence. She argued her case with zeal and with batches of figures that left her poorly briefed interlocutors floundering. But no agreement was reached.

She had higher hopes of the next Council at Brussels the following March. Mitterrand would be in the chair, and he was not ill disposed towards her. But this time Kohl wrecked the proceedings by proposing an unacceptable deal – too small a rebate and for a limited, five-year period. She turned it down flat. No communiqué was agreed, and in retaliation France and Italy promptly blocked Britain's 1983 refund. Mrs Thatcher ordered that consideration once again be given to withholding contributions. But the threat proved superfluous. Europe was now running up against the financial buffers and needed unanimous agreement for an increase in its 'own

---

* John Nott, who was peripherally involved, speculates that Carrington and Gilmour threatened resignation if she did not agree: John Nott, *Here Today, Gone Tomorrow: Reflections of an Errant Politician* (London: Politico's, 2003), p. 188. According to Carrington, Mrs Thatcher started talking about her own possible resignation too (interview for BBC documentary *The Downing Street Years*, 1993).

resources' (from higher VAT contributions). This gave her a more powerful lever than she had possessed three years earlier, and she made good use of it.

Mitterrand, who again chaired the following Council held at Fontainebleau that June, was keen to avoid another row, and no one was minded to allow Kohl to precipitate one. As before, it was left to foreign ministers to come up with a solution in separate negotiations, and once again Mrs Thatcher was loudly critical: she thought Howe had been feeble and told him so. She toughened the negotiating stance and at the following day's plenary session sought a 70 per cent refund. In the end, after more discussion in the margins and then a little pantomime between her and Mitterrand over whether she should have 65 or 66 per cent – 'Shall we give Mme Thatcher her one per cent?' – she received what she had wanted: two-thirds back. Admittedly, it was not quite 'permanent', but it was as near as anyone could make it, because it was specified that the arrangement would last as long as the increased 'own resources' (from a higher 1.4 per cent of VAT) also lasted. So Britain would always be able to secure its continuation, by threatening a veto. And no one doubted that Margaret Thatcher would relish carrying out that threat.

It was the end of an astonishing saga. No other British Prime Minister can be imagined showing such aggression, cunning and financial grasp as Margaret Thatcher did to obtain the deal she won for Britain. And no other European country ever enjoyed such an arrangement. It continues, in modified form, to the present day, when most of the original arguments for it have long since ceased to be valid. But Mrs Thatcher's successors have considered abandoning it too electorally risky.

The process by which success in Europe was achieved also helps explain how the pliant diplomatic patsy of the Rhodesian crisis was transformed into the towering war leader of the Falklands. The return of 'our money' was psychological preparation for the return of 'our Islands'.

10

WAR LEADER

The Falkland Islands have always had some strategic significance, offering usable harbours and tolerable habitation some five hundred miles off Cape Horn. In recent years, the potential exploitation of fishing, energy and mineral wealth has greatly increased their value. But the war which Britain fought to retake them from Argentina in 1982 still seems a little unreal, even to those who lived through it.

In later years, Mrs Thatcher simply refused to discuss the mistakes made by her Government in the run-up to the Argentine invasion. She would refer, often irritably, to the final sentence of the Franks Committee's report into the subject, which reads: 'We conclude that we would not be justified in attaching any criticism or blame to the present Government for the Argentine Junta's decision to commit its act of unprovoked aggression in the invasion of the Falkland Islands on 2 April 1982.'[1] That, as far as she was concerned, was that.

Yet, on closer reading, the body of the report spells out a number of errors. Nott's decision to announce that the symbolically important Falklands guard ship, HMS *Endurance*, would be withdrawn was bound to be understood as a weakening of British commitment.* Similarly, Carrington and FCO officials did not draw the attention of the Prime Minister and the Cabinet to the evident hardening of the Argentine position from early March – the last point at which British submarines could have been sent in time to act as a deterrent. (It took some three weeks to reach the area.) In the longer term, the failure of both Labour and Conservative Governments to act on the 1976 report by Lord Shackleton, recommending the extension of the Port Stanley airfield runway so that the Islands could be rapidly reinforced, created an impossible situation. The Falklands were too far away to be defended by a sizeable permanent garrison; they could not be rapidly reinforced by air; and the dispatch of a naval task force might precipitate an invasion, if one were in the balance, before the ships arrived. So all the weight had to fall on diplomacy, and diplomacy ultimately could not work. This was because the British Government, under pressure from the House of Commons and from public opinion, would not bypass the wishes of the Falkland Islanders. They, in turn, were mistrustful of Argentina and determined to remain British. Argentina was resolved on sovereignty, and the Islanders were resolved that Buenos Aires should never have it – even under a so-called 'lease-back' arrangement, whereby British administration would be retained, though without sovereignty. Deadlock was inevitable.

In all this, Margaret Thatcher was less to blame than some. That said, and despite her indignant assertions, she was not entirely blameless either. The truth is that she was at the time so preoccupied with economics that she took insufficient interest in other matters. She had also pressured Nott into a Defence Review which was too radical and which put too much emphasis on Cold War priorities, above all the defence of Western Europe, rather than on post-imperial

* This is one point where Mrs Thatcher's memoirs are disingenuous, since only the (very limited) military effectiveness of *Endurance* is mentioned: see Thatcher, *The Downing Street Years*, p. 177.

entanglements.* True, her instincts were, as usual, sound, and even before the invasion her actions demonstrated the fact. So she insisted in mid-February that the Argentinians be told that the Falkland Islanders' wishes were paramount.[2] She demanded on 8 March that 'contingency plans' be made to deal with a possible invasion – a comment ignored by the Foreign Office.[3] She took the initiative on the same day with Nott, asking how quickly ships could be prepared.[4] She it was who overruled defeatism and sent the task force.[5] And from then on she was, of course, the linchpin of the campaign to retake the Islands. But she should have exercised a firmer grip earlier and placed less faith in Carrington.

A more nuanced assessment than Franks's is that to be found in the official history of the conflict by Lawrence Freedman. Freedman concludes that the initial Argentine decision to invade was not, in fact, made quite so late in the day as was thought by Franks. So there was more time available than the latter thought within which to make Argentina back down. Above all, Freedman notes, the Thatcher Government and indeed its Labour predecessor should have grasped that a choice had to be made between providing for the defence of the Islands – what the FCO liked to call the 'Fortress Falklands' option – or conceding the sovereignty upon which Argentina insisted. The refusal to make such a choice and act on it was clearly a policy error.†

The account of the Falklands War given in Margaret Thatcher's

---

* Not that he needed pressuring. He was determined to reshape the defence budget, above all by shifting resources from the navy to other services and from platforms to equipment. Both he and Mrs Thatcher were exasperated by the refusal of defence chiefs to accept the need for effective budgeting. Nott defends his approach in his very readable memoirs. Published since Mrs Thatcher's, they also provide a valuable insight into the Falklands War. See Nott, *Here Today, Gone Tomorrow*, pp. 203–44 (on his struggles with the navy) and p. 250 (on Mrs Thatcher's memoirs as 'the most accurate and full historical record').

† See Sir Lawrence Freedman, *The Official History of the Falklands Campaign*, 2 vols (Abingdon: Routledge, 2005), vol. 1, pp. 216–27. Freedman interviewed Mrs Thatcher and – rightly – accepts the account in her memoirs as in good faith and accurate. The copy he gave her is significantly inscribed 'With Admiration, I hope you like the result'. Had she read it, her answer would, or at least should, have been: 'Yes'.

memoirs is partly based upon a memorandum which she wrote in her own hand at Chequers at different times between the summer of 1982 and Easter 1983. It draws upon government records and her personal recollections. As one would expect, the earlier sections written closer to events are more vivid: some were too vivid (and too personal) for inclusion in the memoirs. They reveal Mrs Thatcher's true and raw emotions, and passages are given below.[6] She never explained what motivated her to write her account. It seems likely that there was more than one factor at work. She had to refresh her memory for cross-examination by the Franks Committee. She was also deeply conscious that those eleven weeks as a war leader were the most important episode of her premiership, a view she never changed.

This, in turn, suggests a further reason for writing. Margaret Thatcher did not in her wildest dreams think of herself as on a par with Churchill as a war leader, let alone as a writer – the Chequers document amply confirms the latter judgement – but it would be strange if Churchill's example did not count with her. She notes, for example, her awareness that Chequers, where the Falklands War Cabinet often met, had also been the scene of crucial discussions during the Second World War, and she thought that this atmosphere somehow helped. Indeed, some of the expressions she uses in the memorandum echo that earlier, greater conflict. For example, reflecting after the loss of the *Atlantic Conveyor* container ship, she wrote:

So we learned the deep sorrows of war.

And, after HMS *Glamorgan* was hit:

It is impossible to describe the depth of feeling at these times . . . quite unlike anything else I have ever experienced. In fights for liberty we lose our bravest and best . . . Now we know the sacrifices that previous generations made for us.

And, after the Argentines surrendered:

> Downing Street was full of people, young people. It was their
> generation who had done it. Today's heroes, Britain still breeds
> them.

Not great prose, but proof of a great heart.

The memorandum also conveys how lonely she felt during the conflict. The decision to send the task force was essentially hers. Although it was then endorsed by the Cabinet and backed by the House of Commons, it is by no means clear that any other modern British Prime Minister would have taken it. Many years later she could vividly recall the precise circumstances. On the evening of Wednesday 31 March she was working on papers in her room at the House of Commons when John Nott demanded to see her urgently. Intelligence had just been received that an Argentine invasion of the Falklands was imminent. Carrington was in Israel, so it was Humphrey Atkins and Richard Luce, deputizing from the Foreign Office, who joined Nott at the ensuing meeting. They were accompanied by officials from both departments. The report Mrs Thatcher now received was almost unimaginably bad. The Argentine fleet was already at sea. It could be expected to land its overwhelmingly superior force on Friday. And there was nothing, in military terms at least, that Britain could do to stop it. (In fact, South Georgia and the Falkland Islands fell with little effective opposition.) All she could say was that if the Falklands were lost, Britain 'would have to take them back'. It was defiance of a sort, a foretaste of what was to come, but it sounded lame and whether it made sense at all was debatable when all informed assessments seemed against it. At this stage, the military were absent. The Chief of the Defence Staff, Admiral Sir Terence Lewin, who would have been there, was away in New Zealand. But in his absence the First Sea Lord, Sir Henry Leach, suddenly appeared. He had decided to attend when he learned of the defeatist tone of the advice that Nott had been given. (He was late because the police at St Stephen's entrance of the House had refused to believe who he was.) She would always regard Leach's intervention at this juncture as a kind of salvation. It changed everything. He calmly ignored the Defence briefing and told her that he could and would assemble a naval task force to retake the Islands – if he now received the authority to do so. She immediately gave it, subject to later endorsement by the Cabinet.

And so the frenzied mobilization for war immediately began. Mrs Thatcher was astonished and heartened by the speed at which it proceeded. This too gave her hope that if she sufficiently willed and worked for the victory, Britain's armed forces would be able to deliver it. She was among the millions who watched on television as the two aircraft-carriers left Plymouth the following Monday (5 April). Eleven destroyers and frigates, three submarines, numerous other support vessels – some commandeered from civilian use – and an initial three thousand troops joined them on their way south, to the base on Ascension Island.

Sending the expedition was one thing: supporting its progress and authorizing its use in combat were different matters. Again, Mrs Thatcher was very solitary at the crucial moments. Her decision-making was made easier – indeed, possible – by her wise decision to take the advice of Harold Macmillan to set up a small defence sub-committee, a War Cabinet, and to keep the Chancellor, Geoffrey Howe, off it. This greatly annoyed him.* Howe's memoirs give no idea of the Treasury's true attitude during the conflict. They even suggest that Howe himself was personally supportive of Mrs Thatcher when their paths crossed in the entrance to Ten and Eleven Downing Street.[7] In fact, he and most of his fellow Treasury ministers were hostile to the operation. He joked on the day after

---

* The irony of Macmillan's advice has not been sufficiently appreciated. He was, presumably, drawing on his experience of Suez where, as Harold Wilson remarked, Macmillan (then Chancellor) was 'first in, first out', inheriting the premiership amid the debris of Eden's humiliation.

the Argentine invasion that Britain was at war but that it would probably be 'over by tea time'.* The Treasury's opposition on grounds of cost was magnified by the presence as Financial Secretary of Nicholas Ridley, whose actions at the Foreign Office had helped precipitate the disaster, and as Economic Secretary of Jock Bruce-Gardyne, whose defeatist views surfaced during the war itself – forcing him to make a grovelling public apology.[8] The opinions of other Cabinet ministers outside the War Cabinet should not be assumed to be any more robust than the Chancellor's. Some were known to be strongly hostile; others bided their time.[9] If the mission had failed, Mrs Thatcher would have been overthrown even faster by her colleagues than she was in 1990.

And failure was always a real possibility. From an early stage she was aware of this. It was not the defeatist advice of the Foreign Office but the flow of information from the commanders and from Northwood, the operation headquarters, that frightened her. The logistical problems of getting together and defending from sea and air attack an amphibious force large enough to retake the Islands were truly formidable. In the end, over a hundred ships and more than 25,000 men were sent.

Geography was against the British. So was the weather. The best advice was that from late May the South Atlantic winter could at any time abort the operation. Britain's military advantages over Argentina were radically reduced by these two factors. A run of bad luck could have proved fatal. If one of the aircraft-carriers had been sunk – which was a substantial risk, given the terrible effectiveness of the French-made Argentine Exocets – the political will of the Cabinet might have broken. (Twenty-five years later,

---

* I heard this remark and never forgot it, nor the laughter it evoked around the room. The recollection was one reason why I was determined not to join Howe as a special adviser at the Foreign Office, though his Euro-enthusiasm was hardly more likely to make for compatibility. The Treasury was then a great deal more alarmed by the sinking of the *Belgrano* than by the loss of the *Sheffield*. It was a revelation to me of the dangers of assuming that the twin 'right-wing' causes of sound money and patriotism necessarily went together. This lesson too I did not forget.

on the eve of the celebration of the victory, Mrs Thatcher amusingly described her Cabinet colleagues as having been 'rock solid – afterwards'.) If either of the requisitioned troop ships, the *Canberra* and the *QEII*, had been lost, the public outcry might have been impossible to ignore. Finally, if the Argentine fleet or the thousands of Argentine troops on the Islands had shown a little of the spirit of the Argentine air force, the landings could have been disrupted and effectively opposed, giving the diplomatic termites time to undermine victory. All these possibilities rendered what many in Britain, including MPs, optimistically considered a foregone conclusion anything but. When Mrs Thatcher took a startled President Reagan to task on the telephone for describing the war as a conflict between 'David and Goliath', with Britain in the latter role, her analysis of the military realities was entirely correct.[10]

The War Cabinet consisted of Mrs Thatcher, Whitelaw, Pym, Nott – and Cecil Parkinson, brought in because of his presentational skills and to provide an extra vote for the Prime Minister, whose instincts he shared.[11] The Attorney General, Michael Havers, usually attended. So did several senior officials and Sir Terence Lewin. Whitelaw, though not naturally robust, was loyal and in any case more at home in dealing with military matters than with economics. Mrs Thatcher declared in her memorandum that John Nott was 'splendid throughout', but that does not entirely reflect her view. He was thin-skinned and now felt vulnerable. She had insisted that he stay, because Carrington had gone. But he had put up a poor performance winding up the first, difficult debate on the crisis, on Saturday 3 April. His self-confidence had evaporated and this, along with other practical reasons, was why he let the service chiefs deal direct with Mrs Thatcher on all the important issues. Once hostilities began, however, he was on her side in rejecting the arguments for appeasement that regularly surfaced from the Foreign Office.

Francis Pym's position was crucial. He had been appointed

Foreign Secretary upon Carrington's resignation because Mrs Thatcher felt unable to do otherwise, despite his proven disloyalty and the open speculation that if she had to resign he would take over as Prime Minister. He was weak and not nearly as intelligent as his supporters pretended, but he was also devious and in a position to do great harm.

Mrs Thatcher was well aware, despite her bellicosity, of the need for a calibrated international approach. She took notice of what Sir Nicholas Henderson (ambassador to the United States) advised from Washington and Sir Anthony Parsons (ambassador to the UN) counselled from New York, and she usually went along with both. She recognized, in particular, how important Parsons' achievement had been in obtaining, almost before anyone was looking, the passage of UN Security Council Resolution 502, which demanded immediate and unconditional withdrawal of Argentine forces.

Above all, she focused on relations with the Americans. She had nourished some hope that the United States might be able to persuade Argentina to withdraw. Later, she envisaged that the Americans might act as trustees of the Islands: but on this too she was frustrated.[12] She was irritated by Reagan's unwillingness openly to take her side (until the 'tilt' of 30 April), exasperated by Secretary of State Al Haig's equivocations, and furious at what she described in her memorandum as American UN ambassador Jeane Kirkpatrick's 'very vexing and thoroughly anti-British' behaviour – but she controlled her emotions. Anyway, she knew that Britain had vital support elsewhere within the Administration, above all from Defense Secretary Caspar Weinberger.* He insisted that every British request should come straight to his desk and receive a swift (and in practice favourable) answer, despite the view of his military advisers that the

---

* The most important item provided by the United States was Sidewinder missiles for the Harriers. There was also some (though not crucial) help with intelligence and communications. Weinberger later felt somewhat aggrieved that the full extent of US assistance was not publicly recognized (Nicholas Henderson, *Mandarin: The Diaries of an Ambassador 1969–1982*, London, Phoenix, 1994, pp. 442–4).

British could not win.[13] In the later stages, Mrs Thatcher even came to value Haig's flounderings, because they prevented someone more hostile (and possibly more effective) presenting unacceptable ideas for a settlement. Above all, she played Reagan perfectly throughout, with a mixture of bullying and seductive persuasion.

Nor should it be forgotten how successful she was in rallying European opinion. Spain and Ireland – both temporarily members of the UN Security Council – were strong supporters of Argentina; Italy took the same side, albeit more hesitantly. But by drawing on Mitterrand's hostility to what he deemed a fascist junta, Mrs Thatcher scored a double success: France drew Germany along with it diplomatically; and, above all, it ensured that no more of the lethal Exocets fell into Argentine hands and provided useful information about the missile's capabilities.

So the widely held idea that Mrs Thatcher was hostile to diplomacy as such is misleading. She half hoped for a negotiated settlement, even if she did not expect it. She dreaded the loss of British lives. On that point the evidence is unequivocal.*

The truth is that she differed with Francis Pym on two fundamental questions. The first was whether the return to the *status quo ante* should be ruled out, in other words whether the Falkland Islanders were to be prevented from remaining British and (as its counterpart) whether Argentine aggression should be rewarded. The second question was whether the military side of the campaign should be subordinated – and if necessary sacrificed – to the diplomatic. The tension between her approach and Pym's on these two points was evident throughout. But it reached what she considered a crisis after Pym's return from Washington on Saturday, 24 April.

Ever since Haig's first visit to London (8 April), it had been clear that compromises would be required in the initial tough

* See the account (from a transcript) of her telephone conversation with Parsons before the assault was launched, where she speaks of her horror at the 'waste of young life' if there has to be a 'final battle' (Thatcher, *The Downing Street Years*, p. 218).

public stance adopted by the British if the diplomatic route was to remain open at all. Mrs Thatcher was prepared to be flexible on the declared objective of restoring 'British administration' to the Islands.[14] Different possibilities, variously involving some Argentine role, a role for the UN and (her preferred option) a role for the United States, were discussed. It was, though, vital to ensure that the interim administrative arrangements, whatever they might be, did not provide a cover for an irreversible shift towards Argentine control.

But compromises relating to the task force were a different matter. What appeared the option of using the force to blockade the Islands was no option at all. To keep thousands of troops aboard ship in worsening weather was unthinkable. Withdrawal, even to Ascension Island, would have left the Argentines in a position

"Take heart, Mrs Thatcher! We're right behind you!"

to strengthen and supply their troops. So it was essential to minimize delay to the campaign.

The proposals brought back by Francis Pym from Washington would have passed the initiative straight to Argentina. Even before he went, Pym had publicly, if inadvertently, revealed his thinking. He promised the Commons that force would not be used while the negotiations continued. Since South Georgia was on the point of being retaken, this was grossly irresponsible, and he was forced to make a statement retracting his remarks. In Washington, without Mrs Thatcher's alarming presence, he proceeded to accept terms from Haig that he must have known were at odds with the British Government's aims. The task force would have had to withdraw even further than previously demanded by the Argentines, and do so within a week. Within fifteen days it must be dispersed altogether. Sanctions against Argentina were to be lifted, even before its forces left. Argentine nominees from the mainland were to sit on the Islands' councils. The Argentines would also have been in a position to promote large-scale immigration to change the ethnic balance of the population. Finally, both the possibility of return to the *status quo ante* and the pledge to regard the Islanders' wishes as paramount were effectively sidelined. Mrs Thatcher told Pym that she could not accept these terms. But he insisted, all the same, on putting them in a paper to the War Cabinet.

In her memoirs Mrs Thatcher describes what was proposed as 'conditional surrender'.[15] In her memorandum she is blunter: 'The document [Pym] brought back was a complete sell out . . . A former Defence Secretary and present Foreign Secretary of Britain recommended peace at any price. Had it gone through the Committee, I could not have stayed.'

It did not go through, partly because she exploded the proposals in a firework display of forensic analysis against which Pym could not fight back, but above all because Whitelaw, by prior arrangement, came in behind her. Even then her position was sufficiently weak that she felt obliged to accept a compromise. So she went along with Nott's suggestion that, rather than reject them outright, the Government should ask Haig to put the proposals to the Argentines first. She hoped, of course, that Buenos Aires would do the job for her, and the junta duly obliged. But it might not have worked. She reflected on the outcome: 'So the "crisis" passed, the crisis of Britain's honour.' And her own.

The intensity of her emotions at this time also reflected the fact that the first stage of the Islands' recapture – the return to South Georgia – was already under way. She was kept informed of what was happening. Two helicopters crashed on the Fortuna Glacier while trying to lift off Special Forces in the midst of a snowstorm. She was on her way to speak at the Mansion House when she learned that a third helicopter had succeeded. 'I went out [of Downing Street] walking on air,' she remembered. The Argentines at Grytviken surrendered that weekend. It was a boost to morale, including hers, but she had been shaken by the reminder of the conditions under which troops would have to fight and of the risks they faced. This explains why she snapped at journalists after Nott announced the news from South Georgia, exclaiming: 'Just rejoice at the news . . . Rejoice!' There would be nothing else to rejoice at for some time to come.

Towards the end of April, diplomacy looked ever more hopeless, combat less avoidable. Operational decisions were for the military. The Prime Minister saw the Government's role as ensuring that British forces had the resources they needed, while she and her colleagues kept up morale at home and directed diplomacy abroad. On occasion, she queried whether some decision was correct – as with the dispatch of the vulnerable *QEII* carrying three thousand troops. But when the necessity was explained, she always concurred.

Beyond that, and in recognition of the fact that overall responsibility had to rest with elected politicians, the War Cabinet set the rules of engagement within which the military operated. In the case of the task force, this involved the announcement of 'Exclusion Zones' – first 'Maritime' and later 'Total' – inside which

Argentine forces were liable to come under attack. It also involved authorizations of specific actions, as in the case of the attacks on the Argentine carrier the *25 de Mayo* and the cruiser *General Belgrano*. Only once did Mrs Thatcher and her colleagues ask the military to reconsider. This was when Lewin sought authority to shoot down any aircraft without warning within the Total Exclusion Zone. The purpose was to counter Argentine spying from civilian aircraft. The politicians thought it too risky and the request was withdrawn.[16] In general, however, Mrs Thatcher felt no temptation to second-guess or interfere with military judgements. She even refrained from telephoning Northwood for news, though she made visits. It took some time for the military to understand how unusual this woman was, in being prepared to defend their decisions in public without trying to usurp their authority. This was very unusual and quite un-Churchillian. But in today's wars it is precisely how governments must behave.

This background also provides the essential context to understanding one of the most controversial episodes of the conflict, the sinking of the *General Belgrano*, with a loss of 321 lives, on Sunday 2 May. The attack on the vessel was a military response to a real threat. To appreciate this it is necessary to keep in mind not just the cruiser *Belgrano* but the aircraft-carrier the *25 de Mayo*. Both were elderly and badly maintained. But this did not render them impotent. It simply made them a danger to their crews as well as to the enemy. The *Belgrano* had substantial long-range firepower. But the *25 de Mayo* was even more of a headache. It was the Argentine navy flagship; and the navy, which had pressed hardest for the invasion, was desperate to prove itself. The ship could cover 500 miles a day. Its aircraft could, if allowed within range of Britain's arriving task force, do irreparable damage. And its escorts carried Exocet missiles. From the end of April, when Britain's Total Exclusion Zone round the Falklands came into force, it was upon the aircraft-carrier that the War Cabinet's attention focused. An attack on it was, in fact, authorized, but the ship eluded detection. Now it was the *Belgrano* which became the focus. The Argentine navy was planning a classic pincer attack, and the cruiser was to operate with aircraft launched from the carrier as part of that movement. Only on the morning of 2 May did Argentine commanders finally decide to call off the operation, because of adverse conditions. The *Belgrano* now altered course. The British side did not know this and, of course, could not know either of the enemy's change of mind. Moreover, these intentions might quickly change.*

The cruiser was therefore deemed, in conjunction with the elusive *25 de Mayo*, to pose a clear threat to the task force. That judgement was made by the task force commander, supported by the navy chief and then accepted by the War Cabinet, which authorized the attack. Because of communication difficulties, the message was not received until some hours after it was sent. The submarine *Conqueror* then acted on the order to attack. Contrary to what has been alleged, there was no connection whatever with Peruvian peace proposals, of which the politicians were as yet unaware. The fact that the *Belgrano* was technically outside the Exclusion Zone was irrelevant, because it posed – and was intended to pose – a significant threat. The sinking damaged Britain's international position. But it had one important benefit: the Argentine navy never again posed a threat to the task force.

Argentine aircraft, however, did. On Tuesday, 4 May HMS *Sheffield* was hit by an Exocet and later sunk: forty men died. It was an avoidable loss, the result of mistakes on board and not just bad luck.[17] It was also a terrible shock to the British public. The loss of the *Belgrano* and then the *Sheffield* intensified international pressure on both sides to negotiate. Time, though, was on Argentina's side. To stand a chance of success, a British landing

---

* Freedman, *Official History*, vol. 2, p. 288. An unfortunate element of confusion arose from an honest mistake made by Nott in his statement to the House, where he said that the *Belgrano* when hit was moving towards rather than away from the task force. In any case, the vessel could just as easily have altered course again. The threat did not depend on the direction at the time of the attack.

would have to be made before the end of the month. It was, therefore, vital that diplomacy be brought to a speedy end, though preferably on conditions set by Britain. That meant, in effect, an ultimatum. A long, tense session of the War Cabinet, with Henderson and Parsons in attendance, was held at Chequers on Sunday 16 May. Its task was to draw up the precise conditions to be put to Argentina. Mrs Thatcher clashed repeatedly with her advisers, insisting on harder terms.[18] The form and much of the language of previous proposals were retained, but she succeeded in toughening the details. Thus interim administration was to be conducted largely by the Islanders; South Georgia and the other dependencies were excluded altogether, remaining under direct British control; and insertion of a reference to Article 73 of the UN Charter, which speaks of self-determination, effectively reasserted the paramountcy of the Islanders' wishes. Finally, Argentina was given only forty-eight hours to respond – though there was constant pressure to extend this deadline, while the Argentines argued, haggled and delayed.

On Tuesday, 18 May the War Cabinet, attended by all the Chiefs of Staff, debated whether to go ahead with the landing. The debate was real, because the risks were also real. To land large numbers of troops, who might or might not be opposed, and without having secured air superiority, was extremely dangerous. Yet to hold off any longer would only increase the danger. The Prime Minister summed up: subject to confirmation by Thursday's full Cabinet, the landing would go ahead. As recommended by the military, it would be by night and take place at San Carlos, on the western shore of East Falkland. At the last moment Pym developed doubts, urging postponement on the grounds that Javier Perez de Cuellar, the UN Secretary General, had not yet had a response to his latest proposals. But Pym was overridden, and shortly afterwards Perez de Cuellar gave up his attempts to mediate.

It was now up to the troops. The Prime Minister just had to curb her impatience and wait. She had taken heart from the success of the night raid by British Special Forces on Pebble Island, situated off the north coast of West Falkland, a few days earlier. The Argentines had been taken completely unawares and eleven aircraft were destroyed on the landing strip. It was a demonstration of what could be expected if the odds were evened out. But who could imagine that any such concealment was possible for the major landing that was now planned?

Mrs Thatcher spent Friday, 21 May in her constituency, carrying on with engagements, keeping the secret, desperate for news. All she could gather over the telephone was that the operation was under way. Still in Finchley, she eventually heard, like everyone else from the television, that San Carlos was back under British control. But there was no word of losses. Very late that night, now back in Westminster, she received a report from Nott. Astonishingly, the Argentines had again been taken by surprise, and no British casualties had been sustained.

The landing had been unopposed. But once the Argentine air force was alerted, devastating attacks on the ships began. HMS *Ardent* was lost and HMS *Brilliant* and HMS *Argonaut* were badly damaged, though the vulnerable troop ship *Canberra*, anchored in Falkland Sound, escaped. How and why is still a mystery. If the Argentine pilots had concentrated their efforts on the most, rather than the least, vulnerable targets, the outcome would have been thrown into doubt. They did, though, sink the destroyer HMS *Coventry* and the container ship *Atlantic Conveyor*. Fortunately, the nineteen vital Harriers which the latter was carrying had been flown off earlier. The Argentines also claimed to have hit the carrier HMS *Invincible*, news that shook Mrs Thatcher; but, after desperate enquiries, the claim was proved false.

It was a frustrating and emotionally exhausting time. And the longer the struggle went on, the more difficult the politics became. The commanders and combatants felt under political pressure from London to press ahead more quickly than they believed right, and resented this. Such pressure, it must be added, came through the defence chiefs rather than directly from the Prime Minister. But it accurately reflected her feelings.

Attempts to rally support by the release of information from the front ran the risk of compromising operations. Nott fell foul of this when he briefed backbenchers too fully about the battle for Goose Green, while it was still under way – or at least, that was Mrs Thatcher's clear recollection. When pressed on who was to blame, she said in a stage whisper 'John Nott', though she did not include it in her memoirs. Nott himself wrongly blamed Bernard Ingham for this and every other unfortunate leak.[19]

The hard-fought battle at Goose Green will always be remembered for the heroism of Colonel 'H' Jones, who lost his life in it. But what it demonstrated to both the commanders and their political masters was the danger that lay in exaggerated hopes of a swift and easy victory. Overconfidence and misunderstandings about tactics and timing lay behind the problems of that day, and they could easily be repeated. But at least the objective of breaking out of the bridgehead had, thanks to 'H', been duly accomplished. The job of the Prime Minister and her colleagues was now to give British forces the time and political cover to complete their task.

The Government was facing fresh attempts from the Americans to halt the campaign, to save Argentine face. There was another tense conversation between Mrs Thatcher and Reagan, when he telephoned her on the night of Monday 31 May. She was taken unawares and was highly indignant, demanding to know what he would think if Alaska had been seized by a hostile power, as Argentina had seized the Falklands. It was hardly the most apposite of comparisons, but the President backed down. American diplomacy still wobbled, however, while at the UN support grew for a new ceasefire resolution. When heads of government assembled for the G7 summit at Versailles, Mrs Thatcher used the occasion to bend Reagan's ear, in private and at some length. But though she won his sympathetic endorsement – which he later repeated in public when he came to London to address Members of Parliament in the Great Hall of Westminster – this had no obvious effect on the behaviour of his Administration. America joined Britain in vetoing a UN resolution that demanded an immediate ceasefire; but Jeane Kirkpatrick then announced that she had, in fact, been instructed to abstain, though the message had not got through in time. Mrs Thatcher sought to relieve Reagan's embarrassment when it became clear to the press that he had no idea what had been happening. 'Poor Ron!', she commented afterwards.

On the Islands themselves, the final stage of the campaign was now in preparation. Major-General Jeremy Moore had arrived to take command of the land forces, which had also been further reinforced. The problem now was how to move them forward safely and speedily, with sufficient equipment and ammunition, over forbidding territory and in appalling weather, to ground on which they could finally engage the enemy, who were based at Port Stanley. After some discussion, it was decided to use two routes. Part of the force (3 Commando Brigade) 'yomped' across the north of East Falkland. The rest (5 Infantry Brigade) was dispatched along the south of the island. At one stage, men and large quantities of ammunition were taken by sea to the settlement of Fitzroy in the landing ships *Sir Tristram* and *Sir Galahad*. The operation was poorly handled. Both vessels were attacked by Argentine aircraft off Bluff Cove. Three bombs started a devastating fire on *Sir Galahad* carrying the Welsh Guards. More than forty men died and 115 were wounded. It was a terrible reminder of how vulnerable British forces still were, even as the noose around the Argentine occupiers tightened.

The northern approach, though difficult and exhausting, proved less treacherous. Mount Kent, deep into enemy territory, was seized without too much difficulty on the night of 30–31 May. The Argentines could only hope that the disaster at Bluff Cove had sent British plans awry. But it had not. Perhaps the tragedy even took enemy attention away from the moves that were in preparation to the north-west, from the direction of Mount Kent. On Friday, 11 June,

Moore ordered the start of the attack upon Mount Harriet, Two Sisters and Mount Longdon. It would be the first serious engagement since Goose Green. Now that the conflict had moved on to land, it was more difficult to keep London informed; so, eight thousand miles away, the Prime Minister anxiously waited for news.

The resistance was once more fierce. But the British pressed on. The struggle was hardest on Tumbledown. Argentine morale was not nearly as bad as the politicians back home believed. A ferocious gale was blowing. British mortars sank in the mud. Mrs Thatcher was every minute expecting report of a successful conclusion, constantly checking with the private office for any snippets. But instead she was informed of one last blow. HMS *Glamorgan*, bombarding Port Stanley, had been struck by a land-based Exocet. Fortunately, she was still able slowly to make way out of the area to safety. At last, as Tumbledown and Mount William fell, and with Stanley now surrounded, the end came. After some face-saving negotiation, the Argentines duly surrendered. On Monday 14 June the good news came through at last. That evening Mrs Thatcher told the House of Commons, on a contrived point of order, that 'white flags were flying over Port Stanley'.* Britain had won.

In her memorandum Margaret Thatcher twice uses the word 'miracle' to describe the outcome. Reflecting on the campaign twenty years later, she spontaneously used the same word. It is an odd expression. She was not, in truth, suggesting that God had yet again turned out to be an Englishman. Rather, the word reflects the mood of deep apprehension which had been with her throughout. She never let herself believe in defeat, yet at another level she had not expected to see victory either.

She now felt overwhelmed by relief. She also felt overwhelming pride in the achievement of British forces, and she wished this sense

---

* Oddly enough, the report about the flags seems to have been wrong: if any were waved it was by Argentine civilians, not troops. But the outcome was the same, and the report of surrender was correct (see Freedman, *Official History*, vol. 2, p. 650).

– which she knew was shared by the country as a whole – to be given public expression. Hence her anger at the Church of England's mealy-mouthed attitude to the Service of Thanksgiving and Remembrance in St Paul's. The Archbishop of Canterbury and his advisers were determined to avoid anything that smacked of 'triumphalism', whereas she wished to celebrate a triumph. When some of the clergy refused to take part if members of the armed forces read lessons, she threatened to make this known to Parliament. The turbulent priests backed down.

Nor was she prepared to envisage any more debate about the future status of the Islands. The shedding of British blood had, in her view, changed all that, and permanently. After leaving Downing Street, she remained alert for any weakening of British resolve on this point, and protested vigorously when she suspected concessions to Argentina or depletion of the garrison were being considered.

The changes wrought by the Falklands War extended far beyond policy towards the Falklands. Margaret Thatcher, too, changed. She felt different about herself. Nothing, she was convinced, would ever be so difficult or so dangerous again. She now knew (and knew she knew) how to cope with war – which, like all traditionalists, she saw as the supreme test of statesmanship. Others also saw her differently. Her standing soared. Defeating the enemy overseas cast a new light upon the struggle against enemies of a different kind at home – inflation, union militancy, industrial decline. She was no longer a housewife, she was a warrior. And the economy was also coming round. The next election, still a year away, was all but won – though it would probably have been won in any case, albeit perhaps with a smaller majority. Labour's Michael Foot was, after all, as near unelectable as any leader of the Opposition ever has been.

Margaret Thatcher did not have much historical sense, merely some rather romantic and fanciful historical notions. So it is doubtful whether at the time she thought about the degree to which the Falklands reversed the impact of Suez. (She certainly did so later, when prompted by others.) Yet this, rather than the parallels with the Second World War that came more easily to her, was the most important impact. The military men understood the point.[20] Their predecessors had been let down by the politicians, just as an earlier generation of British politicians had been let down by America. Now Britain was a power to be reckoned with once more – by the United States, but also by the Soviet Union. Mrs Thatcher vividly recalled being told by a Soviet general that the USSR had never thought that Britain would try to retake the Islands or that, if it did, it could do anything other than fail. Its American ally and its Soviet foe both looked at Britain differently now.

Yet she did not let it go to her head. She did not imagine that every other nut would crack so easily. She was not, for example, tempted to try to do for Hong Kong what she did for the Falklands. Realism in this case meant negotiation, and very much on Chinese terms.[21] She did not think, either, that she could go it alone without America. In fact, in the longer term she drew closer still to Reagan, despite his uncertain performance in the South Atlantic conflict. The Falklands War had changed her, and it had changed Britain's standing. It could not change the realities of global power.

11

A SUPPLY-SIDE REVOLUTION

Had she been presented with the title of this chapter, Margaret Thatcher would have put a wiggly line beneath it, as she customarily did in order to register her doubts. She disliked the expression 'supply side' and declined whenever possible to use it.* She was also only half-convinced that she had performed a revolution, preferring to fall back on the banal, if defensible, notion that she had merely restored the British economy to health. Yet 'supply-side' does indeed describe her policy, because, unlike previous governments, influenced by Keynesian analysis, the Thatcher Government was not seeking to achieve growth by pulling levers to regulate aggregate demand. Instead, it was removing distortions and introducing incentives to transform the supply of goods and services. This market-oriented approach was extended from manufacturing industry through the professions and into the workings of government and the public services. The effects were uneven. But the overall outcome of her eleven-and-a-half years in power was a change sufficient to be

---

* She also differed, of course, from the most famous supply-siders in America (where the term originates), such as Jude Wannisky and Art Laffer, in her view of the relative priority of cutting taxes and cutting government borrowing.

qualified as a revolution – and, unlike most revolutions, one with consequences that were overwhelmingly beneficial.

Yet there is a paradox. The single most important impetus for that revolution was not micro-economic reforms devised by the Government, but rather the shock administered, in part unwittingly and for reasons described earlier, by the counter-inflation strategy during its first two years.* The combination of a monetary squeeze and the rapidly appreciating exchange rate, against the background of a wider international recession, administered a body blow to British manufacturing industry. The result was a huge shake-out of overmanning and with it of long accumulated restrictive practices. The effects were felt far beyond the manufacturing giants – by their suppliers and by companies whose performance was not necessarily worse than that of their counterparts overseas. When these firms went to the wall, it marked a real loss to Britain's productive capacity. But, for the most part, the shedding of misused labour and the closure of outdated plant were long overdue. Without the destructive side of Schumpeter's famous 'gale of creative destruction', there could have been no creation – of new and successful businesses and more well-paid jobs.†

Recessions are not, however, of themselves beneficial. It was the unique circumstances of Britain in 1979, as the 'sick man of Europe', which ensured that the shock therapy on this occasion worked. By contrast, the post-Thatcher recession of the early 1990s, which resulted from an overvalued exchange rate within the European Exchange Rate Mechanism (ERM), had no such beneficial effects: British industry was already lean and fit, and the enforced diet risked inflicting starvation.‡ Moreover, even the Thatcher recession of the early 1980s would not itself have inaugurated a British industrial

---

* See above, pp. 173–90.

† Joseph Schumpeter (1883–1950), Moravian-born American economist. The phrase 'perennial gale of creative destruction' occurs in his *Capitalism, Socialism and Democracy*, first published in 1942. For the context see Joseph A. Schumpeter, *Capitalism, Socialism and Democracy* (New York: Harper, 1975), p. 84.

‡ See below, p. 381.

renaissance if a series of supply-side changes had not then been implemented to take advantage of the new economic climate.

Mrs Thatcher's preferred way of describing what the Government was trying to do was to talk in terms of a 'framework'. It was phraseology that she had learned from Keith Joseph and then made her own. Her younger colleagues adopted a rather different tone. They were inclined to speak as if Government programmes – of deregulation, privatization, tax reform, training – were themselves the cause of the British economy's progress. They also waxed lyrical about competitiveness; sometimes murmurings of a 'white hot' revolution seemed audible. She, though, always liked to express the work of government more modestly, seeing its role as holding the ring and ensuring that individuals could get on with the task of wealth creation.

The most politically contentious aspect of reshaping this framework consisted in the reform of trade union law. As has been noted, the 1980 reforms were of little practical effect. They gave employers legal remedies against secondary picketing which were not used and provided public money to fund ballots which was not taken up. The 1980 steel strike was conducted as if the legislation did not exist. Norman Tebbit's 1982 Employment Act, however, did make a difference. It introduced two key changes. It gave employers the right to sue for damages, where no dispute existed with their own employees or where it was not wholly or mainly about employment matters. Most important, for the first time it exposed trade union funds to fines and seizure in the case of unlawful industrial action. The 1984 Trade Union Act then put the emphasis back on democratic decision-making, giving teeth to the approach adumbrated in the 1980 Act. Above all, it provided that union members must be consulted before strike action if the union was to retain immunity. The 1988 Employment Act further strengthened the rights of individual trade unionists and opened union finances to greater scrutiny. Finally, building on a series of earlier measures, the 1990 Employment Act removed all legal protection for the closed shop – thus ending an abuse that even the Conservatives had initially considered an inevitable fact of industrial life. Viewed as a list, these 'step-by-step' measures are impressive. They mark a process by which the trade unions were brought within the same rule of law that applied to other citizens, and they have an obvious liberal, reforming rationale. But in political and economic terms their significance is to be judged according to the effects on raw trade union power.

Mrs Thatcher (and Norman Tebbit) understood, whereas most of their Cabinet colleagues did not, that what really mattered was the balance of industrial power. This analysis was based on the accurate perception that, however trade unions might behave elsewhere, in Britain, the more powerful they were, the more trouble they would cause. This was a function partly of history, partly of the link with monopoly, but it was a fact. The most striking figures about the effect of the trade union reforms are that in 1990 there were fewer industrial stoppages than in any year since 1935, and that just under 2 million working days were lost compared with almost 13 million on average in the 1970s. Naturally, the Government took every opportunity to remind people of the change. Yet there is another, less frequently noted, statistic which provides the explanation: that the percentage of the workforce belonging to trade unions plunged in these years from well over half to about a third. The reason for the decline is obvious. By the end of the Thatcher years, trade union membership was no longer seen as the way to extort higher wages than productivity or profit levels would warrant. So joining a union was less attractive. On top of that, because of the refusal to bail out industrial failures and the privatization programme, what were historically the most highly unionized industries were shrinking or having to exist in the more competitively demanding private sector.

Again, however, it would be wrong to imagine that this was simply the result of allowing markets to operate. Brute force – the force of the union militants – had to be overcome before market-led rationality could intrude. Mrs Thatcher's personal qualities of leadership – one could even say generalship – were as important in that struggle as any amount of diligent attention to the prescriptions of Hayek or Friedman.

The decisive engagement in the war with militancy was the miners' strike of 1984–5. As with the Falklands War, this year-long, frequently violent, conflict could easily have been lost. At several points, above all within the first weeks of the strike, it nearly was lost. Mrs Thatcher and a few key colleagues needed resolve and guile to avoid defeat. But just as Argentina lost more easily because it was led by Leopoldo Galtieri, so the NUM's chances of victory were weakened because it was led by Arthur Scargill. If Scargill had bided his time and launched his strike in the autumn, not the spring; if he had been prepared to moderate his absurd demands that the least economic pits should stay open; if he had courted other trade unions by even pretending to eschew violence – in fact, if he had fought a campaign rather than launching an insurgency – he might have succeeded.

Despite the measures that had been taken since 1981 to increase the capacity to resist a strike – what was known as 'endurance' – the Government was very vulnerable. The problem was, again, not dissimilar to that which had plagued the defence of the Falklands: namely, that all the most obvious such preparations – in this case, moving coal from pitheads to power stations, increasing the use of oil-burn, opening up the market for coal imports or (in the still longer term) enlarging nuclear capacity – were deemed provocative. The avoidance of provocation was even more of an issue once the shape of the strike became clear. For the key to winning it became ensuring that a substantial number of pits remained open, and that the miners there were prepared to keep going to work.

Scargill, for his part, had his own plan. He did not think he could win a national ballot for a strike. But he wanted a national strike all the same. So he had to build up to it.

The process began with an overtime ban in protest at the latest pay offer in October 1983. But it was pit closures which always looked like being the eventual cause of a strike. Some closures were obviously necessary. There was huge overcapacity. Restrictive practices and misuse of the investment poured in over the years had made British coal uneconomic. The potential of those pits which might just have a future was blighted by the refusal to close those which clearly had none. Even the process of slimming down the workforce would yield little benefit, if those who remained were not employed at viable pits. Scargill, though, refused to accept that any pit was uneconomic – when asked by MPs what level of loss-making was intolerable, he replied: 'As far as I am concerned, the loss is without limit.' In these circumstances, the first planned closure in a coalfield where militants of his mindset held sway was bound to be seen as a declaration of war. And so it proved. On 1 March the NCB announced the closure of the Yorkshire colliery of Cortonwood. It was badly handled, but that hardly mattered; any excuse was enough. The Yorkshire miners promptly called a strike. They were soon followed by the communist-led Scottish miners. On 8 March the NUM national executive officially supported both actions.

This marked a further and decisive step in Scargill's chosen strategy. That was to get the militant-controlled executive to endorse strikes called apparently spontaneously by different areas. In these circumstances, there would be no need for a national ballot. It circumvented the NUM constitution's provision that 55 per cent of nationally balloted miners had to approve before an official national strike could be called. One further problem, though, would have to be overcome. It was necessary to ensure that the areas called their own strikes; and that might not happen where the militants were weak, or where miners felt that their coalfields had decent commercial prospects which a strike could harm. The answer was brutally simple. Where there was a risk that a ballot might go the wrong way, there would be no ballot – because squads of militants from other areas would intervene to stop it. And if such a ballot was, in the event, conducted, and if it went against a strike, further squads would be drafted in to prevent by violence those who wanted to go to work from doing so.

The NCB were not much help in resisting Scargill's strategy. Under the commercially effective but politically inept chairmanship of Ian MacGregor, the Coal Board played into the militants' hands by allowing talk of a 'hit list' of closures to pass into circulation. Now and later, the Government agonized about how to allow the NCB to act as independent agents – management left to manage – when a single gaffe or misjudgement could precipitate disaster. As time went by, ministers became increasingly involved.

The strike began on Monday, 12 March and Scargill very nearly achieved his objectives. On the first morning he closed down about half the pits. Soon that had become a substantial majority. By Wednesday, only twenty-nine pits were working. The police had simply been overwhelmed. The violence in Nottinghamshire, where Yorkshire miners swarmed across the coalfield, was shocking, even for those who remembered earlier confrontations. But the Nottinghamshire men refused to accept Scargill's diktat and went ahead with a ballot, which showed more than 70 per cent against a strike. This consolidated the split between the two main coalfields – a split that had its origins in the General Strike, almost forty years earlier – and it frustrated Scargill's plan now. Other areas followed Nottinghamshire's lead. In the Midlands, the North-West and the North-East, ballots returned large majorities against a strike. Meanwhile, the militant heartlands remained Yorkshire, Scotland and Kent. Within a fortnight the geographical battle lines had been crudely and starkly drawn. Scargill, though, was determined to break out, and he still thought he could win.

He was convinced that the police would ultimately fail. For him, the 1972 Saltley coke depot business, which he had organized, proved that in the end brute force would be decisive. Mrs Thatcher also remembered every detail of Saltley, and she was equally determined that it should not be repeated.*

She set up a committee of Cabinet ministers to oversee matters.

---

* She could never have imagined, as Lawson, a former Energy Secretary, did, that Saltley was a feature of the much milder 1974 miners' strike. She had been in Cabinet in 1972 when the news came through that the police had yielded. She was a seasoned general, whereas her colleagues, including Lawson, were at best innovative tacticians. Cf. Lawson, *The View from No. 11*, pp. 147, 159.

A smaller group of junior ministers was specifically tasked with countering NUM propaganda. But it was with Leon Brittan as Home Secretary and Peter Walker as Energy Secretary that she worked most closely. Brittan, whose instincts were robust on matters of trade union coercion, had a particularly tricky job. Under the woolly constitutional flannel that covered British policing, his authority was far from clear. But the wool had its uses, because it concealed from public view what was happening. The Prime Minister thus energized the Home Secretary. The Home Secretary energized the Permanent Secretary of the Home Office, Sir Brian Cubbon. And Cubbon, whose instincts were also robust, then energized the not naturally very energetic chief constables. He told them in a telegram that they should be under no doubt about what was expected of them, namely, to ensure that the law of the land was upheld. Through the National Reporting Centre – the nearest that Britain had to a central police authority in this crisis – they now sought to do so.

But what, in truth, was the law? Mrs Thatcher and Brittan arranged for Michael Havers, the Attorney General, to make its contents clear. In answer to a planted written answer, Havers reaffirmed that the police had powers under the common law – not, that is, any of 'Thatcher's laws' – to turn back pickets on their way to the picket line when there were reasonable grounds to expect a breach of the peace. This ruling was subsequently upheld by the courts. It underpinned all the police operations required to prevent the kind of mass picketing that had forced the closure of Saltley.* Otherwise, Scargill's tactics would have worked.

If the miners' strike marked the climax of Mrs Thatcher's war against militancy, the 'Battle of Orgreave' (as it was dubbed) marked that war's decisive engagement. Scargill's practical objective was to

---

* At this juncture I was special adviser to the Home Secretary. The full extent of the central coordination of the police operation has never been revealed. Had it been so at the time it would have fed the left's paranoia. But even the paranoid are sometimes right – and these paranoiacs had to be defeated.

prevent coke from the Orgreave coke works reaching the steelworks at Scunthorpe. But, like Saltley more than a decade earlier, Orgreave was also intended to demonstrate that the police could not stand out against a mass picket. So at the end of May and through June the nation viewed on television scenes of organized violence that seemed to come from a country in the throes of revolution. More than five thousand miners and assorted troublemakers took on the police, who were pelted with bricks, stones and darts. Officers, clad in protective gear received after earlier riots, charged on horseback into the crowd, while their colleagues pulled out the ringleaders, batons flailing. Mrs Thatcher denounced 'the rule of the mob' and promised that 'the rule of law' would prevail. And at Orgreave it finally did.

But a still more distasteful – because covert – campaign of intimidation was waged by the militant miners against the moderates and their families. Behind the front line, even the wives and children of working miners were considered fair game. Plain-clothes detectives were duly dispatched to the mining villages to offer a degree of protection. But they could not help a Yorkshire miner beaten up that November in his own home in Pontefract by fifteen men. Nor could they save a taxi driver carrying a South Wales miner to work some weeks later, killed by a concrete post thrown on his car. It is one of the more egregious examples of the rewriting of history by the left that the striking miners are now universally portrayed as the victims, not the villains. Many who lived through the period know better. Even Mrs Thatcher, who never entertained illusions about such things, was disgusted by the tactics employed. At the time, she lent strong personal support to the wives of the working miners and she always felt in their debt. She was dismayed when, after she left office, her policy of staunchly defending the Nottinghamshire miners' interests when closures were considered was reversed in the name of desiccated economics.

Brittan at the Home Office oversaw the police response. But Walker's role was also important. He gave little away of what he was doing, but most of it consisted of briefing the press, in which he was, as always, very effective. His manner did not, though, inspire confidence. His colleagues doubted whether his optimism about the prospects for endurance was justified. Ian MacGregor thought him deeply untrustworthy.[1] Mrs Thatcher herself became frustrated at the lack of information she received from the department. She began to have private contacts with MacGregor. She also pored over regular briefing provided by David Hart, whose freelancing activities on behalf of the working miners was highly effective. In cloak-and-dagger style, Hart would meet her political secretary Stephen Sherbourne in St James's Park to pass on what he knew – for it was vital that Scargill should not learn how the Nottinghamshire men were now working to defeat him.

Mrs Thatcher repeatedly toyed with the idea that the employers affected by the strike – the NCB, BSC, British Rail and the Central Electricity Generating Board (CEGB) – should seek an injunction against the NUM under the new legislation. But, as in the Falklands campaign, she never imposed her own judgement. In fact, the 'Thatcher laws' were eventually to have their place in defeating the strike, but without the Government's involvement. Two Yorkshire miners brought a case against the NUM, claiming that the original Yorkshire strike could not be described as official. A writ was duly served on Scargill at September's Labour Party conference. The next month the High Court found against the NUM and its assets were ordered to be sequestrated. It turned out that they had been hidden abroad. But that hardly helped. The foreign connection only emphasized how sinister Scargill's objectives were. It was also revealed that he had been in contact with Libya and that money had been received from the Soviet Union.

Most trade unionists had, in any case, little sympathy with the miners, whom they saw as having been feather-bedded by subsidy, while so many other firms and jobs had gone to the wall. A TUC 'Day of Action' in June had been poorly supported. Within months, the TUC leaders themselves were privately desperate to see an end to the strike that would save Scargill's face (and theirs). But neither the pressure of public opinion nor the expressed wishes of those miners able to vote in a ballot (of 70,000 consulted, 50,000 rejected a strike) sufficed to determine the outcome. The socialist legacy of restrictive practices and monopoly still offered possibilities for militants to defeat the market and ignore democracy.

The National Dock Labour Scheme, which worked through an enforced closed shop, still held many of the main ports in its grip. So when – in July and August – the TGWU called its members out on strike, albeit on feeble pretexts, there was a real chance that the Government might be compelled to yield. The threat was a direct one, to food and other essential supplies. But on each occasion the dispute was resolved. Mrs Thatcher, though, never forgot how serious the danger had been. It made her even more cautious than usual when successive ministers later urged the Scheme's abolition – finally achieved, without any great problem, in 1989.[2]

A second crisis occurred in September and October, when the National Association of Colliery Overmen, Deputies and Shotfirers (NACODS) – the mere title suggests the primitive state of the industry – balloted its members for a strike. The NACODS men had the statutory responsibility of checking that the mines were safe. So if they walked out, the industry must close down – all of it. But it was the NACODS leaders who eventually blinked first: the action was called off.

Christmas was, oddly enough, a source of worry for the Prime Minister as she watched for signs of the strike collapsing. On the one hand, it was likely that some miners would return to work in the New Year, because they needed the money. On the other hand, once pits closed for the holiday period, there was a chance that pickets might assemble to prevent their reopening. The decisive element would be expectations. So, once she was convinced by the figures on endurance, she authorized Peter Walker to state that there would be no power cuts at any stage the following year. Scargill, predictably, disputed the claim. But Scargill's credibility with all but his most blinkered supporters was nil. And if the miners could not bring the country to a halt even in the depths of winter, the strike had in reality been lost. This fact could now sink in.

As the new year progressed, the trickle back to work, though it slowed with each new round of negotiations, eventually became a flood. On Wednesday, 27 February the daily figures which Mrs Thatcher was given showed that a majority of miners were back at work. The following Sunday a conference of the NUM voted for an end to the strike, rejecting Scargill's bluster. Soon even the militant areas were back.

Yet it seemed an inglorious conclusion. Liberal sensitivities, including it seems those of the monarch herself, had been offended by the bitterness and polarization the strike had generated.[3] From another angle, the scenes of violence were an unwelcome reminder that when Mrs Thatcher spoke of 'enemies within' she was all too right.[4] Britain was exposed as a less pleasant and wholesome place than the coddled and nostalgic Establishment had imagined. And though almost everyone thought that Scargill had been to blame, few felt much gratitude towards the Prime Minister. Not that it mattered to her. She was solemnly told by colleagues, officials and advisers that she must not gloat. But speaking, in unscripted remarks, to a Conservative local government conference, she said she had every intention of doing just that.

In truth there was much to gloat about. The defeat of the year-long strike did not necessarily prove that the Government's union reforms were working or that a better economic future beckoned. In fact, to the contrary, the timidity in using Thatcher's laws had been notable, and Britain's coal business turned out to have no large-scale future at all – generous redundancy terms allowed many ex-miners to begin again, but not in mining. Yet the strike proved one vital thing. It showed that no union or group of unions could ever again make the country ungovernable. This demonstration constituted the most important and most beneficial industrial change made during Margaret Thatcher's period in Downing Street. It made – and it still makes – the success of the modern British economy possible.

The taming of the trade unions, along with the taming of inflation, created the conditions for Britain's economic recovery – but these conditions, though essential, were not sufficient. Other aspects of an encouraging framework for enterprise had also to be in place. One of the most important of these was low marginal tax rates.

As has been noted, the 1981 Budget placed the achievement of lower inflation and lower interest rates ahead of low taxes. But as economic growth resumed, tax cuts returned to the agenda. Radical tax-cutting and ingenious tax reforms were to constitute the positive side of Nigel Lawson's period as Chancellor.* In 1984 Lawson restructured corporation tax, eliminating allowances and bringing rates down to internationally competitive levels. He continued Howe's work in cutting and reforming capital taxes. He completed what Howe had started by ending the discrimination against savings income constituted by the Investment Income Surcharge. Above all, in 1988 – admittedly with unfortunate timing, because the economy was already overheating – he sharply cut income tax rates, bringing the basic rate down to 25 pence and the top rate to 40 per cent. The latter was of great importance, because, as exponents of the Laffer curve would predict, it led to a wave of new, or at least newly declared, economic activity. And it finished up by increasing rather than diminishing the share that top-rate taxpayers paid of the total tax take. The deteriorating economic background after Lawson's departure then restricted the opportunity for any more large gestures. But modest improvements were made. John Major's tenure at the Treasury was marked by attempts to increase the level of saving, for example through Tax Exempt Special Savings Accounts (TESSAs – the predecessor of today's ISAs). Progress

* For the negative side see pp. 297–303.

235

towards ending the double taxation of savings was then central to discussions of the economic side of the next manifesto, continuing when Mrs Thatcher left office.

By and large, these initiatives came from the Treasury, not from the Prime Minister. But she had her favourite and less favoured aspects of the tax changes that her Chancellors made. She was, for example – and notoriously, because of the complaints made about it by Treasury sources – a great proponent of mortgage tax relief. She would have liked to increase it. The Treasury under all incumbents wanted to contain and if possible eliminate it. The economic arguments were fairly and squarely on the side of the Treasury. The relief helped fuel house prices and constituted an inefficient form of subsidy. But at another, more important, level Mrs Thatcher knew what she was doing. Her vision of society was one of property owners, constantly trying to move upwards by acquiring assets. Mortgage tax relief was precisely and symbolically framed to that end.

Mrs Thatcher was also a great believer in thrift. She disliked debt of all kinds. One of her greatest sources of pride was that during her last three years in office the country had a budget surplus and was repaying national debt. But, reflecting her early upbringing, she also distrusted the mentality of households who lived beyond their means and she blamed the banks for encouraging it. She was, therefore, fully behind Major's emphasis on saving.

As for tax cuts, she took the view that they were not a give-away. Rather, tax itself was a take-away. There was, she considered, a duty to return the people's money to the people whenever possible. Like Lawson, she preferred straightforward cuts in the basic or upper rates of income tax to the raising of thresholds over and above inflation. Simplicity and incentive effects, she believed, went together. In fact, viewed in terms of the overall burden, the Thatcher record of tax-cutting is somewhat disappointing. Tax did not fall: it actually rose, though this was because of the need to curb and then eliminate borrowing – public expenditure (adjusted for the business cycle) fell as a share of GDP. But, in any case, this tells only part of the story, for two reasons. First, the marginal rate of income tax was reduced at certain crucial points in the income distribution. And second, the overall marginal tax rate (direct and indirect, and including national insurance) of the average worker dropped by two points and that of the top earner by thirty-five points.[5]

The incentive effect of these tax changes was supplemented by changes to benefits. Compared with the reforms later introduced in the United States by the Clinton Administration, or even in Britain those made by the Blair/Brown Labour Government – let alone those planned by the present Coalition Government – the reforms of the Thatcher years look quite modest. One of these changes – the de-indexing of the state retirement pension from earnings (as opposed to prices) in 1980 – although it eliminated major future public spending commitments, led to other problems that are now recognized.[6] In particular, too many pensioners have become reliant on means-tested benefits. The fact remains, though,

"FOR OUR NEXT TRICK WE ARE GOING TO NEED SOME COOPERATION FROM THE AUDIENCE!"

that under Mrs Thatcher some important moves were made to encourage people back into work.* Notably, there was the introduction of Family Credit to tackle the unemployment trap (the situation in which a person earns more on benefit than in work) and of Re-start, a mild version of US-Style 'workfare' which targeted the long-term unemployed to get them back into jobs.[7]

More radical than either tax or benefit changes, however, was the Thatcher Government's privatization programme. The word itself, which Mrs Thatcher did not at first like – she preferred 'denationalization' – was perhaps coined by David Howell.[8] Economic liberals like Howell, Howe, Lawson and Ridley were ideologically even keener on selling state-owned business than was the Prime Minister. She hated nationalization, of course, and she wanted to see the Government out of running what almost inevitably turned out to be loss-making concerns. But her priorities were balancing the books and sound money. She considered the shift of assets and jobs from the public to the private sector as part of a desirable longer-term transformation rather than an immediately attainable goal. In any case, the state of the economy and of the businesses themselves was such that any initial hopes for early disposals were soon scotched, as Britain sank deep into recession.

The concept of sweeping denationalization, including that of the publicly owned utilities, had first been advanced by Enoch Powell. But no one took it very seriously – not even, to judge from some of his answers to objections raised, Powell himself.[9] There were large technical questions to be answered about the accounting systems, share issues and (in the case of the utilities) regulatory

---

* There is a parallel with Ronald Reagan here. Both he and Mrs Thatcher recognized in principle the need to reform welfare, but neither, in practice, did much about it. Both were more interested in the incentive effects of tax cuts than in the disincentive effects of benefit payments. Both came of a generation which assumed a moral stigma attaching to dependency and a moral preference for self-help that applied ever less. Their political successors – on left and right – made and make no assumptions. For Reagan's record, see Andrew Busch, *Ronald Reagan and the Politics of Freedom* (Lanham: Rowman & Littlefield, 2001), p. 103.

regimes that were needed, and the answers differed from industry to industry.

The theory, though, was clear enough. The direct economic benefits of a successful privatization were agreed (by enthusiasts) to be the enforcement of financial discipline and reinforcement of pressure for efficiency by the threat of bankruptcy and the demands of the capital markets. On top of that, the human element was considered, not least by Mrs Thatcher, as equally important: namely, that managers would have to take responsibility for managing rather than pass the buck to government, and that workers would have to face up to the fact that their jobs depended on their own productivity and the firm's profits, not on government hand-outs. Privatization was an element in the wider revolution in attitudes which Mrs Thatcher's strategy was designed to achieve. Alongside ending the money illusion created by inflation and the illusion that union obstructionism saved jobs, privatization would remind the nation that no one owed it a living – a living had to be earned.

A further argument for privatization which Margaret Thatcher deployed increasingly in the later years of her premiership was that it was a means of widening share ownership. Some of the privatizations made special provision for workers to buy shares on preferential terms – in one case, the National Freight Corporation (later Company), there was a management and employee buy-out. Nearly all privatizations encouraged the purchase of small packages of shares by private subscribers. There was, of course, an excellent political reason for this. It made the Labour Party's plans for renationalization more problematic and unpopular. Those who purchased such shares even became one of the early targets of the successful early direct mail 'shots' undertaken by Conservative Party fund-raisers.

In the period immediately after the privatizations there was a large increase in the proportion of the general public owning shares. British Telecom and British Gas were between them responsible for millions of new share-owners (see below). Some of this growth was reversed as people sold to take advantage of windfall gains; but even allowing for this, the number of shareholders still approximately doubled during the Thatcher years. The effects have not, however, been as great in the economy as a whole as enthusiasts hoped at the time. Shares are still, as in the pre-Thatcher era, mainly held through institutions, not directly by individuals. This would not, in fact, have greatly disappointed Mrs Thatcher herself. She knew that for most people dabbling in the stock market was of limited appeal. She thought that it was by building up savings rather than taking risks on the Stock Exchange that the great majority of people would become capitalists – or, as, she liked to say, 'every earner an owner'. And encouraging share ownership was always in her view less important than encouraging home ownership.*

More than forty major businesses were privatized while Mrs Thatcher was Prime Minister.† As a result, the state-owned sector of industry shrank by 60 per cent. The order in which businesses were sold depended on markets, not manifestos. For example, although shipbuilding was mentioned as a candidate for privatization in the 1979 manifesto, for years it could not be given away, let alone sold at a profit. Similarly, although legislation to privatize British Airways (BA) was introduced in 1980, only after it had been streamlined and reshaped by John King could it finally be sold in 1987. The case of BA also illustrates the degree to which the success of privatization needs to be judged not just by the performance of newly privatized companies but by the improvements that occurred while they were being prepared for privatization.

* Another point which received little consideration at the time, but which the subsequent disastrous outcome of privatization through voucher systems in Russia and elsewhere has highlighted, is that the pressure to improve a company's performance is much reduced when large numbers of people own small batches of shares. Corporate shareholders are likely to be more informed, demanding and effective.
† This figure includes the electricity distribution companies, whose sale was launched during the last days of her time in Number Ten but concluded the following month.

In the second term of Mrs Thatcher's Government the revived economy, as well as accumulating experience, allowed privatization to leap to the top of the agenda. It was the sale of British Telecom that marked a radical change of pace, partly because of its size and partly because it was the first of the public utilities to be sold. Planned before the 1983 election, then postponed for the campaign, the sale of the company took place in 1984 – at the height of the miners' strike. It was a huge success, not just through the take-up of shares but through the access the business gained to private capital with which to invest in rapidly advancing technology. British Telecom's near-monopoly position required the creation of an official regulator to control its prices. Price increases were limited according to the formula 'RPI minus X', where RPI is inflation and X represents estimated cost savings. The decision to adopt this approach, which required the company to pass on efficiency gains to customers in the form of price cuts rather than using them to swell profits, dividends and salaries, was replicated for the other utilities. It can be criticized; but the consensus is that it works better than the American model based on a set rate of return on capital. Certainly, the gains to BT's customers in terms of price and service have been dramatic.[10]

A more telling criticism of the privatization programme is that competition considerations were not always uppermost in decision-making.[11] The most obvious case is that of gas privatization, where Peter Walker, with Mrs Thatcher's blessing, was able to argue against all economic logic that British Gas, which ran five separate businesses, should be privatized as a single unit. The interests in the industry were appeased and the timetable for privatization was shortened. The flotation was successfully undertaken in 1986, but then the competitive shortcomings of the new arrangements became evident. Similar political factors were involved in the privatization of the British Airports Authority (1987) – in this case exaggerated safety fears – and of the electricity industry (1990–1), where Mrs Thatcher's gratitude to Walter Marshall, chairman of the CEGB, for his services during the miners' strike was a significant obstacle to an earlier and more radical break-up of the industry.[12]

Despite these shortcomings, the achievements of the privatization programme were impressive. Moreover, it required political courage – on the part of the Prime Minister herself, among others. None of the sales was popular before it occurred. Yet none – except the sale of the railways, which took place after Mrs Thatcher left office, and about which she had reservations, especially in the form actually undertaken – has been substantially reversed. Indeed, the idea of privatization and the fund of technical experience accumulated from it became a significant British export. The British example attracted emulation from different foreign governments for a variety of reasons, some good and some not so good: privatization in ex-communist countries with a weak rule of law has led to large-scale corruption.

For Britain, though, the gains were unqualified – the only serious objection that can be lodged is that they might have been still greater. Nor were they simply economic. Privatization constituted a huge shift away from state to private ownership, strengthening the economic foundations of a free society. More prosaically, it forced both government and the industries themselves to re-examine their assumptions, and this re-examination brought benefits. For example, the privatization of the water companies – the least popular privatization undertaken – prompted Nicholas Ridley to strengthen controls on river pollution.[13] Even the abortive attempt to privatize nuclear power generation usefully exposed the hitherto concealed costs of decommissioning, thus forcing a more rigorous debate about the long-term role of nuclear power and in the long term encouraging cheaper nuclear technology.

In both these cases, one should add, the Prime Minister's new-found enthusiasm for 'green' issues was also at work. Her zeal waned somewhat once the full cost of environmentalism became apparent to her. But she retained her interest in the subject, as well as her belief that sound science was the essential reference point for all environmental policy.*

Making markets work better became the Thatcher Government's signature approach in areas far beyond the manufacturing and service sectors of industry. Restrictive practices upon which previous Conservative Governments had looked with indulgence were now exposed to fresh and critical scrutiny. The City was forced, albeit finally on its own terms, to open up to reform by the changes collectively designated as the 'Big Bang'.† Stock-brokers were livid, but their lunch habits still had to change. The legal profession fought furiously, but unsuccessfully, to resist rationalization. The university lecturers waged a war of attrition against the Government – to the latter's disadvantage but with little gain for themselves – to resist the erosion of tenure (which amounted to the virtual freehold occupation of posts) and to combat pressures for more output and more outside scrutiny. All these reforms brought benefits in terms of efficiency. But the accusation that they were pursued in a manner that showed scorn for professional ethics, freedoms and traditions carries some weight. They took place on territory at the margin where efficiency and standards compete, and perhaps occasionally over-stepped it.

Controversial for other reasons were attempts to bring the disciplines of the market into the work of government and public

---

* The way in which her thinking on the subject evolved – and clarified after Sir Crispin Tickell ceased to be her adviser – can be followed in other published sources, notably: Thatcher, *The Collected Speeches*, ed. Robin Harris (London: HarperCollins, 1997), pp. 326–33 (speech to the Royal Society, 27 September 1988); Thatcher, *The Downing Street Years*, pp. 638–41; Margaret Thatcher, *Statecraft* (London: HarperCollins, 2002), pp. 449–58. The scientific evidence, upon which Mrs Thatcher placed such emphasis, also continues to evolve, and has done so further since *Statecraft* was published.

† Deregulation of financial markets then and since has been blamed for the 2008 financial crash. Even to the extent that is true, it should be remembered that without the 'Big Bang' reforms the City would have lost its competitive edge and the country would be greatly poorer.

services. The contracting out of local authority functions such as street cleaning, and the ending of the inefficient and often corrupt direct labour organizations, beloved of socialist councils, soon proved their worth. But the use of private cleaners in hospitals, though it helped break the hold of a particularly militant public sector work-force, did little to improve hygiene or the welfare of patients. Within the operation of central government, the outcome of the changes was also mixed. In 1988 the 'Next Steps' programme initiated a transfer of much of the administrative work of departments to free-standing agencies, a practice that went further after Mrs Thatcher left office. The evidence indicates that these bodies (which include, for example, the prison service), like nationalized industries before them, do not behave very differently from other parts of government, and they are – again like the old nationalized industries – even less accountable. Another similar body, the Child Support Agency, which was very much Mrs Thatcher's creation and was inspired by her indignation at the failure of absent fathers to pay for their children's upkeep, turned out to be notoriously incompetent.

Also hotly debated at the time, but more positive in their effect, were the supply-side changes introduced in housing, education and health. There were important distinctive factors in the circumstances of each and also in the way Mrs Thatcher herself thought and felt about each of them.

The runaway success of the Thatcher Government's housing policy was the extension of home ownership, particularly first-time ownership, and above all the sale of council houses to sitting tenants. By the time Mrs Thatcher left office, almost 70 per cent of British housing stock was owner-occupied, compared with just over 50 per cent when she came to power. More than one and a half million public sector tenants bought their homes, 1.2 million of these under the Government's right-to-buy legislation. Since the first Act in 1980, attempts had been made to keep up the momentum, by improving the terms and by promoting the sale of (the less desirable) council flats. Mrs Thatcher was proud of the change, but she remained cautious. A proposal to convert (public sector) 'Rents into Mortgages', pioneered in Scotland and then championed by Peter Walker in Wales, would probably have found its way into the next manifesto, if she had had the opportunity to prepare one. But she was still not convinced by the time she left office that the technical hitches had been overcome. She always moderated her desire for more home ownership with awareness that houses, purchased on mortgages, constitute liabilities, not just assets. She would never, for example, have followed the United States in encouraging poor people to take out loans for property they could not afford – the basis of the 'sub-prime' lending fiasco.

In economic terms, the growth in home ownership must be considered a mixed blessing. One can argue that Britain invests too much in bricks and mortar and not enough in business. But the change did at least make those tenants who bought houses more mobile in the longer term, and it provided them with a useful sum of capital.* Still more economically beneficial would have been a revived private rental sector. But at the time even limited measures faced a wall of prejudice, and the Opposition's threats to reverse decontrol deterred new investment in rented property.

The Thatcher education reforms were a more qualified success than her housing policy. What they lacked was coherence. This is exemplified by the Education Reform Act of 1988, the Government's flagship education measure. On the one hand, it introduced a National Curriculum, which greatly increased central government's control over schools. On the other, the Act devolved power by creating self-governing grant-maintained schools, promoting the expansion of popular schools and establishing a network of free-standing city technology colleges.

The centralizing National Curriculum was a failure. It quickly became highly prescriptive, bureaucratic and educationally un-

---

* The immediate effect on mobility was reduced because tenants who bought and resold their homes within a certain period had to repay part of their windfall capital gain.

245

sound. By contrast, the measures to devolve power, which created a wider range of schools, were a great success. The proof of this is that, having initially sought to reverse the changes, the Labour Government then made them its own, albeit with different nomenclature. The approach has been developed further by the Coalition Government with its 'free schools' programme.

Whether the Thatcher changes actually improved the standard of education as a whole is more debatable. But, then, perhaps the success of schooling depends more on cultural, social and personal factors than any government likes to accept. What the reforms did do was to provide the beginnings of an alternative model to the one that had previously failed.

Of the three main social sectors, Mrs Thatcher came latest, and with greatest reluctance, to reform of the National Health Service. Her caution was politically justified. She was aware that the NHS enjoyed a quasi-mythological status. It might look, behave and, indeed, fail like a nationalized industry, but it was widely regarded as a venerable national institution. Yet preservation of the status quo was not, in the end, an option. The demands on the NHS were huge and growing, because people were living longer, because new treatments were becoming available, and because expectations were higher. Such demands could be restrained, in theory, by charging; but any substantial extension of charges always proved politically impossible. Another option was to divert demand by encouraging people to take out private health insurance. This the Thatcher Government did, targeting tax relief on the over-sixties. But it had only a marginal impact, and her successors ended it. When Mrs Thatcher defended her own use of private health care, at a press conference during the 1987 election campaign, she witnessed at first hand how deep the prejudice against it still was.

In the run-up to that election Mrs Thatcher's advisers had, in fact, made a sustained attempt to get her commitment to a radical review of health. But she baulked. She preferred a royal commission, recalling the 1975 Merrison (Royal Commission) Report, which

Victory – MT and Denis respond to cheers at Conservative Central Office, 4 May 1979.

Top left: The Prime Minister works on papers in the flat above 10 Downing Street.

Top right: Cecil Parkinson, Party Chairman, in jocular mood as MT leaves Central Office (1983).

Right: Acknowledging applause for her first party conference speech as Prime Minister, Blackpool, October 1979. Her PPS, Ian Gow, sits on her left; Peter Thorneycroft, Party Chairman, on her right.

Left: *above*, Conferring with Norman Tebbit, Party Chairman (1987); *below*, reflecting with Whitelaw, as Party Chairman John Gummer listens (1984).

Below: The Government front bench at the state opening of Parliament, November 1986: *left to right*, MT, Geoffrey Howe, Nigel Lawson, Peter Walker, Kenneth Baker, Nicholas Edwards, Douglas Hurd.

ABOVE: The 1989 Cabinet – a smiling but divided team (*left to right: front row*, Lawson, MT, Howe; *second row*, Tony Newton, Tom King, Norman Fowler, Hurd, Baker, Nicholas Ridley, John Major, Chris Patten, John MacGregor, Peter Walker; *back row*, Lord Belstead, Peter Brooke, John Wakeham, Kenneth Clarke, Parkinson, Lord Mackay, Norman Lamont, Gummer, Malcolm Rifkind, David Waddington).

FAR LEFT: Charles Powell, foreign policy adviser.

LEFT: Alfred Sherman, early architect of Thatcherism.

ABOVE: With Bernard Ingham, press secretary.

LEFT: John Hoskyns, head of the No. 10 Policy Unit.

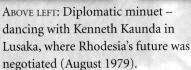

ABOVE LEFT: Diplomatic minuet – dancing with Kenneth Kaunda in Lusaka, where Rhodesia's future was negotiated (August 1979).

ABOVE RIGHT: In the 'bandit country' of South Armagh shortly after the IRA's assassination of Lord Mountbatten and murder of eighteen British soldiers (August 1979).

RIGHT: With Admiral Sir John Fieldhouse, navy chief, and surrounded by British troops on a surprise visit to the Falklands (January 1983).

BELOW LEFT: On a visit to India, Denis in tow, sharing a sunshade with Indira Gandhi (April 1981).

BELOW RIGHT: The 'Battle of Orgreave', during the violent 1984–5 miners' strike.

ABOVE: The Thatchers' bathroom in the Grand Hotel, Brighton, wrecked by the IRA bomb of 12 October 1984.

RIGHT: The devastated hotel.

BELOW: Accompanied by 'Crawfie' (Cynthia Crawford), the Thatchers are driven away to safety – though the Prime Minister would insist on returning next day to continue the conference.

ABOVE: Joviality – after an early meeting with Chancellor Helmut Schmidt (May 1979).

RIGHT: A touch of frost – with Chancellor Helmut Kohl at a press conference (February 1988).

LEFT: Doing business – with President Mikhail Gorbachev on his stopover at Brize Norton (December 1987).

BELOW: Comrades – with Lech Wałęsa, Solidarity leader, at Gdansk, Poland (1988).

Top: At the 1984 G7 summit in London: from the left, Gaston Thorn (EEC), Yasuhiro Nakasone (Japan), Pierre Trudeau (Canada) Ronald Reagan (US), MT, François Mitterrand (France), Helmut Kohl (Germany), Bettino Craxi (Italy).

Above: Cordial – with Mitterrand, celebrating the signature of the Anglo-French treaty for the Channel Tunnel (1986).

Right: Unimpressed – at the inconclusive European Council in Stuttgart, alongside her new Foreign Secretary, Howe (1983).

Top left: First visit to Washington DC as guest of the newly elected President Reagan (February 1981).

Above: With President George H. Bush at Camp David (November 1989).

Left: A very special relationship – farewell visit to Reagan (November 1988).

helpfully concluded that the NHS could potentially absorb the whole national income if it were allowed to do so.

Eventually, not least because of her difficulties during the campaign, she accepted that something far-reaching had to be done to change the structure of the NHS. Various radical options were discarded along the way, not just because of her own caution, but because the Department of Health's officials were unenthusiastic. It did not help that the main proponent of change, John Moore, the new Health Secretary, was ill and below par for much of the time. But that said, the final package – implemented by Kenneth Clarke after Moore's removal – was bold, given the prevailing political climate. The main features were that hospitals were offered the chance to be self-governing; that the Government (in the form of district health authorities) would become the buyer but not the provider of health care; that money should follow the patient rather than be allocated by administrative fiat; and that general practitioners could acquire practice budgets to purchase care on behalf of patients. This approach, the creation of an 'internal market', was attacked by the Labour Party in opposition and partly reversed by Labour in government. Like the education reforms, it is now widely seen as providing the model for NHS reform – though the Coalition Government's U-turn on its proposed radical changes illustrates how treacherous the political territory remains.

In her last months in office, Mrs Thatcher was becoming more open to further change in the health service. She was attracted by the notion of what amounted to a health voucher, which would allow anyone waiting for hospital treatment from the NHS for more than a stipulated period to use the money in the private sector. Fifteen years later, Tony Blair began publicly to toy with the same idea.

This examination of the reforms of the Thatcher years has led the discussion into areas where outcomes cannot be judged on economic criteria alone. Indeed, of the Thatcher Government's housing, education and health reforms, only the first two can be said to have had real economic significance, and then only marginally. And it

is on economic grounds that supply-side policies must primarily be judged.

The extent to which Mrs Thatcher's Government achieved its proclaimed goal of reversing Britain's relative economic decline had been obscured when she left office by the effects of the Lawson boom and by the incipient recession. On the one hand, some of the recent growth was unsustainable. On the other, some of the problems – higher inflation and rising unemployment – looked more intract- able than they in fact were. It was also difficult for objective analysts to allow for and discount the effects of the economic cycle. With the passing of time, however, the evidence is easier to assess, and any fair assessment made today must surely be overwhelmingly positive.

The concept of reversing relative economic decline against which the Thatcher Government chose to be judged is in some respects not a very useful one. Like the concept of 'competitiveness', it treats economic advance as a zero-sum game in which one player's success is tantamount to another's failure. What actually matters to a nation is whether it is getting richer, and at what rate. That said, consciousness of decline was not misplaced. It was understandable that newly industrializing countries in the early twentieth century, and devastated countries after the Second World War, should enjoy higher rates of growth than Britain. But all that had long ceased to be a credible excuse for British failures by the time Mrs Thatcher entered Downing Street.[14]

The obvious measure of a country's economic performance is the growth of its GDP. And here Mrs Thatcher's achievement is not in doubt. Comparing cycle with cycle, between 1973 and 1979 Britain's (non-oil) GDP grew by less than 1 per cent a year, but in the 1980s it grew by 2.25 per cent a year. This was contrary to the international trend. The OECD countries (in other words, the developed economies) as a whole experienced no improvement in growth during that period. The contrast became still more marked, and still less deniable, after Mrs Thatcher left office.[15]

At the root of that improvement has been growth in productivity.

During the Thatcher years British productivity saw both absolute and relative improvement. It was concentrated in manufacturing, and since manufacturing industry's share of total GDP continued to shrink (as in other advanced economies), the effect on the economy as a whole was less marked. But the overall improvement was real and it has been sustained. Using the measure of 'total factor productivity' (the productivity of all inputs involved in producing the business sector's added value), Britain's performance has been transformed. Between the periods 1960–73 and 1979–94, Britain leaped from twelfth to fifth place in the league of OECD nations.[16]

The two blots on Mrs Thatcher's record are inflation and unemployment. But, then, Britain had its own particular, entrenched problems in respect of both. Inflation was first mastered and then, when it was allowed to resume, brought firmly back under control. Unemployment was in large part, though not entirely, the result of concealed overmanning, and from 1986 it too fell swiftly. But it is in the relationship between the two – and the role of supply-side policies – that the Thatcher Government broke the mould. Rejecting any idea of a trade-off between inflation and unemployment, and putting its faith in micro-economic, structural changes within a stable financial environment, Mrs Thatcher's Government permanently altered the terms of economic debate.[17] She refused to be beguiled by the unemployment figure and concentrated instead on creating the conditions for fuller employment. The result was an increase of 1.5 million in the number of jobs (including an increase of 75 per cent in the number of self-employed).

Although she hated such jargon, she tacitly adopted from American monetarists the concept of the non-accelerating inflation rate of unemployment (or NAIRU, otherwise even less attractively called the 'natural rate'). This is the level below which, given the structural features of the economy, any attempt to bring down unemployment by increasing aggregate demand must lead to higher wage inflation rather than to more jobs. Mrs Thatcher's supply-side changes brought down that level – and permanently so, unless any

future government is foolish enough to reverse them. Despite current difficulties, Britain can therefore expect to enjoy in the longer term a lower level of unemployment, with low and stable inflation, than can its main European competitors, because of the reforms she and her colleagues made.[18]

To all of which there is, of course, the riposte: But was it worth it? The doubters have become more vocal in the wake of recent massive government interventions in the banking system to cope with the consequences of imprudent lending. As a result, capitalism's reputation has been damaged; Keynes's has been restored; and the critics of Thatcherism now claim belated vindication. But despite the panics and histrionics, the evidence has not really changed and neither should the conclusions. Free enterprise does not guarantee continuing prosperity; but it does permit it, whereas the alternatives do not. Capitalism certainly does not preclude crises, of which the Thatcher years saw several. The triumph of free markets does not mean the end of economic adjustment, any more than the triumph of democracy meant the 'end of History'.[19] Not everyone understood this, but Mrs Thatcher did. Gordon Brown, not she, claimed to have ended the business cycle of 'boom and bust'. Similarly, no informed exponent of free enterprise capitalism has ever doubted the scope for human error to have catastrophic consequences, particularly when the monetary and regulatory authorities are complacent – as they have been. Margaret Thatcher herself not only loudly and indignantly decried irresponsible borrowing and lending: her private and public expositions of her approach stressed with tedious regularity that unbridled free markets were never part of the system and that government always had a role. But this role, she added, was limited to providing a framework within which private individuals and businesses operate freely. It is, of course, perfectly possible in theory for Britain to reject that model, to revert to a state-controlled economy, and to regress to a collectivized society. But reflection on the events described in these pages

should induce a lively fear of doing so. And it almost certainly will not happen.

That, though, is not the end of the matter. There is a more enduring, if less currently topical, criticism of the Thatcher years. This amounts to a rejection of the whole Thatcher project from first principles as being misguidedly materialistic. In a word, were the social costs greater than the economic gains? Mrs Thatcher herself entertained no such doubts, and again such evidence as exists tends to support her judgement – as will be discussed in the concluding chapter of this book.*

* See pp. 436–8.

12

COLD WARRIOR

The friendly collaboration of Britain and America under Margaret Thatcher and Ronald Reagan is rightly seen as crucial to the outcome of the Cold War. With Pope John Paul II, these two leaders advocated and applied policies that helped bring Soviet communism down.* But Mrs Thatcher's views and actions during these years have also to be seen in the light of British domestic considerations. These were by no means the same as those pertaining in Washington. That was true during the Reagan years; it was truer still during the presidency of George Bush Senior; and it was truest of all when Jimmy Carter was President, as he was when Margaret Thatcher entered Downing Street.

Jimmy Carter and Margaret Thatcher had, in fact, already met, though there had hardly been a meeting of minds. Mrs Thatcher visited the United States as leader of the Opposition in 1977. From her point of view, the visit was successful. But there had been disagreements over nuclear weapons – Carter wanted a Nuclear

---

* The best account of the common purpose and collaboration of these three is that of John O'Sullivan, *The President, the Pope and the Prime Minister* (Washington DC: Regnery, 2006).

Test Ban Treaty – and over Rhodesia. Above all, it was felt in Washington that she was not sufficiently deferential.[1] This is confirmed by the presidential briefing prepared by Zbigniew Brzezinski, Carter's National Security Advisor, shortly after Margaret Thatcher became Prime Minister. It refers to 'her hard-driving nature and her tendency to hector', though Brzezinski, who was in fact well disposed to the visitor, commented on her 'courage and discipline' and concluded: 'We can work with her.'[2] This was, indeed, true, because her warm feelings for America always out-weighed her less warm feelings for Carter. She knew, of course, that he had been close to Callaghan. And while in her memoirs she claims that 'it was impossible not to like Jimmy Carter', it is also manifest that she did not respect him, which he doubtless grasped.[3]

In any case, by the time she made her first visit as Prime Minister in December 1979, with US hostages held by Iran, both America and Carter needed every friend they could find. Oddly, perhaps, she was initially unwilling to articulate her support for the United States in its predicament. She was, in truth, still too timid and too conscious of America's great power status to want to intrude; and she had toothache, which made her uncooperative. But, in the event, her instincts asserted themselves and she spoke out boldly to the press on the White House lawn, thus winning Carter's and, still more important, the despondent American nation's gratitude.[4]

The Iranian hostage crisis was not, though, the full extent of Carter's foreign problems. Later that month, Soviet forces invaded Afghanistan. This threw his proposals for arms control – above all the SALT II agreement – off the rails and effectively consigned détente to a siding.[5] Carter was not impressed by Mrs Thatcher's response to the crisis, particularly her failure to prevent the British team competing in the Moscow Olympics. He noted to Brzezinski: 'UK and other European reaction to SU/Afghan situation are [sic] very weak.'[6] This, it must be admitted, was no less than the truth. But it would take time, and different American leadership, to change it.

Mrs Thatcher was hugely fortunate that Ronald Reagan became President when he did. The two had so much in common. Like her, he was unashamedly and combatively conservative. Both were natural outsiders who had fought their way to the top. Both believed in the power of ideas. More important still, they liked each other – he particularly liked her. There is no great mystery why that should be so. He clearly thought her attractive, and he admired her intellect and courage. She, for her part, enjoyed the attention of a glamorous, albeit ageing, American ex-film star. She also admired his ability to express large and important ideas. She was particularly struck by the way in which he could articulate severe truths in a gentle manner – she knew that her own tendency was to do the opposite, and she fought against it, though with limited success. In fact, she so admired his ability to communicate that she had to be persuaded that commenting solely on this aspect of his statesmanship was not altogether flattering. Thus prompted, she would add that it was the substance of his message that mattered. But she did not instinctively feel this. And she intended no disrespect. Like other successful politicians, she had great professional esteem for those who possess the gift of convincing others. So Reagan's way of speaking, in private and in public, was the core of her regard for him. But, then, he himself always had the same priority – nothing mattered more to him than his speeches.[7]

Mrs Thatcher first encountered Reagan in 1969, as it were by proxy, through a speech delivered by the then Governor of California to the Institute of Directors. Denis heard it and gave her a glowing report, and she later read the text. Justin Dart, a member of Reagan's Californian entourage, then followed her subsequent career. It was he who suggested that Reagan come and see her shortly after she became leader of the Opposition, some six years later. The meeting overran, which was evidence of a genuine rapport, not mere diplomatic politeness – at the time he was just an ex-governor and no one, at least in Britain, imagined that he would ever become President. She knew at once, however, that she had

found someone who agreed with her about what she called 'the big things'. For his part, Reagan was entirely captivated. He wrote a warm letter of thanks, which contains the sort of language she found so powerful: 'I've chosen a dark day to write . . . The news has just arrived of Saigon's surrender and somehow the shadows seem to have lengthened.' He paid a further visit to London in November 1978. The meeting on this occasion lasted still longer and was even more successful, though mainly confined as before to the broad philosophical points which came most easily to him. Later, when Margaret Thatcher won the 1979 general election, he telephoned Downing Street to offer his congratulations. But he was not put through till the following day. Officials did not think he was sufficiently important. Only when the omission was brought to Mrs Thatcher's attention did they learn otherwise.[8] So even before he became President, she had begun to feel towards Reagan an affinity – a personal and political closeness – that she would enjoy with no other politician, perhaps not even with Keith Joseph.

Events would confirm her perception of Reagan's unique genius. In November the following year, this most underrated of politicians was elected in a conservative landslide. Margaret Thatcher understood the opportunities this opened up and was personally delighted. She was even more pleased when she learned that he insisted that she be the first major head of government to visit him after his inauguration in Washington. The circumstances of the visit, in February 1981, were in one sense unpropitious. Mrs Thatcher was very unpopular at home. Britain was deep in recession. Her economic strategy seemed to be failing. Reagan's advisers were keen to distance his approach from hers – and would be even keener after the forthcoming British tax increases in that year's Budget. But neither now nor later was the President willing to treat her as anything other than a friend who was pursuing similar policies to his own. This should be remembered when her own loyalty to him on many later occasions is described. The visit was a triumph. She even found an opportunity for some ballroom dancing: nowadays

few dared ask her on to the floor. Her speeches went down well, too. She spoke at one point, on a theme originally suggested by Airey Neave, about the courage required to face up to responsibilities at the 'lonely hour' of 2.00 a.m. The President, who one imagines had little personal experience of that, was deeply moved.[9]

The practical consequences of all this personal sympathy, real as it was, can, however, be exaggerated. Considerations of mutual national interest remained at the basis of the UK–US relationship, and this is clearly shown by the continuity of British dealings across the Carter and Reagan Administrations. The most important instance of positive collaboration between the two countries was in the provision of Trident. Ever since Kennedy's reluctant agreement to provide Macmillan with Polaris, British dependence upon the United States for its independent nuclear deterrent was the key strategic tie between the two nations. (The sharing of intelligence was – and is – by a short head the second most important.)[10] Carter and his Defense Secretary Harold Brown had shown no reluctance to supply Mrs Thatcher with a replacement for Polaris, in the form of the Trident I (C4) submarine-based system – despite the complications the decision presented for Carter's prized (though doomed) SALT II. One of the early decisions of the Reagan Administration was to switch to the more advanced Trident II (D5) missile. There was not much doubt that the British would have to follow suit. The political opposition was not likely to be significantly greater. But the cost might be. At this point, Reagan's strong personal support for Britain did become a factor. US negotiators knew that there was no point in holding out on some tricky point, because an appeal to the President would go in Mrs Thatcher's favour. That said, whoever had been in the White House, Britain would still have got Trident.

On the debit side, there was also early continuity in areas of disagreement. Just as Carter thought the British feeble over Afghanistan, Reagan found them obstructive over America's response to the 1981 Polish crisis. The United States wished to apply sanctions to the Soviet Union in the wake of General

Jaruzelski's imposition of martial law in Poland that December. The Americans saw Jaruzelski as a surrogate for the Soviet Union and his coup as a means of crushing home-grown Polish opposition to communism without the embarrassment of a full-scale Soviet intervention. The British, though, preferred to see the new regime as something authentically Polish, albeit repressive, and so argued that Moscow should not be singled out for punishment. In this the Foreign Office was wholly incorrect, and the Americans were right. Mrs Thatcher, too, was wrong. But in its reaction, Washington was counter-productively ham-fisted. The Administration unilaterally imposed a ban on the export of material for the construction of the planned natural gas pipelines linking Europe and Siberia. These contracts represented big business for European companies, and the British engineering giant John Brown was particularly badly affected. Mrs Thatcher was furious and her anger boiled over when she learned the following June that, despite much lobbying and various assurances, the United States was applying the ban to foreign companies manufacturing American-designed components under licence. Britain now retaliated with the Protection of Trading Interests Act. Justifying her position, Mrs Thatcher used some of the strongest anti-American rhetoric she ever employed, complaining of bullying by a more powerful country of its allies. It was left to the next Secretary of State, George Shultz, who unlike Haig enjoyed the President's confidence, to smooth matters out. A compromise was reached that November. Mrs Thatcher had acted throughout as a British Prime Minister putting British national interests first – indeed, much as any other British leader would have done in the circumstances. But she hardly covered herself with glory as a Cold Warrior in the face of Soviet-backed aggression in Eastern Europe.*

---

* Mrs Thatcher states her case more fully in *The Downing Street Years*, pp. 251–6. The documentation used by John O'Sullivan demonstrates that the FCO analysis of Polish affairs was wide of the mark (O'Sullivan, *The President, the Pope and the Prime Minister*, pp. 130–5). The question of whether Mrs Thatcher would have acted differently if she had known the truth is now unanswerable.

Her stance reflected her instinctive nationalist priorities, which those viewing events from an exclusively Cold War perspective are inclined to overlook.

It might be thought, and it certainly was thought by many in Washington, that Margaret Thatcher's willingness to bend to American wishes would have increased as a result of the support she received during the Falklands War. In material terms this assistance had been real and important, though not vital.[11] But this is not at all how the situation looked from her angle. She was, of course, grateful to Weinberger personally. But, like most of her compatriots, she also felt that Britain had deserved better from the beginning. She could not forget the pressure Reagan and Haig placed on her to settle on terms that would have left the Falklands in Argentine hands and probably made her own position untenable. The notion that she felt grateful and was thus to become 'an effective partner in the long Cold War battles that lay ahead' is misconceived.* In fact, what she saw as America's culpable equivocation in Britain's – and her – darkest hour made her even less cooperative whenever the Reagan Administration failed to take her views into account. If she was a more effective partner for Reagan after 1982, this is because the Falklands War made her more self-confident, not because it made her more pro-American.

That assessment is amply borne out by the Anglo-American quarrel over Grenada. The incident had many of the characteristics of the rift over Poland and the Siberian pipeline – poor intelligence and flawed advice from the Foreign Office, bad handling by the US Administration, and a large amount of injured pride and resentment from Mrs Thatcher. But while the noise of the disagreement was louder, the substance of the dispute was actually less than that over Poland. This, indeed, is what makes it look so ridiculous today. Margaret Thatcher, though, did not think it small beer at all. Years

---

* The quotation is from John O'Sullivan, who seems to me to be too inclined at this point to press his overall thesis of Thatcher–Reagan collaboration (O'Sullivan, *The President, the Pope and the Prime Minister*, p. 161).

later, when her enthusiasm for all things American and everything connected with Ronald Reagan knew no bounds, she was still not prepared to say that she had been wrong. She also at that time revealed the root cause of her anger. She felt that the decision to invade what she insisted on calling 'the Queen's Island' (Grenada) was a political reaction to the US humiliation in Lebanon. In this, at least, she was demonstrably wrong. Reagan had given the order to go ahead with the invasion some hours before he learned of the death of 242 US servicemen at the hands of a suicide bomber.[12]

It was easy enough to find reasons to justify opposition to the US invasion of the island, and the British duly found them. It was not at all obvious that the violent coup (on 19 October 1983) which brought one band of Marxist desperadoes to power – and which precipitated the action – was inherently different from that (in 1979) which had brought in the Marxists they now displaced. The Americans also played fast and loose with the facts surrounding the request made for their intervention – though the support of Organization of East Caribbean States for it was real enough. Finally, it was a sensitive time, on the eve of the deployment of cruise missiles. Any sign that the United States was throwing its weight around provided material for the peace campaigners. Yet, when all is said, Mrs Thatcher should have understood that America could not permit a second, albeit pint-sized, Cuba acting as a Soviet surrogate in its own backyard. She should also have grasped the flaws in the Foreign Office's briefing, which based its claim that no danger was posed by the major work on Grenada's airport – allowing it to act as a staging post for the real Cuba's intervention in the region – on the fact that the Soviet Union itself had shown no interest in it. Any US analyst would have known that all significant initiatives from Moscow in South America were channelled through Havana. In fact, both over Lebanon – where Britain played a dangerously semi-detached role, even though it contributed troops to the American-led force – and over Grenada, Mrs Thatcher's reactions were again exactly those that would

be expected of any British Prime Minister. In Lebanon, she was pro-Druze and pro-Syrian, while the Americans were pro-Christian and sympathetic to Israel. In Grenada, she was more emotionally committed to the tenuous Commonwealth link (and worried about real Commonwealth headaches) than she was concerned with Cold War geopolitics. And, of course, she was particularly incensed by what, despite Reagan's subsequent disavowal, was a deliberate decision not to inform, let alone consult, her until it was all too late. The US intervention in Lebanon failed. By contrast, Grenada is now a stable, prosperous island. That, though, is no thanks to the British, nor to Margaret Thatcher.

The Thatcher–Reagan relationship survived the Grenada imbroglio. The President telephoned her during a stormy debate on the subject in the House of Commons, but he managed to still any recriminations on her part by beginning:

'If I were there, Margaret, I'd throw my hat in the door before I came in.'

To which she replied: 'There's no need to do that.'

He finished the conversation with: 'Go get 'em. Eat 'em alive.'

And this she more or less did.

Mrs Thatcher's worries about the effect of the Grenada episode on public attitudes to cruise deployment proved exaggerated. That operation went ahead smoothly enough, in November 1983, as planned. Her concerns about the precedent set for invading other people's countries and disregarding (that emerging Thatcher obsession) the 'rule of law' did not convince many others either – certainly none who shared her general political outlook. She did not repent, but she did now shut up.[13]

She seems also to have learned some lessons about what could and could not be achieved in relations with Reagan, at least to judge by the way in which she reacted to the Libyan crisis of April 1986 – with which Grenada may properly be compared. It would have been easy to go down the same route of opposition to US plans. But she did not.

True, the stakes were higher, because international terrorism was the issue. The facts were also clearer. American and British intelligence confirmed that Colonel Qadhafi, the Libyan leader, was sponsoring terrorist violence – bombs in Rome and Vienna airports in December 1985 and, crucially, a bomb in a West Berlin nightclub on 5 April 1986. The shooting of a British policewoman by a sniper from within the so-called Libyan People's Bureau in London in 1984 had not been forgotten either.*

On the other hand, Mrs Thatcher's position at Westminster was very precarious. Her standing had been gravely damaged by the Westland crisis.† There was a strong mood of anti-Americanism in the country. So when, in a message on the night of Tuesday 8 April, Reagan informed her of his plans to launch air strikes against Libya and requested her support for the use of the American F-111s based in Britain, her first reaction was ice-cool. The Defence Secretary, George Younger, was broadly sympathetic to the US request. But he was a new appointment and not a political heavyweight. Geoffrey Howe and the Foreign Office were wholly opposed. The detailed questions now asked by the British side had two purposes. One was to ensure that the Americans had thought through the implications of their action and had refined the targets to reduce the human – and the political – collateral cost. The other was to function simply as a delaying tactic. Yet Reagan persisted. So, with a heavy heart, knowing just what would face her, expecting that something would probably go wrong – as it did; the US targets were far from well defined in practice – Mrs Thatcher lent her support. She proceeded to defend herself in the House of Commons

---

* I was special adviser at the Home Office at this juncture. The murder weapon had, we believed, been secreted in the Libyan diplomatic bag. But opening it would have infringed a long-established international convention of which Britain, like other states, makes various uses which it would not like to have exposed. The only available loophole was to argue that the Libyan 'People's Bureau' did not have full diplomatic status. In the event, *raison d'état* prevailed, the bag was duly dispatched intact and the suspect escaped. For what it is worth, I still consider this the wrong decision.

† See pp. 281–5.

against heavy Tory as well as Opposition criticism and widespread public disapproval. She took her decision because she knew that Britain would never be forgiven by the United States if she refused to cooperate. This made her a heroine for the Americans – not least because her conduct was in marked contrast to the obstruction they faced from other Europeans. (Characteristically, Mitterrand refused the Americans permission to use French airspace, but at the same time urged a heavy attack, not a mere 'pin prick'.)[14] Mrs Thatcher received her reward. She now gained more leverage with the US Administration than any British Prime Minister since Churchill – a leverage which, unlike her successor but one, Tony Blair, she put to effective use.*

Of course, Grenada and even Libya were sideshows when compared with the changes occurring in the overall balance of power between the West and the Soviet Union. Already, the Reagan military build-up was having an effect on Soviet behaviour. In Moscow there was a clear understanding that the Soviet economy, which was far weaker than Western analysts imagined, could not withstand the pressure of a new arms race. Both economic reform and some kind of understanding on weaponry were increasingly seen as essential. This emerging realism led first to the rise of Andropov to succeed Brezhnev and then – after the interval of the non-leader Chernenko – to the emergence of Andropov's protégé, Gorbachev.[15]

Reagan had a number of blind spots. But his insight into the realities of the Soviet Union made up for them. He knew precisely what he was doing with his strategy of piling on the pressure. A revealing but infrequently noticed discussion between him and Mrs Thatcher in September 1983, described in her memoirs, helps

---

* The success of the raid on Libya was both direct and indirect. At least until the downing of a US passenger aircraft in 1988 over Lockerbie with the loss of 289 lives (an atrocity for which, it was initially suggested, Syria rather than Libya was responsible), Libya was intimidated into refraining from the sponsorship of international terrorism. Indirectly, the message to other rogue powers tempted to act against US interests was equally clear: they did so at their peril.

confirm this. He told her then that the Soviet Union, because of its internal difficulties, could not increase its military spending, but that America could double its military output with ease. It also reveals his consciousness of the need to take account of Soviet paranoia. This, after all, is the period when, according to the highly placed Soviet defector Oleg Gordievsky, Moscow was seriously expecting an American nuclear strike.[16]

Mrs Thatcher shared some but not all of Reagan's approach. Although she believed in strong defence, she never subscribed wholly – at least, other than in retrospect – to the goal of outright American military superiority.* She was accordingly more concerned than Reagan with having stable and predictable relations with the Soviet leaders. While she believed that the Soviet Empire would ultimately collapse because communism was fundamentally unworkable, she did not share Reagan's view of its current weakness. The limited figures available at the time suggested that she, not he, was right, though in fact the figures were all wrong, as was subsequently shown. What both of them were prepared to accept – she with somewhat greater alacrity – was that someone might emerge from the Soviet system who could set about reforming it. This was something that hawks in both the United States and Europe were generally unwilling to acknowledge.

Mrs Thatcher was, though, with the Cold War hawks on one other matter as close to Reagan's heart as any other: the Strategic Defense Initiative (SDI), baptized 'Star Wars'. Reagan announced the programme to an astonished world – his own Defense Secretary Caspar Weinberger shared some of the astonishment – in a speech in March 1983. Margaret Thatcher's subsequent role in the politics of its development was crucial and unique. She had a good basic knowledge of the technological potential, especially that of space-based lasers, and unlike most other politicians she had the scientific

* Thus, despite her earlier views when in opposition, she favoured the ratification of SALT II, and when that became impossible it remained British policy to urge the Americans to stay within its limits – a policy which, predictably, failed.

mind that enabled her to make sense of what she read. (The head of the SDI programme, General Abrahamson, once remarked that she was the only politician he had met who did so.) This understanding would later make her a strong advocate of ballistic missile defence systems, a technical offshoot of the SDI programme.

But she also had serious doubts at the time, even more serious than she ever allowed Reagan himself to perceive. Her objections were several. The first was the traditional one that all the believers in deterrence entertained: to decrease the likelihood of an effective nuclear strike, as the defensive shield envisaged by SDI would, was to render deterrence less reliable and thus war – conventional or nuclear – more likely. Her worries on this score never disappeared entirely.* But, on probing, she found that the Americans had some good answers and, acknowledging the fact that Reagan would never drop the scheme altogether, she did not press the point. Instead, she concentrated on the fact that the Soviet Union was already equipped with its own anti-ballistic missile system around Moscow and that it was cheating on the Anti-Ballistic Missile (ABM) treaty with its Krasnoyarsk radar system. America was, therefore, just 'catching up'. In any case, she recognized that the extreme doctrine of nuclear deterrence known as MAD (mutually assured destruction) had already been modified significantly by NATO's then current doctrine of 'flexible response'. Above all, as long as it could be fitted within some credible interpretation of the ABM treaty (and there turned out to be quite a lot of scope for such interpretation), she saw SDI as putting the sort of pressure on the Soviet regime that was central to Reagan's strategy. It was this factor, above all, which by the late 1980s made her more enthusiastic about the programme. Of course, the basis of her enthusiasm was still very different from Reagan's.

Her second worry, which was more fundamental, stemmed from her conviction that SDI could never offer a complete shield. It

---

* She was still arguing the case, though not very forcefully, in Washington in February 1985.

could, therefore, never be a substitute for nuclear weapons. She was careful in what she said to American officials, and more careful still in what she said to Reagan, but in private she was contemptuous. She thought that the President simply did not understand how easy it was to get a ballistic missile through even the most sophisticated defence. She was particularly struck by the possibilities of the so-called MIRV technology – which Trident II and its Soviet equivalents employed.* She would demonstrate the effects with her hands, twisting them round in mid-air to show how complicated was the flight path of the missiles. She considered that Reagan's military advisers were weak in allowing him to continue to entertain illusions of invulnerability.†

Her third objection was to Reagan's vision of SDI as permitting a nuclear-weapons-free world. Mrs Thatcher did not, in fact, want such a world, shocking as that may seem to those who have not thought about the matter very seriously. She believed that nuclear weapons had kept the West free of war, conventional as well as nuclear, since the balance of terror was first created in the 1950s. She was impatient with people who claimed that this state of affairs was immoral. She was particularly grateful when Christian intel-lectuals, such as Michael Quinlan, Permanent Secretary of the MoD, lent their support to her cause. But, in the end, she thought that morality should bend to practicality.

The other point she would make in any discussion of the desir-ability of a nuclear-weapons-free world was that nuclear weapons – like any technology – could not (as she put it) 'be disinvented'. No matter how many agreements were made, no matter how rigorously the conduct of the parties was subject to verification, someone somewhere would have the technology and in the end someone

* MIRV: multiple independently targeted re-entry vehicles.
† I first encountered these arguments forcefully expressed by Mrs Thatcher – including illustrative hand movements – when I was involved in drafting her speech to both Houses of Congress in February 1985. I was – and remain – convinced by her exposition of both the doctrines and the technicalities, which, indeed, I never heard bettered.

somewhere would be tempted to use it. Not only was she right then: her arguments look even more far-sighted now, when the possibility of Islamic extremists or rogue or failing states using nuclear devices is a constant preoccupation.

Finally, there was the matter of money. Only the West's strength in nuclear weaponry allowed Europe to be defended by NATO troops in numbers so inferior to those of the Warsaw Pact. When Mrs Thatcher confronted Reagan with this point he did not blink: he merely accepted that much more would have to be spent by the West on its defence if only conventional forces were envisaged.[17] This, though, was hardly a politically acceptable option, at least in Europe.

In general, she showed remarkable self-control in these circumstances. Having expected that with Reagan in the White House the one thing she would not have to bother about was a sell-out of Western interests, she now feared that the whole basis of Western security would be undermined. But, thanks to support within the Administration, she won some half-victories. At Camp David in December 1984 she demonstrated in virtuoso fashion her ability to get her way. She persuaded the President to sign up to a four-point statement which was drafted by her own officials and largely reflected British rather than American thinking. It stated that the West's strategic aim was to attain balance, not military superiority. It said that deployment (though not 'research', as originally drafted – even the Americans resisted that British ploy) could go ahead only by negotiation. It contradicted Reagan's thinking by affirming that SDI would enhance, not undermine, deterrence. It blandly confirmed the desire to reduce each side's offensive weapons.[18] It was, in fact, a bounce, and perhaps too blatant. It made for good headlines for Mrs Thatcher and briefly settled NATO nerves, but it had no discernible effect on Reagan's real position.

She was more effective in smoothing the way to better relations between Reagan and the Soviet leadership. In her memoirs, Mrs Thatcher claims that her discovery of Mikhail Gorbachev was the

result of deliberation, not just of happenstance. As she puts it: 'I spotted [Mr Gorbachev] because I was searching for someone like him.'[19] And it is true that she had held a seminar in 1983 precisely to try to assess who were the coming men in the next generation of Soviet politicians. As a result, invitations to visit Britain were sent out to three figures – V. V. Grishin, Grigory Romanov and a certain Mikhail Gorbachev. Only the last accepted. This is all accurate as it stands; but it is not the whole truth. The Thatcher–Gorbachev relationship, even more than the Thatcher–Reagan relationship, was from the first a matter as much of chemistry as of calculation. And whereas, with Thatcher and Reagan, he was probably more attracted to her than she by him, with Gorbachev and Thatcher she was the more taken. What the Soviet and British leaders had in common was not, obviously, their views. Rather, it was their enjoyment of an argument and their way of conducting it – at length, with animation, without much attention to what the other party said and without personal ill-feeling. In the end, Gorbachev gained more from Mrs Thatcher than she from him; he knew it; and he was grateful. He rightly felt that she had spotted him before he came to the top of the pile. He knew how much her endorsement had counted with Reagan – to whom he also remained grateful.

Mikhail Gorbachev paid his first visit to Britain in December 1984.[20] He brought with him his lively and elegant wife Raisa, of whom his hostess at Chequers quickly formed a high opinion. Mrs Thatcher knew something of what to expect when she met Gorbachev for the first time. She had received separately from Pierre Trudeau, the Canadian Prime Minister, and Peter Walker the assessment that Gorbachev was 'different'. The formal accounts of the ensuing discussions at Chequers reveal little of their impact. Gorbachev's views, now and later, were not notably different from those of standard agitprop. It was his way of expressing them that marked him out. There was pleasant enough discussion over lunch, though it was slightly stilted because of the presence of Mrs Thatcher's colleagues: Geoffrey Howe, Michael Jopling and

Michael Heseltine, among others. Only later, in a one-to-one discussion with just a pair of note-takers and a translator and over several hours, did she fully take his measure. He was energetic, lively, capable of earthy humour and spontaneous anger, and quite able to keep his end up without hesitation or circumlocution. Above all, he had the sort of charismatic eloquence which Western politicians admire and which they associate – often wrongly – with the spirit of democracy. (By all accounts, Stalin was quite a talker too.)[21]

Mrs Thatcher subsequently delivered a glowing account of Gorbachev's virtues to Reagan. Her recommendation was crucial in winning over the American President and his advisers to the idea that this was a man with whom the West (as she put it) 'could do business'. In one sense, she was too successful. Once the two superpower leaders had established, at their talks in Geneva in November 1985, that they could indeed do business, her importance inevitably waned. Moreover, she understood the risk that Gorbachev might skilfully play on Reagan's idiosyncratic views about nuclear weapons. This is precisely what happened at the Reykjavik summit in October 1986.

Margaret Thatcher was profoundly shocked by what transpired there – and the shock never quite faded. If anything, the accounts now available of the discussions between Reagan and Gorbachev and their advisers show that she was right – as she later put it – to feel that 'the ground had moved' beneath her feet. The Americans, without any consultation with their allies, had been prepared to offer within ten years the abolition not only of offensive ballistic missiles, or even of strategic nuclear weapons, but of *all* nuclear weapons. Far from being the personal whim of the American President, this line was sanctioned by his seasoned Secretary of State, George Shultz. It would have meant the end of Britain's independent nuclear deterrent. It would have given the Warsaw Pact a huge military advantage over the West, because of the communist bloc's superiority in conventional forces. The risk of conventional war would have returned to Europe. In exchange, Reagan would be

allowed to continue researching SDI with (what seemed to Mrs Thatcher) the bizarre objective of then allowing the Soviet Union free access to the technology. Had Gorbachev played his cards better, had he not insisted (against, it seems, military advice) on confining SDI to the laboratory rather than permitting some testing, the outcome of the Cold War might have been different.

Against this view, one can argue that Reagan would never have won the support of the Senate for ratification of such a deal.[22] But Mrs Thatcher could hardly count on that. In any case, she felt that it was now up to her to rescue the West's unity and security, and she rapidly decided to go to the United States. Once again she dominated discussion with the President, and she achieved everything she could reasonably have hoped. In the statement issued afterwards the West's public goals reverted to the elimination of intermediate-range nuclear weapons (INF), a 50 per cent cut in US and Soviet (explicitly excluding British) strategic offensive weapons, and a chemical weapons ban – all of which she could live with. In exchange, Reagan obtained what he was most determined to have: the 'SDI research programme', ambiguously qualified with the phrase 'which is permitted by the ABM treaty'. In any case, he was going ahead with it whatever any treaty said, or whatever Gorbachev or, for that matter, Mrs Thatcher thought.[23]

Reagan's problems now lay not in external but in domestic politics. His Administration was giving every sign of unravelling, as the 'Iran-gate' scandal (the deal whereby arms were offered to Iran in exchange for Middle East hostages) gripped Washington's imagination. Margaret Thatcher was distressed by the humiliation she saw her old friend undergoing. She wrote him a personal letter that December: 'Whatever happened over Iran is in the past and nothing can change it. I fervently believe that the message *now* should be that there is important work to be done and that *you* are going to do it.'[24] Nor did she confine her support to private channels. Her stout defence on American television of Reagan's integrity won

her the unique tribute of being invited by the President to listen to his Cabinet applauding her over the telephone.

Reagan's political weakness in the wake of Iran-gate reinforced Mrs Thatcher's stature as the most effective spokesman for the West. Yet it was still a risky decision to visit the Soviet Union, as she resolved to do on the eve of the British general election of 1987. She had been harsh in her public criticism before her visit, complaining to her Conservative Party audience that in the USSR people were still imprisoned for their beliefs, that Soviet Jews were still forbidden to emigrate to Israel, and that Soviet forces were still in Afghanistan. On her arrival, Gorbachev took her to task, but he then proceeded to allow her complete freedom to express her views. In particular, the Soviet state television interview, shown uncensored, in which she proceeded to demolish her communist-approved interviewers and tell the Russian people many home truths about their system, had a profoundly subversive effect. It was an initial instalment of what the Great Communicator himself would offer, when he too visited the Soviet Union in May 1988.[25]

In November that year Mrs Thatcher paid her most difficult and also most successful visit to a communist country, when she accepted an invitation from General Jaruzelski to come to Poland. It was successful, because it helped advance the legalization of the trade union movement Solidarity and free Polish elections, which in turn assisted the collapse of Soviet rule in Eastern Europe the following year. But it was also difficult – and she had to draw on her resources of experience and intuition to avoid what could have been a terrible blunder.

Poland at the time was faced by Solidarity-led strikes in the Gdansk shipyard, which the Government was threatening to close. The communists hoped to trap Mrs Thatcher into treating the situation as she would treat strikes in Britain's own highly subsidized nationalized industries. In theory, she might well have done this. But in the event she disobligingly refused. Instead, she went to the

heart of the matter, which in her view was not the application of market economics but rather the absence of political freedom. So while she advised the Solidarity leaders to enter into negotiations, she also urged the Government to recognize Solidarity for what it was – a legitimate movement demanding popular rights that were wrongly withheld. Her demeanour throughout – straight-talking but unhysterical, and saying the same to one group as to another – impressed all those with whom she dealt. And she gave both private and public support to the forces of anti-communism. The Poles never forgot what she had done for them: she was henceforth a heroine. The visit equally had a strong emotional impact on her. She had never before seen the combination of religious fervour and patriotism that she found in Poland. It reinforced her conviction that communism was, in Poland at least, reaching the end of the line. At a more personal level it seems to have given her a new insight into Roman Catholicism, whose fighting spirit was so different from that of the supine Orthodox stooges she had encountered on her Soviet visit the previous year.*

Both internally and externally, the Soviet Empire was by now collapsing. Gorbachev's decisions, intended to reinvigorate and restore the system, only accelerated its disintegration. At each step of the way in his unwitting political suicide mission he was encouraged by Mrs Thatcher. In December 1987 – after a brief but substantial discussion with her during a stopover at Brize Norton – the Soviet leader had joined Reagan in Washington to sign the INF Treaty, eliminating intermediate-range nuclear weapons from Europe. It represented a stark reversal of the Soviet position adopted at Reykjavik (no weapons deals unless SDI were confined to the laboratory). In February 1988 Gorbachev unilaterally announced that Soviet forces would withdraw from Afghanistan,

---

* Although the fact that her two main draftsmen – O'Sullivan and I – were both Catholics is not irrelevant to the outcome, it is noteworthy that she was happy in her memoirs to summarize the assessment of her political life in the context of a Polish Catholic mass (see Thatcher, *The Path to Power*, pp. 602–6).

beginning in May: and the last Soviet soldiers duly left in February 1989. The Soviet leader visited Britain in April 1989 and was warmly received. That September began the process, first in Hungary then in East Germany itself, which brought down the Berlin Wall. In November the Velvet Revolution commenced in Czechoslovakia. In Western capitals, amid first apprehension and then astonishment and relief, it was recognized that the Warsaw Pact countries were one by one achieving their freedom – and that, whether from weakness, prudence or forbearance, Gorbachev was doing nothing to stop it.

European and indeed global politics thus entered a period of change and great uncertainty. The automatic reaction in the West to such events was to welcome them. But Mrs Thatcher's welcome, though real, was also qualified. She thought (and often said) that the break-up of empires was always a time of danger. She did not believe that communism was going to be quickly or easily beaten: in this she was over-pessimistic. Nor did she consider that its demise would mean an end to global threats: in this she was correct. In her view, the world was constantly throwing up fresh challenges, and one mark of the statesman was to spot them early.

So she found herself out of step with the wave of euphoria that now swept the West. And matters were made much more difficult by the change in the White House, with whose new occupant she was also temperamentally out of step.

The question naturally arises whether her fortunes would have been different if Ronald Reagan had remained in power. The answer must be 'yes'. Reagan would probably have followed Mrs Thatcher's advice to support Gorbachev for fear of something worse, while being more enthusiastic about the rise of Yeltsin. He would not have shared her deep hostility to German reunification; but he would have handled her differently and better. He would certainly never have behaved like Bush in publicly snubbing her and downgrading the UK–US relationship.

George Bush, though self-consciously a gentleman, was rather

personal and petty. He was over-influenced by his wife, Barbara, whose sharp (and reciprocated) personal antipathy to Nancy Reagan was a factor in her (and so his) resentment of Margaret Thatcher, who was considered altogether too close to the Reagans. Bush was no more able than Reagan to keep up with Mrs Thatcher when she was in full flow. But whereas his predecessor would sit back and enjoy it – and often do the opposite to what she had advocated and he had placidly accepted – Bush became resentful and flustered. He was, in a word, jealous. She was undoubtedly the senior Western leader. He, the head of a superpower, was apparently expected – though actually she did not expect it – to take her instructions. But perhaps the most important complicating personal influence, because it was also political, was that of the new US Secretary of State James Baker. A fixer, a pragmatist, ambitious for himself and his President, Baker had no time for Margaret Thatcher at all. It was Baker who ensured that the US State Department reverted to its policy – temporarily halted by Reagan – of pressing for an ever more closely federated Europe, thus opposing the approach she advocated in her 1988 Bruges speech.*

Mrs Thatcher's caution about events in 1989–90 was, at a rational level, based upon worries about what might happen in Russia if Gorbachev were toppled. For this same reason she was not initially well disposed towards Boris Yeltsin. But she agreed to see him when he came to London in April 1990, recognized his qualities, and then found herself agreeing with his analysis more than with that of his rival. In particular, she agreed that much more power needed to be devolved to the Soviet republics. When she reported her favourable impressions to Bush, however, he was unconvinced. She also had a clearer idea than the President of the limits to what was acceptable in order to keep Gorbachev in power. Thus she refused point blank to accept Gorbachev's demand that the Baltic republics be denied their independence – and repeated that refusal at her last European

* See pp. 305–6.

Council in Rome. She was, it is true, in two minds about Ukraine. This led to some disappointment from her audiences in Kiev, when she visited in June 1990. But both international law and geopolitical fact justified her in making a clear distinction between the Baltics and the other Soviet republics. The internal strife which Ukraine has since encountered while steering a course between Russia and Europe testifies to the country's identity problem.

Where her realism, and indeed basic prudence, did desert her was on the 'German Question' (in that diplomatically taboo phrase). On this, one must simply admit that she was irrational. Attempts to change her outlook failed, to the extent that the conclusions of a seminar she held on the subject in March 1990 had to be reworked by Charles Powell to spare her blushes.[26] (He might have been better advised to try to change her mind; not that it would have been easy.) It is, though, important to understand what was and what was not sensible in her analysis, because there was indeed a German Question to be resolved.

Mrs Thatcher grasped that a reunited Germany would alter the balance of power in Europe, and to some extent outside it. So did President Mitterrand. The fact that she liked the French leader, and had felt close to him ever since his help during the Falklands War, caused her to place too much faith in him. In private talks with her in December 1989 and January 1990 Mitterrand was even more vociferous about Germany than she was. This, in turn, made her imprudent. According too much weight to historical precedent, she now thought that a reunited Germany would revert not just to assertiveness but ultimately to aggression, and she considered the most important task in refashioning post-Cold War security arrangements was to prevent that eventuality. Mitterrand, too, albeit in a cooler fashion, overestimated Germany. To its French neighbours, Germany's population and GDP seemed intimidatingly large and its potential clients in Central Europe worryingly numerous. Accordingly, Mitterrand was keen to tie Germany down within a politically united Europe. Realistic as he was – and as Mrs Thatcher

was not – about the impossibility of preventing German reunification *tout court*, he was unrealistic about the price France would have to pay for his strategy. The near-rejection of the Maastricht Treaty in 2002 and the absolute rejection of the European Constitution by French electors in 2005 showed that the French at large remain more aware of this price than do their political class.

If Mitterrand was to prove an unreliable ally for Mrs Thatcher in combating German reunification, Gorbachev was even worse – and predictably so. She should never have thought she could do a deal with him, and it is still not clear how far she was prepared to go in private to secure his help.* In any case, for a crumbling Soviet Union beset by its own huge internal problems, Germany was a secondary issue. It was also a tempting honey-pot, and the prospect of German aid was probably the decisive consideration in Gorbachev's about-turn on unification in February 1990.

The real objection to Mrs Thatcher's position was that her aims were mutually contradictory. She hoped to halt German reunification and the German dominance in Europe it would bring in its train. Yet she wanted an end to communism in Central and Eastern Europe; she could not come up with a satisfactory argument against democratic self-determination; and she could hardly deny the forces of patriotism and of freedom which brought down the Iron Curtain. On top of all that, there was nothing she could do to stop the Germans coalescing, and once the United States supported the process she could not even successfully influence the timetable. So she created a great deal of ill will for no political gain.

That said, if she was wrong about Germany, she was right about much else. And while Bush was right about Germany, he was wrong about nearly everything else – above all, he was wrong about Britain. It took the First Gulf War, however, to bring that home.

---

* See the account of their discussion in September 1989 given by O'Sullivan, who, doubtless correctly, surmises that what she said about not destabilizing communist Eastern Europe or the Warsaw Pact was distorted or misunderstood by her interlocutor (O'Sullivan, *The President, the Pope and the Prime Minister*, pp. 312–16).

Mrs Thatcher's conduct at this time, with her own fate in the balance at home, rescued the US–UK Special Relationship from the subordinate role to which Bush and Baker had consigned it. It was her final, crucial contribution to the Atlantic Alliance.

Bush won the Gulf War by relying on the military strength built up by Ronald Reagan and on Reagan's old friend and partner, Margaret Thatcher. Whether he would have 'wobbled' at the outset of the crisis remains unclear. In her memoirs Mrs Thatcher diplomatically denies it, and the only known use of the much-repeated phrase appears to have been in a later telephone conversation between her and the President on a secondary issue.[27] This does not, of course, rule out the possibility of her having said it to him earlier. In any case, the circumstance that she was in Aspen when Saddam Hussein invaded Kuwait was very fortunate. She was at once taken into the President's confidence and she boosted his resolve. She was the only one present who had sent troops into battle; she knew a great deal more than the others did about the Middle East and the Gulf; and, as always, she had the right practical, probing questions to ask. (The Americans would soon also find that their preferred 'partner in leadership', Germany, was something less than that.)

Margaret Thatcher played an important and almost wholly constructive role in winning the Cold War. And because from that victory, along with a number of problems, has come a great increase in human liberty, she must be accorded due credit. Yet it is important not to exaggerate her achievement, and she herself never did, even when flatterers tempted her to do so. She was convinced that the main credit should go to Ronald Reagan. She said this privately and also publicly, in office and even more forcefully out of office.* She regarded herself as a partner in Reagan's victory, rather than an independent element. In this she was largely correct. She was very

---

* She also thought that George Bush Senior was remiss in failing to give Reagan the credit he deserved (see the account of these arguments in Prague given in Thatcher, *Statecraft*, pp. 7–9).

independent-minded on some vital issues. But she never failed to accept Reagan's primacy.

In truth, Mrs Thatcher's partnership with Reagan was probably more important than she recognized. She acted as his constant supporter, and initially his mentor, at G7 and NATO summits, where he was often out of his depth. She provided him with mainly good advice – which he took – in dealing with the Soviet Union, and unimpeachably sound advice – which he did not take – in nuclear strategy. She was also, quite simply, a good personal friend when he badly needed friendship.

Her view of Reagan became still more favourable with the passing of the years. Her view of Gorbachev did not, partly because of new facts that emerged, and partly because she was later persuaded that she had taken too much of what he said at face value. From being a champion of reform and even a sympathizer with liberty, he became, in her eyes, someone who as a humane realist had seen that it was better for communism to lose peacefully. In fact, to judge from evidence of the lengths Gorbachev was prepared to go to maintain the integrity of the Soviet Union, resisting by violent means the Baltic breakaway, even this view now appears too favourable.[28]

Like Reagan, and unlike Bush, Margaret Thatcher was the ultimate Cold Warrior. This is not only because of what she did but because of what she thought and felt. Again like Reagan, and again unlike Bush, the Iron Lady had an ideological pedigree stretching from a time when such radically anti-communist thinking was rare and the political courage to enunciate it even rarer.

But there is another side to her statesmanship during these years. For Britain, unlike America, the Cold War was never the exclusive consideration in foreign policy. It is significant that the only war Britain fought while Margaret Thatcher was Prime Minister was one that arose as a residue from colonialism, not as an aspect of the East–West struggle. The same reality is borne out by a study of her foreign visits and preoccupations, as revealed in government papers

and as related in her memoirs. The Commonwealth was just as much of a headache as coping with Soviet threats, while Europe was in the end an even more painful affliction than the Commonwealth. Similarly, managing relations with the Republic of Ireland was often still more troublesome, because it was so intimately linked to British security.

Of course, there were Cold War aspects to each of these areas. The main source of Commonwealth quarrels was South Africa, and, as Reagan fully realized, it was necessary to ensure that such a strategically significant country should not fall into chaos. That was why he backed Mrs Thatcher's determination to resist economic sanctions.* Similarly, Western Europe's commitment to NATO was always an element in arguments about the direction in which the European Community should move. In Ireland, too, the American dimension could never be ignored. Reagan's forbearance, resisting all the Irish lobby's pressures upon him, was not the least of the favours he did Mrs Thatcher.

Yet once these interconnections are acknowledged, the fact remains that Britain's national interests were never – and were never seen by Mrs Thatcher as – synonymous with those of America. She could sharply condemn particular US policies. She could resile from (what seemed to Washington) Britain's Cold War obligations. She could, to George Bush's horror, even speculate about the possibilities of a close relationship with the Soviets to contain the Germans. (If anyone ever subscribed to Lord Ismay's witticism that NATO existed to keep 'the Americans in, the Russians out and the Germans down', it was Margaret Thatcher – though she would not have seen the humour.) In short, she was first and last a British patriot; and in her statesmanship, as in her personal life, for better and worse, everything else took second place. Like de Gaulle she had a 'certain idea' of her country, and this was what always ultimately drove her foreign policy.[29]

* See also pp. 359–60 for her dealings with South Africa.

13

SKIES DARKEN

The events leading to Margaret Thatcher's resignation as Prime Minister on 28 November 1990 have been described on several occasions, not least in her own memoirs, which draw on both contemporary documentation and personal recollections. Since their publication, other participants in the crisis have filled in gaps, while placing – as is the way of things – a more or less self-serving gloss on their personal roles. It seems safe to predict that little new information will surface, though some is adduced in the pages that follow. But in any case the motivations, explanations and consequences of what occurred have not yet been fully explored. And they need to be.[1]

The two opposing poles of the debate about Mrs Thatcher's overthrow can be summed up as (respectively) hubris and treachery. Was she the victim of her own overweening pride? Or was she the victim of a conspiracy? (That does not, of course, rule out some combination of the two.) But before reaching a conclusion to this conundrum – preliminarily in this, but finally in the next chapter – it is necessary to stand back and, indeed, to reach back somewhat further into the past.

In one sense, the primary question is why Margaret Thatcher remained Prime Minister for as long as she did – a question which sympathizers as much as critics should be ready to pose. A Prime Minister with a healthy parliamentary majority is, of course, greatly empowered by his or her office: the ability to recommend a dissolution, the whipping process, the resort to patronage all contribute. But Mrs Thatcher knew that in all democracies time runs against those in power. The media, with their obsessive search for novelty, see to that, as the slow agony of Tony Blair's last months in Downing Street have more recently confirmed. So she was always conscious of the tedium factor. New reasons must be found to justify her tenure of office. It was a constant motive in overcoming her natural caution – a caution which, contrary to the myth, increased rather than diminished as the years went by. 'New occasions teach new duties,' she liked to declaim (quoting one of her favourite hymns).* 'We must renew the beliefs!' she was saying, even as her political world was imploding during the poll tax crisis. Those around her were equally conscious of the dangers that she would look stale – though they were not imprudent enough to tell her that she did, as Norman Tebbit and Michael Dobbs, his chief of staff at Central Office, effectively did in a presentation in 1986, at the cost of her regard. Privately, though, Stephen Sherbourne, her political secretary, was always worried that she would simply look 'past her sell-by date', as he put it.

They needn't have worried. It was upheaval, not boredom, which was the problem. The ordinary laws of politics were suspended, because Margaret Thatcher was not, in reality, an ordinary Prime Minister at all. She was, from the start of her tenure to its tumultuous end, a temperamentally and ideologically disruptive force.

* The couplet runs: 'New occasions teach new duties: Time makes ancient good uncouth; / They must upward still, and onward, who would keep abreast of Truth'. It is a good summary of her philosophy of life, though she would not have sympathized with the cause that prompted it: James Russell Lowell wrote the poem in 1845 in protest at America's war with Mexico.

The Conservative Party, more a part of the wider Establishment than she ever cared to admit, was bound to be ill at ease with her. The longing of her colleagues and subordinates for a quiet life – one quiet enough to enjoy the perquisites of power – was always strong and perhaps ultimately irresistible. Hence her eventual supplanting by the weak, unthreatening and consensual John Major. Hence the ensuing lack of purpose, of discipline, of idealism and of probity.

So why did it not all happen earlier? In fact, it nearly did – as a result of the Westland crisis. Westland is now largely forgotten, and largely deserves to be. When the subject was broached in the course of writing her memoirs, Mrs Thatcher objected to its being given any detailed treatment at all. At one point, she even suggested that it should be 'covered in a footnote'. She was persuaded out of that self-defeating stratagem. Anyone who knew her less well might have concluded that this reticence was a sign of guilt. But it was not. She just hated recollecting the affair because she was so obviously on the ropes and because her antagonist in the struggle – Michael Heseltine – eventually had his revenge four years later. On top of that, she thought that she had exposed civil servants to attack; and she was always powerfully protective of her officials.

The Westland helicopter company, whose future became the occasion for a breakdown of orderly Cabinet government, almost however defined, was of no strategic or industrial importance. It was for the company's board, accountable to its shareholders, to take the decision as to whether it should secure its future by a deal with an American or a European partner – the latter being Heseltine's preferred alternative. There was, it is true, a wider question, which has greater resonance today: whether and how far European defence integration should be considered. It was right that the Government of the day should take an interest in the outcome. But the whole approach of the Thatcher years, albeit one never shared by Heseltine, was to encourage businesses to take business decisions, not for politicians to interfere with them.

Heseltine was from an early stage determined to destabilize the Government. If Mrs Thatcher can be criticized, it is not for pressing the US Sikorsky option, in which she had no political, let alone personal, interest. Nor can she be seriously faulted for the procedures by which ministers took decisions. Perhaps it might have been better to allow Heseltine to put his paper on Westland to the full Cabinet. But the result would have been the same. When Cabinet eventually had to decide – in fact, on the procedural issue of whether statements, including Heseltine's, must be cleared through the Cabinet Office – it decided against him. The most sustainable charge against Mrs Thatcher is, rather, that she allowed Heseltine to flout collective responsibility and to campaign, by press briefings and through various surrogates, for far too long. Had she closed down discussion earlier, he would have resigned. But at least he would not have taken the Trade and Industry Secretary Leon Brittan with him. As it was, she finished up looking both weak and overbearing, and her hitherto unblemished reputation for integrity was seriously – though unjustly – damaged.

'AIEEEEEEEE!'

The effect of Heseltine's campaigning for his preferred option was to provoke Leon Brittan into campaigning too. In this game he was a novice. It was suggested at the time, and the assumption is still unchallenged, that there was something deeply wrong about the DTI's leaking to the media the letter from the Solicitor General, Patrick Mayhew, criticizing Heseltine's behaviour. But it was, at worst, a venial misdemeanour. The convention that the Solicitor's advice is confidential because, though a politician, he is also the Government's law officer, was even then a typically British piece of pseudo-constitutional nonsense. In an advanced democracy, where openness is prized and even the most secret advice can be exposed under freedom of information provisions, it looks quite absurd. Lord Hailsham, the Lord Chancellor of the day, told the Cabinet that he did not find anything wrong in what was done. The Attorney General, Michael Havers, did. But Havers' credibility in such things was non-existent, since he spent his lunchtimes telling journalists at the Garrick Club all the tastiest government gossip of the day: they would then ring up Bernard Ingham for confirmation. (Havers only obtained and kept his position through the friendship of Mrs Thatcher, who had been in chambers with him.)

The political problem came back to Brittan himself. He had already been badly damaged by having to apologize for mislead-ing the House of Commons over the existence of a letter received from Sir Raymond Lygo, the chief executive of British Aerospace. He had tried to be clever and had looked dodgy. But he tried again, instructing the DTI to leak Havers' letter. Unfortunately for Mrs Thatcher, the able but inexperienced DTI press officer, Colette Bowe, thought that alongside Brittan's permission to release the letter she had also received what in the jargon was called 'cover' for doing so from Bernard Ingham at Number Ten. In fact, she had not. The letter had already been leaked before he was consulted. What precisely transpired during the telephone call between the two officials cannot now be proved. But Ingham makes clear that he did not consult the Prime

Minister.* Why should he? Experienced civil servants know what not to ask. And given his mistress's disapproval of leaks and near-obsessive respect for anything connected with the law, he would undoubtedly have received a dusty reply had he done so. The only question still unanswered is: When was the Prime Minister later told by her private office of the leak? And if, as seems the case, there was a suspiciously long delay, does this reflect a cover-up among private secretaries? This intriguing puzzle does not, though, bear on her own position. Her behaviour was honourable; her subsequent account was accurate.

Though dramatic, the Westland crisis was quite short, some two months from beginning to end. That brevity sets it in marked contrast with the final crisis of her premiership, which lasted a full year, from the time of Nigel Lawson's resignation to her own. There were, though, common themes – the loss of senior ministers, complaints about her style of government, the issue of Europe, and an atmosphere worsened by the mid-term blues.

During Westland, the Conservative Party suffered – as it did later – an access of febrility bordering on outright panic. Thus, at the beginning of 1986 there was widespread talk in the media and in political circles of a Cabinet plan to get Mrs Thatcher out. Norman Tebbit, who with Geoffrey Howe had initially backed Heseltine's approach to Westland, was rumoured to be preparing a bid for the succession if she stumbled.[2] But the main common factor between the two crises, of 1986 and of 1990, was Heseltine himself. He had decided that the only way he could become Prime Minister was over Mrs Thatcher's dead body. This was not the first time he had pressed a secondary matter close to breaking point.† He had been

---

* Bernard Ingham, *Kill the Messenger* (London: HarperCollins, 1991), pp. 333–8. The only passage in Ingham's account with which one could take issue is his suggestion that when Mrs Thatcher said she might be out of office by the evening she was joking (p. 337). She did not give that impression five years later; and anyway, she never joked about her political survival. She reproached Ingham for dealing with Westland in such detail in his book, saying that it would 'bring it all back'. But, of course, it did not.

† The issue of where the building of two frigates should take place – Heseltine demanded that one go to Liverpool – had not long before led to a disproportionately bitter row.

preparing his resignation – he had a twenty-minute statement ready to make to the press just after walking out of the Cabinet, and he was a slow writer. For him and for her, the next four years constituted a single duel.

Westland was to prove the most dangerous moment for Mrs Thatcher in the Government's second term; and even afterwards it was not immediately clear that her problems were over. Anti-Americanism, both in the Opposition and in some parts of the Conservative Party, was damagingly apparent in controversy over the proposed sale of BL to an American firm, either Ford or General Motors. It was stoked again by opposition to the Libyan raid that April.* But from the summer of 1986 the Government's and the Prime Minister's political standing began steadily to improve. There were a number of factors at work, including an improving economic situation (especially falling unemployment), the obvious shortcomings of Opposition leader Neil Kinnock, and the world scene, on which Mrs Thatcher cut a dominant figure even when she was on the defensive at home. The crucial development, however – one which failed to occur during the final crisis – was the rallying of the Cabinet. It was, of course, easier in 1986 than in 1990, for Heseltine's behaviour forced even Mrs Thatcher's Cabinet critics into her camp.

A further difference was that by 1990 Norman Tebbit was outside the Government – a loss to Mrs Thatcher at a crucial moment. He had been made Party Chairman in 1985, succeeding the hapless John Gummer (another of her more transparently unsuitable appointments). Tebbit was an inspiration. His selfless commitment to his dreadfully injured wife, his moral and political courage, and his ability to remind the public what Conservatism really meant and why socialism was a threat, accorded him a towering stature in the party. But he was not a good administrator, nor was he a team player, unless it was his own team. He was too big a man for his

* See above, pp. 261–2.

job. He was also inevitably a rival, perhaps even a rival for the leadership.* He clashed repeatedly with Mrs Thatcher, partly because they were two big beasts with similar strengths and weaknesses, but also because of the competing small fry around them. The disagreements, absurdly focusing on rival advertising agencies, would come to a head during the election campaign. Their relationship did not fully recover until the eve of her leaving office.

In the latter half of 1986, however, the tension had two practically beneficial consequences. First, it prompted Tebbit to demonstrate his worth by sanctioning a very successful strategy, implemented by Saatchi and Saatchi but drawn up through the Conservative Research Department, on the theme of the 'Next Moves Forward'. These consisted of new, positive goals for each important department of state, which were duly announced at the party conference. This initiative restored political momentum.

Second, Tebbit's assertiveness encouraged the rest of the Cabinet, including the Prime Minister, to pull together. They were not prepared to see him act as a leader-in-waiting. An indiscreet interview which he gave to the mischievous Anthony Bevins of *The Times* in March was the last straw. In it 'Cabinet level sources' (that is, Norman Tebbit) said that Mrs Thatcher had entrusted him (Tebbit) with work on the next manifesto and that the Cabinet would have no role in it.† This helped prompt the creation of a Strategy Group – effectively an inner Cabinet, popularly known as the 'A Team' – of senior ministers to oversee presentational and policy work in the run-up to the election. The initiative came from

---

* Norman Tebbit has revealed that he had promised his wife that he would leave politics after the 1987 election (interview with the *Daily Mail*, 4 May 2007). The truth of this is not at issue. But no one else knew it at the time, certainly not Mrs Thatcher. The widespread assumption was that he saw himself as a possible successor. If she had fallen, despite what he had told his wife, perhaps he would have been. He would, after all, seriously consider the possibility in 1990.

† I asked Norman Tebbit about the article at his morning meeting and he admitted that he was the source. I said that Downing Street must be told; he did not demur; I then broke the news to Number Ten.

John Wakeham, as Chief Whip. Wakeham was on bad terms with Tebbit, and indeed most of the Cabinet at this time also distrusted Tebbit's judgement and ambitions. Behind the scenes, Stephen Sherbourne was equally keen to see an inner Cabinet formed.* When Wakeham came in to discuss his memorandum, Mrs Thatcher asked if the existence of the group should be made public. He replied that publicity was the real point, even if it never met: she had to be seen to be supported by her senior colleagues. In less troubled times, she would probably have baulked at such collegiality. But now she took the point. (In 1990 there was no such group; but then there was no real consensus, and hardly any loyal heavyweights to mobilize either.) The Strategy Group produced no new ideas. The papers commissioned for it had no great merit. Over time its meetings became less regular. But, as Wakeham predicted, its existence was enough. It undoubtedly stabilized the Government and so prepared the way for the 1987 general election victory, which, in truth, only Tory folly could in the circumstances have forfeited.†

In addition to these differences, the final crisis which Mrs Thatcher faced in the autumn of 1990 was distinguished from that of 1986 by three separate problems, whose conjuncture, along with the human factors in play, ultimately proved fatal. The first of the three was the Community Charge (or 'poll tax' as she refused to call it).‡

The charge was, in its way, perhaps the most radical of all the

---

* I was secretary to this group. I was also close to both the Prime Minister and to the Party Chairman. I was thus in a position to know most of what each was doing and thinking.

† This victory was not a very happy occasion, though Norman Tebbit rightly said, in response to Labour's boast that it had 'won the campaign', that he preferred to have 'won the election'. For a somewhat sanitized account, see Thatcher, *The Downing Street Years*, pp. 569–88.

‡ The Government's refusal to call it a poll tax stemmed from concern that the term suggested it was a tax on voting ('poll'). But it was, indeed, a poll tax, because it was levied per head (which is the meaning of 'poll' in this context). There was an unspoken connection with the electoral register in any case, because it was one source for the names of those liable for the charge. Some of us also privately hoped that it might mean that people determined to avoid paying anything towards their services would not register to vote at all – a useful electoral advantage for the Conservatives. Anyway, why should those choosing to lose themselves in the black economy have a vote?

policies introduced by the Thatcher Government.* This was reflected in the magnitude of the political disaster it created. Much of Margaret Thatcher's earlier political career had been taken up with problems posed by the domestic rating system. She had even been committed to abolishing the rates altogether. But it would be wrong to suppose, as some have, that on this subject she merely finished up where she had started out.[3] Her views changed over the years. It was, in the end, the difficulty of controlling public expenditure which underlay her exasperation with the existing system. Michael Heseltine, Tom King and Patrick Jenkin, successive Secretaries of State for the Environment, devised increasingly complicated, impenetrable and often inequitable schemes to reform local government finance. None had the desired effect of keeping spending under control. This was because the national taxpayer, not the local ratepayer, shouldered most of the burden of paying for what local councils spent. So local electors had little incentive to hold their councillors accountable for local decisions, particularly where a large proportion of these electors lived off welfare. The journalist Simon Jenkins has constructed a superficially plausible and brilliantly argued thesis according to which Mrs Thatcher was an obsessive centralizer.[4] But this is a misreading. Ideology can certainly be linked with the introduction of the community charge – but it is not the ideology of centralization; rather, it is that of classic liberalism, of decentralization and of strengthening links between power and responsibility, taxation and consent.

The fundamental principle was that a charge would be levied at a flat rate on all adults, though with rebates for those on low incomes. So all would pay something for the services they received. Central government would continue to meet some three-quarters of local authority expenditure, and distribute grant on a per capita basis. In a fully fledged version of the scheme, it would theoretically be possible

---

* The abolition of exchange controls, however, also has a claim to this distinction.

to remove central controls, especially 'capping' (centrally imposed limits on increases in rates or charge). Democratic accountability should henceforth suffice to enforce spending discipline. For every extra pound spent, the community charge would rise by four pounds. This four-to-one 'gearing' would, it was envisaged, be sufficient to provoke an outcry and cut back spending. The other large change was that the business rates would be nationalized and the proceeds redistributed, also on a per capita basis. This would prevent local authorities regarding local business as a milch-cow, pushing up levies and driving out jobs from the inner-city areas where they were most needed.

The scheme as it was eventually implemented differed in several important respects from this model. Despite representations from Nicholas Ridley, capping was retained. A range of reliefs were also introduced to make the changes more palatable. These were, in their way, dilutions or even contradictions of the original scheme. The reliefs were also expensive, though not nearly as costly as the Major Government's later changes, which required a 2.5 per cent increase in VAT to pay for them.[5]

Like many political disasters, the charge has found few acknowledged progenitors. The idea was adumbrated by think tanks, devised by William Waldegrave, proposed by Kenneth Baker, modified and accelerated by Ridley, then implemented and further adjusted by Chris Patten. Mrs Thatcher had been won over sufficiently by 1985 to overrule what now look like the prophetic objections of Nigel Lawson.* She would become a great defender of the principle of personal and local responsibility embodied in the charge. She liked to speak of it as a kind of 'ready reckoner', in that it would enable local

---

* Lawson wanted a modified rating system based on capital values – what, when the Labour Party espoused the scheme, the Tories called a 'roof tax', in that it amounted to a tax on home improvement. Lawson's alternative was better than the Community Charge in that it would have been less politically dangerous. It would not, however, have solved the local democratic deficit; it would only have provided a reliable and stealthily increasing source of income, being levied on appreciating bricks and mortar. But then that is what the Treasury (and the Inland Revenue) were bound to find attractive. (See Lawson, *The View from No. 11*, pp. 573–5, for his dissenting memorandum of 16 May 1985.)

electors to know whether their council was overspending or not. But political realities always loomed as large as any theoretical attractions in her mind.

These realities were most pressingly apparent north of the border. The history of the Community Charge in Scotland has been rewritten by journalists and the revised version accepted by politicians – even Tory ones. The Scots have thus been depicted as passive victims of a remote, insensitive and Anglocentric Prime Minister. They were not.[6] It was the furore in Scotland over the rating revaluation of 1985 which convinced ministers that any such revaluation in England must be avoided and that an alternative to rates was required. It was George Younger, Secretary of State for Scotland, reflecting the demands of the Scottish Conservative Party, who pressed for the Community Charge to be introduced a year early in Scotland. It was then his successor, Malcolm Rifkind, who successfully demanded an end to 'dual running' of the two systems side by side, thus maximizing the effects of the change. This turned out to be bad politics. But it was Scottish politics, for a' that.

Similarly, the decision to bring in the charge south of the border without 'dual running' was made as a result of pressure brought to bear at the Conservative party conference in October 1987. True, Ridley was in any case in favour of a swift shake-up, and he persuaded Mrs Thatcher that it made sense. But they went with, not against, the flow of party opinion. MPs were more sceptical. That scepticism expressed itself in several rebellions. But most parliamentarians simply did not understand the system and demanded changes pointing in opposite directions. The most popular proposal, advanced in April 1988 by Michael Heseltine's lieutenant Michael Mates, was that of a 'banded' charge – one which reflected ability to pay. But it was both illogical and pointless. As Mrs Thatcher repeatedly pointed out, three-quarters of the cost of local services would still be met by the Exchequer from national taxation, which did indeed reflect ability to pay. Moreover, the politics of the Mates amendment was wrong. What sank the charge – and the Prime Minister with it – was

not the rationale of the system. It was the large increases in the bills of Conservatives. 'Banding' would have worsened, not lessened, their problems: means-testing always hits the middle classes hardest.

The early projections of the level of the charge were far wide of the mark. This proved fatal. It allowed a degree of nonchalance to enter into the Cabinet's discussions which accurate forecasts would have dispelled. When the truth dawned it was too late. By May 1989, when the Treasury and the Department of the Environment met to plan the level of local authority grant for 1990/1, the projected Community Charge was envisaged as being below a *maximum* of £300. This was already much higher than the previous year's projection. But by January 1990, the DOE was talking about an average of £340 – twice the original figure. A month later, the estimate was up again, to £360. Moreover, in some areas, despite the reliefs available, the bills rose far higher. What had happened?

Underlying everything was, it must be acknowledged, a degree of technical incompetence and political misjudgement, beginning with civil servants and policy advisers, but including the key politicians, which raises awkward questions about the quality of both advice and decision-making at this time.* (It was even worse under John Major, but that is no excuse.) Any huge shake-up of the tax system needs to be challenged, tested and monitored. This was not. Politically hostile councils used the change as a cover for increased spending, and then blamed an unpopular Government for the resultant higher bills. At the same time, the Treasury, which was deeply hostile to the Community Charge, and Nigel Lawson, who wished to be proved right, pursued a very hard line in those May 1989 discussions on local authority grant. The previous year's

---

* I joined the Number Ten Policy Unit at the end of 1989, having hitherto been director of the Conservative Research Department and so, though not at any stage involved in the Community Charge decisions, must accept my share of the collective shortcomings. The experience of my time at Number Ten – a time of assorted disasters – convinces me that the succeeding Labour Government was right to bring in many more and more senior outside advisers to challenge, supplement and when necessary substitute for the 'Rolls-Royce' minds of the civil servants who helped drive this policy on to the rocks.

generous settlement had just been pocketed, and the rates had still risen. But drawing the conclusion that extra money should, therefore, be withheld this time round was politically inept, at best. Given the limited powers of the Government to hold down the Community Charge by capping, the outcome of such an approach was much higher bills. On top of that, inflation was now rising sharply, faster than was known or at least acknowledged. An overheated economy ensured higher local authority wage demands and so rocketing Community Charge bills.

Mrs Thatcher was initially unmoved. As was her custom when she became defensive, she would reel off all the arguments in favour of the new system. In this mood she was difficult to deal with and those seeking a quiet life – above all, civil servants who could count on careers continuing long after she left office – naturally declined to press the point. Nor were her political colleagues in a much easier position. In February, when told by Kenneth Baker about the unhappiness of the 1922 Committee, she fired back: 'They do nothing but complain!' She heard the same message from groups of MPs who came in to see her. One or two of the more intrepid told her bluntly that she should resign. When Baker came in again the following month to warn that the Mid-Staffordshire by-election was looking very bad, mainly because of the charge, she was more reflective, musing: 'I wonder why we didn't tumble to it . . .' The poll in Mid-Staffordshire (22 March 1990) was indeed a disaster, lost with a 21 per cent swing against the Conservatives.

Her longest-standing advisers were deployed to convince her that some change was necessary. The following Saturday (24 March), Tim Bell and Gordon Reece went down to Chequers and delivered the starkest message. Unless she acted, she would be out. She was now in a sombre mood. Staring silently into the fire, she murmured: 'It's the unfairness of it that they don't expect from me.' Neither Bell nor Reece had much of value to offer by way of solution. But their intervention had forced her to articulate to herself what was fundamentally wrong – in her words, the 'unfairness of it'. The

phrase was significant. Unusually, for a right-of-centre politician, Margaret Thatcher had a great belief in fairness (usually a left-of-centre preoccupation) and she considered that she had gone into politics to ensure it – not equality, but what in her more legalistic moments she would call 'equity', or sometimes 'justice'. The treatment being meted out to householders under the charge was, in this sense, plainly unfair. She was henceforth persuaded that cutting the charge bills was imperative, not just for her own political future – important as that was – but because it was the right thing to do. This resolve determined her future actions.

The approach now was highly political – for the first time, and belatedly, politics became the prime consideration – and, even more unusually, the initiative came from within Number Ten.* The plan was to legislate for a new general power to control local government spending. This would be used to set a legal limit for spending, somewhat above the 'standard expenditure level', that is, what the Treasury thought councils needed to spend. Some of the gap between it and actual spending would then be covered by the Exchequer. But real cuts in council spending would make up the rest of the difference.

The Prime Minister's speech to the Conservative Party Central Council that spring was seen as crucial to signalling the new strategy. Unfortunately, because of the unconcern of her colleagues, no specific promises of new measures could be included. Patten at the DOE was opposed to the whole approach. He thought that only much higher public expenditure could suffice. At the Treasury, John Major, on whom success ultimately depended, was simply out of his depth. He entrusted his adviser, Judith Chaplin, with supplying the required passage for the speech. To describe what appeared as a mouse is to exaggerate the significance of mice. All that the Treasury would vouchsafe was that the Government 'would be monitoring the implementation of the charge'. When Mrs Thatcher

---

* In fact, it came from Andrew Dunlop and me (in the Policy Unit), John Whittingdale (the political secretary) and the Prime Minister herself. The officials were given a back seat.

read this she exploded: 'Useless! No Prime Minister was ever so badly served by her ministers!' She went next door to the private office and rang John Major to protest. What was on offer, she shouted, 'wouldn't knock the skin off a rice pudding!' He was in his car and seemed unable to concentrate. In his memoirs he recalls that she was 'in something of a state'.[7] In the end, she told him: 'Very well, the policy will just have to fit the speech.' But in such a complex and costly matter it could not. All that the text eventually said was that people 'would not look in vain' for a remedy.

The tone of another passage did strike a resonant chord – when she promised help for 'the sort of people I grew up with . . . the people whom I became leader to defend'. These people – what a later generation of politicians would christen 'hardworking families' and what Mrs Thatcher herself used to refer to as 'our people' or, more oddly but revealingly, 'the conscientious middle' – were the focus for a new strategy. Radical action on the Community Charge was just to be the start.[8]

The action of the rioters against the poll tax, who spread mayhem in London while Mrs Thatcher was speaking in Cheltenham, somewhat detracted from the message. But in the longer run it might have helped. Polarization of the argument, raising the stakes, was essential. The local election results showed this. In Westminster and Wandsworth, Tory authorities which had levied noticeably low Community Charges, the Conservatives did very well. The Party Chairman, Kenneth Baker, then skilfully talked up the message. During the summer the opinion polls duly improved. Labour's lead began to erode. The difficulties were still great, but they began to appear more of a mid-term phenomenon.*

Underlying the Community Charge fiasco was, as has been noted, the return of inflation. The economy was, indeed, the second

* For a variety of reasons, the new approach was still-born. Among them was some extraordinary legal advice about charge capping, which threw the whole operation into disarray, and the lack of any stomach for reform on the part of key ministers, who were increasingly hopeful of getting shot of the Community Charge completely.

major component of the Government's implosion and of Mrs Thatcher's fall. Understanding what happened requires some understanding of the person mainly responsible, Nigel Lawson.

Lawson was one of the few senior politicians of the day of whom the overused word 'brilliant' can be appropriately employed. The tax changes outlined earlier would alone justify that.* His high opinion of himself, which never wavered, was for many years shared by Mrs Thatcher. She was impressed by his intellectual sharpness, his polemical style and his mastery of economic issues. In all these respects he offered what she found a welcome alternative to Geoffrey Howe. Nor did she mind, as men like Whitelaw clearly did, that Lawson was so obviously not a gentleman in the eyes of Tory grandees. She liked him. But at the same time and at a certain level she seems to have found him lacking in moral stature. This did not matter while they saw eye to eye. It did, though, once they fell out over policy during the later part of his period as Chancellor.

Margaret Thatcher had for most of her life a good memory, and she would recall more than thirty years later how back in 1966 Lawson obtained a local authority mortgage to buy an extremely expensive house in Hyde Park. This had not been dishonest, but it was characteristically brazen. It had created a minor scandal, since public sector mortgages were thought to be designed for poorer people, not upwardly mobile Tories.† She felt that the episode summed up the man. She was persuaded not to include that particular reflection in her memoirs. But it is significant of her view of him that whereas after leaving office she would (eventually) have good working relations with Geoffrey Howe – for example, they cooperated closely over the Scott investigation into the 'arms for Iraq' affair – she never, by contrast,

---

* See pp. 235–6.
† The incident is recorded by William Keegan in *Mr Lawson's Gamble* (London: Hodder & Stoughton, 1989), p. 26. Keegan's opening chapters on Lawson's early career are an indispensable guide to his character. He comes across as a gambler, an optimist, an expansionist, and easily bored. These insights explain much of what later transpired.

had anything to do with Lawson.* That was despite the fact that she and Lawson were a good deal closer politically than she and Howe, especially on Europe.

Nigel Lawson had also been personally close to Mrs Thatcher in opposition. Even though he was not a naturally adept parliamentarian, he was an effective member of the 'Gang of Four' MPs who regularly collaborated with her at Questions.† He also took pains to cultivate her. On 16 July 1978, for instance, he wrote her a personal letter expressing his concern that 'colleagues appear to have swallowed the Labour line that our economic policies, especially on the public expenditure front, would cause massive unemployment'. He added (more optimistically than prophetically, but he was always an economic optimist): 'There is, of course, no reason whatever why this should be so.' This is the sort of message any leader likes to hear.

Hardly less welcome can have been the content of a further letter, of 16 October that year: 'The events of the past week [at the Brighton conference] have underlined how very much the success of the next Conservative Government is going to depend on your faith and your resolve – and how confident those of us who share that faith and that resolve can be in you.'⁹

Since then, Lawson's career had not, in fact, flourished as much as it might have done, or, indeed, should have done. He had supervised shadow public spending operations. He was afterwards by far the ablest member of the Treasury team in government. As Financial Secretary, he more or less single-handedly devised the MTFS and made up for many of John Biffen's inadequacies as Chief Secretary. Lawson was very annoyed when Leon Brittan was promoted over his head to replace Biffen. But his protest to Mrs Thatcher ensured he was not forgotten. At Energy, and so at last in the Cabinet, he was a

---

* After three years' investigation, the arms-for-Iraq inquiry, chaired by the High Court judge Sir Richard Scott, reported in 1996. Both Mrs Thatcher and Geoffrey Howe gave evidence. In 2011 Lawson did come in to see her to present a book he had written on global warming. Whether from genuine amnesia, or half-remembered hostility, or a mixture, she claimed not to recognize him.
† The others were Norman Tebbit, George Gardiner and Geoffrey Pattie.

success, privatizing Britoil and building up coal stocks for the inevitable miners' strike. Now, finally, after the 1983 election, he received from Mrs Thatcher the only job he ever really wanted, that of Chancellor of the Exchequer. No one was ever better qualified. And yet no Chancellor ever destroyed his party's and government's – or his own and his Prime Minister's – reputations more comprehensively.

By the time that Lawson took charge of the Treasury, the apparent – and they were always only apparent – simplicities of monetary policy conducted within the framework of the MTFS had become very complicated indeed. This displeased the new Chancellor, who, unlike his predecessor, had a yearning for intellectual clarity. Even when monetary aggregates other than £M3 were taken into account, the approach still looked a mess. So in setting policy ever greater regard began to be had to the exchange rate, first as a reflection of monetary conditions, but later in its own right. This was the winding path which in 1985 led Lawson back to his earlier enthusiasm for sterling's membership of the Exchange Rate Mechanism (ERM) of the European Monetary System. It was that rekindled enthusiasm that principally lay behind his decision in March 1987 to conduct British monetary policy by reference to sterling's parity with the Deutschmark – without the Prime Minister's or the Cabinet's agreement, and without any public acknowledgement.

The policy was to keep the pound at or below three Deutschmarks (DM3). The background was one of international worries about wider exchange rate volatility. These had led initially to the Plaza and then to the Louvre accords, intended in the first case to force down and then to force up the US dollar. Lawson, through his leverage with the US Treasury Secretary James Baker, exerted a large influence on both decisions. Along with his aforementioned exasperation at the uncertainties of British monetary policy, this experience gave him a taste for a policy of playing the exchanges. In particular, the Louvre agreement of 22 February 1987 provided a smokescreen behind which to conduct his own policy of managing sterling through intervention.

Mrs Thatcher's and Lawson's memoirs provide differing glosses on the interest rate decisions of this period, which can be judged to have ended either, at a theoretical level, with the 'uncapping' of sterling (which thus rose above DM3) in March 1988, or, in more concrete terms, with the steady rise in interest rates that began with the increase from 8 to 8.5 per cent. (The ensuing period of rising rates would only end with the reduction from 15 to 14 per cent on 5 October 1990, when sterling entered the ERM.) Despite the difference of emphasis, the Thatcher and Lawson accounts do not materially differ on the facts – except on one fundamental point. She makes it clear that she did not know about the policy of shadowing the Deutschmark when it began. Lawson claims, albeit with variations, that she did.

In his memoirs, Lawson describes an exchange between the two of them about intervention in the markets. It took place on 8 December 1987. He then comments:

> The whole nature and context of this discussion, incidentally [note that word 'incidentally'!], gives the lie to the extraordinary suggestion, put about by her acolytes [Mrs Thatcher's own memoirs had not by then appeared] after the event, that Margaret was somehow unaware of my policy of shadowing the Deutschmark. It was always an implausible insult to her formidable intelligence to suggest that she could possibly have been unaware of it, even if I had wished to keep her in the dark, which, of course, I did not. In fact, we discussed it openly on a number of occasions, of which the 8 December bilateral is merely one instance.[10]

Once her memoirs were published he could no longer blame the 'acolytes'; so he blamed her. In her book she carefully explained that she had not known of the policy, let alone approved it, until she found herself cross-questioned by journalists from the *Financial Times* on Friday, 30 November. They demonstrated conclusively to her that the pound had over the months been shadowing the

Deutschmark at the DM3 parity. On further investigation, this was confirmed by officials. So, of course, by the time of the meeting 'incidentally' (and disingenuously) adduced by Lawson to support his story, she did indeed know. The question from then on was how she was going to get him to reverse the policy of which he as Chancellor was in control – without dismissing him, which she did not feel strong enough to do.

Lawson's initial response to the charges in her memoirs was to bluster. He did not at first explicitly claim that he had agreed the policy of shadowing the Deutschmark with her. Instead, he (again disingenuously) declared: 'The policy I was pursuing was designed to keep the pressure down on inflation. It was a policy which she was well aware of and it was a policy I discussed with her on a number of occasions.'[11] But it was not the general anti-inflation policy which was in dispute, as he well knew. In a short review of *The Downing Street Years* in the *Evening Standard*, however, he went further. While praising her achievements as Prime Minister (which he believed largely to be his own), he added dismissively:

> Suffice it to say, first, that nothing was kept from her (nor could it have been, even if I wished to do so; she was not that kind of Prime Minister); and second, that insofar as, with hindsight, interest rates may have indeed been too low, all the pressure from her throughout my time as Chancellor was to have them lower – not higher – than I felt was needed.[12]

The second observation is neither fair – all politicians like to keep down interest rates – nor germane – it was Lawson at the Treasury who set interest rates by direction to the Bank, and she never forbade his raising them. It is not even altogether factually correct.* But of

---

* The official papers which I saw when drafting the section of *The Downing Street Years* on these matters appear to confirm that the cut in the interest rate from 8 to 7.5 per cent – to a level which was hopelessly adrift as regards counter-inflation policy – was Lawson's proposal. The Prime Minister accepted it as the price to pay if sterling was to be uncapped and Lawson was not to resign (see Thatcher, *The Downing Street Years*, p. 705).

the first observation one can only say that it is highly misleading, as Mrs Thatcher's public and private accounts confirmed.

The fact that she discovered the policy under the circumstances she did also helps explain why she belatedly decided that she needed, once more, her own personal economic adviser – paving the way for the return of Alan Walters in July 1988. Unfortunately,

Walters' arrival only compounded the problem. The economic damage had already been done. And Walters' caustic observations about the ERM provided Lawson with a timely excuse to jump ship. From a lack of creative tension, the tension suddenly became explosive. But there would have been an explosion in any case.

The serious inflationary consequences of this period of heavy intervention and very low interest rates (it is debatable how much weight should be accorded to each) were only slowly grasped. In the wake of the worldwide stock market crash of October 1987, the consensus had been that governments must loosen monetary policy to avoid a recession. In fact, the consensus was probably wrong. Stocks

and shares bounced back, with little long-term effect. But some increase in the risk of inflation was to be assumed and discounted. Of course, the effects of Lawson's policy of shadowing the Deutschmark went beyond that. Rising inflation would now need to be countered by much higher interest rates. Politically, the timing could hardly have been worse. Governments can sometimes afford to reflate as they approach elections. But they should never reflate after them, otherwise the economic and political cycles go awry. The coincidence of renewed inflation and higher interest rates with the introduction of the new Community Charge was to prove fatal.

Between the summer of 1988 and Lawson's resignation in October 1989 a state of undeclared war existed between him and the Prime Minister.* Each side strove to place its own interpretation on why inflation and interest rates were rising, while periodically negotiating an unconvincing compromise formula to bridge the gap. Naturally, it did not work. At the time Lawson largely had the better of the argument, because he enjoyed close links with the world of journalism, particularly City journalism. Moreover, from the time of her tenth anniversary in power in May 1989 Mrs Thatcher was felt to be fair game for the media, always anxious for novelty. But Lawson must have known that the blame for his mistakes could not be dodged for ever. The extraordinary quasi-coup which he and Geoffrey Howe attempted before the June 1989 Madrid European Council – better regarded in the context of European policy, where it is considered below – has also to be understood in this light. By the time of that autumn's party conference a lethal minuet was being performed between the two neighbours in Downing Street.

Lawson was by now strongly suspected by the Prime Minister's advisers of trying to find a suitable early occasion to resign, while

* It was so well known that I suggested making a joke of it in Mrs Thatcher's 1989 party conference speech, with a line to the effect that (in the context of crime prevention), 'We have a very effective neighbourhood watch scheme in Downing Street. I watch Nigel and he watches me.' It was not included.

leaving Mrs Thatcher to bear the blame and face the consequences. (We did not at this time know what had transpired before Madrid: that would have transformed suspicion into certainty.) Lawson was, or at least appeared to be, enormously sensitive to anything his colleagues said about sterling or indeed economic policy generally. The recently appointed Party Chairman Kenneth Baker thus found him in an extremely difficult mood.[13] Lawson was jaded and low, and with no ambition for any other post – even that of Foreign Secretary, for which Chancellors usually long – he must have been wondering, anyway, what was the point of carrying on.

Mrs Thatcher's attempts to demonstrate her support for Lawson were honestly meant, if not appreciated. They were also unconvincing. She was not, except when placed under extreme pressure and then only temporarily, prepared to blame the onset of inflation on external factors or on the decision to drop interest rates to counter the 1987 stock market hiccup. So, to compensate, she indulged in exaggerated praise of Lawson personally. At the Conservative Agents' Dinner on the first evening of the party conference she improbably described herself as Lawson's 'foremost fan'. Along with her repeated description of his position as 'unassailable', this had a hollow, even ludicrous, ring. But then she was never good in such circumstances. By contrast, the *Daily Mail* reflected what a large section of Conservative opinion truly thought when it demanded the departure of 'This Bankrupt Chancellor'. The relevant passages in the Prime Minister's speech and his were the subject of textual criticism and dispute by each side which would have been more appropriate to a linguistics seminar. In the end, and somewhat improperly, it fell to her principal private secretary (and ex-Treasury official) Andrew Turnbull to draft what she said. It all showed that a fatal breakdown of trust had occurred which could – and should – result in an early vacancy at the Treasury: one that was, indeed, long overdue.

The conference ordeal was not long over before Lawson finally jumped. He was annoyed by the appearance in the press of Alan

Walters' description of the ERM as 'half baked'. But it stretches belief that he did not know Walters' comments were contained in an article written the previous year, long before he returned to advise Mrs Thatcher. There was nothing improper about them, however embarrassing. But one must add that Walters was not naturally discreet and his return would have led to more stories. In any case, Lawson saw his opportunity and took it.

So on Thursday, 26 October, he demanded to see the Prime Minister. She was under the hairdryer, having just got back from a difficult Commonwealth Conference in Kuala Lumpur. Her mind was on that afternoon's Questions. She just wanted to focus on her briefing. But then Lawson arrived and told her that unless she sacked Walters he would resign. She played for time, pretending not to take him seriously. But he insisted – and then left the room. He turned up at Cabinet, but just before Questions he appeared again and said he was going. She now explicitly refused to sack Walters, asked Lawson to think again, and went on to the House. Ten minutes before Questions began she was told by Turnbull that Lawson wanted the news of his resignation out at once. She refused to agree, knuckled down to Questions and then delivered a statement on the summit. It was courageous professionalism of the sort at which she excelled. That evening Lawson saw her again, his resignation was made public and a still stunned John Major – alerted a little earlier – took over as Chancellor.

What Lawson would have done if she had complied with his demand to fire Walters is unclear. He would probably have found some other excuse, perhaps demanded a public assurance about future behaviour that she could not give. In any case, he gambled on her personal loyalty to her staff and he gambled correctly. When she thought about it afterwards, she was sure that he had forced the pace that day for fear that Walters, who was still in America, might find out what was happening and resign before Lawson himself could do so. If so, he was right to be afraid on that score: for Walters did, indeed, resign once he heard what had

transpired from the head of the Number Ten Policy Unit, Brian Griffiths.

The damage which resulted from the falling out between Mrs Thatcher and her Chancellor was severe. Norman Tebbit has since suggested that it was her single greatest mistake.[14] But mistakes are by definition avoidable, and it is difficult to see how this could have been avoided, given Lawson's behaviour and character. Certainly, most of the harm had already been done before his departure. Lawson was a hero to the BBC when he was boldly standing up to the Prime Minister. But afterwards he really ceased to matter. He became, almost overnight, an insignificant presence on the back benches, his reputation shattered in the City, unsuitable for any useful international role. Even those who wanted Mrs Thatcher's scalp did not, for the most part, regret the loss of his. The *Sun* reflected a common view of Lawson in its headline: 'Goodbye and Good Riddance'.

Mrs Thatcher did not help herself, though, by her fumbling explanation of what had transpired. Interviewed by Brian Walden for London Weekend Television, she claimed not to know why Lawson had resigned, nor whether he would have stayed if she had dismissed Walters. Lawson, the following week, said that she must have known. Her ever-censorious biographer, John Campbell, suggests that this shows she was not telling the truth, though he adds, as a kind of concession, that 'if she really did not understand why Lawson had resigned . . . she was too insensitive to continue long in office'.[15] Her mistake was, in fact, quite the opposite. She had been persuaded that she must be emollient. But she was convinced that Lawson's demand for Walters to go was no more than an excuse. She was, therefore, not willing to admit that if she had given way on this matter Lawson would have stayed. That explains what looked at the time like equivocation.

Lawson's departure was also part of a larger problem. She was thought to be overpowerful. In fact, she was not fully in charge of her own Government's policy. And she could not admit the fact. If

she had revealed the depth of the disagreement on economic policy – notably Lawson's unauthorized shadowing of the Deutschmark – she would also have revealed that policy was being conducted against her wishes. Similarly, if she had referred to the Lawson–Howe ambush before Madrid, she would have tacitly acknowledged that the Cabinet was in a state of civil war. Her fault was that she should have sacked Lawson earlier. It would have been better now to admit that. It would have cleared the air. But in the panic-stricken atmosphere that surrounds political crises it is difficult to think straight. And a serious problem, now evident, was that too many of those who had the Prime Minister's ear knew little or nothing about politics.

The same lack of political nous in Number Ten and other key departments was also important in the third aspect of the crisis – policy towards Europe. Without the discontent created by the poll tax and the return of inflation, Mrs Thatcher would probably have been able to withstand hostility to her rejection of European Economic and Monetary Union (EMU). But that said, Europe was the most dangerous of the three challenges, because it divided Mrs Thatcher from the senior members of her Cabinet – and it was the Cabinet which would overthrow her.

Mrs Thatcher's critics, including Geoffrey Howe, her Foreign Secretary since 1983, were right to see her Bruges speech, delivered to an unappreciative Europhile audience on 20 September 1988, as marking the beginning of a new policy. Yet like many novelties it began as a reaction. It reflected Mrs Thatcher's exasperation at what she still preferred to see as silly rather than dangerous features of the Euro-federalist project which was taking shape.* She did not, therefore, advance anything more radical than a return (as she

---

* Charles Powell was the main draftsman. I also had an input. I find it amusing to reflect upon the fact that whereas Powell provided the Euroscepticism, I supplied the more enthusiastic passages about Europe at the end. I thought the speech was explosive enough already. But I doubt whether anyone at Number Ten understood that, at least before it was delivered. The speech is reproduced in Thatcher, *The Collected Speeches*, pp. 315–25.

saw it) to the idea of a group of sovereign states loosely cooperating, primarily for economic reasons. The Bruges speech was, in part, a reaction to a speech given earlier that month by European Commission President Jacques Delors to the TUC, which promised a new wave of interventionism. Delors had also predicted in the European Parliament that 80 per cent of economic, fiscal and social legislation would soon be coming from Europe. Still more important was the evidence that the Single European Act of 1986, aimed at creating a European single market, was in fact serving to impose regulation and to impose socialism 'by the back door' (as Mrs Thatcher put it). She now felt duped and betrayed; and among those who had persuaded her that the single market was a fulfilment rather than a negation of free-market goals was, of course, Geoffrey Howe.[16]

Howe, for his part, must have felt equally peeved by her attitude. Unlike Lawson, he could with justice claim that he had not misled her. Any mistakes in negotiating the Single European Act were hers as much as his – not that he perceived any. Howe had always been a passionate Europhile. Even in his Treasury days, he would remark that support for Europe was a mark of 'decency' within the Conservative Party. He found Mrs Thatcher's new tone offensive, even if it was difficult to point to any particular point on which he and she parted company. He was not, after all, able to admit that he would welcome a single currency; she, for her part, was not able to admit that she wanted a renegotiation of existing treaties. This is why the essentially secondary issue of the terms and timing of sterling's entry into the ERM took on such importance.

Lawson, with Howe's support, had been pressing the case for the ERM since 1985. Whatever the problem – whether sterling was too high or too low – the ERM seemed the solution. Moreover, the official policy throughout the Government had been that Britain would enter 'when the time was right' (or sometimes 'ripe'). But by now, influenced by Alan Walters' analysis, Mrs Thatcher was convinced that the ERM, far from being a force for stability and

confidence, would prove to be quite the opposite – in which she was subsequently proved correct.

The fundamental objections to the ERM could not be avoided. Because it involved targeting sterling against the Deutschmark (subject to very occasional, collectively agreed revaluations), ERM membership effectively meant abandoning monetarism. British monetary conditions might demand changes in British interest rates. But such decisions were now subject to the exchange rate target. On top of that, any such target constitutes an open challenge to currency speculators. Arguably, a 'pegged' rate, that is, one which purports to be fixed but (unlike a single currency) is in the last resort moveable, appears even more inviting. And in the end the markets will prevail.

In truth, by 1988 the economic arguments had receded somewhat into the background. It was now the Foreign Secretary who was most enthusiastic about setting a firm date for ERM entry and consequently Howe – as Mrs Thatcher was well aware – who initiated the 'ambush' before Madrid. For the Foreign Office, the ERM had adopted the significance of a pledge of European good faith.

The background to the 'ambush' was the British Government's failure to find allies to support its opposition to EMU. The Hanover European Council in June 1988 had set up a committee of European Community central bank heads, under the chairmanship of Delors, to draw up proposals. In April 1989 its report appeared, with recommendations just about as bad as they could be. It called for a three-stage approach to full EMU and then, crucially, insisted that embarkation on the first stage – the coordination of currencies – entailed irrevocable commitment to the third stage – a single currency. Howe, supported by Lawson, argued that Britain could avoid this prospect if it demonstrated its *communautaire* credentials by signing up to the ERM. Mrs Thatcher, who anyway disliked the Mechanism on economic grounds, preferred to fight it out and ultimately, if necessary, use the veto – for a new treaty would at some stage be required and could only be voted through by unanimity. The confrontation between her and Howe and Lawson

on the eve of her departure for Madrid, when they demanded she set a date for signing up to the ERM or they would resign, was the result. She felt that they had ganged up on her – and throughout her career she reacted very badly to such tactics. But, as Howe has argued, he and Lawson also had a grievance, because they had been excluded from discussion of the policy.[17] Both sides had a point. Yet one side or the other had to prevail – which should have meant dismissals or resignations.

She decided that summer of 1989 that it was Howe who must be moved. But she was persuaded by David Waddington, the Chief Whip, to leave him in the Cabinet, as Leader of the House. It was a bad idea, badly executed. Howe never forgave her. He acquired overnight the status of victim. And he was still dangerous. The exact details of who offered and who demanded what are still not altogether clear, perhaps because negotiations about Howe's country house (he received Dorneywood in place of his beloved Chevening) and his role as Deputy Prime Minister (which Bernard Ingham insensitively but accurately described as of no constitutional significance) were conducted via intermediaries. In any case, various versions of it all got out.*

The summer reshuffle also brought in Kenneth Baker as Party Chairman. Baker was an odd choice in many respects. Hailing from the Europhile, wet wing of the party, he had risen through the Cabinet mainly because of his skills as a presenter of policy. As a policy formulator, his touch was less certain. He must share the blame for the Community Charge. He then allowed the National Curriculum to become a bureaucratic tangle. He was, though, a

---

* There is no way of reconciling the two accounts given respectively by Howe in his memoirs and Mrs Thatcher in hers. She certainly believed that it was Howe's friends who leaked the details to the press. He believes that Bernard Ingham set out to rubbish his role as Deputy Prime Minister, which Ingham denies (see Ingham, *Kill the Messenger,* pp. 332–3). Indeed, from this point on it is impossible to reconcile Howe's account of his motivations with anything that was believed in Number Ten, or that I believe (see Thatcher, *The Downing Street Years,* pp. 756–7, and Geoffrey Howe, *Conflict of Loyalty,* London, Macmillan, 1994, pp. 586–95).

polished handler of the media; and such polish was scarce in the last years of the Thatcher Government. Many thought he would turn out to be disloyal. But in the end he proved his critics wrong.* He showed character and he went down with the ship, having struggled to keep it afloat. His weaknesses were that his judgement was some-times bad, that he was subject to political panic attacks, and that he had a tendency to indulge in wishful thinking. The last flaw was exemplified by his decision to choose for the 1989 party conference the slogan 'The Right Team'. Since it was common knowledge that the 'team' was soon likely to be altered by resignations or dismissals, this was extremely foolish. His lack of judgement was also evident in the fact that in October 1989 he recommended Tim Renton as Chief Whip to please Geoffrey Howe, to whom Renton was close.† He thus helped place a committed enemy of Mrs Thatcher in a strategically crucial position, for which she (and Baker too) paid a very high price.

Baker's strategy, which was not unintelligent, was to secure the existing compromise on Europe and then turn the party's guns against Labour, thankfully still in the incapable hands of Neil Kinnock. But events were against it. Above all, events in Europe were against it. Euro-federalist pressure grew from summit to sum-mit, ending with the fateful Rome Council of October 1990. There Britain was entirely isolated, pressing for free trade, which others were not inclined to discuss, and standing alone against proposals for EMU and for 'political union' (that is, stronger central institutions), as well as against an enforceable Social Charter. Mrs Thatcher found herself ambushed by the other leaders at Rome,

---

* On a personal note, I was among those critics. After a few weeks of Baker, I told Mrs Thatcher that I could not work with him. She said I must come to the Policy Unit. The agreement was that I should leave Central Office without a fuss. Needing the money and lacking alternative offers, I did.

† Baker seems to suggest that someone else put forward Renton's name and that he then urged caution. But Renton clearly states: 'Kenneth Baker . . . told me later that he had put my name forward to be Chief Whip' (Tim Renton, *Chief Whip: People, Power and Patronage in Westminster*, London, Politico's, 2004, p. 14; cf. Kenneth Baker, *The Turbulent Years: My Life in Politics*, London, Faber & Faber, 1993, p. 309). Renton was unsuitable on other grounds too: he had never before been a whip.

just as she had earlier been ambushed by her then Foreign Secretary and Chancellor before Madrid. But the feasibility of Baker's strategy would ultimately be determined (and negated) in the Cabinet.

In truth, Mrs Thatcher's Cabinet was not for the most part supportive, many members not even sympathetic. Joseph and Tebbit had gone. Successive Cabinet reshuffles in 1988 and 1989 had then helped swing the balance against her. She sacked John Moore and she downgraded Cecil Parkinson (from Energy to Transport), both her supporters. The arrival of Tony Newton, John Gummer, Chris Patten and Kenneth Clarke shifted the balance of the Cabinet further to the left. The only new right-of-centre arrival in 1989 was Norman Lamont (followed in 1990 by Peter Lilley). Renton's promotion, already noted, was full of danger. She thus created the conditions for her own overthrow. Strangely enough for an ideologue, she had forgotten that in politics, particularly the politics which she had encouraged, ideology matters. It was not hubris but naïveté which was ultimately her undoing. It would also undermine her legacy, because she had not brought on any like-minded successor.

The final straw was the departure of Nicholas Ridley in July 1990, as a result of what he had thought were off-the-record comments made to Dominic Lawson, Nigel's son and editor of the *Spectator*, to the effect that EMU was a 'German racket designed to take over the whole of Europe'.* He had not, in fact, been suggesting a re-emergence of the Third Reich, and it was the *Spectator*'s cartoonist Garland, not Ridley, who had him comparing Helmut Kohl with Adolf Hitler. Ridley thought that the Germans wanted a European single currency in place of the overpriced Deutschmark so as to make it easier for their industries to compete. It was, in fact, the sort of thing that a Trade and Industry Secretary should be

---

* Nicholas Ridley later described how the interview took place and why he was so indiscreet: he knew the tape recorder was on but he did not expect that Dominic Lawson, who said he wished to be 'helpful', would quote him verbatim. He does not add, but it is relevant, that Lawson was the son of a former colleague and also a guest in his home. Lawson behaved poorly but not unethically, and Ridley was traduced, though he was also naïve (see Nicholas Ridley, *'My Style of Government': The Thatcher Years*, London, Hutchinson, 1991, pp. 223–4).

concerned about, though, naturally, only an indiscreet one would express the thought in such a fashion. Ridley's closeness to Mrs Thatcher – who, unlike him, certainly was viscerally anti-German – also compounded the damage. Nor did it help that the colourfully written account of her seminar on Germany was at about this time leaked to the press.*

The Prime Minister fought hard to keep Ridley. She was distressed and depressed because he was a friend, because she thought he had been betrayed, because she essentially agreed with him. She defended him robustly at Prime Minister's Questions – though telling her advisers before she went to the House that she 'hoped she would be alive at the end'. She was. But Ridley was doomed. The Whips reported that a clear majority of Tory MPs wanted him out. Baker was among them, furious, complaining that Ridley had 'destroyed the compromise' [over Europe] and exclaiming: 'Ridley must go!' So he went.

And she still had to cope with Geoffrey Howe. He was now raddled with bitterness, having lost all hope of entering Number Ten, where

* On her views of Germany, see p. 365.

311

he thought he belonged. He was keen to assert himself and, though temperamentally incapable of expressing his views without endless nuances, he took the strongest exception to everything that the Prime Minister said or did on the subject of Europe and sought, as far as he dared, to make his feelings known. It is, indeed, impossible to doubt that he was henceforth seeking a chance to bring her down and was increasingly keen to surrender his thankless and pointless role – one rendered still more unwelcome by Mrs Thatcher's scorn for him at Cabinet.

Howe did not, though, come fully out into the open. As a wily, experienced politician, he knew how to remain just on the right side of positions that might have prompted calls for his resignation. He preferred to gloss Government positions in such a way as to contradict what everyone knew, or thought they knew, the Prime Minister really wanted and believed. Thus in the wake of Nigel Lawson's resignation in October 1989 he publicly warned against withdrawing from the line on ERM which she had announced at the Madrid Council. The Press Association caught his intention with its headline: 'Howe Takes the Initiative in Cabinet Crisis'. It was known that he had consulted the Foreign Secretary, Douglas Hurd, and the Chancellor, John Major, before he spoke, adding to perceptions of her isolation. His motives were transparent to the Prime Minister and those around her. She and Baker speculated at the time that Howe might run against her in that year's leadership election, though in the end it was Sir Anthony Meyer, the 'stalking horse' candidate, who stood. She survived the challenge, but it did her damage. Meyer secured only thirty-three votes, but there were twenty-seven spoilt ballots and abstentions and she was told by her campaign manager, George Younger, that up to a hundred MPs were shaky in their support.

In the spring of 1990 it was the poll tax rather than Europe that was the main source of worry. But in July Howe deliberately widened the rift with a speech in which he downplayed the difficulties of accepting a European Central Bank, just days after

Mrs Thatcher had rejected it in the Commons. He also, in a theme to which he would return, said that the 'hard ecu [European Currency Unit]' scheme – essentially the idea of a common but not single currency, which was being proposed as a stalling action by Britain – might lead to 'the emergence over time of a single currency'. He well knew that Mrs Thatcher and, for that matter, his colleagues completely rejected this.*

On Friday, 5 October, Mrs Thatcher finally had sterling enter the ERM. But she insisted that monetary conditions, not the level of sterling, must remain the final determinant of interest rates. As a demonstration of that, and because monetary policy had clearly tightened, interest rates were reduced simultaneously. It was the eve of the party conference. Not just the timing of ERM entry, but the decision itself was a shock to most of her advisers. Brian Griffiths, himself a leading monetary economist, had been kept in the dark. Having wavered (as had many in the Policy Unit) between accepting entry on political grounds and rejecting it on economic ones, he had just firmly concluded that sterling should not enter – when he was informed that it had. At one point that afternoon Mrs Thatcher looked at her watch and proudly announced what had happened to her speech-writers, sitting around the Cabinet table as they worked on her conference speech. The grumpy response did not just reflect the fact that the economic section now had to be redrafted. We knew in our hearts it was wrong.

Nor, of course, did it save her premiership. It did not buy time in resisting the rush to EMU – she had been right about that: indeed, it probably encouraged the other European leaders to believe that in

* Worthy of a footnote mention here is the odd textual compromise that had been reached in order to try to reconcile Howe's and Mrs Thatcher's opposing attitudes to the eventuality that the hard ecu might eventually lead to a European single currency. This was the assertion in all party documents that we would not have a 'single currency imposed upon us'. The weasel-worded phrase 'imposed upon us' was dropped in the last months of the Government and attention focused instead on whether and in what circumstances one might cease to 'issue the pound sterling' – the power to do so being a clear attribute of sovereignty. Hence Norman Tebbit's question to the Prime Minister on the fateful day of her 'No, no, no!'. See below, pp. 315–16.

the end she would fold.[18] Although it did not in itself create the subsequent deep recession – it was Major's, not her, approach to the exchange rate which was to blame for that – it did set policy off in the wrong direction. It rendered her reputation after leaving office more difficult to defend. It was, in retrospect, the worst error of her time at Number Ten.

One might have thought that this enormous concession to the Europhiles would appease Howe. But it did not. Far from evoking congratulation, it prompted him to gloat and make more trouble. He had no opportunity for a platform speech at the party conference, but he told a meeting of the Bow Group: 'The next European train is about to leave for a still undefined destination, but certainly in the direction of some new form of EMU. Shall Britain be in the driving seat? Or in the rear carriage?'

Mrs Thatcher's final conference speech was jinxed. There was an early panic when her marked-up text disappeared, to be discovered by Crawfie packed away in Denis's suitcase, under his shoes. When she finally spoke, the sound system failed altogether at one stage, and it continued to malfunction after that. A good joke about the Liberal Party – likened to *Monty Python*'s 'dead parrot' comedy sketch – became an embarrassment, as the parrot revived to win the subsequent Eastbourne by-election. But at the time there was a nine-minute ovation, as enthusiastic as anyone had ever seen, a sharp reminder to her Westminster critics that the party faithful, at least, remained loyal.[19]

It was not until she was in the car on the way back from Bournemouth that she read the text of Howe's speech. Her staff had kept it from her until she had made her own. She saw at once what he was doing and was shaken. It was now clear that his enmity could only result in his departure – or hers. And so it proved. A few weeks later, when she was in Rome, fighting desperately to hold the line against other European leaders, Howe used a television interview to undermine her stance. His final, and fatal, blow – to which we must now turn – can only be understood against this background.

14

THE FALL

The story of Margaret Thatcher's removal from Downing Street has through frequent telling acquired a certain aura of inevitability. There is drama, of course, even melodrama. But the received wisdom is of a disaster long in gestation: it was waiting to happen; and in the end it did. That, though, is a misleading view, encouraged in the aftermath by the main players in order to minimize their responsibility – and culpability – for what happened, and then taken up by others. The truth is more complex. As has been noted, a crisis was certainly brewing – not the first but undoubtedly the most serious of Mrs Thatcher's premiership, which was always by its nature prone to crises. And this time the conjuncture of events was against her. But the dangers need not have been fatal; the crisis need not have been terminal. The end was man-made, though it was woman-made too.[1]

The legend also has it that it was precipitated by Mrs Thatcher's threefold denunciation in the Commons of the Euro-federalist agenda of Jacques Delors. He had argued (to use her words) for 'the European Parliament as the democratic body of the Community . . . the Commission [as] the Executive, and . . . the Council of

315

Ministers [as] the Senate'. To which she responded: 'No, no, no!' But this episode was not too significant. Geoffrey Howe in his resignation letter of Thursday 1 November certainly attacks 'the mood' she had struck both in Rome and in the House. But it is her position on EMU rather than on Delors' institutional federalism which Howe specifically singles out. Even then, the point of his criticism is elusive. He complains that 'the risks of being left behind on EMU are severe'. But he stops short of saying whether he supports a single currency.

Nor was Mrs Thatcher's rejection of EMU in the House of Commons as unconditional as it would become. In answer to Norman Tebbit, she said that she wanted to keep the pound. But she did not rule out some future Parliament deciding to surrender it. She added, though, that this must happen only 'after the greatest possible consideration'. That was a first hint of her view that a referendum would be required. But most commentators did not think that she was saying anything new.

Neither – to rebut a further misconception – did Mrs Thatcher's bad behaviour towards Howe at Thursday morning's Cabinet make any difference. Colleagues were surprised that he failed to defend himself against her patently unfair criticism of his allegedly slack preparation of Government bills. But he had no need. He had already decided to take his revenge later that day; he could wait. That evening he handed her his letter of resignation at a stiffly formal private meeting.

Howe's departure in such circumstances was bound to be damaging. But, again, not quite in the way that was later assumed. Brian Griffiths, when told, exclaimed: 'Tremendous news!' (He had said the same about Lawson's exit.) Elsewhere in Number Ten there was also a sense of relief. If another twelve months could be secured to sort out the Community Charge and the economy and to develop a new brand of popular Euroscepticism, the break with Howe might be a turning point – a new beginning.

But it was a large 'if'. Heseltine was in the wings. The

parliamentary party was fractious, though it was enthusiastic about the stand on Europe. The political complexion of the Cabinet had changed. And if the Prime Minister did indeed have to fight a leadership campaign, she was not well placed to do so.

All Prime Ministers in office for any length of time get out of touch with their parliamentary supporters. Critics like to put this down to arrogance. But it largely comes from pressure of work. A leader who gossips in the tea room is not one who can get on top of his brief or take the right economic decisions or conduct diplomacy, let alone fight the occasional war – and the second of Mrs Thatcher's wars was already in the making. On top of that there arises a kind of timidity – the very opposite of 'hubris'. Leaders feel uneasy with their MPs. What is one to say to backbenchers who criticize matters of which they know little and understand less? And when one fails to 'listen' (which inevitably means fail to agree) there are recriminations, possibly press stories. In any case, since the 1989 leadership election Mrs Thatcher had regularly met groups of MPs, nearly all of whom complained bitterly about the poll tax. Much good did it do her.

Her experience was not unique. John Major was more skilled than she was at such internal party diplomacy. He habitually told people what they wanted to hear and so was regarded as a listening leader. He had an uncanny ability to read character, particularly character weaknesses. Yet even Major, after a much shorter time at the top, was soon radically out of sympathy with his MPs. In the end, what succeeds in politics is success, especially electoral success, and 'keeping in touch' is more important in theory than in practice.

Mrs Thatcher, though, had allowed herself to be weakened by three other developments. The first – the failure to procure a loyal majority in Cabinet – has been mentioned and its consequences will be described. But the second – an excessive reliance on government officials – is less frequently remembered.

No Prime Minister had done more than Mrs Thatcher to remodel the top ranks of the Civil Service. None was more successful in

securing the loyalty of her officials. But she had been captured by the system. The influence of Charles Powell and Bernard Ingham was singled out for criticism. And, despite their notable merits, it would have been better, for her if not for them, had they moved on. But the essential problem was deeper. She had grown to think primarily about the problems of government, not of governing; about policy rather than politics. The bureaucracy reacted as bureaucracies always do. The private office excluded outside advice and minimized outside engagements right to the end – as any inspection of the Prime Minister's engagements diary in her last months in power will show. The joke in her Policy Unit – itself half filled with civil servants more loyal to the system than to her – was that she couldn't campaign in the House because she had to see the Deputy Defence Minister of Singapore. It was not particularly funny, but it was all too accurate.

A further problem was the appointment as her parliamentary private secretary of Peter Morrison. Mrs Thatcher had a strange if endearing view of what made a suitable candidate to be her PPS. The job typically requires someone personally loyal, in touch with parliamentary opinion, a natural gossip who can, when necessary, control his tongue: in vulgar terms, a 'nark'. Several of her PPSs did not satisfy all or even any of these criteria. Some she admired for some virtue or other that did not necessarily have any political value. Others were appointed because she felt sorry for them, when their ministerial careers had stalled. This was the case of Peter Morrison, appointed in 1990 as an alternative to relegation to the back benches. In other circumstances, he might perhaps just have done. He was loyal, a supporter before she even became leader. He liked the House of Commons, though he was a terrible speaker and claimed to suffer vertigo at the Dispatch Box. He also quite liked to gossip, at least over a drink. But that was the problem. He not only drank: he was an alcoholic. By lunch time he was drunk on vodka and tonic, and even sober he was intellectually incapable, often woozy, sometimes asleep. Perhaps to compensate, he had developed

an insistently jovial manner and had convinced himself that any problem could be solved by cheering people up. From his optimism stemmed complacency, which added to his general inadequacy. He had no judgement, though he prided himself on having it, and so he was constantly surprised by events. And it was on Morrison that Mrs Thatcher would have to rely in her darkest hour.

Howe's resignation at 5.30 on that Thursday evening, 1 November, came at a logistically difficult time. Mrs Thatcher had to attend a reception, so it was some while before she could think through the necessary reshuffle. During this period two sharply contradictory views emerged. The political advisers in Downing Street – Whittingdale, Griffiths, Dunlop and I, with Morrison's support – wanted to retake the initiative and saw Norman Tebbit's return to the Cabinet as crucial to this. He was the only senior Tory politician with the instincts, intellect and guts to fight alongside Mrs Thatcher in what increasingly looked like a decisive, possibly terminal, struggle. We wanted him at Education and the Prime Minister herself was easily persuaded. The alternative candidate, supported by everyone else, was Kenneth Clarke. (The current incumbent at Education, John MacGregor, was widely seen as lacking the presentational skills for such a crucial post.) Similarly, there were alternative candidates for other jobs. For Health (assuming that Clarke vacated it for Education, in the case of Tebbit's refusal) we wanted Michael Portillo or Francis Maude (the latter still thought to be loyal). Every one else wanted either William Waldegrave, wetter than whom none could be imagined, or possibly John Patten, only marginally less so.

At this point Tim Renton, the Chief Whip, was away: Alastair Goodlad, his amiable but also distinctly wet deputy, stood in for him. When Renton returned and found out about the plan he was furious and argued against it – proof, if any were needed, that the prospect of Tebbit's return seriously frightened the Prime Minister's enemies. But the agitation was pointless. Tebbit turned down the offer. He has since explained why, but also admitted that

he was 'utterly torn'.[2] Virtual history is not usually instructive. But in this case it is reasonable to conjecture that had he decided otherwise the future might have been very different. Mrs Thatcher would have had a serious ally in the Cabinet when the final crisis came. She might then have survived. And whether she did or did not, Tebbit himself would have been in a position to run for the leadership later, rather than leaving the field to Major.

As it was, Clarke took the Education job. He would prove Mrs Thatcher's most determined opponent and quickly showed his colours by denouncing the prospect of education vouchers that she had raised in her conference speech. Meanwhile, Waldegrave, at Renton's urging, got Health.[3] Thus at the end of the reshuffle the Prime Minister was still less in charge of a Cabinet where even the power of patronage had slipped from her grasp.

The next day (Saturday, 3 November) was spent speech-writing in Chequers. She was in sombre mood. A stolid Civil Service draft was on the table. John Whittingdale tried to raise the general political situation by saying, 'I am worried . . .'. He got no further, as she exploded: 'You're worried? *You're* worried? What about MY worries!?' After a while, she apologized for being 'scratchy'. The rest of the afternoon was then spent discussing possible leadership challenges, though to no great effect.

The weekend had a bad feel to it, and not just at Chequers. Heseltine had issued an open letter to his constituents about the current crisis. It was seen as testing the water for a leadership challenge. In fact, it backfired. The Henley constituency officers were annoyed and wrote an open letter back, proclaiming their loyalty to the Prime Minister.

But then a serious misjudgement was made – the origin of much that was to follow. The view was formed by Mrs Thatcher and Peter Morrison, without consulting any other political figures, that matters should be brought to a head. Bernard Ingham was, therefore, authorized to brief the press with the message that Heseltine should 'put up or shut up'. This was dangerous, because Heseltine's pride

was as swollen as his ambition. Initially, though, it seemed to work.

Unfortunately, a still more fateful step had been taken. Mrs Thatcher and Morrison – again without wider consultation – called in Cranley Onslow, the chairman of the 1922 Committee, and proposed, as the rules allowed, that the deadline for any possible leadership election be brought forward to 15 November. The argument was that this would cut short the uncertainty which was damaging the Government and the party. But it was pure folly. It meant that she would be abroad in Paris, at the forthcoming CSCE summit, at the time of any contest.* It also took no account of the effect of Geoffrey Howe's future resignation speech. The assumption was that the bluff against Heseltine would work. But if it did not – if she had to fight for her political life – there would be no time to prepare. Though whether Morrison could have prepared an effective campaign in a month of Sundays is doubtful.

At the same time she provoked her enemies. Her speech in the House on the Loyal Address went well. But she also took the opportunity to deny 'significant policy differences on Europe' with Geoffrey Howe. This was justifiable. He had not, after all, explained those differences, despite penning a four-page resignation letter. But it made him look foolish, and it doubtless helped concentrate his mind and sharpen his attack.

The following day Baker told a 'political' Cabinet to expect very bad by-election results at Bootle and Bradford. The expectations were fulfilled. In Bradford the Tories came third. The weekend press was terrible. Howe let it be known that he would give his reasons for resigning in a speech to the House early the following week. After the memorial service at the Cenotaph, Mrs Thatcher told Baker that she now expected Heseltine to stand.

On Monday evening she delivered the traditional address at the Lord Mayor's Banquet. This is one of the occasions when civil

---

* The Conference on Security and Cooperation in Europe (CSCE) summit was widely seen as marking the end of the Cold War and inaugurating a new era of peace and freedom in Europe.

servants write and tightly control the speech. The private office included a passage designed to demonstrate resolve – a strained cricketing metaphor, hardly appropriate for a woman in any case. She promised that the bowling, 'which had been pretty hostile of late', would 'get hit all around the ground'. It was the wrong tone: it smacked of bravado, and it provided Howe with an opportunity for more nastiness. Not, of course, that it made much difference in the long run.

Her position was already becoming unstable. In the background, big and usually somnolent Tory beasts were moving. Carrington had taken the opportunity over dinner in April to convey his view – clearly also the view of others – that she should leave office with 'dignity', in other words, soon. Now Baker, whether in search of solace or advice or just through lack of judgement it is hard to say, went to see Whitelaw, who told him that though this was not the right moment for her to go, she would have to if a third of the party voted against her – a good indication of what was in the wind.[4] The Tory establishment was preparing to abandon her, while she was playing Boadicea.

Howe was due to make his statement after Questions on Tuesday, 13 November. She had an inkling of what was coming. She was hopelessly distracted during her briefing and became obsessed with all possible variations of the tiresome cricketing metaphor. She did not perform well, failing to find any response to the inevitable jibe about Clarke's public dismissal of education vouchers. The House was geared up to enjoy Howe's humiliation of her, and it was not disappointed.

He mocked the idea that he had resigned without a serious difference of opinion over policy. It was again the abstruse question of the hard ecu on which he dwelt, claiming that Mrs Thatcher had undermined the case for it by her remarks: 'It is rather like sending your opening batsmen to the crease only for them to find, the moment the first balls are bowled, that their bats have been broken by the team captain.'

Clearly, Howe's speech was a better performance than he usually managed. But its legendary qualities have been bestowed in retrospect. It still failed to spell out differences of substance. It is not, in truth, difficult, if one has a mind to do so, to deliver a wounding speech at the expense of a close colleague whose every quirk and weakness one has known for years. It is just that most people, however annoyed, would not do it. It was this aspect that made it so damaging. It suggested that he had been driven to it; that she was both personally odious and politically unworthy; and that she must be removed. And to avoid any doubt, it ended with a call for 'others to consider their response' – that is, for Heseltine to stand and force her out.

She remained stony-faced throughout, ignoring the theatrical intakes of breath which greeted each barb. In her memoirs she was persuaded to praise Howe's performance.[5] In fact, she thought the talk about 'broken bats' was silly. She knew enough about cricket to grasp that it was most unlikely that a batsman could find himself in such a situation, and her literalness did the rest. She was shocked, though she made every effort not to show it. But others began to panic, including her family. Carol was soon back in the flat needing reassurance. Mark was in tears on the telephone. Nick Ridley promised Mrs Thatcher to be 'even more vicious' in his forthcoming statement than had Howe, though this did not prove possible.

Although her enemies crowed, many others shared her revulsion at Howe's behaviour. That most mild-mannered and forgiving of men, Keith Joseph, told him that they were no longer friends, turned his back and refused to speak to him for three more years.[6] Joseph would write of Geoffrey Howe's 'spiteful and misleading speech'.[7] Perhaps even Howe developed second thoughts about his conduct. At his eightieth birthday party, held in the Locarno Rooms of the Foreign Office, with Mrs Thatcher seated in front of him, he mystified his guests with a long and rambling speech explaining why there had been a parting of the ways. One of those present leaned over to Mrs Thatcher's aide, Mark Worthington,

and whispered: 'Guilt!' Perhaps it was. Howe was a good Christian and he had a conscience. Temperamentally, he always shrank from conflict – it was why he had fared so badly with Mrs Thatcher, who preferred (in Keith Joseph's words) 'destructive dialogue' to pleasantries and who was scornful of passivity. Above all, Howe did not like to be hated. And henceforth that was his lot from many who had over the years been well disposed towards him.

By the time Howe sat down, the tumbrils were on the move. Heseltine immediately began campaigning, openly approaching Tory MPs in the lobby. The following day (Wednesday, 14 November) Cranley Onslow confirmed to Number Ten that he had received Heseltine's formal nomination. At the time, Mrs Thatcher was meant to be discussing the setting up of policy groups in preparation for the next election. It had been decided in the spring that, following the model of 1986, it was essential to restore momentum. With the Gulf War approaching, it was even possible to envisage a snap 'khaki' election in the wake of victory – though she would have taken some persuading to agree to it. Naturally, the renewed slump in the party's fortunes that autumn – the Conservatives were now over twenty points behind Labour – made that less likely. In any case, her mind was not on the subject in hand. She reflected angrily on Howe's speech. He had been 'embittered and vicious', she said, before adding more questionably: 'After all I have done for him!' She was also worried about her campaign. 'I hope the 92 Group [of right-of-centre Tory MPs] are mobilized!' Her staff tried to manage her mood. A copy of the *Independent* had been carefully laid face down, so she would not see it. Absent-mindedly she picked it up and read the headline: 'Howe Indictment Could be Mortal Blow to Thatcher'. Whittingdale then broached a subject which others such as Morrison would not, telling her that she must run in a second ballot if she did not win outright in the first, an eventuality which he feared all too possible. She did not reply.

They both knew that the hurdle was higher than it seemed. By the somewhat bizarre rules – originally conceived for when the

party was out of power and not intended to displace a sitting Prime Minister – to win outright on the first ballot she needed a super-majority of 15 per cent of the 372-strong parliamentary party (i.e. fifty-six) over the next candidate. This meant that, while she required a minimum of 187 votes, the actual number of votes she needed above that would depend on Heseltine's own score (and abstentions, if any). On the second ballot, an absolute majority of those able to vote was enough. So if she stayed in and others kept out, victory became easier. But, of course, others might come in; her first round vote could erode; and pressures could be brought to bear.

The following day's press summary prepared by Ingham was full of Heseltine's prospects. Reading it upset her and was a bad preparation for that afternoon's Questions. But, as so often, she confounded expectations and put in a superb performance against an inadequate Kinnock. The problem, as she sensed, lay elsewhere – in the campaign itself.

Morrison had already been authorized to appoint a campaign team. Unfortunately, the line-up was more impressive on paper than in reality. It was based on the team which had delivered a comfortable majority the previous year, though with one or two additions and subtractions. The names presented to her were: George Younger, Norman Fowler, Michael Jopling, John Moore, Norman Tebbit, Gerry Neale and Michael Neubert (keeping the 'tally'). Younger was meant to head the campaign, as he had in 1989. But he was heavily involved in business (he was chairman of the Royal Bank of Scotland) and could spare little time. Fowler was inactive. Jopling, who as a former Chief Whip would have been useful, at once dropped out. Tebbit gave himself wholeheartedly to the enterprise, but he was not universally popular. Neale and Neubert did their bit, but neither was of influence. So the main responsibility was Morrison's.

Conservative Members of Parliament constitute the most elusive and mendacious electorate imaginable. To learn, let alone to influence, their opinions requires reserves of guile and unremitting effort of

the kind Airey Neave exercised on Margaret Thatcher's behalf in 1975. Morrison was no Neave. There was a further problem. The Tory Party, it is said, only panics in a crisis. MPs were now in a panic. Rumours of switching and speculative calculations rippled back and forth. Conspiracies were hatched and then dissolved to be replaced with new ones, for politics in such circumstances always functions through plots, even if a single Plot is absent. In this atmosphere, Morrison's job was still more difficult; but the difficulty never seems to have impinged upon him or alarmed him. He kept his head. But as a result she lost hers. His first figures available that Friday (16 November) were: Thatcher 177; Heseltine 76; don't know 112. These were not particularly revealing either way, given the number of (apparently) undecided.

It had been agreed – presumably early on by Mrs Thatcher and Morrison, because an alternative strategy was never discussed – that she would not campaign personally. Nor would she do radio or television. Instead, she would give a number of press interviews and write a signed article. There were good and bad reasons for this approach. The problem about approaching MPs personally has already been outlined, though she should have done more of it, and probably would have done if she had been in the country. The risk of television, which was Heseltine's main campaigning medium, was that the interviewing would have been very hostile and she could have seemed defensive, aggressive, shrill or all three. That said, risking televised interviews might have impressed MPs with her powerful personality and could have frightened them back into grumbling servility. The newspaper interviews and article were the most easily controllable means of projecting a message. But Mrs Thatcher herself was never very controllable. Baker was later critical of the use she made of her interview with Simon Jenkins for *The Times* to attack Heseltine as a 'corporatist'. He thought this went down badly with MPs. He then acted to tone down the article for the *Daily Telegraph* to make it less aggressive. He may have been right in arguing that attacking Heseltine created a bad impression.

But if it had ceased to be possible for her to criticize her opponent for his published views, while he was allowed to denounce her for her real and imagined shortcomings, then no public campaign was possible anyway. In truth, Baker shared the same panic that had swept through the rest of her supporters and had helped paralyse the campaign.*

What caused more dismay was the way in which, in interviews with Michael Jones for the *Sunday Times* and (still more explicitly) with Charles Moore for the *Sunday Telegraph*, she promised a referendum before sterling was ever abandoned in favour of a European single currency. This did not quite come out of the blue. She had hinted at it, and she had thought deeply about the use of referendums in general. The pledge was subsequently taken up by both major parties. From it results the fact that sterling is still Britain's currency and looks likely to remain so. But at the time it was an imprudence. It had been discussed with no one. No one had been lined up to support it. Some colleagues, even including the loyalist Parkinson, disowned it. It seemed to exemplify her waywardness and lack of collegiality. It made the Cabinet still more wobbly.

These interviews had not yet appeared when Mrs Thatcher met her team and their spouses at Chequers over supper on Saturday evening (17 November). Present were Denis, Mark, Carol, Whittingdale, Morrison, the Bakers, the Wakehams, McAlpine, Reece, the Bells, the Neuberts and the Neales. It was a large gathering – too large, because it meant that real business had to be done in corners. This, after all, was the last general discussion of the campaign before the result, for the following afternoon she was due to fly to Paris. Not that there was anything to worry about, according to Morrison. He told Mrs Thatcher that the figures now stood at: Thatcher 224 ('the worst case' figure, he assured her); Heseltine

---

* I was primarily responsible for having her attack Heseltine in *The Times* and I drafted the *Telegraph* article, so my judgement is not unbiased.

110; the rest (most improbably) abstentions. Later he revealed that he had, in fact, 235 pledges. She, though, was uneasy. 'Tuesday will be the worst day of my life,' she said. She was wrong. Wednesday would be worse.

On Sunday the press interviews won mixed reviews. But she was already preparing to leave, trying to concentrate on the forthcoming summit that she should never have been attending. (Baker tried even now to get her to stay in London, but it was too late for that.) She had lunch in the flat at Number Ten with Crawfie, Powell and Whittingdale. Morrison rang to say that the figures were 'if anything somewhat better than last night'. Tebbit also rang to say that Heseltine had levelled new accusations at her over Westland.* Just after five o'clock she left for the airport.

Elsewhere the subject of discussion was the 'lines to take', by the Prime Minister and by her supporters at home, in the event of differing outcomes of the first ballot. A good deal of thought had been given to this. Andrew Turnbull, unbeknown to Mrs Thatcher, had drawn up a grid diagram illustrating the significance of different combinations of figures, and cross-referencing to the form of words to adopt. It was agreed by Morrison, Wakeham and Tebbit – with dissent from Baker – that she must speak to the press immediately she heard the result in Paris. Tebbit argued that this was crucial in the case of her failing to secure victory. Doubts about her intention to contest the next ballot might lead in her absence to a haemorrhage of support. Baker, though, was worried that it would reinforce the impression that she was unwilling to consult colleagues. Both were correct in their analysis. The real problem, though, was that she was in Paris at all.

On Monday and Tuesday it was as if two different worlds turned on their own unconnected axes. In Paris, Mrs Thatcher was fully involved in diplomatic and quasi-social engagements. Monday was

---

* Heseltine said that she had read out the minutes of a meeting that had never taken place. This was presumably intended to cast doubt on her sanity as well as her veracity. His bizarre behaviour during these days did not serve him well in the second round.

spent in discussions with Bush and Kohl, who were sympathetic –
there is a kindred spirit among national leaders, who sense the
fragility of their own positions as they contemplate another's
demise. Tuesday morning was passed with Gorbachev, Mitterrand
and the Turkish President Ozal, followed by lunch with the Dutch
Prime Minister Ruud Lubbers, and afterwards by discussion with
the Bulgarian anti-communist President Zhelev. Meanwhile, back
in London those who had their fate in her hands were preparing to
resolve it.

Morrison had decided that he would come out to Paris later on
Monday (19 November) so that he could (as he put it) 'deliver the
good news' in person. But first he attended a meeting with the rest
of the campaign team and others in the Prime Minister's room in
the House. As over the weekend, the discussion focused on what
she should do once the first ballot result was known. Younger,
Tebbit, Baker, Moore, Neale and Whittingdale were there. But so
too were Cranley Onslow and – at his own insistence – Renton.[8]
The discussion focused on the 'grey area' lying between a majority
of 187 and the required super-majority of (depending on abstentions) 214. Morrison was adamant that she would not be in this
territory at all. His latest estimate was that her position had
improved. It stood at: Thatcher 236; Heseltine 78; don't knows 58.
He had learned that the Heseltine camp was 'jittery' and that their
figures were: Thatcher 220; Heseltine 120; the rest don't knows.
But Baker was far from confident. Though personally committed to
her, he had already begun to think it likely that she would not win
on the first ballot and his mind was turning to other possibilities. So
he reiterated his view that she should consult before saying she
would go into the second round, adding that, if the worst came to
the worst, 'we must not hand the party to Heseltine'. This injunction would gain wider currency in the hours that followed, until it
became a chorus. Younger added that in the case of her failing to
win on the first ballot there would be members of the Cabinet who
would say that she should not go on. This too was a foretaste of the

future. Renton, the only one present who was truly hostile – he did not even vote for her – now joined in by asking whether Denis would want her to go on either. He thus revealed another point of vulnerability. But Tebbit and Morrison were immoveable. The lines to take were endorsed. Morrison added that whatever happened she must stay in Paris for the ballet being organized by President Mitterrand.

The same group met again the following morning – Tuesday, 20 November, the day of the vote. There was a reprise of the arguments. Baker said that he had heard of Cabinet ministers unwilling to back her. He was proposing a rather weak statement of support: Tebbit had him toughen it up. But all that mattered now was the result. Morrison was in good spirits, jovially chiding John Whittingdale as 'Doubting Whitto', before leaving for Paris.

There, others shared his confidence. A sweepstake was organized among her entourage. Bernard Ingham plumped for 220 votes. Charles Powell took 230. President Bush's chief of staff, who probably had about as much useful insight as the other two, chose 228. But Mrs Thatcher was not confident. She often feared the worst; now she expected it. She went up to her room at the Residence to wait. One telephone line was open between Powell and Whittingdale. The other connected Morrison and Renton. Powell received the news first but waited for Morrison to give it to her: Thatcher 204; Heseltine 152; abstentions 16.

She had failed to reach the required majority. If two votes had gone the other way she would have been safe. Such a margin is what effective campaigning can secure. But there had been no such campaigning.

Mrs Thatcher never lacked courage, and she showed it now. As planned, she went straight out to tell the press, who were not expecting it, that it was her 'intention' – a word whose ambiguity was not fully grasped – to 'let my name go forward for the second ballot'. Douglas Hurd then came out and gave her strong public support.

It is worth noting that, unlike most of the Cabinet, and unlike Major, Hurd behaved impeccably throughout. He was not of her wing of the party. He knew that he had long been kept out of the Foreign Office because she thought him unsound. He had, it is true, been prodded by Powell and Ingham to go outside and declare for her.[9] But he need not have done so, and certainly not with such good grace. He had signed her nomination papers: he thought it was now a matter of honour to stand by her. He would go on to sign her papers for the second ballot, without grumbling or delay.

Back in London a tumult of plotting, rejoicing, rage and recrimination shook an already near-demented Tory Party to its core. Four groups of players were involved. At one end of the spectrum were the committed supporters of Mrs Thatcher. The members of this group were all ideologically driven. Among the older figures, Tebbit and Parkinson were most notable. There was also a sizeable number of junior ministers and younger MPs, whose enthusiasm was not tapped until it was too late.

The second – more shadowy – group consisted of those to the right of centre who were keen to retain the changes made during the Thatcher years but not necessarily to retain her. These were the people whose influence would be decisive in persuading her not to contest the second ballot. Norman Lamont, the Chief Secretary, who would become Major's campaign manager, was perhaps the most significant. But the number also included much of the party establishment and most of the whips – the Chief Whip had never, of course, supported her; how far it even included her campaign team is to this day debatable. Some of these people simply gave in to panic. Some made a rational calculation and convinced themselves that she could not win. Some hoped for advancement under a successor, which from their point of view had to be Major. All regarded with foreboding the prospect of Heseltine arriving in power with his egomania, his support for EMU and his bevy of odd lieutenants.

Hostility to Heseltine was also, however, shared by a third group, those on the Europhile left of the party. They had always disliked

Mrs Thatcher and regarded her as a liability, but had usually managed to conceal it. Kenneth Clarke and Chris Patten were the key figures. John Gummer can also be included. This group was to be the most active in bringing Mrs Thatcher down; but it then proved too weak to elect its own man, which had to be Hurd.

Finally, there was the Heseltine campaign, energetically led, formidably well organized, enjoying a tailwind from the first ballot result. These were classically the disappointed and the embittered – into which category fell Geoffrey Howe. Despite his disagreement with Heseltine's economic interventionism, Howe not only supported him but persuaded Lawson – an even more doctrinaire economic liberal – to do the same. Lamont, as Major's campaign manager, was incredulous when he learned this and had a furious if fruitless row with his old boss.

An important role in undermining confidence in Mrs Thatcher was played by a large meeting of MPs, including five Cabinet ministers, called together by Tristan Garel-Jones in his house in Catherine Place on the evening of Tuesday, 20 November, after the first ballot. Most of those present were supporters of Hurd. But a significant presence was that of Norman Lamont, who had hitherto been an effective and enthusiastic Thatcher backer. He now wanted to see Major stand. A Eurosceptic opponent of EMU, he was desperate to stop Heseltine. He had also not received as fast advancement under Mrs Thatcher as he might have expected. All of those present agreed on one thing: that she could not win and must be persuaded to withdraw. Cecil Parkinson – the strongest of her Cabinet supporters – believed that this meeting was crucial in destroying support for the Prime Minister before her return. He was undoubtedly right.[10] Norman Lamont has written – and confirmed to the author orally – that there was no Major campaign before Mrs Thatcher withdrew.* Doubtless

* Norman Lamont, *In Office* (London: Little, Brown, 1999), p. 16. This conflicts with Major's own account, in which he is shocked to discover from an equally shocked Tristan Garel-Jones that Lamont had been campaigning (cf. Major, *The Autobiography*, London, HarperCollins, 1999, p. 183). Of course, by the time this was written Major and Lamont were enemies.

this is true. But in politics it is not only (as the saying goes) 'the wish that is father to the thought' but the thought that is father to the wish. Those who sincerely doubted whether Mrs Thatcher could beat Heseltine were easily led along the path of hoping for something better – and different. Major's campaign already existed in Tory minds. And in Major's mind too.

Hurd and Major had proposed and seconded Mrs Thatcher's nomination for the first round. Hurd had then done the same for the second. Major's position was different. He was not, of course, in Paris. Indeed, he was in his constituency recuperating from an operation to have his wisdom teeth removed. Its timing was convenient. It gave him a perfect excuse to avoid campaigning on her behalf, while physically isolating him from plotters who might have embarrassed him. Major's account of his sentiments at this time is on the record: his support for Mrs Thatcher, his reluctance to contemplate succeeding her, his stern injunctions to others not to campaign for him.[11] It is not inherently incredible. He was a modest man with much to be modest about, and the prospect of taking over as Prime Minister from a titan brought low in such circumstances must have been intimidating. But not every one was or is convinced. One of Major's senior government colleagues still speaks simply of a 'Treasury Plot'.[12]

What is indisputable is the impression others gained of his reluctance to support Mrs Thatcher in the second round. Several of her supporters rang urging him to speak out for her on television. But he answered: 'I'll have to think about it.' Perhaps the after-effects of his dental operation prevented his agreeing to speak, but it is an odd reply.[13] When Mrs Thatcher herself telephoned to ask him to second her nomination, she too found his hesitation 'palpable'.[14] Morrison then spoke to him and gained the same impression. Major was apparently annoyed that he had not been asked to give his advice: it is not difficult to guess what it would have been.

Sticklers to the last, the Civil Service would not allow a government car to take the nomination papers out to Major's home in

Huntingdon. So Whittingdale arranged for Jeffrey Archer's driver to do it and then rang Major to repeat the request. To this Major replied: 'Well, I suppose so.' When the driver got there, he had to wait for two hours before the nomination papers were signed. In fact, Major did not sign them until he had been told by Morrison that the Prime Minister would almost certainly not be standing.* Major had been kept in touch with what other Cabinet colleagues had been telling her. He had held his hand until he was sure that her will had failed.

Mrs Thatcher had returned from Paris, worried but determined, shortly before lunchtime on Wednesday, 21 November. She at once sat down with Tebbit and Wakeham. They agreed that she should fight on. There was then a wider meeting at which, as she had been warned, more dispiriting voices were heard. Already the tone had changed. The issue had become who was best able to defeat Heseltine. She seems not to have registered this; but it opened up a porthole through which those minded to abandon ship might slither.

There had already been angry discussion about the campaign. Morrison's role was harshly criticized. Tim Bell told Mrs Thatcher (in Paris) that John Wakeham should be put in charge. It was the obvious choice. Wakeham was not very good at presenting policy, as a fumbling television performance in the 1987 campaign had confirmed; but he had been a powerful and successful Chief Whip, a post which offers unique opportunities to get to know one's fellow MPs. Hitherto he had been on the fringes of the leadership campaign because, as Energy Secretary, he was in the middle of electricity privatization. But was he still loyal? At the time, Mrs Thatcher had no doubts on the subject. Wakeham's marriage to her

---

* Major's own account suggests that he signed the papers but did not send the driver back because he was preparing a letter for his PPS, Graham Bright, declaring his own candidature (see Major, *The Autobiography*, pp. 187–8). The difference between this and Morrison's account, followed here, is not, though, critical to the judgement one forms of Major's behaviour.

former constituency secretary, Alison Ward, served to cement the bond. But doubts would later surface, because of the advice he gave in her final days. When asked straight out at the time she was writing her memoirs whether he had been loyal to her, she paused and said that she did not know. This explains the slightly odd reference to him in the text.* Later she forgot her doubts, and the Wakehams remained personal friends. The truth is that Wakeham was indeed loyal. But he was distracted by other duties and he lacked the physical energy to deliver the campaign she needed – he was still affected by the injuries he had sustained from the Brighton bomb.† That said, he was undoubtedly the best available choice.

Not everyone thought so. Peter Morrison again demonstrated his lack of judgement by proposing that Kenneth Clarke should head the campaign. Clarke was the most forceful of the group of Cabinet ministers who wanted her to stand down. Not surprisingly, he declined the offer, and Wakeham took charge.

Wakeham duly received the message from Mrs Thatcher, then still in Paris, that he should run her campaign. He had first to launch the prospectus for electricity privatization. But he wanted to know how the political land lay. He was convinced that Morrison's calculation had been adrift because of a defection of junior ministers. So he asked John MacGregor to sound out Cabinet ministers about the opinions of their respective teams. In the course of this exercise, MacGregor discovered that Cabinet ministers themselves were

---

* 'I had already seen Cecil Parkinson after returning from the tea-room. He told me that I should remain in the race, that I could count on his unequivocal support . . . Ken Baker had made clear his total commitment to me . . . *And John Wakeham was my campaign manager*. But all the others I would see in my room in the House of Commons' (Thatcher, *The Downing Street Years*, p. 851, emphasis added).

† Alan Watkins' account of a meeting held before the first ballot, at which Wakeham allegedly told one of those present (in fact Kenneth Clarke) that she 'was not going to make it', might suggest otherwise (see Watkins, *A Conservative Coup*, London, Duckworth, 1991, p. 4). But whatever precisely Wakeham said at this juncture was in order to appease Clarke, who was already threatening trouble. Wakeham was not in a position to know what would happen, and anyway he wanted her to win.

starting to defect. They wanted Major or Hurd to be freed to stand.[15] Wakeham was also told by other ex-whips that Thatcher support was collapsing.

His reaction to this news was that she must steady the Cabinet by seeking their personal pledges of support. Like so many bad decisions, that to see Cabinet ministers individually came originally from Morrison. But Wakeham was no less clear that it was right. His view was that without their personal pledges she could not survive. He even advised them to tell her clearly what they thought, not to take refuge in evasion.

MacGregor, who knew how bad things looked, was part of the wider meeting over lunch, but he did not wish openly to say what he knew. This is hardly surprising, given that Renton was also present (along with Cranley Onslow). Renton said that her support was slipping. His assessment was that twenty-five of her supporters would switch to Heseltine, though this was not based on any firm evidence. Norman Tebbit rescued the situation, repeating that she was best placed to beat Heseltine; and so, though further demoralized, she decided to fight on – and said so to the press.

Already, though, she had subtly changed her position. She had told the meeting that she would stay 'until the end of the Gulf War'. This was, in fact, what the defence establishment wanted. The advice had been relayed by her security adviser, Percy Cradock, and was echoed later at her meeting with the Defence Secretary, Tom King. (If she had survived and the war been a triumph she could, of course, have reconsidered.) Another thought in her mind was that she might stay as Prime Minister but stand down as leader of the Conservative Party. She had probably been reflecting on the precedent whereby Chamberlain and Churchill had briefly divided those posts during the Second World War. Later, she would angrily say that she could have simply refused to resign as Prime Minister, whatever the outcome. As a constitutional purist, she believed that she was chosen by the Queen, not by the Conservative Party. This was not as far-fetched as it now seems. If she had threatened her

Cabinet with recommendation of a dissolution and an immediate election, her enemies would probably have crumbled – at least for a time. But she would never, in fact, have done this. She had too great a sensitivity to the monarch's position. And she would not have wanted to weaken the Gulf War effort.

In any case, she now gave another fine performance in the House. MPs appeared to rally. She then went with Norman Tebbit round the tea room – her first, last and fatally overdue visit – to seek support. She was shaken by what she found. But the fight returned to her once she was doing something on her own behalf. She went back to Number Ten in better spirits. Yet it was the Cabinet that mattered.

The signs here were ominous. Extraordinarily, no means had yet been found to warn her about the views of a sizeable minority or perhaps majority of those she was going to meet. She did know, however, that Whitelaw had given his advice to Renton, who helpfully asked him for it, and it was that she should go. He even offered to come in and tell her so.* The group of Cabinet ministers who had attended Garel-Jones's Catherine Place cabal were also issuing warnings and ultimatums. Clarke was even threatening to resign. He warned that if she tried to face down the opposition to her he would not allow it and that he had 'a high embarrassment threshold'. Two other Cabinet defections were, though, more significant. One of which she did now know was Peter Lilley, the right-winger who had replaced Nicholas Ridley at Trade and Industry. He had refused point blank to help while she was in Paris, saying she was finished. She never knew, however, about the second defection, because it was thought by her advisers that it would merely poison future relations: accordingly, it is not mentioned in her memoirs. On Wednesday morning, Tim Collins, Michael Howard's special adviser (and future MP), came to see John Whittingdale in a great state. He said that Howard had decided that she could not win and

* What right Renton thought he had to make such an approach is unclear. Presumably none, since he pretended at the time that the initiative had come from Whitelaw (Renton, *Chief Whip*, p. 98).

had resolved to see the Chief Whip to say that support must now be switched to Major.*

Nor had Wakeham been able to launch a campaign. He needed deputies, so he now asked Tristan Garel-Jones and Richard Ryder to take on the job. Both refused. Garel-Jones's refusal cannot have been too surprising. But of Richard Ryder, her former political secretary, who surely owed her at least the chance to fight for her life, more might have been expected. He replied: 'I would lose my political credibility if I attached myself to such a hopeless cause.'†

She would see Cabinet ministers individually in her room in the House. It was a bad location. In the Cabinet corridor above, ministers milled and gossiped and strengthened each other's nerve, so as to break hers. Kenneth Clarke was the most active. The order in which ministers were seen, Clarke among the first, also helped this strategy. Soon she was in tears and incapable of fighting her corner. Because of other engagements, the meetings began late – at about six o'clock – and they ended about half-past eight. By then her will to continue had been crushed. Andrew Turnbull was present and took a note of the discussions. There is no serious disagreement about who said what.[16]

In they came, parroting almost exactly the same formula – namely that she could not win, though they supported her.‡ Only Clarke and Rifkind made clear their personal hostility to her continuation at Number Ten. Some wept real or crocodile tears. The common factor was a loss of nerve. Once that had occurred the rest merely followed.

Back in Downing Street, Mrs Thatcher went up to the flat and spoke to Denis. He had already given his view and it was now more

* In fact, Howard seems to have rung Renton (ibid., p. 99).
† John Whittingdale's contemporaneously written diary provides the basis of this account, along with my own recollection.
‡ Francis Maude, a Treasury minister, was the first to come in and mouth the agreed formula. His otherwise inexplicable presence lends some credibility to the 'Treasury plot' theory.

emphatic – she should not go on. This time she agreed. The rest of the evening was spent working in the Cabinet room with her advisers on the speech she was to make in the no confidence debate that Labour had ill-advisedly tabled for the next day. Around the table sat members of her private office, John Whittingdale and I. Norman Tebbit was there, as, for no apparent reason, was John Gummer, who had not long previously cheerfully added his signature to her political death warrant. She would try to concentrate, wipe away a tear, deal with interruptions – younger MPs, like Michael Portillo and Michael Forsyth, coming in to urge her to continue – before getting back to the work in hand.

Before going up to the flat, and after consulting Wakeham, she told Andrew Turnbull that she intended to resign but that she would sleep on it. The following morning, Thursday, 22 November, she telephoned through to confirm the decision. The last rites could now be performed.

The first of these was the Cabinet. It was an embarrassed but excited group that met her – earlier than usual that day – and sat through her tearful statement of what they knew had already been decided. Soon, after formal tributes from James Mackay, the Lord Chancellor, from Baker and from Hurd, they adjourned for coffee. She regained her composure. Many of those present were anxious to slip away to devote themselves to their campaigns. The consensus, with which she enthusiastically concurred, was that Heseltine must be stopped. Hurd and Major would be candidates in the race to stop him. One minister showed just a little too much brio by suggesting that they would pin the blame on Heseltine as 'her assassin'. She looked puzzled and then replied, in that unnerving way she had of stating a truth that every one else would rather forget, that it was the Cabinet, not Heseltine, who were responsible.*

Mrs Thatcher's performance that afternoon in the debate on the

* The precise wording is disputed. Parkinson's account is the most dramatic: 'Oh no, it wasn't Heseltine, it was the Cabinet' (Cecil Parkinson, *Right at the Centre*, London, Weidenfeld & Nicolson, 1992, p. 4). But cf. Renton, *Chief Whip*, p. 107.

motion of no confidence has, like Geoffrey Howe's resignation statement, acquired the status of a 'great parliamentary occasion'. Such judgements are ones of taste. This occasion was, as a spectacle, signally lacking in it. Her speech was not particularly good. It was, though, delivered with such energy and courage that it dumb-founded all expectations. Kinnock's liverish and ungracious contribution helped, as did her treatment of the interruptions. But the adrenaline that fired her made her seem almost insane – which, of course, some of her critics thought she was in any case. At one point she exclaimed: 'I am enjoying this!' The bellows of approval from the Tory benches that greeted her performance were also expressions of shame and relief. As the crowd at a bull fight roars when a fine, combative specimen breathes its gory last, so the parliamentary Conservative Party roared as it now dispatched its leader.

Mrs Thatcher's remaining days in Downing Street were probably no more melancholic than those of other departing prime ministers. She bucked herself up by urging support for Major. He alone would maintain her 'legacy', a word incessantly on her lips. Not all around her were convinced. She might, some of us thought, have been better persuading Norman Tebbit to stand, though he would have been defeated. Even a Heseltine victory would have clarified issues and allegiances in the difficult years that lay ahead. And the ensuing election would almost certainly see him go down to defeat, which also might have suited the long-term interests of the party. But she could not bear too much reality – and who can blame her? Major duly secured the leadership, albeit with fewer votes – 185 to Heseltine's 131 and Hurd's 56 – than she had obtained when losing it. He then brought both his opponents into his Cabinet. So, in the short term at least, every one could be happy.

In conclusion, some judgement must be made of the role of those involved. This was not a Greek tragedy. Hubris was not punished; Mrs Thatcher was insensitive but she was not hubristic. Betrayal there was, but it was more the result of weakness than of malice, and though design entered into it, there was not a single conspiracy,

let alone a coordinating conspirator. In politics, it is legitimate to withdraw support from a leader who fails; and because failure is relative, assessments of it will differ. Yet, making all due allowances, Margaret Thatcher was shabbily treated by people who owed her a debt of personal loyalty. She might not have beaten Heseltine. She might not have won the next general election. But she had a good chance of doing both, and she deserved the right to try. The Cabinet denied it to her because most of its members preferred interest over honour. And not even interests were in the longer term served. Dispatching a Prime Minister, still sound in mind and body, who has won three general elections out of three – and doing so by Cabinet cabals, without reference to the electorate, on the eve of a war – is not the obvious route to legitimacy and stability.

15

AFTER THE FALL

Anyone who can yield great power easily and painlessly is probably ill suited to exercise it. As a case in point, nothing became John Major so well as the cheerful manner, indeed the patent relief, of his resignation.[1] He was never up to the job, and by the end somewhere inside himself he recognized the fact. By contrast, for Margaret Thatcher leaving Downing Street was more than a wrench: it was a personal catastrophe. She had driven herself so hard, excluding so much else from her life, that all she was now made for was to lead. Suddenly she found herself, indubitably and irreversibly, on the political scrapheap. Some of those around her thought, with varying degrees of optimism, of a possible return to power. But she never did, and, contrary to whispered allegations, she always discouraged such imaginings. She knew she was out for good.

Events themselves conspired to maximize her frustration. Britain was on the eve of a war in Iraq, one that was of her devising almost as much as Saddam Hussein's or George Bush's – Saddam having hoped to acquire Kuwait without a fight, and Bush having initially hoped to dislodge him by diplomacy. It was the

second time that Margaret Thatcher had authorized British troops to be mobilized for war. She half thought that she was indispensable to victory. She feared that if she were not there to take decisions, the allies would lose their nerve and the campaign would go wrong. Although there was, in fact, no such outcome, her fears proved far from groundless. Kuwait was freed. But the pursuit of international consensus, which she so despised, resulted in a premature end to campaigning that left Saddam in place: it would then take a new war, with terrible consequences, to oust him.

She took the closest interest in the progress of the campaign, watching news ceaselessly, poring over maps and studying commentary. She was proud of the contribution made by British troops. But she thought the allied political and military leadership was weak. She admired the grit of General Norman Schwarzkopf, commanding Operation Desert Storm on the ground. But she was critical of the ultra-cautious US Chairman of the Joint Chiefs of Staff, Colin Powell. She spoke with derision about his warnings against a 'turkey shoot' of defeated Iraqi forces. Mrs Thatcher never believed in worrying about enemy casualties while a campaign was in progress, and not greatly afterwards.*

She was even more tortured by her successor's handling of Europe. Guilt-ridden by her own slowness of perception, she felt she had to alert the country before Britain was inextricably drawn into a United States of Europe. Once she was out of power that sense of urgency consumed her.

It was natural that Major should feel hurt and betrayed by her behaviour. He complained, and frequently raged, about her attacks

---

* In fact, when she came to know Colin Powell better she developed respect and even liking for him. Oddly enough, given the importance ascribed to Powell's colour in American politics, she had to be persuaded after their first lengthy discussion that he was black at all. (He has quite a light skin.) But then, she was not only racially unprejudiced, she never thought about the subject.

on his European policy. In his memoirs he suggests that she should have made her views known to him privately, respecting proprieties.[2] But that would have been pointless: shifts of government policy are not achieved by polite exchanges behind closed doors. Moreover, it would have denied her the only significant weapon she still possessed: the power to command media attention and to use it in order to mobilize public opinion.

What she can be blamed for is her indiscretion. She was too free with her opinions about Major's failings, and her observations were mischievously but predictably passed on to the press, often in an exaggerated form. It is, however, worth noting that, unlike less honest and more media-savvy politicians, she never used the device of 'friends of' or 'sources close to' as cover to brief the press with her own remarks. This sort of poisonous briefing against her, by contrast, flowed regularly out of Downing Street.

On one occasion, though, she did seriously embarrass herself. Frustrated by the discipline of keeping her mouth shut during the 1992 general election campaign, she used a written interview with the US magazine *Newsweek* to break free of that constraint. She wrote out at home the replies to the questions asked and managed somehow to fax them back – she was not usually so good with office machinery – while concealing the whole affair from her staff. The worst passage was in response to the question whether Major would now be his 'own man' – itself a reference back to her clumsy, but not maliciously intended, remarks shortly before leaving Downing Street, when she referred to herself as a 'back seat driver'. She now replied that she didn't accept that Major could possibly be his own man, because he had only 'been Prime Minister for seventeen months and he inherited all these great achievements of the past eleven-and-a-half years'.[3] The effect was worsened because the questions actually asked were not printed and the piece appeared as a seamless article, thus making it more offensive. When it was published, there was a brutal confrontation with her staff. She was initially indignant but soon contrite, at

least about her unprofessionalism. In future, only the European issue would prompt her to make personal attacks on Major, as when she chastised him for his 'arrogance' in refusing a referendum on the Maastricht Treaty.[4] Otherwise, she tried to hold her peace.

In any case, these two *idées fixes* – the Iraq War and the European threat – dominated Mrs Thatcher's thoughts in the period after she left office. She repeatedly complained to those around her of the timing of the move to bring her down, when she was representing Britain abroad and when a war was to be fought. This was no mere pose, though, naturally, it also contained an element of special pleading. She genuinely considered her removal in this manner as unpatriotic, and it added greatly to her bitterness. The ensuing rows about Europe stoked the same flames, and over a much longer period.

She had other complaints about Major too. She believed, for example, that the Community Charge could have been salvaged and was displeased, if not surprised, when it was abandoned in favour of a new version of the old domestic rates, the Council Tax. She deplored the Government's relaxation of control over public expenditure, which she correctly predicted would lead to economic and political trouble. Something else that grated was the return of Michael Heseltine to the Cabinet. She was being unrealistic in thinking that Major would volunteer to inherit her enmities. But she rightly foresaw that Heseltine's influence meant an adoption of policies she could not stomach. Major's later appointment of Heseltine as Deputy Prime Minister, as part of the deal to win his support when apparently under threat from John Redwood's candidature in 1995, provided confirmation that his Government would always go in an anti-Thatcherite direction.* This, it should

* Major's denial that he did such a deal with Heseltine is at best disingenuous. Whether it was sealed with words or merely by mutual understanding, it was done, and no one with any understanding of the politics of the day seriously questions it (cf. Major, *The Autobiography*, p. 642).

be added, was despite her reluctantly giving Major public support against Redwood.*

Beyond all that, Mrs Thatcher increasingly disliked Major's pursuit of consensus, his wooing of interest groups, his chippiness and, of course, his constant attempts to distance himself from her. Although it involves a jump forward in time (before another jump backwards), mention should here be made of her Keith Joseph Memorial Lecture, which she delivered to a CPS audience on 11 January 1996, because its contents encapsulated her objections to the general course Major was pursuing.[5] At the time it was already clear that, barring a miracle, the party was on course for an electoral drubbing. The question was: Why? Was it because the Government since she had left office had moved too far on to the Opposition's ground? Or was it failing because it was still too 'Thatcherite'? More than a decade later, the question still has resonance.

In her lecture, Mrs Thatcher contended that the principles adopted in the late 1970s, and given effect during the 1980s, were as relevant as ever. She argued the case for limited government. She also argued for 'self-government', attacking moves towards closer European integration. The forthright language placed the speech on the front page of every newspaper. That was, indeed, her intention. It was, after all, a rallying cry; and she, at least, still believed that it might be heard.

By now she had become hopelessly frustrated. She had genuinely

---

* She issued a statement on 23 June 1995: 'I fully support the Prime Minister and would vote for him if I were still a member of the House of Commons. I hope that the matter will be resolved by a ringing endorsement of the Prime Minister as soon as possible.' At the time I was working on Redwood's campaign and had tried to prevent this endorsement. But she was not, in fact, personally close to Redwood, or he to her – a matter of temperament, not policies. In any case, Seymour, working with his old friend Robert Cranborne (later Marquess of Salisbury), Major's campaign manager, got the statement out of her before dispatching her abroad. He was acting in her interests, of course, and he was right in so far as her reputation was concerned. But Major was almost forced to resign and would have gone had just a few votes swung against him. If he had, the future of the Thatcher project might have been very different. Naturally, Major felt no gratitude, and even complained that she had not done more to back him (Major, *The Autobiography*, p. 636).

if perhaps unrealistically believed that she could play a role in encouraging a Tory revival. She expressed the view in a letter written soon after leaving office: 'It would perhaps be true to say that we have just come to the end of the *first phase* of our work. So short a time, but even now the fires need re-kindling, and that will be my main task.'[6] Unfortunately, the 'second phase' was rejected with varying degrees of irritation by the Conservative leadership and, as a result, the 'fires' she had hoped to 're-kindle' proved destructive, not creative. She kept on talking about setting up groups to encourage fresh thinking, only to be told not to do so because it would be portrayed as plotting. She had hoped for so much more. Major never understood this, and such misunderstanding was fateful and perhaps fatal for the Conservative Party.

Nor could Major understand her at a deeper level. He focused obsessively on her bad behaviour. She, for her part, concentrated on his lack of principle. One should add, however, that she did not hate her successor, while he does seem to have hated her. She would never, for instance, have used 'foul language' about him, or cried, 'I want her isolated! I want her destroyed!', as Major's political secretary records that he did of her.[7] The words she was most likely to use about him were ones of exasperation – 'How *stupid*!', 'How *petty*!', 'What a silly little man!', or (screwing up her face, and using a stage Scottish accent) 'Puir wee bairn!' She did not even really dislike him, though unfairly she disliked his wife (she rarely saw the best in spouses). The worst that she ever felt for Major was a mild contempt, and even that was tinged with a sort of affection, which perhaps came from the knowledge that she, after all, had chosen him (something she claimed she did not regret).

Immediately after her departure from Number Ten, her mood was black: she was prone to tears, she was difficult and ill-tempered, sometimes she seemed unhinged. She was almost certainly clinically depressed. Perhaps she should have taken some medication, but she did not. It is also to this time that can be traced another problem in her life, namely her drinking.

Contrary to later legend, Mrs Thatcher had never drunk heavily in office. She enjoyed relaxing with a whisky and soda (no ice) and continued to do so. She was not knowledgeable or even particularly enthusiastic about Scotch, but it was her favourite, because it was less fattening than gin and tonic. (In later years, though, the latter became her regular tipple.) She had not been tempted to drink heavily in Downing Street, for two very good reasons: first, she always had a low threshold for alcohol, so a little went a long way; and second, even the mildest inebriation would have dulled her mind during the extremely long hours she worked on her papers. And one thing she never lost from Grantham was the conviction that work came before everything else. Now, however, the demands of work were far less – and, like many unhappy people, she undoubtedly hoped that a drink would make life bearable. Most important, she was now reliant on Denis to pour the drinks; and he filled her glass as he did his, with the equivalent of quadruple shots of spirits.[8] Naturally, people began to notice that Margaret was often plainly intoxicated. Nor did she take drink well. She quickly became loud, argumentative and unpleasant to those who crossed her, or who she merely thought had crossed her.

Nor, unfortunately, was this the end of the complications. Other factors meant that people thought she was a secret drinker, even perhaps a full-blown alcoholic, neither of which was true. A year or so after leaving Downing Street she discovered, or at least persuaded herself, that she had put on weight, and she determined to lose it. This meant that she cut down heavily on lunch. So she would be up at six, have her hair done, hold meetings or read and dictate all morning, and then restrict herself to soup and fruit, with or without a large drink poured by Denis. The lack of food meant that when he poured her next drink – and in DT's view the sun passed 'over the yard arm', as he put it, as early as a quarter past five in the afternoon – it went straight to her head.

Worse still, she had major work on her teeth. She acquired cumbersome plates, and began to mangle her words. She now

slurred and sometimes hissed. This had nothing whatsoever to do with alcohol. She did it when she was stone-cold sober. But many drew the conclusion that she was continually drunk. And because the dental work hurt her, she felt even less inclined to eat and so the drink had even more effect. Finally – as will be considered further later – the effect of her growing deafness and her more serious mental deterioration was to render her conversation repetitive and on occasion barely comprehensible. Again people assumed that the bottle was to blame, and those who did not really assume it pretended to do so and sneered openly in order to damage her reputation and belittle her opinions. The tactics were unpleasant, but they were effective.

At least she was not friendless. Friendship with Mrs Thatcher came in very different forms, and it was important to understand in which category one fitted. She did not encourage people to call her by her first name, though she accepted it when they did.* She was uneasy with intimacy, though not a prude. She continued to use her appearance to get her way, and she was still a remarkably good-looking woman in her late seventies. She had fine legs, and knew it, hitching her dress up a little as she folded them. Her concern to look attractive explained her impractical and much discouraged attachment to high heels. Many exaggerated accounts of her 'frailty' resulted from her tottering shakily up or down a staircase, clutching at banisters for support. This was the result of vanity, not decrepitude – though she did in her eighties suddenly become less sure-footed and more uncertain on stairs. She liked in an innocent way to flirt. But she did not much like to be kissed, though she suffered it with good grace. Norman Stone, who was a great admirer and helped her with speeches, was a kisser. This privilege was, however, withdrawn after a misadventure in Taiwan. Late one

* For some years after her ennoblement she was not at ease being addressed as Lady Thatcher. She specifically instructed me to go on calling her 'Mrs Thatcher', and I stuck to this to the end. Everyone else in the office called her 'Lady Thatcher' (or in later years 'Lady T') – never 'Margaret'.

evening, when Mrs Thatcher was entertaining guests in her magnificent hotel suite, the professor appeared in her doorway to pay his respects but promptly collapsed, full length and senseless, on the marble floor. He was then unceremoniously carried out. Mrs Thatcher was not puritanical in such matters, but she thought this indecorous, and the relationship cooled.

A small group of friends tried hard to make the transition to private life less stressful for her. Alistair McAlpine organized lunches and dinners. Other stalwarts joined in the task of filling her time. Cecil Parkinson, Nicholas Ridley, Charles Powell, Bernard Ingham, Gordon Reece, Tim Bell, David Wolfson, George Gardiner, Jeffrey Archer and Stephen Sherbourne were among those who offered the balm of friendship when it was most needed. Crawfie, Alison Wakeham and Caroline Ryder provided female company, as, from the older generation, did Margaret Thatcher's old friend Lady Glover, with whom she spent holidays in Switzerland. A rota of friends ensured that the Thatchers had somewhere to go at Easter and Christmas. Archie Hamilton, Mark Lennox-Boyd and Alexander Hesketh had them to stay: when they visited the Heskeths at Easton Neston they would go to Towcester races, where Mrs Thatcher enjoyed a bet. Christopher Bailey and his wife took them regularly to the opera, which she liked well enough, though Denis was the opera buff. And Peter Morrison entertained them in style at his house in Bruton, in more or less conscious reparation for his earlier shortcomings.

Nor, by and large, did the intellectual right forget what they owed her. Paul Johnson came in to talk and even set up a Thatcher-supporting Tory group (later merged with Conservative Way Forward). Alan Walters was back in touch. Brian Griffiths, who received a peerage in her resignation honours, paid his respects. He had hoped to serve as a minister under Major, though he was disappointed. Mrs Thatcher, always keen to see that her former staff were looked after, had him appointed to succeed Hugh Thomas as chairman of the CPS. But the CPS board resented her

intervention and some of its members henceforth distanced the Centre from her, a course which Griffiths soon proved content to follow.[9]

John O'Sullivan, Robert Conquest, Norman Stone, Patrick Minford and others commiserated and consoled. This group, which expanded over time, also provided practical advice and drafting help with the prodigious number of speeches and articles, and several books, that filled the next decade of Margaret Thatcher's active life. There was even a sense, for a time, that though Thatcher was out Thatcherism was a creed whose time had come. Certainly, there was a contrast between the world-weary cynicism of Major's Government, committed to stitching up deals and with a thinly disguised contempt for anything that smacked of ideology, and the fervour of the enthusiasts who gathered around Mrs Thatcher and fought the causes – above all the Eurosceptic cause – that she espoused. The transitional section in *The Path to Power* entitled 'Beginning Again' catches the feel: 'nearly all the cleverest conservatives, those who had something to say and much to offer, were of my way of thinking'.[10] So it seemed. It was an illusion. Conservative Party politics always rests in the end on power and patronage, not on ideas. But it was pleasant for a while to think otherwise.

An infrastructure for Mrs Thatcher's life had rapidly to be created. McAlpine was the central figure in doing so. He provided a house in Great College Street, close to the Palace of Westminster, for an office. Mrs Thatcher was duly ensconced in a little sitting room on the first floor: secretaries and other staff worked above and below her, detectives dwelt in the basement. John Whittingdale (ex-political secretary, future MP and lifelong Thatcher devotee) organized the work.

More problematic was finding somewhere suitable for the Thatchers to live. Denis and Margaret had bought a house on a private estate in Dulwich in 1989. She had always been anxious to avoid finding herself in the position of Ted Heath in February 1974, bundled out of Downing Street with no house of his own. But it

was less an intimation of political mortality, more an eye for a good investment, that prompted the purchase, and it is hard to imagine that she ever seriously envisaged permanent residence there. (Luckily, the Thatchers sold it before Major's ERM-induced recession caused house prices to collapse.) Dulwich was simply too far out of town. There were other problems associated with no longer living 'over the shop'. Suddenly deprived of staff, Mrs Thatcher had to make her own phone calls and had no idea how to use a push-button telephone. She had to get advice from the police to do so. While preparing to put Dulwich on the market and find somewhere else, the Thatchers borrowed a flat owned by Mrs Henry Ford in Eaton Square, Belgravia. It was suitably grand and central but dark, and Denis in particular disliked its gloom. Mrs Thatcher, sitting beneath a painting of Queen Isabella of Spain, hosted sometimes lachrymose and slightly mad lunches here, while her friends and advisers around the table lamented bitterly the turn of events.

The Thatchers eventually bought a Georgian house in nearby Chester Square, and moved in during the summer of 1991. It was smart and convenient. There was a small formal dining room in which to entertain, though routinely she and Denis ate below stairs in the kitchen. There were no live-in staff, at least not until she fell ill – just a cleaner and an odd-job man. So she was compelled to do more cooking. Denis in general ate little but was extremely demanding about his breakfast. He required five kinds of toast. He also liked boiled eggs, but since she rose early and he late she usually overboiled them. On one memorable occasion, however, she forgot to boil them at all and Denis's reaction as he sliced the top off his raw egg was unprintable. The new house was also somewhere to put her possessions: the basement had a strongroom for the valuables – or, if necessary, for her own security, in case of terrorist attack.

But 73 Chester Square was not ideal. There were too many stairs for Denis, though almost to the last he struggled up them to his sitting room on the third floor. The couple's bedroom was on the second.

Also, though there was a small patio at the back, the house became very hot in the summer months. Planning restrictions prevented the installation of both a lift and built-in air conditioning, and the Thatchers' stinginess precluded the purchase of portable air cooling units. She preferred to swelter, even though she hated the heat, and would endure sleepless nights that interfered with her ability to work.

In addition to providing her with office accommodation, Alistair McAlpine also conceived the idea of a Foundation, to promote Margaret Thatcher's vision and perpetuate her legacy – and, in his private view, to provide a basis from which she might return to office, if events moved in that direction. From the start the project was dogged by problems. The purposes of the Foundation were established without sufficient regard to whether it would be able to gain charitable status, which was essential if it was to attract sizeable tax-beneficial donations. Above all, it was not understood how much political bias would enter into the Charity Commission's final decision. In truth, no Foundation bearing Mrs Thatcher's name was ever going to be granted charitable status, because it was a red rag to too many leftish bulls. But the rejection was a blow all the same. Eventually, a halfway house was found by which money for specific purposes that counted as 'charitable' was funnelled through the Charities Aid Foundation. But the donations in Britain were disappointing. Foreign donations were much more significant. Most of these went into the Foundation's US account – many in lieu of fees for speaking which Mrs Thatcher could otherwise have taken for herself.

One reason why British donations dried up lay in the behaviour of Mark Thatcher. His swaggering and shifty manner, his demands that businessmen 'pay up' for gains that business had made during his mother's premiership, and his wrongly presumed presence on the Foundation's board, or at least influence behind the scenes, did irremediable damage. Only in February 1991, when Julian Seymour (a business colleague of Tim Bell's) was recruited to run the Thatcher office and the Foundation, was the shadow of Mark's

presence lifted. Indeed, this was the main reason why Bell and other friends pressed for Seymour's appointment.

Under Seymour, the Foundation became a modest success. It concentrated on funding projects to assist students and entrepreneurs from behind the old Iron Curtain to make the most of the freedoms that Mrs Thatcher had helped win for them. The funds were liquidated as her retirement approached. The British money went to endow a chair of enterprise studies at the Judge Institute in Cambridge and to the Churchill archive centre, also in Cambridge, where her papers would be stored alongside those of her great hero. The bulk of the American money was used to set up a Margaret Thatcher Center for Freedom at the Washington-based conservative think tank the Heritage Foundation. The Center is committed to a cause that was always close to her heart: cementing the Anglo–US Special Relationship.

It was, above all, work that saved Margaret Thatcher's sanity. It was also a necessity. She was poorer than many imagined – scandalously so by the international standards of former heads of government. At Number Ten she had scrupulously paid all her private entertainment and dining expenses. DT made no contribution. She had also refused to take successive salary increases as Prime Minister, and that reduced her pension. This situation prompted her to complain ceaselessly and disagreeably about how much she had forgone. But, leaving aside personal obsession, she certainly needed to earn a good salary during the rest of her active life if she was to retire in comfort. DT could not afford to keep them both, and such a course was never envisaged. Now, despite his directorates, she was soon once more keeping him, because, from 1994 when he lost his office at the Conservative Small Business Bureau, he had to be found a place and staff in hers. On top of all that, she could expect to subsidize her two children, neither of whom seemed capable of earning a reliable, trouble-free income. The speech-making circuit obviously beckoned.

She was fortunate in that abroad at least her reputation was still at its height. Her favourite stamping ground was the United States,

where conservative audiences – much larger and richer than in Britain – offered her not just cash but love and veneration. The Washington Speaker's Bureau organized tailor-made visits for the few years following her departure from office. She enjoyed these tours and continued making them, often addressing far from distinguished audiences, until her health prevented it. Some of her speeches in the United States were, though, of considerable importance, for example those in which she set out a conservative vision of foreign policy in the post–Cold War world. She argued the case for ballistic missile defence at a time when the approach was highly controversial, thus demonstrating her willingness to move away from Cold War paradigms. She also spoke about the shared values and history of Britain and America, arguing for a reinforced Special Relationship.[11] She was intrigued by the concept of an 'Anglosphere' of English-speaking nations, an idea championed by John O'Sullivan. In private, her enthusiasm went further and she admitted that she would welcome Britain becoming the fifty-first State of the Union. She succeeded Chief Justice Warren Burger as Chancellor of William and Mary College in Virginia, a position which involved a good deal of fund-raising and more speech-making. (She also consented, at the prompting of Max Beloff and Ralph Harris, to be Chancellor of the independent University of Buckingham, her ability to say 'no' in private being the inverse of that in public.) She was chairman of the Institute of US Studies at London University, whose director Gary McDowell helped with her American speeches, arranged meetings for her with top US politicians and academics visiting Britain, and rapidly became a friend. She stood up effectively for the Institute in internal academic politics: significantly, it was wound up soon after she left the post.

Margaret Thatcher was also greatly admired in Asia, where her combination of power and femininity proved doubly intriguing. The focus of her speaking tours was Japan, at least until that country fell into economic crisis at the turn of the century. If you asked Margaret Thatcher what she thought of the Japanese she

would initially dwell on their 'infinite courtesy', though what she really meant was formality. She also had a high view of their industrial and engineering capacity. Beneath the surface, though, she was distrustful. She did not launch into attacks on Japan's wartime conduct in the way she did in respect of Germany. But she was quite open, even in Japan, in saying that she did not think the Japanese should be given a permanent seat on the UN Security Council.

Similarly, her attitude to China was more complicated than would appear on the surface. She probably understood the Chinese better than she did the Japanese and, indeed, better than most Western statesmen do. This was partly the fruit of experience in dealing with them over Hong Kong. But she also had an instinctive rapport. She admired their entrepreneurial spirit, and she was not in the least repelled by their often crude nationalism. She believed China would become a superpower, before such prediction became a platitude. She did not think that the Chinese she met were all the same, as some Westerners do even after years of diplomatic contact. She treated her interlocutors as individuals; thus she disliked Li Peng, thought Jiang Zemin empty, but enjoyed meetings with the (relatively) open-minded economist and former mayor of Shanghai, Zhu Rongji. Whenever she visited China she brought with her a stylish silk tie for the disgraced former Prime Minister Zhao Ziyang.

She had two golden rules that governed her personal dealings with China. First, she would never compromise her position by accepting money, either from the Chinese or from pro-Chinese figures in Hong Kong, for any speeches she delivered. Second, she did not say one thing to the Chinese in private and another in public. The account of her harsh encounter with Li Peng in 1991 given in *Statecraft* is entirely accurate and vouched for by another source present. It contrasts with the approach adopted by John Major at about the same time, which was to say nothing awkward to the Chinese in private but act the British lion in front of the British media.[12] In public, she weighed her words. A great deal of thought

went into her speech to an *International Herald Tribune* conference in Beijing in 1996. She was persuaded with reluctance not to talk about the *laogai* (Chinese political prison camps), largely on the grounds that the evidence for them was disputable (though she believed it). But she had just met the Chinese dissident Harry Wu and she was absolutely determined to mention publicly the case of two persecuted freedom activists, Wei Jingsheng and Wang Dan, which she did. The Chinese protested angrily, though they did not actually walk out.[13]

Naturally, both she and Major were compelled to be cautious because of Hong Kong. She had disapproved of Major's appointment of Chris Patten as Governor of the colony. She thought that he was too political and that a ceremonial Governor, an official, would have been more appropriate. Her instincts turned out to be correct: Patten behaved like a politician and so within months earned the distrust of the Chinese. But she lent strong support to his intro-duction of limited democratic reforms there, arguing that they were in line with, and not a breach of, the Anglo-Chinese Joint Agreement. She need not have done this, and, given the fact that her former adviser Percy Cradock was fiercely opposed to the strategy, it was not an easy decision. She was able to smooth out some problems, such as those with the airport and the courts, and she retained the respect of the Chinese after Patten had lost it, which was good for the people of Hong Kong. She also defended him robustly in the House of Lords against the old China hands. But the reforms were never accepted by China and have since been swept aside. Rarely has more effort been invested with less result.

Elsewhere in Asia, her visits had a purely private significance. She made speaking tours to all the main countries, including Taiwan despite protests from Beijing. South Korea she did not find congenial. Thailand was exotic, and she was friendly with General Prem, who had been the military ruler. In Singapore, and whenever he came to London, she enjoyed discussions with Lee Kwan Yew, for whom she had great admiration, but with whom she disagreed

about how to treat China. Indonesia was another port of call. She had always got on well with President Suharto and was perhaps overimpressed by features of his apparently enlightened authoritarian rule. She was prepared to accept that special circumstances warranted a large measure of intervention, both politically and economically, and she was completely and culpably blind to the treatment of East Timor.* On the other hand, she was quite aware that the Suharto family was corrupt. She would affect shock but then laugh when Denis referred to Mrs Suharto as 'Mrs Ten Per Cent'. Her favourite Indonesian was, without doubt, Dr B. J. Habibie, Suharto's right-hand man and briefly his successor as President. Mrs Thatcher knew him as Minister of Technology and he always considered himself more of an engineer than a politician, which perhaps he was; she, who liked to consider herself a scientist, enjoyed his technically baffling conversation.

Undoubtedly, India was Margaret Thatcher's favourite Asian country. But then, in her eyes it was hardly Asian at all: rather, an outpost of the old Empire and, at the same time, a leading member of the English-speaking community of nations. As so often, her views were a curious mixture of the archaic and the prophetic. She had always had a penchant for India, more than for Pakistan, though she got on well enough with the latter's leaders. As a young girl, she had entertained the thought of entering the (then still exclusively male) Indian Civil Service. But her father had told her that India would probably no longer be British by the time she was eligible and he was, of course, correct. Reading and rereading Kipling's verse continued to nourish her romantic ideas of India. It was only after she left office that, under the direction of the Finance Minister (and later Prime Minister) Manmohan Singh, India decisively took the path of economic reform that would begin to release its vast potential. Margaret Thatcher was fascinated by

---

* But, then, nobody else, apart from the Vatican and the Portuguese, cared much about East Timor, until Suharto's fall meant that the 'international community' could pontificate without its members losing trade concessions.

what she saw on her visits – and she was very impressed by Singh. She regarded the rise of India as a powerful and valuable balance against Chinese hegemony. She also saw the country as a force for stability and peace, because it was a democracy and because of its inherited British tradition of liberty and constitutionalism. She thought it was perfectly logical that India should be a nuclear power. She was in two minds about whether it should also be a permanent member of the UN Security Council.

Africa was bound to be less appealing than Asia, because so much of it was grindingly poor, or embarrassingly corrupt, or both. South Africa was the exception and came to play a significant role in her life. She visited in May 1991, as she had planned to do as Prime Minister, and was royally received by the (still minority white) Government. She had excellent relations with F. W. de Klerk, and it is often thought – not least by David Cameron – that this meant that she had bad relations with black leaders.* By and large, she did not. It is worth recalling why.

Margaret Thatcher's views of South Africa were influenced by Denis. He knew and loved the country and admired its achievements. But, like her, he thought that apartheid itself was as stupid and cruel as the Boers who devised and applied it. Mrs Thatcher understood black grievances, but she believed that change would eventually come through economic development. Hence enforced isolation through sanctions made no sense and would hit hardest the living standards of poor blacks.

She wanted, above all, a peaceful transition and she consistently worked to secure it. This involved being much harder on the South African Government in private than in public – precisely the opposite of the policy pursued by most other Commonwealth leaders. Thus when President P. W. Botha came to see her at Chequers in 1984 he was subject to some of the strongest face-to-face criticism

---

* After a well-publicized meeting with Mandela, David Cameron spoke of 'the mistakes my party made in the past with respect to relations with the ANC and sanctions on South Africa' (*Observer*, 27 August 2006).

he ever encountered. But the bullying had a purpose. This was to encourage secret negotiations in Britain between representatives of the South African Government and the ANC. These duly took place in locations provided by MI6. She pressed vigorously for the release of Nelson Mandela from detention. She saw that he alone had the authority and character to negotiate peace. Her demands for his freedom grew still more frequent and more forceful once de Klerk became President in 1989. Mandela himself knew perfectly well what he owed her. After his release, she had MI6 provide a safe house in which he could relax and recuperate. He visited her in Downing Street in July 1990 and they had a long, courteous, substantial discussion – to the fury of the Labour Party, who considered that he was their political property.

By now Mandela had developed a personal rapport with Mrs Thatcher that continued once she left office, when, obviously, he could simply have ignored her. Instead, he and his (second) wife visited her in London on several occasions. The Mandelas would have coffee with the Thatchers downstairs – Mandela found the long, steep staircases in the Belgravia houses too difficult to climb. They also met when she spent Christmas with Mark in South Africa. Mrs Thatcher made a generous donation to Mandela's charity. He was at this time deeply unhappy with what Robert Mugabe was doing in Zimbabwe, which he considered could also destabilize South Africa, and he poured out his worries to her. Relations with Mandela's successor as President, Thabo Mbeki, were less cordial. This, though, reflected Mbeki's shortcomings as a leader, not his views of Margaret Thatcher. He was a weak man, and for that reason more inclined to appease the ANC's hard-line communist wing.

Of all the South African black leaders, it was Chief Buthelezi, the Zulu leader, to whom she was closest: he can indeed be accurately termed a personal friend. She thought his contribution to ending apartheid had been much underrated. And she always had a romantic sympathy for the Zulus; as warriors and traditionalists, they represented her kind of Africa.

In 1995 Mark Thatcher purchased a fine house in Constantia, a wealthy suburb of Cape Town. Margaret and Denis took to going there for Christmas and the New Year and for occasional other holidays. Denis, in his old age, hated the British winter and sought the warmth. Margaret was interested in the plants and spent hours walking and sitting in the garden. Evenings were passed dining with dignitaries. Sometimes they made lengthy trips inland. Mrs Thatcher had mixed feelings about her South African stays. Despite her affection for her son, he got on her nerves when she had to spend long periods with him. Nor was his wife, Diane, keen to have her mother-in-law around too often or for too long. Also, Mrs Thatcher fretted about a lack of political news and gossip and often made abortive plans to return early. She did pay for Mark to have a separate house built in the grounds in which she and Denis would stay; but it was never completed. Mark failed to obtain the requisite planning permission and her security team decided that anyway it was unacceptably vulnerable to intruders. By the time he had to sell his house in 2006 to pay the fine levied by the South African Government – and to repay the bail money advanced by his mother – what Mrs Thatcher plaintively called 'my little house' had never been occupied, except by policemen.[14]

It was Margaret Thatcher's visits to the countries of the old Warsaw Pact that brought her into contact with perhaps her warmest admirers. Of these, the most enthusiastic were the Poles. The reception on her visits to Poland (to Warsaw, Poznan, Gdansk and Krakow) had a completely different quality from her welcome anywhere else in the region: not just enthusiastic but passionate. She appealed not only because she was seen as anti-Soviet but because she was also known as anti-German. The admiration was evident right across the political spectrum. As far as possible, though, Margaret Thatcher was committed to helping anti-communist Solidarity politicians whenever she discreetly could, and planned the timing of her visits and content of her speeches to that end. She was close to the young conservative Polish politician

(later foreign and defence minister) Radek Sikorski. The Thatcher Foundation opened an office in Warsaw, and thanks to the efforts of another British-educated Pole, Marek Matraszek, some useful work was done there.

Her best political friend in the region, however, was Vaclav Klaus, Prime Minister and later President of the Czech Republic. He was, if anything, even better versed in free-market economics than she was, though his government's actual performance was more questionable. In 1999 she made a very successful visit to Prague, ten years on from the 'Velvet Revolution' that ended communism in Czechoslovakia, to unveil a statue of Churchill. She was taken aback by the size and enthusiasm of the crowds she encountered.[15]

In Russia, the position was more complicated. She steadfastly refused to distance herself from Mikhail Gorbachev, even after his replacement by Boris Yeltsin and the collapse of his (always fragile) popularity. On the other hand, she had no doubt that Yeltsin deserved support, as she proved during the short-lived coup in the summer of 1991. While the Major Government and Bush Administration wavered, she did not. She received at Great College Street Yeltsin's representative, Galina Staravoitova, accompanied by the MEP Lord Bethell. Mrs Staravoitova put Mrs Thatcher through on the telephone to Yeltsin, besieged in Moscow's White House, and they spoke while Lord Bethell translated.* Mrs Thatcher then went outside to denounce the coup and call on the Russians to reject its leaders. This was precisely what they did, but she found herself as a result the target of some venomous briefing from Downing Street, resentful at her intervention.

She remained fascinated by Russia, not least by its sheer size – 'nine time zones', she would remind her audiences. She always believed in its potential, and she held frequent meetings in London

---

* Mrs Staravoitova was subsequently murdered in a classic KGB-style operation. After a meeting with the family, and at their request, Mrs Thatcher wrote to President Yeltsin demanding that the killers be brought to justice. They are still at large, doubtless enjoying high-level protection.

with the Russian economic reformers. Their policies are now widely regarded as synonymous with kleptocracy, a view which unfortunately contains some truth. Like everyone else, she was too easily persuaded that the fundamentals in Russia had changed. But she was right in insisting that the essential condition for meaningful economic reform was a rule of law. The lack of it, then and since, has squandered the opportunity to turn Russia into a 'normal country'. She also had an eye for young talent, particularly when it was combined with good looks, as it was in the case of her favourite young Russian politician, Boris Nemtsov. She met him in 1993 on her first tour of Russia after the break-up of the Soviet Union. He was then Governor of Nizhny Novgorod, which he had turned into a highly successful experiment in free enterprise. Nemtsov admired her hugely, though she would not have been flattered to know that he referred to her as his *babushka*.

Later, people like Nemtsov sought to reassure her about the emergence of Vladimir Putin. Others with whom she had contact, including the heroic former dissident Vladimir Bukovsky, thought differently. Bukovsky and she had had a serious disagreement about Gorbachev. He told her bluntly that she had been duped by the former Soviet leader; she did not agree and was angry. But she privately shared Bukovsky's feelings about Putin.[16] Typically, she complained about the Russian President's face, but she was, as always in such cases, thinking about his character – and her instincts were right. When in November 2006 Alexander Litvinenko was assassinated in London in what still looks like a Kremlin-authorized operation she sat down and wrote a strong letter to Tony Blair, urging that police protection be given to other likely targets – such as Bukovsky.

With the break-up of the Soviet Union, the old pattern of contacts had inevitably changed. But Margaret Thatcher had the reputation and mindset to cope with the new circumstances. She did not think that the Russians should be accorded an unfettered sphere of interest in the new Community of Independent States. Indeed, she strongly

supported the Chechen independence movement, at least until it turned to mass terrorism: she had discussions and dinner with the Chechen leader Aslan Maskhadov in London in 1998 – at which, however, she was very firm in demanding an end to hostage-taking.

In the Central Asian republics, the individual closest to her was Kazakhstan's President Nursultan Nazarbayev, the sort of wily authoritarian figure she understood. They spoke during the crisis of 1991, when he was trying to steer a middle way between the old USSR and an entirely new array of sovereign states; and later, whenever he came to London, they would meet. In Azerbaijan, the reformist President, Abulfaz Elchibey, looked to her as an example – until he was overthrown through Russian intervention. His regard for the former Prime Minister yielded substantial benefits to Britain. In the summer of 1992 BP was negotiating a huge deal with the Azeris to exploit their oil reserves, in the teeth of powerful American-led competition. Only one thing was required by Elchibey for him to confirm the contract: he wanted Margaret Thatcher to be present at the signing to demonstrate in that highly corrupt environment that it was all fairly and honestly done. At BP's and the British Government's request, she therefore agreed to stop over in a baking hot Baku on her return flight from Hong Kong. When the American ambassador saw her arrive unexpectedly at dinner with the President, his face fell, for he guessed the significance. The United States had indeed lost – and Britain had won – the vital contract.

In fact, of the states of the old USSR, only in Georgia, where Mrs Thatcher and Shevardnadze had never got on, and in Ukraine, where she had been unsympathetic to a break-away from the Soviet Union, was she without much of a following. She had, though, been much tougher about the Baltic states, refusing to countenance moves to force them to remain subject to Moscow. Here a new generation of politicians threw up people of her way of thinking – above all the young, dynamic Estonian Prime Minister Mart Laar.

Visits to Western Europe, where her well-known hostility to

Euro-federalism counted against her, were more of a problem, though even here she could count on a warm reception from the conservative-minded bankers and businessmen likely to constitute a paying audience. But it is worth noting what she felt about the Europeans themselves. Margaret Thatcher was often accused of being prejudiced, xenophobic and narrow-minded. Taken as a whole, these accusations are wide of the mark. She did not categorize people at all, at least when she met them personally, and their origins never mattered to her. But on one count she did warrant what was said, namely in her attitude to Germany and the Germans. Thanks to the efforts of others, her speeches put her views into a reasonably persuasive strategic context – that of the problem of a reunified Germany wielding excessive power in Europe. On one occasion, a speech in Frankfurt in November 1992, she even managed to praise Germany's monetary policy and post-war democracy.[17] In practice, Germany has proved much weaker than Mrs Thatcher, or many others, feared. More of a problem, indeed, has been the country's unwillingness to pull its international weight. But, in any case, in private Margaret Thatcher's views were much cruder. She believed that the German character had not changed and that it was essential to keep Germany weak if Europe and the world were to know peace. She expressed these opinions in terms that did no good to her reputation.

About the French she felt differently. It is true that in her last years, as towards Germany, her prejudices hardened. She would snort contemptuously and declare, 'the French never fought' (meaning in the Second World War). She even convinced herself that de Gaulle, for whom she initially had a certain admiration and with whose views and temperament she had more in common than she knew, fell into that category. She would inform gullible guests that he had been rescued by the British and evacuated from Dunkirk, pointing to a famous cartoon of a dripping General borne ashore by Churchill that hung outside her office. But in her way she

loved France, admired French style and enjoyed the company of Frenchmen. In particular, she liked and was too indulgent towards François Mitterrand, who received her as graciously after she left office as before.

Like many a British politician, she had a low view of her Italian counterparts, whom by and large she thought corrupt – with some exceptions. Francesco Cossiga, at different times Prime Minister and President, she considered a kindred spirit. Of the younger politicians, she knew and respected Antonio Martino, the economist who became Italian Defence Minister under Silvio Berlusconi. She also enjoyed Berlusconi's own company when he came in to see her. She particularly appreciated his anti-communism, though whether she would have admired his record in government is doubtful. In any case, once safely elected, he preferred to focus his charm on Tony Blair, not her.

This wide-ranging network of acquaintance meant that Margaret Thatcher was able to find points of contact in most of the world where she travelled, and if some lucrative speaking occasions could be arranged she could engage in a little personal diplomacy as well. Once Julian Seymour arrived to run her affairs, he saw that she gained proper reward for her labours.

She was an authoritative and powerful speaker. Although she demanded and received extensive briefing before any foreign visit, she generally spoke from scribbled notes. It was her forte, because it allowed her to ad lib and to seduce or provoke her audience. But the extempore technique also contained dangers, particularly when her health became precarious and her memory worsened. Because the performance depended on delivery at least as much as content, she had to fire herself up and rely on her nerves to such an extent that her staff never knew whether she would collapse or excel. She almost always excelled, and audiences received their money's worth. On the rare occasion that she failed to shine, as before a Chase Manhattan Bank audience in New York, she was only with difficulty prevented from returning her fee.

The standard speech, usually entitled 'Challenges of the Twenty-First Century', was a peculiar mixture of the trite and the profound, the anecdotal and the philosophical, the practical and the grandiose. It included sections on the 'advance of science' (which might include anything from nuclear fission to, if not quite the kitchen sink, at least the washing machine), on Russia, on Asia, and on current international crises. There was some discussion of the importance of capitalism and of the family. There was always a passage extolling the role of America and the vocation of the 'English-speaking peoples', even in front of audiences whose first language was not English. She would summarize the history of the twentieth century as a struggle between two systems – one based on the individual and the other based on the state, in which the habitually used labels of right and left had little or no significance. (She also particularly resented the label 'conservative' being accorded by the BBC and others to hardline communists.) She often liked to speak of a 'tripod' of liberty – oddly illustrated by raising three fingers to her audience – the 'legs' (or fingers) being respectively 'democracy', 'free speech' and (above all, incessantly and repetitively) 'the rule of law'. From such a summary, it is difficult to explain why the speech worked at all. But it did. Her voice carried well and was modulated to perfection, sometimes loud and harsh and sometimes sweet and girlish. She used her spectacles to great effect, pulling them off her nose and waving them to make a point. Jokes did not come naturally to her, but she had a fund of prepared humorous anecdotes, which she practised and delivered with aplomb. Her audiences, above all those in America, were spellbound.

Speaking tours were the main source of her income, but not the only one. She could have earned enormous sums had she sat in an executive role on main company boards, as her colleagues and successors would do. But she avoided it. She did take a place on the Hollinger advisory board, but only to please Conrad Black, who owned the *Telegraph* newspaper group: no one then knew what the future held. By contrast, it was a mistake, though a well-remunerated

one, to become a consultant to the tobacco giant, William Morris. Mrs Thatcher had no sympathy for the anti-smoking lobby, and DT chain-smoked with no obvious ill effects, but the connection did not help her standing. Another profitable but relatively short-lived source of remuneration was her presence on the advisory board of the New York-based Tiger Asset Management hedge fund. Here again she had no executive role, though she was asked to give her views about large international issues. She briefed herself extensively for this, though her judgement on Russia proved wrong – she was overimpressed by the reforms and believed, as did so many others, that neither the Russian Government nor the IMF would permit a default.

The single biggest project of her retirement was the writing of her memoirs. This, like so much else, was badly handled at the start, and for the same reason – namely, the role of her son, though Peter Morrison's incompetence also contributed. Morrison had at this stage pulled himself together enough to try to help organize her life, and like Mark he was motivated by great affection (and in his case, as previously noted, guilt). But he was not sober, clever or forceful enough to do anything other than add to the chaos. For example, it was Morrison who allowed Alan Clark to imagine that he was being asked to co-write Mrs Thatcher's memoirs, which she would never envisage, rather than merely draft them for her, which he would not even consider.[18] Mark entertained hopes of an unrealistically large sum for the commission and turned in search of it to Macmillan (then owned by Robert Maxwell) rather than HarperCollins (owned by Rupert Murdoch). Despite the offence this caused, her literary agent, Marvin Josephson, in due course secured a first-rate deal with HarperCollins, worth £4 million. The publishers also proved highly professional and, at the end when her health failed, extremely kind.

Mrs Thatcher knew nothing of writing books – why should she? – and she was initially seduced by flatterers who told her that she could simply sit down and write her memoirs herself with some

research assistance. She was also assured that what the world wanted to hear were her thoughts rather than her experiences. Neither, of course, was true. As a result, the work on the memoirs stalled and there were lengthy and acrimonious rows. After spending several days trying to draft a passage describing what she ate at her first (take-away) meal in Downing Street – Was it Chinese? Was it Indian? Who went out to get it? – she grumpily accepted that the procedure would have to be that used for her speeches: namely, to use drafts prepared by others – but on the basis of her thoughts and subject to her correction.

The work finally began in November 1991. The full memoirs team was then assembled – me to write the main draft, Chris Collins to do the research, and John O'Sullivan to provide lightness and humour and, when necessary, to help browbeat the author herself.[19] A stream of figures from her past were summoned to recount their memories and so stimulate hers. She would study chronologies of events and extracts from other published sources and then give her reflections, which were typed up. She paid visits to the Cabinet Office to study papers. The old boardroom downstairs at 35 Chesham Place (her new office premises) now became the 'memoirs room', where row upon row of boxed files climbed the walls. Mrs Thatcher came down to give her verdict on the latest drafts.

Special 'retreats', as she called them, were organized at which she and the memoirs team would go through groups of chapters. These events were held in circumstances of some luxury in Gstaad (Switzerland), at Lyford Cay (the Bahamas) and in a variety of British country-house hotels. Denis came too and pretended he was on holiday. But the gatherings were tense, unpredictable affairs. One problem was that Mrs Thatcher, though personally generous, hated to see conspicuous consumption at her expense. She was particularly outraged when members of her party ordered Pimm's, and complained about it for weeks. But more often the tension arose from the drafting process. She had her own views about style, but

would, after some argument, accept advice. She was, however, rigid and often irascible if she suspected that anyone was underplaying an achievement or misrepresenting an event. The most difficult chapter of *The Downing Street Years* was that concerning the Iraq War, precisely because she was so sensitive about her role in it. As a result, it is one of the least revealing, because everyone gave up trying to coax interesting insights out of her.

By far the worst row concerned her dealings with Deng Xiao Ping over Hong Kong in 1982. She wanted to emphasize how tough she had been in the negotiations – and she had indeed been tough. But she did not wish to admit that she had lacked effective leverage and that, because the Chinese could not have been stopped from walking in if they decided to do so, they had been given almost all they demanded. Wrongly considering this a suggestion of weakness – it was, in fact, simply a tribute to realism – she erupted with fury and continued to shout, glare and strike out text, until John O'Sullivan announced that he was catching a flight back to the United States and left the room. The point in question was later resolved with little discussion, and soon forgotten.

The Downing Street Years was written in just eighteen months. Many of those Mrs Thatcher criticized in it themselves wrote critical and self-serving reviews. Other reviewers simply allowed their prejudices full scope, and most of the media was at this time still strongly prejudiced against her. But the book was a commercial success. It sold more than half a million copies, earning HarperCollins a good return and Mrs Thatcher substantial royalties – in marked contrast to some modern high-profile political memoirs. Because of its veracity and frankness, it has also stood the test of time and will continue to do so as more information is revealed. One of her less sympathetic biographers describes it as, despite 'its *longueurs* . . . by far the most comprehensive and readable of modern prime ministerial memoirs'.[20] The judgement is fair – on both counts.

Both volumes of memoirs, but above all *The Downing Street Years*, were intensively and exhaustingly promoted by Mrs

Thatcher through interviews, speeches and book signings in Britain, America and Asia. She excelled in this. Her speeches drew large, rapturous audiences. Particularly remarkable was a high-octane performance in the Barbican in London. When she signed books, at enormous speed and without a smudge of her large signature, crowds arrived and waited for hours. At Harrods, the queue wound around the tableware department, entirely obstructing ordinary business. At Hatchards, it stretched down Piccadilly. The public already knew, even if most of the political world as yet did not, that they were in the presence of a great historic figure.

Because of the requirements of the market, the two volumes of memoirs were published in inverse order, so *The Path to Power*, which deals with her early life, came later. It was completed still more briskly. But, then, it was shorter and bound to be of less interest. She remembered a great deal about Grantham, but not that much about Oxford, and she evidently had no wish to dwell on the Heath years. Nor did she think that she had shone as leader of the Opposition, so she was reluctant to think about that period much either. The last section of the book consisted of essays on topics of contemporary importance, but these – aside from her observations about Europe – did not gain much publicity, mainly because the publishers wrongly concentrated all their promotional efforts on the early life. There was at about this time also the first evidence in private of a dimming of her previously very acute mental faculties. Her concentration was inclined to flag and she found it more difficult to master complicated data – though Margaret Thatcher at half throttle was still more impressive than most of her political contemporaries at full power.

By now the framework for her professional and personal life was fully in place. While Julian Seymour ran her financial affairs, Mark Worthington, a former researcher to Tory MPs who was to serve as her indispensable aide to near the end of her life, arrived to provide political advice and briefing. In early 1992 Seymour organized a move into spacious offices in a fine Georgian house in Belgravia at

35 Chesham Place. In 1996 she would move into the smaller house next door, Number 36, on a short lease. In both, her own office was arranged to look very much like her study at Number Ten. There was an old leather-covered desk, whose drawers were stuffed with papers relating to speeches or her personal affairs. But usually, as in Downing Street, she worked in a high-backed chair by the fireplace, looking at papers with the help of a huge magnifying glass – she wilfully refused to wear reading classes – underlining, marking marginalia, gathering odds and ends together in files, and then forgetting where she had put them. (There were only, in fact, a few possibilities, and Worthington or a secretary could quickly locate what was later required – in a desk drawer, in the brown leather briefcase she carried around with her, or even, if of small format, within one of the famous capacious handbags.) As in Number Ten, there was a written programme prepared for the following day. This too she would often lose, to the extent that weekly programmes were prepared and stuck on to the wall of her kitchen at home where, naturally, she never consulted them.

She took great care of the decoration of the offices, particularly of the combined sitting room, study and office in which she worked. Here were kept the items that meant most to her. On top of the desk was a fine writing stand, and by the side of the desk a large globe. Over the mantelpiece was the wedding painting of her dressed in blue, with her ostrich feather hat. On display around the room were busts of Ronald Reagan, of Winston Churchill and also of Denis. A rather unnerving bronze impression of her own hands, sliced off at the wrists, perched on a ledge. On one side of the fireplace was a copy of a headless Neanderthal dove, from Vukovar in Croatia, across from a South Atlantic stone walrus. Bowls, dishes and statues were frequently moved around as the fancy took her. She needed no help with this, being immensely strong in the arms. There was not a box or pot she could not carry, nor, indeed, a stuck window or jammed door she could not shift – and, being impatient, she would sometimes use this strength in disregard of her personal

security – as when she would go out on to the balcony at home to force open the french windows, presenting herself obligingly pro-filed for any sniper.

In her office a glass-fronted bookcase with cupboards was full of her favourite volumes. These were selected for inspiration rather than continuous reading, which she rarely practised, preferring to dip into books and extract whatever she found useful in them with-out worrying too much about what the author's conclusions actually were. For example, in the opening section of Paul Kennedy's *The Rise and Fall of the Great Powers* the passages arguing that political diversity in Europe had allowed the West's progress – and thus that a single European state would impede it – were heavily underlined. She never seems to have got to the main argument that America was a declining power, which she would have roundly rejected. She liked volumes of history. Hugh Trevor-Roper's *The Rise of Christian Europe* was a favourite source, though again for a special passage – this time relating to the West's cultural capacity for tech-nological advance – as was Barbara Tuchman's book on the Holy Land, *The Bible and the Sword*. There was theology too: for example, books by the Catholic neo-conservative theologian Michael Novak, whom she admired. She would consult a large-print King James's Bible to check her scriptural quotations.

Other sources to which she turned for inspiration included Ronald Reagan's *Speaking my Mind* and books by two other American conservative figures, Ben Wattenberg and Alan Bloom. In her handbag she always carried around a tiny volume of extracts from Churchill's speeches and broadcasts. She was, in truth, over-fond of quoting, not realizing that what she herself had to say was more noteworthy or at least more apposite than the sources she quoted. She used several dictionaries of quotations and shortly after leaving office became enthralled by a book of sayings from American Presidents. She was very annoyed, but her staff relieved, when Denis threw the volume out with the rubbish – by mistake, or so he claimed. Many of her most heavily thumbed books were of

poetry: Kipling (naturally), *Palgrave's Golden Treasury* and an anthology compiled by Lord Wavell called *Other Men's Flowers*. The lower cupboards were stuffed full of pamphlets and photocopied articles and speeches. When in search of ideas, she would get down on her knees and rummage through them.

The offices had a distinctive femininity. Sir John Carter, a stalwart but unobtrusive friend, every week sent beautiful flowers and plants which were placed on tables or taken home. In summer their perfume filled the air, adding to Mrs Thatcher's own, for she wore a heavy scent, usually Chanel No. 5. The offices reflected her life in and out of power. She was not modest about her achievements, and the offices reflected this. They were packed with memorabilia of past glories and triumphs. Cabinet and G7 summit photographs lined the downstairs walls. Inside her study were two watercolours of Chequers. But the room was dominated for several years by an extraordinary painting of her by the Russian artist Sergey Chepik. She liked it – mainly because it made her look very thin and intellectual – but no one else did. Her staff referred to it as Nosferatu. Just outside it were highly prized, though in several cases amateur, paintings of the Falklands campaign. In one, soldiers yomped across country; in another, marines landed at San Carlos; the *QEII* and the *Canberra* were depicted, as were *Endurance* and *Invincible*; a Harrier was shown refuelling in mid-air.

At home in Chester Square, her sitting room was also full of prized possessions, though, unlike that in her office, this display looked a little showy. Among rows of snuffboxes, silver and china stood framed photographs. She was particularly fond of one showing her, looking a bit overdressed, with the Queen and the Queen Mother at Balmoral. It is worth noting that she got on much better with the Queen than is frequently imagined, albeit with greater warmth in her last years. But she had greatest regard for the Queen Mother, who reciprocated it. The Thatchers were always invited to the annual lunch organized for her by Walter Annenberg.

On one wall of the sitting room at Chester Square was a

Overture to a riot – the London poll tax protest (31 March 1990).

LEFT: With her PPS, Peter Morrison, at the memorial service for Ian Gow, assassinated by the IRA (22 October 1990).

BELOW: Howe delivers his devastating resignation statement in the House of Commons (13 November 1990).

TOP: Michael Heseltine reacts with elation to news of MT's decision to resign (22 November 1990).

ABOVE: Last speech in the Commons as Prime Minister, defending the record on a motion of no confidence (22 November 1990).

RIGHT: Final remarks to the press, as she and Denis leave Downing Street (28 November 1990).

ABOVE: Examining produce
in Zagreb market, on a visit to
Croatia in September 1998.

RIGHT: Unveiling a statue of
Winston Churchill in Prague
in November 1999 to mark the
tenth anniversary of the fall of
communism. On the far left is
Vaclav Klaus.

LEFT: Speaking at a rally for the release of
General Pinochet held in October 1999
during the Tory party conference. Her
enemies were apoplectic.

LEFT: Out of step – with her successor as PM, John Major, in Teesside during the disastrous general election campaign of April 1997.

BELOW: Major's successor as leader, William Hague, listens uneasily as she takes the microphone at a meeting during the 1998 Conservative party conference.

BELOW: Greeted by Tony Blair at a Falklands veterans parade in June 2007.

BELOW RIGHT: Returning to Downing Street, as a guest of Gordon Brown, in September 2007.

LEFT: Dressed in her ceremonial robes for Garter Day at St George's Chapel, Windsor (June 2002).

BELOW: More robes – and capacious handbag – in the House of Lords for the State Opening of Parliament (November 2002).

BELOW: Touching Ronald Reagan's coffin at his lying in state in the Capitol Rotunda, Washington DC (June 2004).

LEFT: A tear for Denis at his funeral in the chapel of the Royal Hospital, Chelsea (3 July 2003).

BELOW: With the family at Denis's memorial service: *from the left*, Mark, Amanda, MT, Michael and Carol (30 October 2003).

Old soldiers – with Chelsea Pensioners at the Royal Hospital (February 2008).

magnificent portrait by the American artist Nelson Shanks, in which she is shown in imperious pose, dressed in deep red and black, like some ambiguous Renaissance cardinal. On another wall was Nick Ridley's painting of Downing Street. She hung a fine portrait of Denis by Michael Noakes downstairs in the dining room. A mixed bag of other paintings of different styles, some surprisingly risqué, and her large collection of porcelain, adorned the entrance hall and bordered the staircase.

In these surroundings, year by year after leaving office, she worked at an immense pace to accumulate the capital she needed, for the furtherance of her ideas, and to advance British interests overseas – no one was more effective at securing a contract for some British firm than Mrs Thatcher. Needless to say, she neither sought nor received any benefit from doing so.

Had she confined herself to this activity, her reputation would now undoubtedly be more favourable than it is. The biographies would conclude with a comforting description of virtuous decline. But this was not the end of her story, and even the most dismissive accounts have had to contain at least one additional chapter. Ex-leaders are expected to employ their celebrity to replenish – or swell – their bank balances and permitted to offer their wise (or not so wise) thoughts about the world while doing so. But if they interfere with the running of their former domain, if they challenge the interests of the generation that thinks it has come into its own, then they run into trouble. This convention she now brutally breached, and the response was equally brutal. Her former Cabinet colleagues, in particular, were unforgiving. They had ditched her because she threatened their continued enjoyment of office. Now her activities threatened to embarrass them more. And when, in 1997, their own mistakes and misconduct led to the worst Conservative defeat in the party's history, they and their successors sought to pin the blame on her.

16

THREE LAST CAMPAIGNS

Mrs Thatcher's last active years were taken up with three campaigns which involved her in often bitter conflict with respectable opinion. She offended the Government over Europe. She outraged diplomats over the Balkans. And she shocked human rights enthusiasts over General Pinochet. She did not embark on any of these initiatives lightly. She did so because she believed in each case that without her involvement some vital principle would be surrendered.

The division between Margaret Thatcher and the rebels against the Maastricht Treaty on the one hand and John Major and the bulk of the Cabinet on the other was fundamental. This is still not widely understood, and that misunderstanding in turn has led to a good deal of irrelevant commentary. Attention has focused, as Major sought that it should, upon tactics. The passages in Major's memoirs complaining about those of his opponents are a prolonged, occasionally snarling, whine.[1]

The problem for both sides lay in the Government's narrow majority. It meant that every disagreement became, at least potentially, a question of the Government's survival. Major had not

fully taken this into account when he negotiated Maastricht. He just thought that the rebels would back down. The rebels, for their part, thought that he would prove flexible. Each side was wrong about the other. In the end, the treaty's critics were not prepared to precipitate the general election which Major threatened. But until that point was reached – and Major did the party harm by using the threat so publicly – the rebels would go to any lengths to stop the measure. Obviously, if all that was at stake was a marginal disagreement, such behaviour would be culpable. Major, himself, suggests that the basest motives drove the rebels on. That is not the case.

Major also suggests that Mrs Thatcher was at the heart of the rebellion. This, too, is false. She certainly hoped to see Maastricht defeated. But she did not engage in the systematic lobbying of waverers that he suggests. A few she did see, summoned in by John Whittingdale – who also at the last moment wavered and received a dressing-down for his pains. (She told him: 'Your spine doesn't reach your brain!') More active was Gerald Howarth who, though not at this time a Member – he had lost his seat in 1992 and returned in 1997 – served as a sort of PPS to her. 'Sort of' is a necessary, if inelegant, qualification, because, not being a sitting MP, his scope for activity was limited, and much of that activity was, anyway, undertaken on his own account. Margaret Thatcher herself did not much like lobbying for support: it was one reason she was no longer Prime Minister. In any case, she was heavily involved in writing her memoirs.

But she did use speeches – both at home and abroad – to make the anti-Maastricht case. It was the theme of her last speech in the House of Commons, on Wednesday, 20 November 1991. It was a powerful performance, but she felt uneasy making it – an unease reflected in her uncharacteristic refusal to take interruptions, which she usually enjoyed. She found herself ostensibly speaking in support of Major's approach to the negotiations, which she already knew must lead to a deal that she would not accept. And MPs knew this too.

The experience helped convince her that she should leave the

Commons altogether and accept the peerage that awaited her whenever she wished, as a former Prime Minister, to claim it. She could, indeed, by precedent have expected an hereditary title. But by an unsatisfactory compromise it was Denis who had finished up with that, as a baronet, and she who, in the 1992 Dissolution Honours, took a life peerage. According to Carol Thatcher, her father did not think that people from their background should have hereditary peerages.[2] But Mrs Thatcher had, after all, reintroduced them, in part because she rejected what she termed the 'one-generation society'. Not to take such an honour herself, when other Prime Ministers had, weakened the newly set precedent. It also made it easier later to remove the hereditary peers from the Lords altogether.

Mark, though, was the real problem. Gaining public acceptance of him as a baronet was bound to be difficult enough; but if he had inherited, say, an earldom it would have been worse. His mother was conscious of this, and it was decisive with her. So she took a life peerage. At least, she felt, she would now be free to speak her mind without people suggesting that she was trying to return as Prime Minister: by a constitutional quirk, life peerages, unlike hereditary ones, cannot be renounced.

She did not regret the decision itself, but she was never happy in the Lords, whose atmosphere she found soporific and whose ponderous style offended her taste for argument. The House was also full of the left-of-centre great and good, whom she disliked, and not a few of the Cabinet colleagues whose careers she had ended, or who had ended hers. She did find a few friends there among the anti-Maastricht peers on both sides of the House, and in later years Michael Forsyth (Lord Forsyth of Drumlean) showed great kindness in escorting her whenever she appeared. But, all in all, she would have agreed with only the first element of Disraeli's celebrated remark on entering the Lords, that he was 'dead – dead, but in the Elysian fields'.[3]

Between Margaret Thatcher's leaving the House of Commons and entering the Lords, the 1992 general election was held – and

Major unexpectedly won it. Contrary to some suggestions Mrs Thatcher always hoped that he would. She played only a limited part in the campaign, visiting the seats of friends and supporters, avoiding the wider stage. Naturally, she saw the outcome as a vindication more of her record than of the decision to throw her out of Downing Street.

By the time the new Parliament met, she had had plenty of time to think about the Maastricht Treaty, which was now due to be ratified. She had already decided that she would fight it. All the pressure on her had been to do the opposite. Her staff privately hoped that she would be persuaded by Major's arguments, because the consequences of her opposition were bound to be damaging, not least for her. But she would not be moved. The day after Major announced the results of his negotiation he and his wife attended the Thatchers' fortieth wedding anniversary party at Claridge's. Outside afterwards, in a flush of gratitude and when questioned by the press, she inadvertently said that Major had done 'brilliantly', which was taken as signalling her acceptance of the Maastricht deal. When she read the following morning's newspapers at home, she was appalled. Overriding all pleas for reflection, she insisted that a clarification to the press be issued, as it duly was. Now the row was public, and people began to take sides.

Charles Powell took Major's. He even claimed that had she been in office she too would have signed Maastricht. This was repeatedly quoted against her. But Powell was wrong. He would undoubtedly have counselled it. But she would have refused. There are three reasons why this can be known. First, before leaving Downing Street she had already become convinced that any further steps towards integration with the European Community must be resisted, that Britain had already lost too many powers. Second, she had decided that the veto should be used, or at least threatened, to prevent treaty changes that further restricted British sovereignty. Third, she no longer believed the assurances she had received about the use to which European Community institutions would put their

powers. As she would state in a speech in the House of Lords on Monday, 7 June 1993 – in a phrase explicitly designed to rebut Powell's assertion – 'I could never have signed this treaty.'

Margaret Thatcher not only scrutinized the Maastricht Treaty's wording herself, she also drew on the expertise of others, like the brilliant young barrister Martin Howe (Geoffrey's nephew). Her objections to Maastricht were the stronger because the text was so explicit about its aims – the creation of a new 'Union', with its own 'citizenship', having the objective of 'economic and monetary union, ultimately including a single currency', and involving 'the implementation of a common foreign and security policy, including the eventual framing of a common defence policy, which might in time lead to a common defence'. None of this, however interpreted, was acceptable to her or, indeed, to a substantial section of the Conservative Party. It was also her view that resisting the tide of federalism, which Helmut Kohl now publicly admitted would result in a 'United States of Europe', would be very popular and could restore the party's fortunes. Her overriding concern, however, was the preservation of British national and parliamentary sovereignty.

Against that, Major and his colleagues also had a case, though they made it poorly. The early suggestion, advanced by the Foreign Office, that the incorporation of the concept of 'subsidiarity' into the treaty would lead to a devolution of power to nation-states was manifest nonsense: no one now attempts to suggest that it did or could.[4] Rather, it was Britain's exemptions from Maastricht, not the substance of it, which provided Major's most persuasive arguments. He (or more precisely Michael Howard) had secured for Britain an opt-out from regulations issued under the 'Social Charter'. More important, and more robust, was the opt-out which he (or, again, more precisely Norman Lamont) had obtained from the European single currency, whenever it materialized.[5] But how does the argument between the two sides look now in the light of events?

On balance, Margaret Thatcher and the Maastricht rebels have been proved correct, but not in exactly the circumstances they

envisaged. The Social Charter opt-out was in any case abandoned in 1997 by the new Labour Government. But the opt-out on the single currency has not been challenged. The interest rates that govern the level of sterling are set by the Bank of England without reference to Brussels. This seems to negate many arguments used against Maastricht at the time. But a closer look reveals a different picture.

What has prevented Europe from encroaching upon sterling, or a Euro-enthusiastic government from abolishing it, is what Harold Macmillan famously termed 'events', rather than anything in the Maastricht Treaty. The Major Government's experience of the ERM and the pound's precipitate departure from it on Black Wednesday, 16 September 1992, changed everything. Thereafter it was politically impossible to envisage sterling rejoining the mechanism, let alone being abandoned in favour of a single currency. Under pressure from Clarke, Heseltine and Hurd, Major refused publicly to recognize that reality, and this provided the opportunity for endless hypothetical but bitter argument. Moreover, the Labour Party's pledge to hold a referendum before abandoning the pound – a referendum for which Mrs Thatcher had pressed, but which Major and his colleagues (including alleged Eurosceptics like Portillo) rejected – has since put a block on the process.*

Mrs Thatcher had not herself foreseen that sterling would be driven out of the ERM. But she had publicly warned about attempts to use membership as a means to create the conditions for a single currency. She had also specifically attacked the Government's pledge to reduce the band within which sterling moved from plus/minus 6 per cent to plus/minus 2.25 per cent.[6] The ensuing financial and political crisis was thus the result of a policy which she had condemned. It was also inextricably tied up with the concept of Maastricht's goal of economic and monetary union. Michael Portillo was content to be used by Major as the

---

* Major, *The Autobiography*, pp. 275, 688. In a revealing aside, Major notes that his colleagues would not accept a referendum, because it was Mrs Thatcher who had asked for it – an indicator of the pettiness that characterized his Cabinet.

Government's voice in the media to dispute this connection. And Major would gleefully point to the fact that it was Margaret Thatcher herself who had entered the ERM. But it was his, not her, conduct that led to the débâcle.

In attacking Maastricht, however, she knew that she was opening herself up to counter-attack, less because she had entered the ERM than because she had negotiated the Single European Act. The speeches she made in the House of Lords were thus largely concerned with defending herself against the charge that she, not Major, had sacrificed sovereignty. Here she scored no better than a draw. In practice, more restrictions on Britain have probably flowed from the Single European Act than from Maastricht. (But, then, one could also point out that the original Treaty of Rome led to a still greater loss of sovereignty than either – notably over trade policy, agriculture and fishing.) The important difference is, however, that for her the Single European Act turned into a wake-up call against further integration. But her successor, by signing Maastricht, accepted what was, indeed, a 'new stage' in progress towards a European megastate, with its own international presence, citizenship, currency and defence. (The last dog only barked later, when Tony Blair agreed to integrate British defences under the Anglo-French St Malo agreement in 1998.)

Mrs Thatcher also attempted to gain support for an alternative 'Bruges-style' vision of Europe. This failed. On taking office, the Blair Government adopted as its own Major's objective of putting Britain 'at the heart of Europe'. But her attempts to argue for a different model have historical interest.

The most important speech she delivered on the subject was at The Hague on 15 May 1992.[7] It contained a lengthy analysis of the disadvantages of a federal Europe which, she suggested, was both the answer to 'yesterday's problems' and itself a problem for the future. She argued for a return to the politics of the balance of power in Europe, and dismissed the idea that a united Europe was required to tie down an overmighty, reunited Germany. She argued

against the model of top-down, centralized bureaucracy, and in favour of a regulatory market 'in which the players [were] Governments'. Competition between independent countries would supply the momentum for economic and institutional progress. The speech was ill received by her Europhile audience, but it succeeded in provoking debate in Britain.

Her speech to a CNN conference in Washington on 19 September – three days after Black Wednesday – won still more media attention and thus greatly infuriated Major.[8] Without actually saying 'I told you so', she argued that sterling's recent departure from the ERM was something to be welcomed, not lamented, as long as the correct lessons were learned. The main one was that governments should not try to 'buck the market' in currencies, or they themselves would be 'bucked'. So there must be no return to the ERM. She mischievously added that the U-turn on economic and monetary union should now be followed by a U-turn on Maastricht, since the philosophy – and the errors – of both were the same. And she woundingly quoted Kipling:

> Let us admit it frankly,
> As a business people should,
> We have had no end of a lesson,
> It will do us no end of good.

But it didn't, because no one in the Cabinet was listening.

Maastricht accordingly reached the statute book. The Conservative Party was divided and its reputation damaged. The following general election was lost. Looking back some years later, Mrs Thatcher believed that if Major had vetoed Maastricht and then got out of the ERM when the pressure began to bite, the Conservatives would probably have won in 1997 – despite the reputation for 'sleaze' (a term she hated) and the evident tiredness of the Government (which she never admitted). Her reasoning was that the country was hostile to Europe and so were most Conservative MPs. Moreover,

the worst of the recession would have been avoided – as would the frittering away of reserves and the resultant unedifying ministerial panic. There would still, of course, have been the threat from a formidable new Labour leader, Tony Blair. But the Tories would have been in with a chance. As it was, the scale of Major's defeat shattered the party at every level.

Before leaving Mrs Thatcher's abortive campaign for an alternative Europe, it is necessary to mention the extended discussion contained in *The Path to Power* and *Statecraft*. The former, based on the speeches she had made on the subject, concluded that it was necessary to renegotiate the treaties that underpinned Britain's membership, whereas the latter called more starkly for Britain to leave. In the intervening seven-year period (the dates of writing being respectively 1994 and 2001) her attitude had, indeed, hardened against the EU, though more in style than in substance. Even in the early 1990s she was seeking ways of disengaging Britain from a system that she believed would continue to work against the country's interests. But she realized the unwisdom of saying this too explicitly. To do so would have played into not just Major's but the Labour Opposition's hands.

Later, she was less bothered about this. In her old age Mrs Thatcher's thought processes became cruder and her vituperation about the Europeans more intemperate. But she was still absolutely clear in her mind about the fundamentals. She was convinced that more important than the balance sheet of advantage, which she anyway felt meant net disadvantage, was the question of future direction. All the momentum, she saw, was towards further integration, involving the loss of more powers from the British Parliament to Brussels. Each setback for the European federalist cause – for example, problems of enlargement, the collapse of the ERM, the later rejection by electorates of the proposed European Constitution – merely slowed rather than derailed the train. She wanted the British people to see that a viable, and a better, future was possible outside the EU. Otherwise, the scaremongers would

always outgun the sceptics, and the future was lost. Of course, the great majority of active politicians – including those in the Conservative Party – did not agree. Understanding this, her advisers discussed how to finesse her message so as to minimize the inevitably hostile response. But she would not budge on the essentials. She was convinced that Britain should leave the European Union. She also sensed she had little time left. She wanted her conviction to be on the record before she died. And so it was and is.[9]

Saving Bosnia was the second cause to which Mrs Thatcher devoted her energy in these years. That this was so is indicative of why hers was a more complex political character than either friends or critics frequently grasped. She had, after all, no experience of the Balkans. Her dealings with Tito had been peripheral and pass-ing.[10] Her anti-German prejudices might easily have thrust her into the camp of those who saw the break-up of Yugoslavia as a German plot and who espied swastikas under every stone. She could equally have been envisaged swallowing, as did others, the propaganda which suggested that the strongly secular Bosnian Muslims were Islamic fundamentalists. But, in fact, she did none of these things. Unlike many on the right of the Conservative Party, she ap-proached what was happening in the former Yugoslavia neither as an exercise in great power politics nor as an opening round in the Clash of Civilizations. She surprised many by her stand.

It is true that some of those around her had strong views and that these had an influence, but they were not decisive.* She never for a moment doubted that a great moral issue was at stake in both Croatia and Bosnia, and she could not have been prevented from speaking out about it, no matter who tried – as some did. And, perhaps more clearly than on any other issue, she can now be seen to have chosen the right side in the fierce debate that erupted throughout the West. Although the scale of the conflict was different, as was the outcome,

* I myself became very closely involved in the issue, an involvement which led to a book and various articles. But Mrs Thatcher did not always follow my advice.

the crisis in the former Yugoslavia, above all the genocide in Bosnia, divided the political and intellectual worlds much as did the issue of appeasement in the 1930s. This, indeed, was precisely how she saw it. And, just as her family had been then, so she was now, on the side of the victims, while so many others chose complicity with the aggressor.

Mrs Thatcher was not in the usual sense of the word a humanitarian. She thought that victims deserved protection or the means to protect themselves, not humanitarian aid. She reserved special scorn for those like Linda Chalker, the Overseas Aid Minister during the crisis, who argued in sanctimonious tones against the use of force on the grounds that it would make the aid operation unviable. At the same time, Margaret Thatcher was easily and deeply moved by the plight of civilians engulfed by violence, particularly when the victims were women and children. She had been indignant at the way in which Saddam Hussein after the first Gulf War was permitted to slaughter the Marsh Arabs and the Kurds. She vigorously and successfully demanded that the latter be protected and had several meetings with Kurd leaders.

The war in Croatia, which began in earnest in the late summer of 1991, brought more victims of aggression in to see her and to tell their tales. The mothers of young men killed or missing when the Serbs besieged and slaughtered the inhabitants of the Croatian city of Vukovar that November were greeted with more than tea and sympathy: she made their cause hers, with great vigour and to considerable effect.

In the early 1990s Margaret Thatcher's was, in Britain at least, one of the few voices protesting at the Greater Serbian ambitions which gripped Belgrade and which she saw as an unholy mixture of Nazism and communism.* She believed that the West was wrong to

---

* In Britain probably only Michael Foot, who was similarly haunted by appeasement, expressed the same degree of outrage. He was even heard to express grudging admiration for her, though it did not last. He sent in a video of the powerful documentary film which he and his wife made about the crisis. But she was never patient enough to sit down and watch it. This was her loss: she would have appreciated it.

impose an arms embargo on 'all sides' and to refuse any dealings with the Slovenes, Croatians and later Bosnians unless they ceased their demands to leave Yugoslavia. She was convinced that every nation has the right to defend itself and grasped at once that the stance of the US Administration and of the British Government was playing into the hands of the Yugoslav army and thus encouraging it to advance as far and as fast as possible. She believed that a military ultimatum or a short, sharp air attack would have prevented the aggression. In August 1991, watching on television the columns of Yugoslav army tanks making their way towards Zagreb, she declared unequivocally: 'This has to be stopped!' She felt that if she and Ronald Reagan had been in power it would have been. Considering how fragile Slobodan Milošević's hold on power in Belgrade then was, her judgement was undoubtedly correct.

Pressure was placed on her to remain silent in public. She was, though, allowed the opportunity to shout and protest with indignation to the Foreign Secretary, Douglas Hurd, over the telephone. He always behaved with courtesy – which is more than could be said of his successor – but he also took no notice. He was entirely of the Foreign Office view that international negotiation was the answer to the problem and that nationalism, not communism, was the threat. She was exasperated. But she was also trapped, because their discussions occurred on the implicit understanding that she would then keep her views to herself. The point was finally reached, with the horrible siege of Vukovar, when she could continue to remain silent no longer. The Foreign Office got wind that she planned to state publicly that Croatia should be internationally recognized and allowed to acquire weapons in self-defence. The FCO duly persuaded Charles Powell to get out of bed at 4.00 a.m. in Macao, where he was on business, to plead with her on the telephone to hold back. But it was in vain. From now on she and the Government were at loggerheads on yet another high-profile issue. Hurd's later response that allowing the (now Bosnian) victims to acquire arms would

merely create a 'level killing field' she would denounce on television as 'a terrible and disgraceful phrase'.[11]

Margaret Thatcher's involvement with the former Yugoslavia brought her into contact with a wide group of experts, campaigners and interested parties. In the early stages, when the focus was on Croatia, she received regular briefings from the Croatian Government's representative in Britain, a doctor called Drago Štambuk, whom she quickly came to trust. The two most important figures, however, were Chris Cviić, a highly anglicized ethnic Croat, journalist and foreign policy analyst, and Noel Malcolm, the polymath author of seminal histories of Bosnia and Kosovo. Both became her friends. She was particularly interested in the military options; indeed, she always saw the crisis in essentially practical, military terms. She received advice from Norman Cigar, a US military analyst and expert on the region. General Sir Anthony Farrar-Hockley came to give his assessment. So did the former Croatian Defence Minister, General Špegelj. But perhaps the meeting which had most impact was one with a group of Bosnian politicians which included General Jovan Divjak, number two in the Bosnian army and an ethnic Serb. Mrs Thatcher had by now come to believe that the Serbs were a thoroughly malign people. She would sometimes remark of them: 'They're really just like the Nazis, aren't they?' But Divjak impressed her. From now on, she was always liable to interrupt people who criticized the Serbs en bloc by saying: 'Don't forget the *good* Serbs!'

On these occasions, Mrs Thatcher would call for maps of the region, which were then laid out on the coffee table or across the floor. They were not easy to decipher, because they were necessarily of the old Yugoslavia and reflected neither ethnic nor current military realities. And then there were the names. Mrs Thatcher was not a natural linguist, but she made a great effort. She would, at least, not have muddled Slovenia with Slovakia, which Major did, asserting to a representative of the former that he had just returned from visiting its capital, Bratislava (not Ljubljana). Indeed, she

became rather a know-all, asking when someone mentioned Slavonia (part of Croatia): 'But do you mean *Eastern* or *Western* Slavonia?'[12]

Others from the region itself visited frequently as well. She did not warm to either the Croatian or the Bosnian leaders, though she did not countenance the Foreign Office black propaganda about them. Franjo Tudjman, the Croatian President, visited her shortly before she left Downing Street and then again in August 1992, when the different factions were invited to one of the British Government's counter-productive conferences. Tudjman was starchy and self-important, spoke no English and was determined, it seemed, to make the worst of a good case by talking about history, ethnicity and frontiers, rather than concepts like liberty and justice which have a wider appeal among Westerners. The following year she had her first meeting with Alija Izetbegović, the Bosnian President. Quite the opposite of Tudjman, he was smoother, an intellectual, capable of charm, but at the same time lacking the Croatian leader's realism and toughness, sardonic where Tudjman was abrupt. She did not much like him either, but she did what she could to support his cause and Bosnia's territorial integrity. Her dealings with others were more friendly and productive. Among the Croatians, the Foreign Minister Mate Granić, whose time was spent piecing together the political china that Tudjman dropped, commanded her confidence. His Bosnian counterpart (and later Prime Minister) Haris Silajdjić she found eloquent and impressive. But she did not fail to note that when he was in London he was ferried everywhere by Iranian cars and guards: it confirmed her conviction that if the Bosnian Muslims were abandoned by the West, Islamic radicals would be the gainers, as has indeed happened.

Mrs Thatcher's favourite Bosnian Muslim was Bosnia's Vice-President Ejup Ganić. He was a tall, striking man with a mop of black hair, a scientist educated at MIT: the sort of person she felt at home with and a genuine admirer of her achievements. But it was

the circumstances of their first meeting which marked him out. While she and her memoirs team were staying in Gstaad in August 1993, by courtesy of the shipping tycoon Captain Latsis, she learned of the imminent arrival of Ganić, who had been smuggled out of besieged and bombarded Sarajevo on a returning Red Cross aid flight. His wan, exhausted presence – she fed him everything she could find in her chalet before he left – crystallized her decision to make a public appeal directed not at the British Government, of which she despaired, but at the US Administration and American public opinion. She wrote a powerful article for the *New York Times* and gave a companion broadcast on US television. The impact of her intervention was huge, and at one point it looked as if Bush would be shamed into changing his approach. But, having wobbled one way, he wobbled back again, under State Department pressure. The killing and persecution then continued unabated. The article itself is still worth reading because it offers the clearest alternative approach to the crisis. It calls for an ultimatum to Belgrade to stop supporting the Bosnian Serbs' aggression, allow aid through and permit the return of refugees. If these demands are not immediately heeded, it asserts, they must be followed through with a full-scale aerial bombardment, extending into Serbian territory. This, indeed, is precisely what happened to great effect three years later – after thousands more had died or lost their homes.[13]

In late 1992 and 1993, despairing of any outside intervention to relieve the pressure of the Serb advance, the Bosnian Muslims and Croats fought their own murderous civil war – a conflict which, unlike the others that blighted the former Yugoslavia, genuinely deserves the title. At one point an informal suggestion came from the Bosnian Muslims that Mrs Thatcher mediate between the two sides. This she wisely declined to do. Only the United States had the authority to bring them together. The Americans did so the following year, promising technical support and military co-operation. Meanwhile, the plight of Bosnian civilians subject to Serb shelling grew worse.

It was an attack on Srebrenica in April 1993 that prompted Mrs Thatcher to utter her fiercest criticism of British policy, accusing the international community of being 'little more than an accomplice to murder'. In this she was echoing words of the Vatican Secretary of State, Cardinal Sodano. But, despite widespread public support, she was denounced by the Defence Secretary – later Foreign Secretary – Malcolm Rifkind for 'talking emotional nonsense'. With Douglas Hurd she could at least have some kind of dialogue. He knew her well and, though she thought him hopelessly weak, she appreciated his courtesy. Rifkind she found not merely rebarbative but incomprehensible. She would express disbelief that a Jew who had lost members of his family in death camps could be so indulgent when evidence surfaced of very similar persecution. 'But he's *Jewish*!', she would exclaim, as if that said it all.

She also found herself subject in absentia to vitriolic abuse in the House of Commons and in private from the influential Serb lobby. At a lunch organized by Jonathan Aitken and his Serb wife she was ambushed by the very young Russophile Tory MP Harold Elletson and denounced as an ignoramus. In the House of Commons he urged that her remarks be 'treated with the contempt they deserve'. Such behaviour, though in this case extreme, was not untypical of the reaction of many other Conservatives, variously motivated by spite, isolationism, anti-Americanism or just prejudice against Muslims.[14] By contrast, in other circles, including many on the left, she was for the first and only time viewed with reluctant admiration.

She increasingly turned to others outside the UK in her crusade. In April 1993 she wrote a long letter to Jacques Chirac, the former French Prime Minister (and future President) who was at this time Mayor of Paris, who had recently (and temporarily) advocated air strikes against the Serbs. She set out her views and urged a coordinated campaign of speeches: not surprisingly, perhaps, Chirac, though he wrote back a flattering letter, resisted this temptation. She discussed with the French philosopher and journalist Bernard-Henri Lévy how to draw attention to Bosnia's plight. She contacted

Helmut Kohl to urge support for the heroic Catholic bishop of Banja Luka, Franjo Komarica, whose flock was being expelled and intimidated. She wrote to the former Polish Prime Minister and current UN Human Rights Commissioner for the former Yugoslavia, Tadeusz Mazowiecki, who shared her views and who finally resigned in disgust after the Srebrenica massacre in 1995. Whenever she went to the United States she spoke publicly of the shame of Bosnia. She met Senator Robert Dole when he visited Britain in November 1994 to call for the lifting of the arms embargo and the commencement of air strikes, and she supported him in the media when he was publicly insulted by Rifkind. Pressure from Dole, as the leader of the Republican-dominated Senate, was important in persuading the Clinton Administration to act decisively the following year. It was during Dole's visit that Mrs Thatcher was put through by a BBC link to speak to the mayor of the embattled 'safe haven' of Bihać (one of six so designated by the UN and never properly defended). She made it the occasion for another attack on the British policy of obstruction. The fate of Bihać, too, would be decisive in 1995 for Western policy in the region.

By now, she had started to gain the upper hand in public debate. The British and French governments, though grumbling loudly, were forced to recognize that they had no answers and to accept that US public opinion required action. It was not, though, soon enough to save Srebrenica. On 12 July 1995, the day after it was overrun as UN forces looked on, Mrs Thatcher spoke in the House of Lords. She pointed out that UN resolutions relating to the 'safe havens' had been taken under Chapter VII of the UN Charter and thus bestowed powers of enforcement. She warned that there were 'many potential aggressors looking at and learning from what [was] happening in Bosnia' and called for 'stern, calmly calculated, effective action'.

In fact, action was now taken – to save the Bihać pocket from falling to the Serbs, as Srebrenica had fallen. But it was military action in the form of Operation Storm, undertaken by Croatian and

Bosnian forces with strong American support, and despite howls of anger from the Major Government. In August, heavy NATO air strikes – which for years the British had prevented – swiftly broke the Serb grip on Sarajevo, freeing UN hostages and driving Milošević and the Bosnian Serbs to the negotiating table. That autumn the Dayton settlement brought peace and stability, if not justice. Margaret Thatcher had been proved right and her Conservative Party critics wrong. It was something else for which they would not forgive her.

Mrs Thatcher was never able to visit Bosnia. She would have liked to go to Sarajevo, even when it was under siege. There was, for example, a proposal that she should visit along with Benazir Bhutto, to draw attention to the city's plight. But she would always drop such ideas, despite their symbolic value, when it was pointed out to her that she would be putting others, including British troops, at risk.

She did, though, in September 1998, finally visit Croatia. By then her health was already starting to give cause for concern. But Croatia was a less stressful and less complicated destination than Bosnia. She had a long-standing invitation to collect an honorary doctorate from the University of Zagreb – she had cancelled her earlier visit because of the Muslim–Croat conflict in 1993. Tudjman still had a somewhat dubious reputation, but she thought it possible to give moral support to Croatia without becoming hostage to the political interests of his HDZ Party. In fact, her hosts behaved impeccably. She received a rapturous reception from the crowds. As she moved around Zagreb market buying cream cheese, sausage and assorted vegetables, she was mobbed by women astonished to find a politician who engaged in ordinary conversation about the humdrum elements of life – and one with an eye for a bargain.

But the most moving and memorable part of the visit was that spent in Vukovar. She had insisted on going, though the journey by helicopter was not entirely safe. A missile from Serbia could have paid off an old score and nothing could have been done about it. When she arrived she met some of the women who had visited her

years earlier. She joined them at the mass grave in a muddy field at Ovčara where patients from the hospital had been led out and slaughtered by Serb paramilitaries. She also visited a newly unearthed mass grave at Sotin. The Croatians had been told not to show anything too shocking, but one pulled back the black plastic to uncover a victim's leg bone. Here and elsewhere she lit lamps which joined scores of others to mark the scenes of carnage. She also made speeches intended to convey some thinly coded – and widely deciphered – messages about corruption to the Tudjman Government. But the most important was a warning to a wider audience that even now the problem of Greater Serbian expansionism was fundamentally unsolved and that its new focus was Kosovo. This proved prophetic.

Kosovo was where the story began, with Milošević's exploitation of nationalist passions in 1989, and it was where it would end a decade later. Margaret Thatcher's concern for Kosovo was reinforced by a meeting in April 1995, shortly before Operation Storm, with the self-styled Kosovan President, Ibrahim Rugova. A gentle, courageous intellectual, always seen wearing a trademark, somewhat incongruous, silk scarf, he explained to her the plight of the majority ethnic Albanian Kosovars. She was persuaded by what she heard that the only answer was independence. Unlike Tony Blair, she saw the Kosovo campaign of 1999 less as an humanitarian venture and more as a continuation of unfinished business.

By the time that the NATO campaign against Serb ethnic cleansing in Kosovo was launched in 1999, Mrs Thatcher's health was in decline and she was clearly nearing the end of her active political life. With the change in government of 1997 and the corresponding collective nervous breakdown of the Conservative Opposition, her role would anyway be reduced. But she made great efforts to encourage Tony Blair in his determination to save the Kosovars from the fate that otherwise awaited them. She visited him in Downing Street, she wrote to him, and she spoke to him over the telephone. But, recognizing how difficult his position was, knowing

that any suggestion that she had influence with him would create problems with the Labour Party, she strictly respected his confidence. When any word of the contacts got out it was through Number Ten, not through her. She did, however, use a speech at a dinner celebrating the twentieth anniversary of her becoming Prime Minister to pledge public support for Blair's policy and to handbag wobbly, partisan Tories back into line.[15] Her intervention bought Blair time and political space, before finally, and unexpectedly, Milošević suddenly crumbled.

By this time Margaret Thatcher was already involved in her third and final campaign, one which was to attract more opprobrium and provoke more personalized attacks even than the other two: for she had dared to undertake the defence of Augusto Pinochet. The circumstances, which have been widely misreported even by sympathetic sources, need to be clarified, because they alone can explain her reasoning and her actions.

Chile had been of great assistance to Britain during the Falklands War. But the help was largely kept secret. Mrs Thatcher herself had forgotten many of the details by the time she came to writing her memoirs; hence the failure to mention Chile's role. She did, though, always recall that Pinochet had taken risks to assist Britain, and this was what motivated her support for him when he was arrested on a visit to London in October 1998. Shortly after his detention, she drafted in her own hand an affidavit stating that he had been 'most helpful' in the conflict.* But it was never used, and the lack of specific detail in the document bears witness to the dearth of hard information she had available. It was not until she read a memorandum written in March the following year by the Commander-in-Chief of the Chilean

---

* It is dated 27 October and reads: 'To whom it may concern: During the war to free the Falkland Islands from occupation by Argentina General Pinochet was most helpful. His action was courageous. He is a man who keeps his word meticulously. His support was crucial to our Armed Forces who would otherwise have had to operate from the Fleet in the inclement waters of the South Atlantic.' In fact, Pinochet specifically forbade operations from Chilean territory, though the prohibition was disregarded at least once; so the draft statement misses the point. It is, though, of historical interest.

air force in 1982, General Fernando Matthei Aubel, that she had at her fingertips the facts – she had, obviously, not felt able to seek access to them from government documents, because the British Government was a party to Pinochet's arrest. Matthei's memorandum revealed that, at Britain's request and with President Pinochet's permission, the Chileans had installed a powerful military radar at Punta Arenas, within range of the Argentine air base of Comodoro Rivadavia. There a British air force officer was given minute-to-minute intelligence on Argentine aircraft movements, which he then communicated to the British task force.* The day the radar was shut down for overdue repairs Argentine aircraft got through and hit the troop ships *Sir Galahad* and *Sir Tristram*. Pinochet was taking a big risk, though he obviously believed that it was in Chile's interests to do so. If Argentina had won, Chile would have been next.

The press then and since have assumed that General Pinochet and Margaret Thatcher were friends, or at least regular acquaintances, by the time of his arrest, but this is not the case. They never communicated directly while either was in government. Their first meeting took place when Mrs Thatcher made a speaking tour of South America in March 1994. Pinochet, still Commander-in-Chief of the Chilean armed forces, was invited to a reception at the British Embassy in Santiago, where he arrived in a white uniform covered with medals. As well as exchanging pleasantries, the two former leaders discussed the benefits of low taxation. During her visit to Chile Mrs Thatcher collapsed in the middle of a televised speech, creating panic among her hosts and alarm back in London. It has been suggested that this was her first stroke. But that is not so.[16] She had, in fact, eaten too much rich seafood, and it had the predictable consequence. The text of the speech which she issued but was unable to deliver is of some significance, because it reveals what she already thought about the Pinochet years. She praised Chile for its

---

* This provided vital early warning, so that British aircraft could be scrambled and ships prepare their defence against missiles. I revealed the existence and substance of this document, after Pinochet's death, in an article in the *Daily Telegraph*, 13 October 2006.

successful free-market reforms. In response to the charge that these policies had under the military government been 'pursued at the expense of political freedom and social justice', she refused (as she put it carefully) to 'justify all that happened in [Chile] over these years', but insisted that 'economic freedom is real freedom' and it had 'provided the soundest possible basis for democracy'.[17]

The next meeting between Pinochet and Mrs Thatcher, back in London, has also been misrepresented. It was not one of many, and was not even scheduled. He was in Britain in the autumn of 1998 on a mission to Europe connected with arms purchases. He already had a diplomatic passport but he was waiting in London for a visa to go to France. It was eventually refused – the French Government having heard something of what was in the wind and behaving more honourably than the British. While lunching with a friend in White's, the General was spotted and approached by Michael Forsyth, who suggested that he pay a call on Margaret Thatcher. This was arranged, and Pinochet and his friend duly came in to see Denis and Margaret at six o'clock on the evening of Monday, 5 October. While his ADC and bodyguard went for a drink in the kitchen, Pinochet and his companion, who translated, climbed the stairs to the Thatchers' sitting room. She and Denis drank gin and tonic, the abstemious Pinochet just water.* His back was already painful, and he told Mrs Thatcher that he had arranged to have an operation on it in a London clinic. The conversation was amiable enough, though a little stilted, because Pinochet spoke no English. They discussed Chile's economy, about which he expressed confidence, and Chilean politics, where a left-wing President looked likely to take office – news that prompted laments from Margaret Thatcher. After an hour he and his party departed. It was by now dark, raining hard, and there was an endless traffic jam in the King's Road. In the car, Pinochet spoke warmly of the meeting, and

---

* He would sometimes drink a pisco sour or a malt whisky before lunch and perhaps a glass of wine with it; little else. But he had a sweet tooth and liked pastries.

of Britain. In some famous last (or almost last) words he remarked: '*Me encanta este país!*' ('I love this country!')[18]

The General was arrested in the clinic at about midnight on Friday–Saturday, 16–17 October.* Mrs Thatcher was due to depart on Monday for a speaking tour in the United States, but she fired off a letter of protest to *The Times* before she left. This was the first indication that Pinochet's entrapment was not going according to plan. In retrospect, it was probably her single most important contribution to his release. Her criticism of what had occurred rested at this point on her sense that Britain, in the form of the Labour Government, had broken faith with an ally, who had trusted that he was safe on British soil. Her belief that Britain owed him a debt of honour was at the root of her actions over the next eighteen months.

It is worth recalling that there was a strong feeling on the right-of-centre of British politics, not just among a few British Pinochetistas, that what had been done was at best a mistake and at worst a scandal. The press was for the most part very critical. Conrad Black was annoyed at Mrs Thatcher's choice of destination for her letter. But the *Telegraph* group was henceforth vocal in attacking the arrest. For most critics, it was in the precedent that the principal danger lay. Pinochet was, after all, carrying a diplomatic passport at the time of his arrest – though on a technicality it was ruled that he had no diplomatic immunity. He enjoyed the benefit, too, of sovereign immunity, having ruled Chile for seventeen years. In Chile, he also benefited from an amnesty, which itself was part of the Constitution. His alleged victims – all torture cases, not deaths, because it was under the international Torture Convention that the action was brought – were none of them Spanish. Yet a Spanish judge claimed the right to extradite him to answer for them in Spain.

How far would this precedent reach? The answer is still unclear. The assertion of universal international jurisdiction over the actions

---

* The original warrant was later ruled unlawful because incorrectly drawn up. The authorities knew this was so soon after the arrest. But they contrived to delay Pinochet's release so that a new warrant could be obtained.

of heads of government and high officials has extended much further since the Pinochet case passed into history. Mrs Thatcher believed that such risks would make Western leaders less likely to act in ways that were deemed provocative. Because she thought current leaders were inclined to be spineless anyway, she considered this very retrograde. If and when Tony Blair comes face to face with what Pinochet endured in London he may be inclined to agree.

But what really shocked her was the connivance of elements of the judiciary with a politically motivated operation. She could not believe what she witnessed, and kept asking for confirmation that she had not misunderstood. The bare facts were enough, and still are. The warrant on which Pinochet was arrested was unlawful and he was held for six days illegally. The Divisional Court ruled that he enjoyed sovereign immunity, but on appeal and after political protests the Law Lords decided by a majority that he had no immunity at all. One of these judges was then found to have failed to declare an interest in the case, and for the first time in British legal history a decision of the House of Lords was set aside. When they reheard the case, the Law Lords came up with a completely different decision: namely, that Pinochet had immunity for crimes of torture, but not after 1988 when Britain adhered to the Torture Convention. If justice had prevailed he would now have been released. As Pinochet's (politically hostile) successor as President publicly confirmed, there was, in fact, no systematic torture in Chile by that date, when the country was well on the way to full democracy.[19] But new cases were suddenly discovered, the source being Chilean and Spanish communists. And so the embarrassing saga continued. The final decision by the Home Secretary that Pinochet was unfit to stand trial was made on the basis of professional and impartial medical opinion. But there was a widespread assumption that this too was a political fix to avoid a continuing diplomatic crisis with Chile. So the case managed to damage the respect held by people across the political spectrum for what Mrs Thatcher had so frequently boasted as the uniquely just 'rule of law' in Britain.

Margaret Thatcher also believed that Pinochet's rule had been beneficial to Chile. The Chilean armed forces had acted, reluctantly and at the demand of most Chileans and the lower house of the Chilean Parliament, to prevent a bloody revolution which would have turned the country into another Cuba. In power, Pinochet backed economic reforms that turned Chile from a Third World basket case into the economic success story of Latin America. She was not naïve about the cost in terms of abuse of human rights. But she understood that civil wars are never bloodless and that the suppression of insurgency is rarely clean. Furthermore, she was not being asked to give a judgement on every aspect of Pinochet's rule. She thought such an assessment was for Chileans, not British or Spanish courts. But, in the end, it was a simple matter. She had a good instinct for a political set-up when she saw one. And she knew that this was a set-up.

The criticism was made then, and since, that she should have been cooler in her defence of Pinochet and louder in her condemnation of abuses under his government. In other circumstances, as her earlier speech in Santiago shows, she might have sought to strike this difficult balance. But in Britain Pinochet was fighting for his life. He would never have come back from Spain. He had no chance of a fair trial. He had few other high-profile defenders. She had to be at her most strident. And if there is one thing harder than arguing the case for a man branded as a torturer it is to argue for just a little bit of torture. She was not foolish enough to try. Naturally, if she had been concerned for her own reputation she would not have supported him at all. But having no such concern, she supported him throughout.

One further point should be made about her attitude: she was not squeamish. No mature head of government can afford to be, and those who pretend otherwise are play-acting. Especially during the Cold War, Western democratic leaders embraced many a ruthless, undemocratic counterpart with blood on his hands, opponents in gaol and ill-gotten money in his bank account. It was the price of victory. And it still happens when a British Prime Minister

travels in Asia, Africa, the Middle East and elsewhere. Against this background, she did not feel the need to enquire into every dark cranny of Pinochet's past.

But, in fact, she thought better of him than that. Indeed, she came rather to like him. When he was under house arrest on the Wentworth Estate, she sent down Christmas presents – a game pie and some malt whisky – because she was essentially kind-hearted. She made her first visit in March 1999 because she wanted to make a point. She came away angry that he was not allowed even to walk out on the terrace: presumably someone thought he would throw away his stick, take to his heels and break through the armed police. She had found him charming, dignified and without rancour. On the way back, she remarked that he was 'easy company'. On her second visit in June he was showing marked signs of the mental deterioration that helped convince the doctors that he was incompetent to stand trial. He was obviously clinically depressed and lost track of conversation. In fact, he had been suffering from a series of small strokes – as, indeed, had she, though she did not yet know it. She distracted him by engaging him in talk about Chile. He recounted his problems with the country's hostile neighbour Argentina, explaining how he had created mock-up tanks which were prominently displayed to convince the Argentines that Chile was militarily stronger than it was. His aides then brought out a map and he pointed out with his stick the course of the *Autopista Austral* (motorway) that his government had built, while she got down on her knees to look more closely. It was the last time they met. But by the time he left Britain they were, in a certain fashion, friends. And when, to a renewed chorus of disapproval, she pronounced herself 'saddened' by his death in 2006, she meant it.

The main value of her public activity in relation to Pinochet, after that first letter to *The Times*, was simply to keep the case on the front pages. There was a risk that the authorities might contrive to have him sent off to Spain in a shroud of secrecy. But the prime mover of the campaign to free Pinochet was not Mrs Thatcher; it

was Norman Lamont. Unlike her, he was not particularly interested in Pinochet's role in the Falklands: what outraged him was the manifest injustice of which Pinochet was the victim. It was Lamont who initiated the debate in the House of Lords in July 1999 in which Mrs Thatcher spoke – to be repeatedly interrupted. Lamont, too, organized and persuaded an initially reluctant Margaret Thatcher to speak at a fringe meeting at the Conservative party conference in Blackpool that year. This event was subsequently regarded by the modernizing wing of the party as proof of the damage she did. The speech certainly stole the headlines. But it was mainly because the party leadership had none to offer themselves.

The Conservative Party had by this point fallen into a state of self-regarding self-doubt. As a political vehicle, it was quite useless. So, despite the rally in Blackpool, her attempts to secure Pinochet's return to Chile were mainly pursued elsewhere. She brought it up directly with Tony Blair, who was not unsympathetic to her arguments, but claimed to be powerless. She wrote to the Spanish Prime Minister, Jose Maria Aznar, who had the constitutional power to override the Spanish prosecuting judge who had initiated the crisis. But he merely replied with the sort of flattering banalities that she found irritating. She did not, in any case, nurture a favourable view of Spain. She would mutter about Franco and fascism and complain about Gibraltar at the slightest provocation. When she sent her present of a silver Armada dish to Pinochet – then in a Chilean jet on the point of take-off – she accompanied it with a note drawing attention to the symbolic significance – 'another victory over the Spanish', it read – and she meant the insult. She was then delighted when the Spanish Foreign Minister lost his temper and declared that she was madder than Pinochet.

Her communications with the Vatican, however, were more constructive. She wrote a long letter to the Pope drawing his attention to the danger that Pinochet's arrest posed to the stability of Chile, to the benefit that flowed from respecting amnesties, and to the hatred with which he was pursued by his communist enemies. Cardinal

Sodano wrote back a private letter on the Pope's behalf completely endorsing her analysis.[20] This letter also revealed that the Vatican had intervened with the British Government to seek Pinochet's return to Chile. The difficulty posed by the personal nature of the correspondence was overcome when Norman Lamont was prompted to ask whether any such representations had been made. Thus the Vatican's intervention became public. Not just Margaret Thatcher, but John Paul II too, thought that Pinochet's detention was wrong.

Lamont joined Mrs Thatcher to watch CNN's coverage of Pinochet's return to Chile. When the General, to the outrage of the commentator, rose from his wheelchair to embrace the Commander-in-Chief of the Chilean armed forces on the tarmac, Lamont cheered. But Mrs Thatcher thought that Pinochet should have played along with the stories of his fragile health. In fact, of course, it was his mental not his physical condition that prompted his return: the wheelchair was irrelevant. But since he would soon be facing more difficulties from judges in Chile, her instinct was probably right.

These three last campaigns – Europe, Bosnia and Pinochet – formed a turbulent conclusion to Margaret Thatcher's active political life. In different ways, they expressed a good deal about her. They demonstrated, above all, that she was courageous to the point of imprudence, that she was loyal to a fault, and that no cause was completely hopeless if she took it up. She did not succeed in pulling Britain out of Europe, but she helped solidify opposition to Euro-federalism. She was disregarded by most of the British political class over Bosnia, but she appealed to the conscience of the world, and in the end Bosnia was saved. She did not make most people (outside Chile, which was evenly divided) think that General Pinochet was other than a villain, but she kept up the pressure for his release, and he eventually died in a Chilean hospital bed not in a Spanish gaol. She was, to the core of her being, a fighter for truth and justice, when so many others did not care much for either; and she fought to the end.

17

SILENCE

The paradox has often been remarked upon that Margaret Thatcher had a greater long-term effect on the Labour Party than on the Conservatives. This judgement is accurate, and she herself recognized the fact. But her view subtly changed over the years. She began by merely remarking (repeatedly, and in particular by way of explaining Tory defeats to foreign visitors): 'The trouble is that we converted our opponents.' She finished up by grasping the other part of the paradox, though happily not all of it, that her legacy was now regarded with strong disfavour by the Conservative leadership.

At one level this contrast is not very surprising. The Labour Party recognized that the economic changes she had made were irreversible and, indeed, beneficial. Running a free-enterprise economy required compromises, and the Labour leadership willingly made them. As for the Conservatives, a new generation, dazzled by Tony Blair's success and forgetful of their own under Margaret Thatcher, considered that the only way to restore the party's image was to prove that it had 'changed'. This meant breaking with Mrs Thatcher herself, who, after

all, was the only recent Tory leader that anyone took seriously.*

Some break with the past was clearly necessary. The last days of John Major had seen the lowest ebb of Conservative fortunes in the party's history. Its reputation for incompetence, corruption, sniping and cynicism had altogether obscured the reality of earlier achievements. The 1997 general election campaign fully reflected the problem, being devoid of strategy and beset by ill-considered improvisation. Mrs Thatcher had, naturally, to be part of it; fortunately, the Party Chairman Brian Mawhinney was someone she liked and respected, and he treated her impeccably. Her election tours were prudently kept well away from Major's, as she visited the constituencies of candidates of whom she approved, like Iain Duncan Smith in Chingford.

Exceptionally, at Stockton on Wednesday, 16 April, she and Major were set to campaign together. They were to fly up separately, and when Mrs Thatcher arrived at the airport she found that Major was absent. Only after she had waited for an hour and a half did Tim Bell, deputed by Major for the task, telephoned to explain that the Prime Minister had at the last moment decided to scrap the planned party election broadcast and record a new one to camera explaining his thinking about Europe. At this she flew into a fury, not least because Major's 'thinking' was diametrically opposed to her own. She denounced what she saw as his unprofessional behaviour – 'an insult to the people of the North', she called it. So the mood was tense when Major eventually arrived. Nor did it then improve. He was distracted, not even looking out of the windows of the campaign bus bearing the current and former Prime Ministers to their destination, and quite ignoring his predecessor's stern injunctions: 'Voters to the left – wave! Voters to the right – wave!'

After this it was clear that they could not collaborate, even briefly. Fortunately, they did not need to. It had been arranged that she should spend a few days out of the country, in Hong Kong, where

---

* That view was also based on a number of fallacies. See pp. 433–5.

she had agreed to open the monumental bridge which constitutes a link with the new airport. She returned to London shortly before polling day, when she watched the results on television in her office, surrounded as usual by a few friends and staff. From the first results it was clear what the outcome would be. She was particularly shocked when Michael Portillo lost his seat.

Major's sudden announcement of his resignation as leader now plunged the party into even greater chaos. She thought that his decision was precipitate. She reckoned he should have been prepared to face at least some of the music, instead of effectively deserting his post. But her attention now, like every one else's, was focused on the new occupant of Ten Downing Street.

Margaret Thatcher had met Tony Blair on several occasions over the years, though never one-to-one. She had watched his performance closely since and had been impressed. She admired the way in which he had abandoned so much of the socialism that she and Keith Joseph had identified many years before as (in Joseph's phrase) 'the poison' in Britain's system. In public, of course, she had to pretend that Blair's conversion was skin-deep: otherwise, why vote Conservative? But she delivered such lines only with reluctance.[1] Privately, she believed he had seen the light. On top of that, she liked his style and already saw him as a powerful defender of Britain on the world stage. It was this sense of his robustness and patriotism which led her in an unguarded moment to make the remark 'Tony Blair will not let us down' – which got out. And finally, as usual, there were other factors: he was, after all, good-looking, and he knew how to treat her as a woman. There was from the beginning a genuine warmth between them, which grew over the years. He admired her qualities as a leader, and sought to emulate them. She found she understood the difficulties he faced, particularly in dealing with what were for both of them the ultimate issues of war and peace. She had long hoped for a worthy successor. Perhaps he had at last arrived?

Shortly after taking office, Blair asked Mrs Thatcher in to

Downing Street for a private meeting. It was a mark of respect, which she appreciated. When they met alone in the flat, her main warnings were about the threat posed to British independence and interests from Europe. Blair was, naturally, unmoved by this. The meeting had, though, a wider significance. It demonstrated Blair's early intention to try to combine consensual internationalism with robust neo-Thatcherism. Trying to bridge that unbridgeable chasm would lead him, and Britain too, into no end of trouble before the close of his premiership.

This was not the end of their personal contact. She paid a further private visit and there were also several telephone calls, all at his initiative and all concerning Kosovo – as already mentioned. She urged him to be bolder in the bombing campaign against the Serbs. He valued her advice and seems to have acted on it.*

There was also what remained of the Conservative Party to concern her. The party had been pulverized. Not just its parliamentary representation but its constituency organization had been shattered. As would swiftly become apparent, the blow to its intellectual self-confidence was greater still. And now there was an immediate leadership campaign to be faced. Would-be leaders beat a path to her door. On Monday, 2 June, the Thatcherite Alan Duncan brought a rather less Thatcherite William Hague in to see her. She was friendly but withheld her blessing. On 6 June I brought in Michael Howard. She soon reached the view that Howard would be the best candidate for the situation in which the party found itself. She admired his intellect, believed he had been a good Home Secretary, valued his experience and remembered his loyalty – which she thought greater than it actually was.† But it was not clear whether her endorsement would hurt or help, and the news that she backed him was only, in fact, leaked when his campaign had already been holed by Ann Widdecombe's assault on him as tainted by

* For the Kosovo campaign, see pp. 394–5.
† See pp. 337–8.

'something of the night'. In retrospect, had Hague stuck by his original agreement to back Howard, the party would have benefited. Hague lacked the experience and, worse still, lacked the humility to ask others to provide it. Howard, if only temporarily, would have managed the transition to a new generation; and there was no real expectation of winning the next election anyway.

Of the other candidates, Clarke never hoped for her endorsement or even neutrality, and his assumption was correct. (It was not just his views that offended her, but his lack of application: 'He's a lazy hound,' she would complain when his name was mentioned, and then shake her head.) Redwood, though, was definitely annoyed that he did not secure her support. Peter Lilley had perhaps more reason for disgruntlement, because Mrs Thatcher's closest allies, including Tim Bell and Cecil Parkinson, backed him as a substitute for his friend Portillo, who was out of the race. But despite their intercessions she remained unpersuaded. She had little time for Lilley. He had let her down in her last days; he had not impressed her since. And he would more than vindicate these doubts once Hague gave him responsibility for policy development.

In view of the frequent suggestions that Margaret Thatcher behaved badly towards William Hague as leader, it is worth recalling just how much he owed her, and how little he repaid it. The first round of the Tory leadership election that year saw Clarke and Hague emerge as the front-runners. They and Redwood went into the second round. Redwood was then eliminated, while Clarke again emerged ahead of Hague. If Redwood's supporters now backed Hague, Clarke would lose. But Redwood made a surprise pact with Clarke; and if he successfully brought his supporters with him, Clarke would clearly win. It was immediately clear that there was only one person who could ensure this did not happen – Margaret Thatcher. Hague therefore sought her public intervention on his behalf. Both Alan Duncan and Norman Lamont urged her to support him, but still she did not commit herself. She had never intended to become involved and she remained reluctant to do so.

She went off to the hairdresser and left her advisers to think about what to do. There was little time, and all the gossip and news reports suggested that the Clarke–Redwood ticket would triumph. After some hard persuading, she decided to demonstrate her support in the most newsworthy way available – by proclaiming it on the steps of the Palace of Westminster before the assembled media. The performance dominated the headlines, dispersed Redwood's backers, brought out other critics of his unholy alliance with Clarke, and thus, against the predictions, ensured Hague a decisive victory.

This was gratifying, but it also contained dangers. Despite his extrovert demeanour, Hague lacked self-confidence. Precisely because of his youth and inexperience, he feared being overshadowed by his benefactress. She, for her part, was this time round determined not to be seen as a 'back seat driver'. But it was difficult. At party conferences she dwarfed the new leader. Even when visiting the exhibition stalls she stole the headlines, as when she solemnly covered up with her handkerchief some modernistic tail-fin designs on a model of a British Airways plane to express disapproval of BA's dropping the Union flag. (This was characteristic play-acting, with a large element of self-mockery.)

But when Hague started, from this very first conference, to signpost a rejection of the past, the situation became more tense. She was outraged when there was public talk of throwing Norman Tebbit out of the party because of his unreconstructed views. She contacted Tebbit and offered her support, which was not in fact needed. Yet, contrary to reports, she never spoke disparagingly about William Hague himself – who was the butt of plenty of press criticism, without any assistance from her. More specifically, she never referred to him as 'Wee Willie', despite this canard doing the rounds. She only ever spoke of Whitelaw as 'Willie', and the nearest she came to using 'wee' about Hague was her all-purpose, overused mock-Scottish phrase 'puir wee bairn', directed at anyone, however distant or close, who she thought was being feeble.

In truth, she did not know Hague at all well. Nor did she get on

with Michael Ancram, the Party Chairman, who, unlike his predecessors, made a point of never setting foot in her office. But the real problem at this time – and not just for Mrs Thatcher – was neither Hague nor Ancram; it was Michael Portillo.

It has been widely said that she considered Portillo her natural successor. This is not the case. Her view of him when she was Prime Minister was certainly favourable. She had high hopes of what he might become. But she was immune to the fabled Portillo charm. Indeed, when others mentioned it, she would look surprised. Nor did she think that he had charisma, though it is true that she was never very good at seeing that quality in others. And he did have charisma. Mrs Thatcher had first encountered him when, as a young man, he briefed her for the 1979 general election press conferences. She thought he did it well, and she was told then and later, and had no reason to disbelieve, that he was of her way of thinking. Portillo came into the House of Commons in 1984, fighting a by-election in Enfield Southgate caused by the IRA's murder of Tony Berry. He was later made Minister for Local Government with responsibility for the poll tax. His great claim to Mrs Thatcher's gratitude and to the right of the Conservative Party's support was his last-ditch attempt to persuade her to fight on, as the vultures gathered.*

But Portillo owed his real advancement to Major, not to her. Under the new leader he entered the Cabinet, first as Chief Secretary, then at Employment and finally at Defence. Any residue of loyalty to Mrs Thatcher was soon abandoned. He was also profoundly hostile to her viewpoint over both Maastricht and Bosnia. On the latter, he was, indeed, among the most fervent Serb apologists.

In fact, the notion that he and Margaret Thatcher ever had anything much in common is erroneous. It is difficult to think of two more different characters. He was not completely English. She was very much so. He had a remarkably easy ride to the top of

* See p. 339.

politics, and then fumbled. She had to fight against all the odds, and then triumphed. He was a fanatical Wagnerian. She preferred Mozart, Verdi or Puccini. He was sensitive and his wounds did not quickly heal. She was prosy, down to earth, tough-minded and thick-skinned. Portillo was rash, but he also wavered. She was instinctively prudent, cautious by nature, weighing every real and even the odd imagined risk; but when she decided to act, she did not look back. She was 'not for turning'. He turned with facility into the opposite of what he started out.

Ejected in 1997, Portillo returned to the House of Commons in 2000, and Hague immediately appointed him Shadow Chancellor. But he showed no interest in his portfolio and instead, in collaboration with Francis Maude, set about destabilizing his leader and preaching a doctrine of social liberalism manifested in media opportunities. Mrs Thatcher could not understand what he was doing or why. It was not that she radically disagreed. It was simply that what he was saying seemed either obvious or irrelevant. For example, when Portillo agonized about the need to be compassionate towards sexual or ethnic minorities, she did not scoff or protest. She merely thought that since their rights had been adequately protected in law, there was nothing more to be said on the subject. There was only one difference of substance between them. She believed that, since children were obviously better brought up by two parents, single parenthood should be discouraged: this was strictly taboo to Portillo and the early modernizers.

In any case, by the time the crisis caused by Portillo's campaign within the Conservative Party came to a head in 2001, Margaret Thatcher's health had begun to fail – as will be described. She was no longer a major player, merely a useful victim. She was not at all responsible for the so-called 'lurch' to the right which was subsequently blamed for Hague's problems.

Hague had begun by accepting the modernizing agenda pushed by Portillo and Maude. The high (or low) point of his attempts to cast off the shadow of Mrs Thatcher was reached in April

1999, when, at the dinner organized to celebrate the twentieth anniversary of her becoming Prime Minister, he delivered an ill-judged address urging the party to move on. At the same time, and still more crassly, Peter Lilley delivered at another venue a speech, approved by Hague, which was an outright rejection of her legacy and beliefs. The reaction was hostile, not so much from Mrs Thatcher, who was just mildly contemptuous, but from her supporters, who thought the timing outrageous. Above all, by the criterion that mattered to its authors, the strategy failed. The restiveness provoked in the rank and file of the party was not compensated for by any gain in favour among non-partisan voters. Hague's and the party's support slipped further. His subsequent switch towards extreme Euroscepticism and right-wing populism was a desperate attempt to shore up his own leadership and the party's ratings. This tactic too failed to convince. It did, though, provide an opportunity for Portillo to turn directly against Hague and, *en passant*, Mrs Thatcher.

By the time the 2001 general election came into view, the Conservatives were desperate for Margaret Thatcher to play a significant part in the campaign. But they were also wary. So were her staff, who understood that her capacity to contribute had diminished. She could not now be relied upon to remember the line to take, and while her instincts were good enough to see her through most of the time, there was a latent risk.

It was decided that the safest option would be an interview with Simon Heffer for the *Daily Mail*, which she duly gave on Wednesday, 16 May. Heffer seemed, and in many ways was, the ideal interviewer. He was probably her greatest admirer in the press. However, he also carried, albeit inadvertently, a real disadvantage: he was too close to her. He had even drafted articles that appeared under her name in the *European* newspaper. She therefore treated him more as a friend than as a journalist, and was accordingly unguarded. She was also unfocused. The only newsworthy points she made were precisely the ones she would have been advised not

to make – about race and culture. Judicious editing ensured that several ill-thought-out remarks were removed; but by common agreement between the paper and her office, her denunciation of 'multiculturalism' was included. In retrospect, the line she took was ahead of the political game. Since then, similar criticisms have been expressed by Trevor Phillips, Tony Blair and even Conservative spokesmen. But at that time she fell foul of the Tory modernizers. When the content of the interview became known in advance of publication, Conservative Central Office even tried unilaterally to have the text altered. For his part, Portillo fell into a lather of real or contrived indignation.

Mrs Thatcher was due to address an election rally in Plymouth the following Tuesday in the presence of Hague and the Shadow Cabinet. Portillo now demanded either that the invitation be withdrawn or that Hague stand up after she had spoken and denounce her. Whether he was sincere in predicting that her remarks would provoke a storm is unclear. If so, it confirms his lack of judgement. Hague, for his part, was frightened of Portillo, but even more frightened of the effect of what Portillo demanded. The Tory high command's semi-public agonizing quickly got back to Mrs Thatcher's advisers, who put her in the picture. She was at first incredulous. But after some discussion, it was decided that it would be best if she simply withdrew from Plymouth and, necessarily, from the rest of the campaign, and this news was conveyed to Central Office.

Now the Tory leadership collapsed into a further panic. Archie Hamilton was dispatched by Hague to persuade her to come after all. Hamilton was a clever choice. He was not only a close personal friend; he was also someone for whom the term 'Honourable Gentleman' might have been coined. He could not tell a lie. But unwittingly he deceived Mrs Thatcher on this occasion. Sitting opposite her and asked point blank whether there was any risk that the party would disown her if she appeared, he swore that there was none. In truth, this was still a possibility. Only later

did Hague finally assert himself in the face of Portillo's tantrum.[2]

Thus falsely reassured, Margaret Thatcher duly appeared in Plymouth. Her performance was a triumph, giving rise to still more irritation to her enemies in the Shadow Cabinet. One line, which was probably in the circumstances a joke too far, was taken particularly amiss by the Portillo party. Alluding to a film running in a local cinema, she proclaimed: 'The Mummy Returns!' The laughter was as strained among the party leadership as it was genuine in the hall.

The Conservative Party's 2001 defeat was probably inevitable, but its failure to make any gains at all was not. A full debate about direction was required, but Hague's immediate resignation, like Major's earlier, effectively pre-empted this. Instead there were three contrasting options on offer, each embodied in one of three (in their different ways) unsatisfactory leadership candidates.

Kenneth Clarke cast his trilby into the ring. Michael Portillo's sombrero followed. As irritation with Portillo rapidly grew, Iain Duncan Smith finally emerged as the traditionalist right-wing alternative. Portillo should have won. Despite his record of disloyalty and flakiness, he had the highest public profile. He was fluent. He looked good on television. He had a devoted group of followers. But he threw it away. Mrs Thatcher was at this point unaware of how badly Portillo had behaved towards her. He telephoned her when he announced his candidacy. He did not seek her support, nor did she offer it. But she wished him well.

As time passed, however, and she learned more of Portillo's views, she started to feel uneasy. He had clearly changed, and she could not fathom what precisely he had become. By contrast, she knew all too much about Clarke, and she strongly opposed his statism and Europhilia. So Portillo still seemed preferable. But once Duncan Smith belatedly entered the race, her preference shifted to him. Even then, her support was not unqualified. She understood IDS's weaknesses. He had had no experience in a senior post. He was not particularly intelligent. His conversation was boring. She knew he was sound and honest – but where was the talent? So, while

privately favouring IDS, she still hoped to stay out of the contest.

Charles Powell inadvertently brought her in. Mrs Thatcher was by now ill disciplined in private conversation – which rarely remained private for long. She was also inclined to agree with what people said to her, simply because she could not remember some contradictory argument that had been put on a previous occasion. Powell gained from her the impression that she would back Portillo over Duncan Smith, and he passed this information on to Dominic Lawson, editor of the *Sunday Telegraph*, which also backed Portillo.

It was the weekend before the ballot of Tory MPs, and thus a crucial moment. All three candidates had roughly equal support among MPs. Charles Moore, editor of the *Daily Telegraph*, who backed IDS, informed the Thatcher office of the headline that the Sunday paper was planning to run. This would bluntly state that she preferred Portillo to Duncan Smith. With Mrs Thatcher's authority, the *Sunday Telegraph* was told on the record by her office in no uncertain terms that this was not her view. But the paper refused to print the disavowal. So a statement of direct rebuttal appeared instead in Monday's *Daily Telegraph*. This did Portillo great harm, because it suggested that he and his supporters were prepared to lie in order to win. This may have been unfair: the *Sunday Telegraph*'s editor may merely have been engaging in private mischief. In any case, the episode seemed to highlight the nastiness that the Portillistas' tactics had already conveyed.

The damage proved decisive. Portillo failed by just one vote to get into the final ballot, and promptly announced that he was leaving politics. Now that she had been forced to intervene, Mrs Thatcher decided that she might as well go all out to try to stop Clarke. She accordingly wrote a letter backing Duncan Smith to the *Daily Telegraph*. He showed no gratitude then or later. Probably rightly, he thought that he would have won in the constituencies without it. But she had certainly finished Portillo.

Margaret Thatcher's dealings with the Conservative Party were henceforth much less important to it, or to her. By mutual

agreement she no longer attended party conferences. She did not try to save IDS when he floundered in a job for which he turned out to be ill suited. She thought he had been badly treated. But she welcomed Michael Howard's becoming leader, and he for his part always treated her with consideration. He was not intimidated or resentful, and so she was able to deal with him as an equal. He even went so far as to declare in a speech at yet another celebration of her past – this time a dinner held to mark the twenty-fifth anniversary of her becoming Prime Minister – 'What you stood for then, we stand for now.' Admittedly, the sentence was carefully omitted from the press release, but it was a gracious gesture all the same.

How Howard squared that statement with his later support for David Cameron, whose whole approach was to distance himself from Margaret Thatcher and her works, is unclear. But she was not, in any case, interested in Cameron, and he was interested in her only as an element in his public relations strategy. He even managed to avoid the ritual of coming in to meet her, which might have been embarrassing, though to what extent this omission was contrived or fortuitous is unclear.

In either case, Charles Powell lent a helping hand. In November 2005, shortly before the votes were counted in the Tory leadership election, he took Mrs Thatcher out to dinner at the Ivy, while his daughter was entertaining friends at her birthday party. Among these friends just happened to be David Cameron, already the overwhelming favourite to be the next Tory leader. Powell naughtily suggested that his dinner guest might like to drop in, which she was happy to do. Here she was introduced to a young man in an open-neck shirt and jeans who, she was told, was the next leader of the Conservative Party. She thought that she must have misheard, and asked with a smile: 'So you want to become a Conservative MP?'

Cameron proceeded to define his position as the opposite of hers. There was little reason for them to have contact, and they barely did. She still had friends in the parliamentary party; but their

commitment to her was now more personal than political. By tacit mutual agreement, she and the Conservatives had simply parted company.

In fact, it was from Gordon Brown, once he became Prime Minister in 2007, that she received the sort of treatment she might have expected from her own party. Brown was, naturally, being mischievous when he so publicly invited her to Number Ten. His aim was to embarrass Cameron, and he succeeded. But, in any case, by now, like other New Labour figures, he had developed a certain regard for her achievements. He turned out to have read her books. He said she had been right about the most important issue of her times, the Cold War. They discussed their families. The son of the manse and the lay preacher's daughter turned out to have something in common, in background if not politics. After this, the Cameron camp suddenly became anxious to stage a similarly warm encounter for the cameras. So she obliged. And when Cameron's team discovered that, contrary to their fearful predictions, association with the former leader helped, not hindered, the current leader's standing, there began a kind of competition between Conservative campaign headquarters and Downing Street to offer praise or sympathy or good wishes on the slightest pretext.

By now there had begun a more general reassessment of Margaret Thatcher's role. The news, in 2002, that for reasons of health she was retiring from public life had prompted a flood of quasi-obituaries, mainly favourable, already bearing traces of nostalgia. The inescapable conclusion was that Britain's history was now impossible to write, impossible even to imagine, without her. Margaret Thatcher was, quite without knowing it, well on her way to becoming a national institution – not a treasured or beloved one, perhaps, but an institution all the same.

She was already, formally at least, part of the Establishment. The Garter had been awarded her in 1995. In the same year the Queen attended her seventieth birthday party. But it was with her eightieth, held at the Mandarin Oriental Hotel in Knightsbridge, that her

new status was sealed. The list of those attending this event, beginning again with the Queen and including Tony Blair, but also numbering most of her former Cabinet, a galaxy of international figures and a sprinkling of the better class of celebrities, constituted a unique tribute. She was late for the party because she was detained by a telephone call of congratulations from President George W. Bush. Peter Carrington spoke wittily and Mrs Thatcher, to widespread surprise and some trepidation, replied with style. Her delivery was faultless. Only those who knew her best perceived that she was not quite clear what the event was about.*

In the preceding years she had suffered, and the suffering had left its mark. De Gaulle writes in his memoirs: 'Old age is a shipwreck'; at times she had seemed to be drowning.[3] Every ageing politician discovers sorrow and humiliation as his or her mental faculties decay, but it is worse when those faculties have been outstanding, as in the case of Margaret Thatcher. Relating the details is upsetting; but it is also necessary, partly because the period coincided with significant events in which she had a role, and partly because no true portrait of her can be drawn that omits the dark reality.†

Mrs Thatcher had enjoyed exceptionally good health. She had huge stamina, physical as well as mental. She was subject to colds, but she quickly got over them, with generous resort to vitamin C – on which she also relied to provide a boost before speeches. As Prime Minister she took remarkably little exercise, but she made up for that with a healthy diet. She was even prepared to embark on more adventurous ways to stay healthy – like the electric baths about which the media eventually learned, to public amusement and her annoyance. She had had just one serious health problem in Downing Street: a detached retina, from which she had been lucky

---

* The one jarring note came from Michael Portillo who, for old times' sake, had been invited. On leaving, he coldly informed the press that Mrs Thatcher 'was influential in her day but not now'. The two did not meet again.

† Carol Thatcher also lifted the curtain on this issue during her mother's lifetime: See p. 429.

to recover without losing the use of her eye. But she left office in remarkably good shape.

Her closest advisers were convinced, though the doctors were not, that it all then began with her teeth (which have already figured in this account).* They were the one aspect of her appearance which she felt had let her down, and she had always had trouble with her gums. She was given free treatment by a dentist in north London and, as is the way with unpriced services, she and Denis – who was not going to pay if he could help it – spent hours in traffic going back and forth for largely unnecessary work. But she then concluded that something more drastic was required and settled on a radical solution. She had major dental surgery elsewhere. It was not a success, with results already described. So the whole exercise had to begin again. In summer 1994 she underwent three further operations in the Wellington Hospital in St John's Wood, spending hours under a full anaesthetic. The treatment roughly coincided with the completion of work on the first volume of her memoirs and the early stages of work on the second, and it was immediately noticeable that her mental faculties were suddenly much less sharp. Whatever the full explanation, the difference was undeniable. For over a year she was very noticeably below par.

This mental deterioration was neither continuous nor fatal to her public performance. Nor was it easy to distinguish its effect from other problems. For example, in 1996 she also became much deafer. She initially tried to wear hearing aids, but could not get on with them. They hurt her ears, and she said that she could hear her own footsteps as she walked along. So she did not persist with them. As with other people who are hard of hearing, people began to shout at her, or ignore her, or treat her as a fool.

In later years her memory seriously started to fail. Again, it is possible to pinpoint the beginning of the decline, because it coincided with the writing of her final book, *Statecraft*, in 2000–1. She would

---

* See pp. 348–9.

not have started on the project if she had thought she was incapable of completing it, nor would others have let her. And, as a book, it undoubtedly works, constituting an authentic and clear account of her thinking on foreign affairs, punctuated with vignettes drawn from her travels.* But by the time it was complete her short-term memory had all but disappeared. She would open the draft and reach the bottom of the page, then start to read the same page from the begining again, desperately trying to recall the argument, and failing to do so.

Statecraft was written when the war in Afghanistan seemed won and an invasion of Iraq looked likely. Opinions are divided about whether she would have supported the latter, and on what conditions, had she been in full command of her faculties, let alone had she been in Downing Street. She did, indeed, lend public support to the Bush–Blair strategy. She could hardly do otherwise.† She thought that Tony Blair had been right to ally Britain closely with America; she despised Conservative attempts to finesse their support when things became difficult; and she even wrote privately to Blair in February 2005 to congratulate and encourage him when the Iraqi elections were declared a success – just about the last such success, as it turned out.

But in private she was more cautious and more critical. It was with some difficulty that her worries were concealed from the wider world, where they would have undermined the war effort – which she certainly would not have wanted. Nor was it easy to be sure what she really meant – for example, by her oft-repeated complaint: 'We just don't have enough information [about Iraq].' This, of

---

* Some reviewers quibbled about the title, claiming that it was misleading. But they failed to understand that for conservatives the art of statecraft can only be derived from action, not theory. By examining developments in different continents and drawing conclusions about how to deal with them, the book pursued an authentically conservative approach and one that Mrs Thatcher, who was a pragmatist in these matters, herself adopted in power.

† Designedly, her support centred more on the struggle against Al-Qaeda and Islamic militancy than on Iraq. But she was also clear in public that Britain had to back Bush's wider strategy. See, for example, her article in the *New York Times*, 'Advice to a Superpower', 11 February 2002.

course, turned out to be all too true. The campaign was based on a lack of intelligence about the country to be invaded. People who had occasion to talk to her also found her declaring, 'I just don't like it,' before, during and after the campaign. But what did she mean? Was it prophecy? Or amnesia?

Probably a bit of both. One must, in reaching a judgement, recall her underlying approach, honed and developed during years in power. She thought that force must be used unflinchingly when required. She was by temperament belligerent. But she was also cautious. She was not a 'neo-conservative' (at least as usually defined), in that, though she believed that democracy was a boon in itself and that it led to other benefits, she did not think it could successfully be imposed by fiat. Nor did she consider that every society was ready for it. Values and habits had, in her view, to precede institutions, if these were to function and last. Although she certainly wanted to see the back of Saddam Hussein, she would not have assumed that anyone much better would automatically emerge. She would probably have settled for an alternative friendly dictator; her sympathy for the personal rulers of the Gulf and military rulers elsewhere suggests as much. She would equally have been prepared to envisage a break-up of the country into three ethnic and/or religious units: she had always argued that Iraq was an artificial entity and so not robust. One can also add with some confidence that she would never have accepted at face value the flimsy evidence that Saddam had at his disposal operational weapons of mass destruction; and so, like John Howard in Australia, she would have avoided putting every egg into that fragile political basket. Finally, anyone who knew her would also know that she would have probed more deeply than did Tony Blair Washington's plans for the operation.

In any case, it is hard to imagine a more treacherous background against which to promote a book on international affairs than that obtaining in the spring of 2002. And she was simply not equipped for it. Providence now intervened, although others lent a hand as

well. At the insistence of her staff, now seriously worried about her health, she had been repeatedly sent to her doctor for check-ups. But she was a bad patient. She regarded appointments with the doctor as opportunities to prove that she was indestructible. When she entered the consulting room she would summon up all her power of domination to demonstrate that nothing was wrong and to dismiss the anxieties that friends had privately passed on. But, in the end, reality intruded.

On holiday over Christmas and the New Year 2001–2 in Madeira with Denis – it was his decision that they should revisit the scene of their honeymoon – she was taken ill. The Thatchers and their security team were drinking coffee outside a café up in the mountains when it suddenly became clear that she could not string her words together. The symptoms bore every sign of a stroke, though she persisted in claiming, then and later, that she was suffering from altitude sickness. Denis was in an even more defiant state of denial. But a doctor was called when they returned to the hotel, and a scan and other tests were done.

Back home in London, she was examined seriously for the first time by a specialist and more extensive neurological tests were performed. She was then allowed to travel to Washington and South Africa. By the time she returned the results were available: they showed that she was suffering the effects of a series of minor strokes which had already irrevocably affected her brain and would continue to do so. Moreover, the risk of a major stroke was high if she continued her current stressful life.

Serialization of *Statecraft* began, as planned, in *The Times* on 18 March. But the next day the doctors summoned up courage to say not just that she would have to cancel the speaking engagements planned to promote the book, but that she should not speak in public again at all. It is a tribute to the regard in which Rupert Murdoch held her personally and to the professionalism of HarperCollins that they accepted the news without protest. She, for her part, fought against it. She undoubtedly hoped to reverse the decision

and would try, on occasion successfully, to escape the ban. But in the wake of the doctors' advice, she agreed to issue a statement which was immediately interpreted to mean, though in deference to her resistance it did not specifically say, that her days of public speaking were over.[4] She had been silenced. Was it in her best interests? Yes. The painful circumstances of the next few years would amply testify to that.

The diagnosis was in one sense a relief. The name 'Alzheimer's', like the word 'cancer' for previous generations, had already acquired a terrible resonance. She certainly seemed to show classic signs of dementia. Was she suffering from Alzheimer's? If so, how, if at all, would the announcement be made? In the light of Ronald Reagan's courageous final letter to America, a precedent of openness had been set. But she was not Reagan; and, in any case, such intimate expressions of weakness are probably easier for men. To complicate matters, she was patron of the Alzheimer's Trust and regularly helped raise funds for it. One of her last engagements before she was silenced was at such an event. In fact, she was spared the indignity. Alzheimer's was never diagnosed, and she probably did not have it, though the effects were similar.

The quality of medical attention she received, once a specialist had been brought in, improved greatly, because it now focused on the real problem. But the 'small' strokes continued, and some were not that small. She would suddenly feel unwell at home and the doctor would be called. After such an incident she would then arrive in the office, able to articulate only with difficulty. Her face would have the ravaged, lop-sided look that strokes leave behind. The medication was incapable of preventing them, even though the strain had been taken out of her schedule.

In fact, the problem from now on was how to fill her time. Her memory continued to worsen and she was often seriously confused. If she went abroad – which she now rarely did – or even if she stayed with friends, care had to be taken to ensure that she did not get disorientated and leave her bedroom during the night. As in

previous years, a police officer always sat in the corridor, which helped. It was also necessary to install full-time nursing staff and a housekeeper in 73 Chester Square. It fell to Mark Thatcher and Mark Worthington to see that her life was re-established on a new and inevitably more expensive footing. It was some time before she accepted it. And in the meantime there was more tragedy in store.

In one way, seeing one's contemporaries die is a privilege, because it testifies to one's own robustness, and Margaret Thatcher was still, in physical terms, extraordinarily robust. But it is also depressing, and the round of visits to those struck down by fatal illness, to their funerals, and to their memorial services, became all too regular. Nick Ridley died in 1993, Keith Joseph in 1994, Willie Whitelaw in 1999. But death struck younger friends as well. She joined a courageously cheerful Gordon Reece for his valedictory party on Wednesday, 12 September 2001, and attended his funeral mass a fortnight later.

Denis, ten years older than Margaret, greatly disliked such intimations of mortality. At least he did something practical about it. From about 1998, he ensured that the two of them went to church every Sunday. Initially, they tried St Michael's in Chester Square. But it was very evangelical, and no one was less happy-clappy than the Thatchers. They then tried out the Chapel Royal in St James's and the Guards' Chapel in Birdcage Walk, before finally alighting on the Royal Hospital Chapel in Chelsea. They became very fond of it and of the institution it served. The Hospital embodied a traditional concept of service, it was authentically British and patriotic, and they liked both the staff and the pensioners, who reciprocated the attachment. She made a generous donation to the chapel and was vice-patron of the appeal for the new infirmary that now bears her name. Denis would be buried in the Hospital graveyard.* And so, finally, was she.

---

* A third of Denis's ashes were scattered from Table Mountain in South Africa; the rest, several years after his death, were quietly interred in the Royal Hospital cemetery.

Denis seemed to defy his years. He gave up his directorates, but kept up with his rugby and his lunches. He spent much of his time carefully adding up the totals in his bank statements, in search of an elusive, beneficial error, or reading history and biographies. Yet appearances were deceptive. He put on a good show for outsiders, but he was not in reality so happy. He had pressed his wife repeatedly ever since she left Downing Street to retire for good and – he fondly if unrealistically hoped – to stay at home and look after him. When she did not, he insisted on joining her on foreign tours, where his physical inability to keep up constantly threatened schedules. She worried about him. 'Where is DT? Where is my husband? Is he all right?' was her constant cry. But she worried about him at home as well, concerned that he would not take taxis because they were too expensive, trying to have him use her official car, which she knew was not allowed unless they were travelling together. Her concern was justified. On one occasion he tried to jump on to a Routemaster bus in Piccadilly after lunch, fell off, hurt himself and smashed his gold watch. She was furious.

The two were now spending much more time in each other's company. But, as is often the case, the more the elderly couple were together, the more spiky were relations between them. What made the situation worse in the case of the Thatchers was her fading mental capacity. Her forgetfulness and repetitiveness irritated Denis terribly. He had always had limited patience, but now he showed none. He shouted at her and she became angry and felt humiliated. The resentments grew. She also suddenly developed a strange obsession that he was unfaithful, based perhaps upon some old memory or at least past suspicion, but obviously now a cruel delusion resulting from her illness or from the medication. So by the time Denis's own health suddenly collapsed their marriage was going through a difficult patch.

They spent their last Christmas, that of 2002, together in Tenerife. The holiday had been intended to extend to the New Year

but was cut short because Crawfie and her husband had been unable to join them as planned and, with no outside company, time dragged intolerably. She did not yet know that Denis had been told by his doctor that he was in need of a heart by-pass. On 9 January the operation was successfully performed. She was still resentful and suspicious but at the same time frantically anxious about his health and guilty that she might have neglected him. It was a bad combination, and it made her badger him when he most needed rest. He was accordingly dispatched first to a luxurious hotel in Devon, far enough away to make visits more difficult and rows less frequent, and then to South Africa, where he spent April with Mark. She later flew down to join them. For some reason, the clouds suddenly lifted. She, Denis and Mark enjoyed a wonderful holiday. But it would be their last.

Denis was now in good spirits and in apparently better health. The prognosis on his return appeared encouraging. But suddenly he became listless; his physical strength ebbed. Tests were done: the heart was sound, but terminal pancreatic cancer was diagnosed. On Thursday, 26 June 2003, in the Chelsea and Westminster Hospital, surrounded by his family, friends and the Royal Hospital padre, Denis died, with Margaret holding his hand.

Some of those around her who had seen the reality of the last few months thought that she would take the loss in her stride. They were wrong. If love amounts in the end to mutual need, she and Denis had loved each other more than they ever conveyed, and more perhaps than they ever knew. She was devastated with grief. What was worse, she kept thinking that he was still with her. Her hold on reality weakened. No one could predict where the crisis would end. For seven months she was in a trough of terrible and unrelieved despair. She could not work, sleep or function, and in her disorientating misery she made life impossible for everyone around her.

Finally, in January 2004, at Mark Worthington's prompting, her medication was reassessed, and she started to receive a better mix of

treatment, both for her immediate and for her long-term condition. Life became bearable again. But the improvement, though noticeable straight away, was slow at first.

In particular, new losses, like that of Ronald Reagan in 2004, sharpened the pain of the one she had already borne. She had been worrying about Reagan for years. Each year until his withdrawal from public life in 1994 she had attended and spoken at his birthday party. She would never refuse an opportunity to honour his name. Once she found out that he wanted her to deliver his eulogy – the first time a foreigner had been asked to do such a thing for a former President – she worried constantly about whether she could do justice to him. Whenever some titbit of news of the old man's health was conveyed to her, she would go into a panic. In the end, Reagan's death coincided with her own enforced silence. So she was unable to deliver in person the fine eulogy which John O'Sullivan had drafted. But she recorded it in advance in London with solemn eloquence, and then had the curious experience of listening to herself in Washington Cathedral, before attending with Nancy, family and friends the final interment at the Reagan Library in California. The trip was a great strain, and sometimes she was more confused than her hosts understood. But, buoyed up by instinct and willpower like the old trooper whose memory she had come to celebrate, she gave a performance that intellect alone no longer could deliver.

It was, in fact, a further two years before she emerged completely from the interior darkness that descended with DT's death. But she eventually did – partly because somewhere inside her the old resilience still lurked, and partly through the bitter-sweet blessing of a forgetfulness that dulled the pain. The effect was now very noticeable. She smiled more. She slept properly. Despite going for regular walks in London's parks, she put on weight, becoming quite tubby with all the chocolates she was given and not, of course, being able to remember how many she had consumed. She still had no short-term – and not much long-term – memory, though this, at

least, spared her understanding what the new Tory leadership thought of her. Most importantly, she had ceased to be so confused and was often unnervingly shrewd in her observations. It was no longer necessary to shout in order to be understood, because she had become highly proficient in the art of lip-reading. But she still felt lonely. She had always liked animals and she would have liked to have a dog – Denis and then Mark hated dogs, so it was never possible. But in 2007 she acquired a rescued tomcat called Marvin, which she had to be prevented from overfeeding.*

In fact, the only regular source of worry was her son. She had been away in Virginia when Mark was arrested in South Africa in August 2004 on suspicion of involvement in an attempted coup in Equatorial Guinea. Her staff kept the news from her for three days, fearing the consequences. She was only told at Dulles airport in Washington, just before boarding the flight home. She managed to retain her composure on that occasion, but for the following six months she was constantly taken up with his plight. She provided money for his bail but was advised that any political pressure for his release would be unavailing and probably counter-productive. Although muddled about the exact nature of the charges, she felt a deep sense of shame. She told friends that she was glad that DT had not been alive to see it. Nor did Mark's eventual release solve the family's problems. Diane had early on taken the children back to the United States, after threats were made against them. But the State Department denied him permission to join them. Instead, he spent eighteen months in and out of his mother's house. She never knew where he was or when he would return. She was concerned that he would be unable to earn a living. She was dismayed when his marriage to Diane broke down and he formed a liaison with a married woman (who

* The cat followed her around and people became worried it would trip her up. When she was in hospital it was spirited away 'on holiday' (so the line was spun to her), in fact to the care of a good owner. Soon she had no recollection that Marvin had ever existed.

eventually became his wife). Although married to a divorcee herself, Mrs Thatcher had always taken a very stern view of adultery. (And, obviously, she had not known Denis during his first marriage.) She had, it is true, never enjoyed close relations with her daughter-in-law. But she always believed her to be a good mother. And now she would see even less of her beloved grandchildren. Mark's departure to Spain in 2006 was, in these circumstances, a blessing for all concerned.

By contrast, and to some extent in compensation, she was extremely proud of Carol's success in the television reality programme *I'm a Celebrity, Get Me Out of Here* in December 2005. She did not watch every episode, and friends ensured that she avoided some of the less tasteful bits, but she was glued to the screen for the final and was ecstatic at Carol's triumph. She was equally proud of the way in which she turned her success to financial advantage. Those who did not know Margaret Thatcher well would have been surprised by this. But she respected courage and she saw it now in her daughter's performance. Despite her image, she was not averse to vulgarity if it went with success and rewards, as in this case it did. Sadly, this rapprochement did not last.

In the summer of 2008 a Sunday newspaper published extracts from a book by Carol which revealed intimate details of her mother's mental condition.* The headlines describing the symptoms of Margaret Thatcher's 'dementia' (Carol's word) aroused public sympathy, at least for the mother. But it was now wrongly assumed that the former Prime Minister was in an advanced state of Alzheimer's. People thought that she could not even be invited to attend private functions, which she still enjoyed. There were even rumblings about whether someone apparently mentally incompetent should be allowed to vote in the House of Lords. Confusion and embarrassment descended. For a few days Mrs Thatcher's staff

* *Mail on Sunday*, 24 Aug. 2008, serializing Carol Thatcher, *A Swim-on Part in the Goldfish Bowl: A Memoir* (London: Headline Review, 2008).

kept the piece from her, but in the end she had to know. When she read it, she was shocked at seeing in print facts about her condition which she only half-acknowledged, but above all wounded by the thought that her own daughter could behave in such a fashion.

The last occasion on which Mrs Thatcher played a major public role was, as she would have wished, on the occasion of the twenty-fifth anniversary of the Falklands War in June 2007. She was fit enough to undertake a taxing programme of engagements to mark the celebrations, though by the end she was exhausted. How much she grasped what was happening at each event is unclear. But she was passionate in her pride in what Britain had achieved in that perilous venture. The most moving event was a service in Pangbourne, where she spoke to young people whose fathers had been killed in the Falklands campaign. But the noisiest was a 'Heroes' Dinner' for decorated veterans, held in the Painted Hall at Greenwich. On departing, she turned to wave from the top of the great staircase, and more than a thousand male voices roared their approval. The thunderous bellows might have reminded her of her party conference triumphs; but if they did, the impression quickly faded. The following morning she had no recollection of what had occurred.

The final years of Margaret Thatcher's life were particularly sad. The underlying problem, of course, was her mental decay. Physically, she was fitter than outsiders assumed, while mentally she was a good deal worse. Of the physical mishaps – passing out in the House of Lords in March 2008, breaking her arm in a fall at home in June 2009, and contracting what was described as flu in October 2010 – only the last was dangerous. And this was because, on investigation, it turned out that she had been suffering great pain from a serious, weakening rheumatic condition ('polymyalgia') which had gone undiagnosed. The ensuing steroid treatment cleared it up, but also caused her to put on a lot of weight.

The mental decay, which Carol claimed to have spotted in 2008, was linked to the continuing strokes. She had a quite serious one on

the morning of her (last) Christmas party in 2009. She should never have attended, but she did, though she sat down throughout and left early. The effects, and perhaps those of other new strokes, became very noticeable in her speech the following year. She could no longer string a sentence together. This only partly righted itself, and not for long. By 2010, it was difficult to know what she was talking about. By 2011, meetings with her had become heart-wrenching. She would earnestly seek to make some point – even now she had no taste for small talk – but then trail off, and look hard at you. Then she would try again, with the same intent, but to no more avail. The quandary about whether to reply cheerfully without any comprehension or to hesitate and try to make sense was ultimately irresolvable. It was hard to know which she preferred. People easily assumed the first. But they may have been wrong. Nothing is worse for someone like Margaret Thatcher than to feel patronized. Was there sometimes a gleam of contempt in her eye, as she saw one slithering? Or was that just memory and imagination playing tricks?

Mrs Thatcher's last years were also, to some extent, overshadowed by worries about money. She and Denis – and, indeed, their children – had always been preoccupied with the topic. At the time she retired, it looked as if she would always be comfortably off, and indeed she was never by any definition poor. But her outgoings were much larger than foreseen. The nursing staff were expensive, and (as she had forecast in quite another context) she went 'on and on'. There was also a problem about the house. The sub-lease to her from the family trust on 73 Chester Square expired in 2010, and Mark would have liked her to move out so that the property could be sold. But this was regarded by everyone else concerned as out of the question, given her age and health. So she eventually stayed, but the argument aroused tensions. There were also difficulties created about Mrs Thatcher's appearances in public and even whom she should see at home. On this matter Carol was the most concerned. There were practical arguments for some restrictions: but the end

result was that Mrs Thatcher finished up more isolated than ever.

Quite what she felt about it all is hard to tell, because she was no longer articulate. She did, though, read the newspapers. In early 2012, she certainly noticed a large picture of Meryl Streep, playing Margaret Thatcher in the highly successful film *The Iron Lady*. 'How elegant!' was the delighted response – though whether this was a tribute to the actress or to the Prime Ministerial original was unclear. She was unaware of the intrusive and distasteful elements of the film – focusing on her own dementia – which she would certainly have found humiliating and distressing. Others carefully kept them from her.

The rhythm of Mrs Thatcher's days was by now well established. She seemed, indeed, in reasonably good physical health. Then suddenly, just before Christmas, she began suffering abdominal pains and was stealthily rushed into hospital. The operation to remove a growth in her bladder was not difficult and after some days she was allowed out. She could not manage the stairs at home, however, so she was provided with a suite at the Ritz, through the generosity of Sir David and Sir Frederick Barclay, the hotel's owners. Here she enjoyed a period of luxurious recuperation. But it was not for long. The end when it came was mercifully quick, a massive stroke – the last of so many smaller ones that had remorselessly destroyed her faculties, though never her self-respect.

18

CHARACTER AND ITS
CONSEQUENCES

While still in her twenties, Margaret Roberts was informed by an enthusiastic fortune-teller at a fête in Orpington that she would be 'great – great as Churchill'.[1] Although she never entertained the comparison herself, the claim has validity. Greatness exists, to some extent, in the eye of the beholder and can be very differently assessed. But Mrs Thatcher's claim to the accolade, like Ronald Reagan's, has grown ever stronger as the years go by, and done so in the view of former foes as well as friends.*

The breadth and depth of her imprint on Britain are not simply or even mainly to be explained by the length of time – eleven and a half years – that she occupied Ten Downing Street. Of course, if she had not won three general elections, she would now be viewed differently: she needed more than one term in power to make changes of the scale she set out to accomplish. Yet time alone is not

---

* Evidence for this comes, for example, from a Reuters/Ipsos MORI poll of July 2011. This showed that voters reckoned Mrs Thatcher the most capable British Prime Minister of recent decades (36 per cent), followed by Tony Blair (27 per cent). John Major came bottom (7 per cent). See report in *Daily Telegraph*, 4 July 2011.

enough, as the few, faint traces left by Tony Blair's ten-year stint serve sadly to confirm.

Part of the explanation of Mrs Thatcher's impact on the national psyche must be attributed to the tumultuous, and often traumatic, events with which she was involved. The national miners' strike, the Falklands War, Irish terrorist attacks, the fall of communism in Eastern Europe, the circumstances of her taking and then of her losing the Tory leadership – these would invest the story of any politician who lived through them with a special drama.*

But the essential criterion by which national leaders should be judged is not what they endured but what they changed. Here it is no exaggeration to say that Mrs Thatcher transformed the British political landscape, fundamentally and probably irreversibly. Her four successors as Prime Minister – John Major, Tony Blair, Gordon Brown and David Cameron – have with greater or lesser ease had to live in her shadow and accept her legacy.

Her disagreements with Major were intense and over matters of substance. But when one compares them with what was disputed in the Conservative Party in the 1970s and early 1980s, they look marginal. That is because Mrs Thatcher purged more completely from the Tory system than anyone could have foreseen the corporatism which the Heath Government had embraced. Major did not – and had no wish to – reverse that change. As for the Labour Party, Blair and Brown accepted, and even in the early years in certain respects consolidated, the changes she had implemented. Notably, the Labour Government's early decision to give the Bank of England the power to set interest rates should – despite the recent rise in inflation above target – allow price rises to be kept down better in the long term than under Mrs Thatcher. The later years of the Blair Government, however, saw a sharp rise in public spending. After Brown became Prime Minister in 2007, there was a further splurge. Brown's policy, moreover, adopted in response to the

* On the Brighton bomb, see below, p. 448.

banking crisis and recession, was explicitly based on Keynesian, indeed socialist, assumptions and sacrificed the public finances to a programme of bail-outs and boosting economic demand. Brown's rejection of economic Thatcherism was itself rejected at the 2010 election, to the benefit of the Conservatives. This can be attributed in large part to the sea-change of opinion effected during the Thatcher years. Despite their anger at capitalists, the British people had not forgotten the lesson Mrs Thatcher taught that capitalism works, and that large, intrusive government does not.

Now the Conservative-led Coalition Government, though desperate to adopt a very un-Thatcher-like rhetoric and to nod vigorously in the direction of social justice, is pursuing policies quite similar to those adopted in the early Thatcher years, notably by giving top priority to reduction of the budget deficit. The sharpest difference is between the Thatcher Government's belief in the incentive effect of marginal cuts in income tax and the implicit rejection of this tax-cutting philosophy by David Cameron and his colleagues. Whether that will continue in the event of anaemic economic growth will be interesting to see. Meanwhile, the underlying gains from the Thatcher trade union and regulatory reforms and from privatization have been and will continue to be felt under Labour and Conservative-led Governments alike.

These changes have not only been good for Britain, underpinning stability and prosperity; they have also, after a period of painful transition, benefited the Labour Party. Labour were forced to face up to reality and then gained the electoral rewards for doing so. The Conservatives were less fortunate. For some years, the party's unpopularity and its defeats were widely blamed on Mrs Thatcher's legacy. A detailed refutation of this thesis – which is, indeed, fundamentally misguided – would be inappropriate here. Many of the arguments concern not the Thatcher Government's policies or even Mrs Thatcher's actions since leaving office but an exaggerated or distorted version of Thatcherism. The continuing debate between neo-Thatcherites and modernizers in today's Conservative

Party, though interesting in its own terms, is not part of her story.

Just one point needs to be made. While it is true that Mrs Thatcher was highly unpopular by the end of her term as Prime Minister, this was not, by and large, because of what she stood for, or even what she was thought to stand for. For example, it is stated as a fact that her caricatured remarks about there being 'no such thing as society' did the Conservative Party great harm.* But no hard evidence to support this assertion is evinced. Indeed, the notion that the Conservatives became unelectable because they were deemed uncaring is simply a myth. Throughout the 1980s, opinion research showed that the party was thought to be hard-hearted and tight-fisted. But it was also thought to be technically competent, good at running the economy and reliable in a crisis, offering strong leadership and a sense of direction.† Once that reputation was lost under Major's misgovernment the long-standing Tory weaknesses on social policy also became a problem. Yet the key challenge facing the Conservatives remains how to reclaim its old reputation, not how to contrive a new identity. Of course, in so far as Mrs Thatcher's Government mismanaged the economy and mishandled the poll tax in her last years, she must, it is true, share responsibility for later Tory difficulties. But otherwise, blame for the party's failures should fall on other shoulders.

The second way in which Margaret Thatcher changed Britain was through the country's sharply improved economic perform-ance. The successes, the shortcomings and the final triumphant transformation have already been described.[2] What needs to be stressed here is the extent to which this turn-round was the result

---

* This, for example, is the starting point for Kieron O'Hara's interesting and influential, but for me unpersuasive, analysis *After Blair: Conservatism beyond Thatcher* (Cambridge: Icon, 2005). Having fairly described what she said and meant, he asserts as if it were obvious: 'However that may be, the quote was disastrous for the image of the Tories, and they have been living it down ever since' (p. 210). David Cameron was clearly persuaded. He spent his first two years as leader repeatedly intoning: 'There is such a thing as society.'
† I saw both internal and public polling at the time and this was the clear – and clearly understood – message.

of the single-minded application of a coherent economic philosophy as clear and as radical as the socialism of which it was the opposite and to which it was the antidote. The programme edged two steps forward before taking a step back – sometimes, though not often, two steps back. But while its progress was irregular, the direction was not. It propelled Britain from near the bottom to near the top of the Western industrial nations. It ended decline. It reshaped industry. It transformed attitudes. It restored the nation's prospects and expanded its influence.

While Mrs Thatcher's critics are often sceptical about the economic effects of her policies, they have been keen to assert the scale of their social impact, which, naturally, they see as wholly bad. Thus we are urged to lament the fate of 'Thatcher's children' – and, in one bizarre variation, to blame these 'children', now themselves parents, for a further generation's misbehaviour.[3] Such criticism usually comes from the left. But a variant of it can also be heard on the traditionalist right, where the accusation is that she destroyed the institutional fabric of the nation. This is neither fair nor sensible.

Margaret Thatcher could, it is true, talk as if all that mattered was efficiency, but she did not really believe it. She simply wanted to remind people in all walks of life that no one owed them a living. She was in many respects a romantic patriot. In seventeenth-century terms, and despite her puritanical streak, she always thought of herself as a Cavalier and not a Roundhead. She favoured the monarchy, the aristocracy, the armed forces, elaborate ritual, venerable tradition, the 1662 Prayer Book, field sports – even the Royal Mail, which she could not envisage being privatized. She was, in fact, a Tory, philosophically conservative in most respects, only in economic affairs a liberal. She was an individualist; but her individualism was asserted against the state, not against the prevailing values of society. When the historian Andrew Roberts publicly dedicated his biography of Salisbury to her as 'Thrice-elected "illiberal Tory" ', he hit the spot.[4]

The left's criticism of the social effect of her policies is that they

produced inequality and impoverishment.[5] On the first, Mrs Thatcher would have harboured no regrets. It was not her aim to create a more equal society, only one where there was more opportunity. She agreed with Keith Joseph that inequality was the concomitant of liberty, and she placed liberty first.[6] She did not, therefore, have any final plan for society at all. She occasionally talked about a 'classless society', but it was only a way of attacking class-based politics.* Her primary interest was in economic, not social change; and, as will be discussed, the broader social changes that did occur in the 1980s owed rather little to her.

As for the accusation that she increased poverty, the significance of the official figures is disputable. The currently prevailing definition of poverty in relative, not absolute, terms – officially the 'poverty line' is regarded as 60 per cent of median income – renders the debate almost meaningless. On that basis, if the general level of wealth increases, the number of people in poverty may also increase, even if their living standards have not in fact fallen. Mrs Thatcher had no time for such nonsense, even if her successors have. She recognized that poverty exists, of course, and (contrary to some accounts) she never believed in or referred to the 'trickle-down' theory in explaining how to relieve it.† She thought, however, that only a very small number of people in society lacked the ability to improve themselves if they made the effort. By the time she left office, and still more afterwards, she also agreed with those American social policy experts who argued that the causes of poverty in modern societies were essentially behavioural.

* To my knowledge, she proclaimed her belief in a 'classless society' only twice. In her final party conference speech she listed ways of increasing opportunity and concluded: 'And that's the kind of open classless Britain I want to see.' (I drafted that section: it was a misjudgement.) Her instinctive view was better expressed in her Central Council speech in Buxton on Saturday, 19 March 1988: 'The socialists speak of a classless society. But their every action betrays their class consciousness.' When Major then took up the slogan his background and outlook lent it a more socially radical overtone.

† According to that view, wealth automatically 'trickles down' from the top to the bottom of society. In fact, this only happens if markets work properly. And anyway, in a functioning market economy wealth is created and incomes rise at all levels, not just at the top.

Mrs Thatcher did not have a social policy as such. But her economic policies did have social effects. Economic change – including disruption, mobility and prosperity – was bound to have social consequences. But this does not mean that the overall outcome for society was either willed by or welcome to her. Materialism, egotism, vulgarity and irresponsibility have all come to be associated with the 1980s. But five years of John Major's consensual Toryism and more than ten years of New Labour have hardly delivered a great improvement. In any case, in the longer run cultural factors, shifts in religious and moral values and the impact of technology are more important than politicians in changing society. The trends towards family break-up and single parenthood, alongside the rise in crime, continued during the Thatcher years. But they did not begin with, and were probably not accelerated by, Mrs Thatcher's policies. One can argue that her government was rather too interested in the economy, not enough in society.[*] But the idea that government has the power to fix a 'broken society' (in the vogue phrase) as it has to fix a broken economy is unrealistic. The parallels are not exact and the possibilities are not commensurate.

It is easy to assume that, as Britain's first woman Prime Minister, Margaret Thatcher had a large impact on the role of women in society. That assumption should be resisted. The reality was more complex. It was, doubtless, reassuring for women to witness another woman more than holding her own in a position traditionally the preserve of men. Moreover, Mrs Thatcher obviously possessed to a high degree skills that were valuable outside the world of politics. She was the ultimate professional, capable of organizing herself and others in pursuit of clearly defined goals. She would have made a superb chief executive of a multinational company. She showed men what a woman could do.

She was in some respects a feminist, but of an old-fashioned middle-class kind. As has been noted, her early pronouncements on

---

[*] I felt this at the time. It is the underlying theme of my *The Conservative Community: The Roots of Thatcherism and its Future* (London: Centre for Policy Studies, 1989).

the role of women were very much those of the aspiring and frustrated professional woman of the 1960s. Some of these attitudes remained with her. She had been an early supporter of liberalizing abortion and did not regret it. Her attitude would have been incomprehensible to her American conservative admirers, and she was usually sensible enough to avoid the subject with them. But she did not fit into the stereotype feminism of the 1970s Women's Liberation movement. When asked, at an early press conference as leader, about Women's Lib, she scoffed: 'What's it ever done for me?'[7] No one was less likely to 'burn her bra' than Mrs Thatcher. She was the opposite of the unwomanly woman. She was attractive and she had no reservations about using her femininity. She also had a high if somewhat incoherent regard for motherhood, which had an impact on her Government's policies.* She rejected schemes which went beyond encouraging women to aspire. She knew that quotas and promotion by merit were mutually incompatible, and she was (with some reservations) a meritocrat. She was proud to have succeeded against the odds, and she thought that other women could do so too.

Margaret Thatcher's greatest impact during her years in office was undoubtedly on Britain's international standing. This in part reflected the economic turn-round, which by the mid-1980s was well known and by the time she left office was widely emulated abroad. But it principally stemmed from the use and development of military power. Victory in the Falklands War was fundamental. The decisions to upgrade the independent nuclear deterrent and to deploy cruise missiles upheld Britain's military significance. Above all, Mrs Thatcher's decision to throw in her lot with Reagan's strategy led to the defeat of communism. Her relationship with Gorbachev then added glamour to this prestige. Generally, her forceful presence and undiplomatic brand of diplomacy gave Britain a world role which it had not played for a quarter of a century.

* See p. 51. * See p. 51.

Most, though not all, of this legacy has survived into the post-Cold War world, which she also helped shape. Britain's closeness to the United States preceded Mrs Thatcher, but she made it central to British strategic thinking, and despite the odd hiccup it remains so. This was a conscious choice made at the expense of relations with Europe. Despite rhetorical changes and symbolic initiatives under her successors, that directional shift has not been revoked.

One can legitimately question the benefits that have flowed from her approach in foreign affairs. The debate about the merits of US-led interventionism overseas ebbs and flows, and at present it ebbs. But the fact that Britain still has the will and (just about) the resources to play such a role at all stems from the confidence she gave the nation in its capacities and from the priorities she set. The present arrangements in Europe would seem unsatisfactory to Mrs Thatcher – who wanted Britain out altogether – and to the Euro-enthusiasts – who want it much further in. But the status quo, largely her legacy, has its advantages, in that it ensures influence without, so far, much loss of autonomy. All in all, because of Mrs Thatcher's leadership, the United Kingdom is now probably the world's fourth or fifth most powerful nation. What the country chooses to do with that is up to her successors; but without her, they would not have the luxury of deciding.

The Thatcher effect does not, however, lie in government measures alone. Without her extraordinary personality, many of the changes would not have occurred. Certainly, their cumulative effect and the impression they left behind would have been less, and different.

Her character contained elements which were not in themselves unusual. It was the combination, often the contradictory combination, that made them so. She was not subtle. She was not, for example, good at, or interested in, making distinctions or adding qualifications. But at a certain level she was indeed complicated. She combined reserves of cunning with personal naïveté. She was tactically brilliant – as in timing her trade union reforms, in pressing the budgetary case

in Europe, and in combining force and diplomacy in the Falklands. Yet she was inclined to take people at face value, a particularly dangerous trait in a radical leader. This helped undo her.

She was also at one level extremely modest. She never thought that she was a child of destiny, even if she would not quite have settled for being one of those 'unprofitable servants' who merely do their duty.[8] Asked by John O'Sullivan whether she thought that she had been spared by God for a higher purpose, when she nearly died as a result of the Brighton bomb (on which see below), she simply replied: No she didn't think that. (O'Sullivan's other two subjects, Ronald Reagan and John Paul II, by contrast, did think in these predestinarian terms.[9]) On the other hand, she could be arrogant. She would claim to be an expert on some policy matter of which she knew little. She would become absurdly defensive when faced with mild criticism. Anyone who exercises great power for a long period is likely to become big-headed. This made her difficult. But her pride never severely got in the way of her judgement and – as noted above – she avoided the dangers of outright hubris.

Her mood and behaviour could change quickly: at one moment she could be brutal, harsh, coruscating, at the next soft, sensitive and charming. This capacity to surprise kept those around her on their toes and was probably meant to do so. Her ability to attract loyalty from her staff, which was intense, and her capacity to persuade less amenable people to put up with her at all, both depended on her deep personal kindness. There are countless examples, which others have recounted.[10] She was invariably prompt to offer consolation for a loss or misfortune. She was unswervingly loyal to friends and colleagues who made a mess of their lives. She did not judge them when they fell into disgrace; she just tried to get them out of it. She remembered tiny details about people's circumstances. Invitations to Christmas lunch at Chequers went to those she found out by discreet enquiry would otherwise be alone. (Every year the staff at Chequers and at Downing Street all

received Christmas presents from her – even in 1990, when she was thrown out of office.) She was constantly writing letters of praise or sympathy or thanks. For someone who agonized endlessly over the drafting of public statements, she had a unique gift for writing personal notes, finding the right words and tone without second thoughts or alterations.* Admittedly, some of this sympathy was a little forced. She would use such gestures as a way to make up for her bad behaviour. There was, though, nothing artificial about her love for children.

Margaret Thatcher could not bear to see children labelled. She remembered how in Grantham she had been distressed to see children from the local orphanage – who, everyone assumed, had been born out of wedlock – dressed up in their distinctive, Victorian uniforms. She thought it cruel to stigmatize children (even involuntarily) for their parents' faults. Similarly, in later years, she would not even use the word 'illegitimate', though no one was otherwise less politically correct. Her care for children took practical forms. She took seriously her role as patron of the NSPCC and made substantial donations to it. She would give vent to her sorrow whenever she heard or read of children suffering. She was horrified by child abuse and tried to do something about it long before it became a staple of tabloid shock. She gave private and public support to ChildLine, the telephone helpline for abused children, and she introduced the Children Act, which strengthened powers to intervene when abuse was suspected. People were always bringing in children to see her – and did not stop doing so after she left Downing Street. When a group of cancer-stricken children from Chernobyl came to visit her in her new office she fussed around endlessly and gave them juice, cakes, T-shirts and food parcels to take away.

All this made her lovable to some and at least tolerable to rather more. But the most politically important attribute of her mature

---

* These letters will doubtless come to light as the years go by – she did not keep copies. Any forgeries will be clearly evident if they contain the words 'thank you' properly divided. She always wrote the expression as one word.

personality was its sheer power. She could bewitch and she could terrify, sometimes both at once. Her eyes would blaze and her voice louden and deepen when she was angry or passionate on some essential point. (Even when irate, though, she never swore.) All political leaders acquire an aura which is in part the effect of office, mainly the result of how they are seen by others. But long after she had left government, she still filled a room. That elemental force was what made her unique.

One result of this force of personality, which media concentration magnified, was that what she did and said seemed larger than life, or, at its worst, exaggerated. She was frequently clumsy in her choice of words, which also contributed to the 'over the top' effect. 'Rather swamped', 'no such thing as society', 'the great car economy', 'our money', 'Rejoice!' and 'frit' are among the more memorable of her extempore remarks.* All could have been better expressed. She had, indeed, despite her music lessons and knowledge of poetry, something of a tin ear. Certain words she would always mispronounce, no matter how many times the correct version was explained.†
Recognizing her deficiencies, she sought to overcome them. She would ask others to read drafts of speeches aloud for her several times, so she could catch the rhythm. She had a code which she used to mark up speech texts, indicating (by dots) the proper speed of delivery and (by *grave* or acute accents) whether to lower or raise her voice. A problem with both her ad lib and her prepared remarks was her literalness. Off the cuff, she was inclined to explain over-clearly what she meant, which made people think she was talking down to them – which she never consciously did. In written material, it affected her style by prejudicing her against adverbs or even adjectives – she considered such elaborations frivolous and redundant – and making her wary of employing any term that could be misunder-

* 'Frit', used by Mrs Thatcher of the Labour Opposition in the House of Commons at Questions on 19 April 1983, means in the dialect of Lincolnshire 'frightened'.
† For example, Renaissance (a word she liked) she pronounced 'Ren-ássence'. Hawaii (which she visited on speech tours) she called 'Hi-Wi'.

stood, especially if it might be thought naughty. *Double entendre* was one of the few French phrases that crossed her lips.*

Mrs Thatcher always made great efforts to improve her performance, both as leader of the Opposition and as Prime Minister. In fact, her capacity to learn quickly was one of her greatest strengths. Even the most experienced MP has almost no training for the party leadership; the tasks of a Cabinet minister are very inadequate preparation for Number Ten. So having the instincts, humility and intelligence to learn 'on the job' is essential – and Margaret Thatcher had them.

But in the end it is character that counts. It was her virtues and weaknesses – she had no characteristics that can properly count as 'vices' – that ultimately determined the nature and extent of her achievements. She knew this. She thought that inner strength was required to accomplish great things. She needed no prompting to talk about the 'Victorian virtues' (not 'values', a word she rarely used). She tried to practise them. Shirley Letwin, who knew Mrs Thatcher and understood her, described the Thatcher project as all about encouraging the 'vigorous virtues' which in recent times had been forgotten. These qualities are listed by Letwin as 'uprightness, self-sufficiency, energy, independent mindedness, adventurousness, loyalty and robustness'. They were exemplified in Margaret Thatcher's own life – at least when she was at her best.[11] After she left office and through her reading, she became interested in the four 'cardinal' virtues of classical and Christian thought – prudence, justice, temperance and fortitude.[12] They offer a useful framework for examination of her as a politician.

Prudence in the sense of practical wisdom, not merely caution –

---

* Among the words which were often banned or accepted only with loud protests were 'sex' (meaning gender), 'bloody' (meaning gory) and 'just' (meaning only). There were endless discussions about whether the Iron Curtain would 'rise' or 'fall'. The most famous, indeed legendary, incident is her prolonged refusal to understand why, in a party conference speech, she could not advise James Callaghan, who had compared himself to Moses, to keep on taking the pills rather than, as her draftsmen had written, 'tablets'. I wish I had witnessed this.

though she was also cautious – she had in abundance. She had a large fund of common sense, an attribute of which she anyway thought women had more than men. It deserted her only rarely, and then not for long. It allowed her to keep matters in perspective and to exercise judgement about what could and should be done in particular circumstances. Her favourite sayings reflected her determination to be practical. So she would remind people that 'life is a matter of alternatives': that is, be realistic. And she would talk about 'Thatcher's law', to the effect that 'the unexpected happens': that is, be prepared.

Justice was also one of her strengths, though her critics would doubtless argue that her policies were unjust. She placed an unusually high value on fairness. She thought that people should receive everything to which they had a right, as a result of their own efforts, not only what government found it convenient to bestow. She saw government's task as maintaining a framework of law that was equitable to all. She so disliked trade union privileges because they breached this principle. She also felt guilty about the effects of the poll tax when she became convinced that the conscientious were suffering from its effects. She was extremely upright. She habitually told the truth, and if she did practise some trivial act of deception her guilty demeanour almost always gave her away. She was also scrupulously honest.* The only attacks made on her probity all concerned the indulgence she showed towards her son, who was, indeed, allowed on occasion to get too close for comfort to sensitive intergovernment business deals. The circumstances of the multi-billion-pound Al-Yamamah defence contract with Saudi Arabia, negotiated in 1985 and 1988, are in some respects obscure and likely to remain so. But two points are clear. First, Mrs Thatcher as Prime Minister never allowed hope of personal gain to influence her behaviour; and second, neither then nor later did she benefit financially from securing this coup for British business. In the present context, that is all that counts.

---

* She was honest and honourable during the Westland crisis: see pp. 281–4.

Temperance, the third of the virtues, has a slightly odd and antiquated ring to it. For someone with Margaret Thatcher's Methodist background it was associated with abstinence from alcohol. In this sense, she was not always temperate. Nor was she temperate in any sense when a bout of rage took her. In a wider sense, however, she was. She generally exercised iron self-control, disciplined her tastes and faculties, consciously pushed herself to the limit, denied herself rest and even minor pleasures, in order to devote her time and energy to duty. She had a great distrust of inactivity, whether her own or other people's. She disliked the expression used by Major – and not just because it was he who used it – about wanting to see 'a nation at ease with itself'. She said no one should feel at ease with himself: we should all be dissatisfied and try to do better. She quoted with approval Teddy Roosevelt's 'doctrine of the strenuous life'.* She would similarly applaud the sentiments of the hymn:

> Not for ever in green pastures
> Do we ask our way to be;
> But the steep and rugged pathway
> May we tread rejoicingly.[13]

There was something of her upbringing in all this. It had its advantages, but also drawbacks. She would have made better decisions if she had slept longer than five hours a night. She would have had a healthier and happier old age if she had earlier learned to relax.

Fortitude (or courage), the last of the cardinal virtues, was the defining and, indeed, inspiring mark of her character. Shortly before his death, Disraeli remarked that throughout his career he

---

* The passage runs: 'I wish to preach, not the doctrine of ignoble ease, but the doctrine of the strenuous life, the life of toil and effort, of labour and strife; to preach that highest form of success which comes, not to the man who desires mere easy peace, but to the man who does not shrink from danger, from hardship, or from bitter toil, and who out of these wins the splendid ultimate triumph.' Speech by US President Theodore Roosevelt to the Hamilton Club, Chicago, 10 April 1899.

had suffered 'from the timidity of colleagues', adding that 'courage is the rarest of all qualities to be found in public men'.[14] Margaret Thatcher would have understood and agreed. She was herself sometimes downhearted, temporarily querulous, occasionally over-timid. But when confronted with large and dangerous matters she invariably displayed great and sustained courage.

Usually this meant moral courage. She could not have ridden through the 'Milk Snatcher' and 'hoarding' campaigns, overcome Cabinet opposition, pushed through trade union reform, reined back public spending, faced down Scargill, defeated Galtieri, won back 'our money', denounced Balkan genocide, defended Pinochet or repeatedly crushed her opponents in the House of Commons without it. But she needed physical courage as well when she visited Ulster during the troubles. Above all, she needed it when the IRA tried to kill her with the bomb that wrecked the Grand Hotel, Brighton, in the early hours of Friday, 12 October 1984. Had she been in the bathroom of her suite she would have been dead. She stayed completely calm. Robin Butler was appalled to see her, to the sound of falling masonry, walk back without hesitation into the darkened bedroom to check on DT. Her only concern was for others. But her fortitude was an act of will, not an absence of fear. For years afterwards, she was convinced that the IRA would eventually kill her. 'They'll get me in the end,' she would murmur. When she was under stress the worry returned. At her last party conference she had net curtains placed on her hotel window because she felt exposed. She remained the terrorists' prime target, but they never got another chance.*

---

* Robin Butler's account is to be found in Iain Dale, ed., *Memories of Maggie: A Portrait of Margaret Thatcher* (London: Politico's, 2000), pp. 106–7. I do not otherwise cover the Thatcher Government's policy towards Ireland, but it is worth noting that in later years she had doubts about whether the 1985 Anglo-Irish Agreement on cross-border cooperation had been worth it. In any case, no one seriously thought that she had been moved to sign it by fear of the IRA. Only when the terrorists at length discovered they could not win did they consider compromise. Today's peace in Northern Ireland thus reflects Margaret Thatcher's implacability as much as it does Tony Blair's flexibility. Even after the Provisional IRA's ceasefire, the breakaway Real IRA continued to target her.

Mrs Thatcher's toughness was, though, allied to aggression. She was a warrior even when there was no war to be fought, and she did not take hostages. This was one reason why she was feared and hated. Indeed, the depth of the hatred she provoked resulted in her enemies behaving in ways that made them seem somewhat deranged. She was anathema to the self-righteous and self-opinionated world of 'the Arts'. She kept the BBC licence fee, despite Denis's protests, and she continued to feather-bed the British film industry, to no obviously beneficial effect, but the country's artistic and intellectual elite were convinced they were her helpless victims. Their bile knew no limits. The playwright Denis Potter thought her 'repellent'. The theatre's jack-of-all-trades, Jonathan Miller, called her 'loathsome, repulsive'. Academe felt no more kindly. Oxford University unprecedentedly refused her an honorary doctorate. Baroness Warnock, head of Girton College, mocked Mrs Thatcher's dress and appearance as 'not exactly vulgar, just low'.[15] Seldom has snobbery been less abashed.

The left luvvies were not, of course, representative of the country as a whole. But the fact remains that Mrs Thatcher was a profoundly divisive figure. Her personality and her policies ensured it; and, though she did not enjoy it, she was resigned to it. Whether this divisiveness should be accounted a weakness is another matter. It was surely impossible to find common ground with the defenders of the over-blown public sector, which had to be deflated. Nor did the opponents of change seek any middle way. In any case, it is the mark of great leaders that they do divide: indeed, it takes such divisive qualities to save the nation in a crisis. In their different ways, the careers of David Lloyd George, Winston Churchill and Charles de Gaulle all testify to that. And so, again in a different way, does Margaret Thatcher's.*

Mrs Thatcher certainly had her weaknesses as a leader. She was

* Ronald Reagan appears to offer an exception to the rule. But though Reagan was not hated, he was often despised. In any case, the political atmosphere of America is simply nothing like that of Europe.

not good at long-term planning. She was secretive and distrustful of her colleagues. She paid insufficient attention to bringing on people who would value and continue her work. Yet even these deficiencies are all, in their way, understandable. She had to improvise and seize the moment in order to catch her adversaries off guard and so get her way. She had good reason not to rely on others, because she knew their support was unreliable. She worked so hard that the day after tomorrow seemed just too many red boxes away to justify bothering with what and who would follow on. She did not set out to destroy potential successors for fear they might become rivals – she was simply not like that. If Cecil Parkinson had not had to resign because of scandal; if John Moore's health had been better; if Norman Tebbit had not left the Cabinet to care for his wife – and if John Major had had time to destroy his reputation at the Foreign Office, as he would have done – the overall outcome might have been different.[16] But probably in the end her failure to establish successors comes back to the recurring fact that she was a woman surrounded by men. Attracting devotion is possible – it is even easier – across the sexual divide. But the joshing camaraderie from which political teams are formed, and from which new team leaders emerge, is much more elusive.

Margaret Thatcher rose, she prospered, and she eventually fell more or less alone. Her legacy is all around us. But she has no heir. Perhaps she did not need one. She slew the dragons. Now the meek can inherit the earth.

PERSONAL AND POLITICAL
CHRONOLOGY

MR = Margaret Roberts; MT = Margaret Thatcher; DT = Denis Thatcher.

1925   MR born in Grantham (13 October)

1943–7   MR at Oxford

1949   MR selected as Conservative candidate for Dartford

1950   General election (23 February): narrow Labour victory

1951   General election (25 October): Conservative victory

1951   Marriage of MR and DT (13 December)

1953   MT gives birth to twins, Mark and Carol (15 August)

1955   General election (26 May): Conservative victory

1956   Suez crisis

1957   Macmillan succeeds Eden as PM

1958   MT selected as Conservative candidate for Finchley

1959   General election (8 October): Conservative victory: MT
        elected MP for Finchley

1960   MT's maiden speech in the House of Commons
        (5 February)

1961   MT given first government post as Parliamentary
        Under-Secretary at Ministry of Pensions (9 October)

1963   Douglas–Home succeeds Macmillan as PM

1964   General election (15 October): Labour victory

1965   Heath succeeds Douglas–Home as Conservative leader;
        MT moved to shadow Housing and Land

1966   General election: Labour victory; MT moved to be
        Macleod's deputy Shadow Treasury spokesman

1967   MT joins Shadow Cabinet at Fuel and Power

1968   Powell sacked from Shadow Cabinet; MT's CPC Lecture,
        'What's Wrong with Politics?'

1969   MT appointed Shadow Education Secretary

1970   General election (18 June): Conservative victory; MT
        becomes Education Secretary

1972   MT produces White Paper, *A Framework for Expansion*

1973   Britain joins the EEC

1974   General election (28 February): Labour victory (minority
        government); MT becomes Shadow Environment Secretary.
        Second general election (10 October): Labour victory

1975   MT becomes Conservative leader (first ballot 4 February;
        second ballot 11 February)

1976   IMF crisis package (15 December)

1977   Lib–Lab Pact (23 March)

1979   General election (3 May): Conservative victory; MT becomes PM. Howe's first budget (12 June); exchange controls abolished (23 October); USSR invades Afghanistan (December)

1980   Steel strike (January to April); Reagan elected US President (4 November)

1981   Austerity budget (10 March); major ministerial reshuffle (14 September)

1982   Falklands War (2 April to 14 June)

1983   General election (9 June): Conservative victory; US invasion of Grenada (25 October)

1984   Miners' strike begins (March); Brighton bomb (12 October); Hong Kong agreement (19 December)

1985   Miners' strike ends (March); Gorbachev becomes Soviet leader (March); Anglo-Irish agreement (15 November)

1986   Westland crisis (January); US raid on Libya (15 April)

1987   MT visit to USSR (March–April); General election (11 June): Conservative victory

1988   Bruges speech (20 September); MT visits Poland (November)

1989   Lawson's resignation (26 October); destruction of Berlin Wall (November)

1990   Iraq invades Kuwait (2 August); Howe resigns (1 November); Conservative leadership first ballot (20 November); MT resigns as PM (28 November)

1991   First Gulf War (January–February)

1992   General election (9 April): Conservative victory; MT stands

down as MP and is awarded life peerage in Dissolution Honours. 'Black Wednesday' financial crisis (16 September); MT intervenes publicly over Bosnia (from August)

1993   Maastricht Treaty legislation passed; publication of *The Downing Street Years*

1995   Publication of *The Path to Power*

1997   General election (1 May): Labour victory; Blair becomes PM

1998   Arrest of Pinochet (16/17 October)

2000   Pinochet released and returned to Chile (March)

2002   Publication of *Statecraft*

2003   Death of DT (26 June)

2004   Death of Ronald Reagan (5 June)

2005   General election (5 May): Labour victory

2013   Death of MT (8 April)

BIBLIOGRAPHY

I list here published volumes that I found of direct use and to which, therefore, reference is made in the notes. Articles and unpublished documents on which I have drawn can, unless indicated otherwise in the text, be found in the Margaret Thatcher papers contained in the Thatcher Foundation's Churchill College archive, accessible either on its website, www.margaretthatcher.org, or on the CD-ROM entitled *Margaret Thatcher: Complete Public Statements 1945–1990*.

Abse, Leo, *Margaret, Daughter of Beatrice* (London: Jonathan Cape, 1989)

Anderson, Digby, ed., *The Loss of Virtue: Moral Confusion and Social Disorder in Britain and America* (London: Social Affairs Unit, 1992)

Baker, Kenneth, *The Turbulent Years: My Life in Politics* (London: Faber & Faber, 1993)

Beckett, Clare, *Thatcher* (London: Haus, 2006)

Bennett, William J., *The Book of the Virtues* (New York: Simon & Schuster, 1996)

Blake, Robert, *Disraeli* (London: Methuen, 1966)

Booth, Philip, ed., *Were 364 Economists All Wrong?* (London: Institute of Economic Affairs, 2006)

Bukovsky, Vladimir, *Jugement à Moscou* (Paris: Robert Laffont, 1995)

Busch, Andrew, *Ronald Reagan and the Politics of Freedom* (Lanham: Rowman & Littlefield, 2001)

Butler, David, and Sloman, Anne, *British Political Facts 1900–1979* (London: Macmillan, 1980)

Campbell, John, *Margaret Thatcher*, vol. 1: *The Grocer's Daughter* (London: Jonathan Cape, 2000)

Campbell, John, *Margaret Thatcher*, vol. 2: *The Iron Lady* (London: Pimlico, 2004)

Carrington, Lord [Peter], *Reflect on Things Past: The Memoirs of Lord Carrington* (London: Fontana, 1989)

Cecil, Lady Gwendolen, *Life of Robert Marquis of Salisbury*, 4 vols (London: Hodder & Stoughton, 1921–32)

Clark, Alan, *Diaries*, 3 vols (London: Weidenfeld & Nicolson, 1993)

Cockett, Richard, *Thinking the Unthinkable: Think-Tanks and the Economic Counter-Revolution 1931–1983* (London: HarperCollins, 1994)

Congdon, Tim, *Keynes, the Keynesians and Monetarism* (Cheltenham: Edward Elgar, 2007)

Cosgrave, Patrick, *Thatcher: The First Term* (London: Bodley Head, 1979)

Crafts, Nicholas, *Britain's Relative Economic Decline, 1870–1995: A Quantitative Perspective* (London: Social Market Foundation, 1997)

Crafts, Nicholas, *The Conservative Government's Economic Record: An End of Term Report* (Institute of Economic Affairs, 1998)

Dale, Iain, ed., *Memories of Maggie: A Portrait of Margaret Thatcher* (London: Politico's, 2000)

de Gaulle, Charles, *Mémoires de guerre: l'appel, 1940–1942* (Paris: Plon-Pocket, 1954)

Djilas, Milovan, *Conversations with Stalin* (London: Rupert Hart-Davis, 1962)

Donoughue, Bernard, *Downing Street Diary: With Harold Wilson in No. 10* (London: Jonathan Cape, 2005)

Donoughue, Bernard, *Prime Minister: The Conduct of Policy under Harold Wilson and James Callaghan* (London: Jonathan Cape, 1987)

Falkland Islands Review: Report of a Committee of Privy Counsellors, Cmnd 8787 (London: HMSO, January 1983)

Fowler, Norman, *Ministers Decide: A Personal Memoir of the Thatcher Years* (London: Chapman, 1991)

Freedman, Sir Lawrence, *Official History of the Falklands Campaign*, 2 vols (Abingdon: Routledge, 2005)

Gardiner, George, *Margaret Thatcher: From Childhood to Leadership* (London: William Kimber, 1975)

Harris, Robin, *Beyond Friendship: The Future of Anglo-American Relations* (Washington DC: Heritage Foundation, 2006)

Harris, Robin, *The Conservative Community: The Roots of Thatcherism and its Future* (London: Centre for Policy Studies, 1989)

Heath, Edward, *The Course of My Life* (London: Hodder & Stoughton, 1999)

Henderson, Nicholas, *Mandarin: The Diaries of an Ambassador 1969–1982* (London: Phoenix, 1994)

Hoskyns, John, *Just in Time: Inside the Thatcher Revolution* (London: Aurum, 2000)

Howe, Geoffrey, *Conflict of Loyalty* (London: Macmillan, 1994)

Hurd, Douglas, *Memoirs* (London: Abacus, 2004)

Ingham, Bernard, *Kill the Messenger* (London: HarperCollins, 1991)

Jenkins, Simon, *Thatcher and Sons: A Revolution in Three Acts* (London: Allen Lane, 2006)

Joseph, Keith, and Sumption, Jonathan, *Equality* (London: John Murray, 1979)

Keegan, William, *Mr Lawson's Gamble* (London: Hodder & Stoughton, 1989)

Kissinger, Henry, *Years of Renewal* (New York: Simon & Schuster, 1999)

Lamont, Norman, *In Office* (London: Little, Brown, 1999)

Lawson, Nigel, *The View from No. 11: Memoirs of a Tory Radical* (London: Bantam, 1992)

Letwin, Shirley Robin, *The Anatomy of Thatcherism* (London: Fontana, 1992)

McAlpine, Alistair, *Once a Jolly Bagman: Memoirs* (London: Weidenfeld & Nicolson, 1997)

MacGregor, Ian, with Tyler, Rodney, *The Enemies Within: The Story of the Miners' Strike, 1984–5* (London: Collins, 1986)

Major, John, *The Autobiography* (London: HarperCollins, 1999)

Matlock, Jack F., *Reagan and Gorbachev: How the Cold War Ended* (New York: Random House, 2004)

Middlemas, Keith, and Barnes, John, *Baldwin: A Biography* (London: Weidenfeld & Nicolson, 1969)

Millar, Ronald, *A View from the Wings* (London: Weidenfeld & Nicolson, 1993)

Minford, Patrick, *Markets not Stakes* (London: Orion, 1998)

Minford, Patrick, *The Supply Side Revolution in Britain* (Cheltenham: Edward Elgar for Institute of Economic Affairs, 1991)

Mount, Ferdinand, *Cold Cream: My Early Life and its Mistakes* (London: Bloomsbury, 2008)

Murray, Patricia, *Margaret Thatcher* (London: W. H. Allen, 1980)

Nott, John, *Here Today, Gone Tomorrow: Reflections of an Errant Politician* (London: Politico's, 2003)

O'Hara, Kieron, *After Blair: Conservatism beyond Thatcher* (Cambridge: Icon, 2005)

O'Sullivan, John, *The President, the Pope and the Prime Minister* (Washington DC: Regnery, 2006)

Parkinson, Cecil, *Right at the Centre* (London: Weidenfeld & Nicolson, 1992)

Pepper, Gordon T., and Oliver, Michael J., *Monetarism under Thatcher: Lessons for the Future* (Cheltenham: Edward Elgar for Institute of Economic Affairs, 2001)

Powell, Enoch, *Income Tax at 4/3 in the £*, ed. Anthony Lejeune (London: Tom Stacey, 1970)

Prior, James, *A Balance of Power* (London: Hamish Hamilton, 1986)

Reeves, Richard, *President Reagan: The Triumph of Imagination* (New York: Simon & Schuster, 2005)

Renton, Tim, *Chief Whip: People, Power and Patronage in Westminster* (London: Politico's, 2004)

Ridley, Nicholas, *'My Style of Government': The Thatcher Years* (London: Hutchinson, 1991)

Roberts, Andrew, *Salisbury: Victorian Titan* (London: Weidenfeld & Nicolson, 1999)

Schumpeter, Joseph A., *Capitalism, Socialism and Democracy* (New York: Harper, 1975)

Shepherd, Robert, *Iain Macleod* (London: Hutchinson, 1994)

Sherman, Alfred, *Paradoxes of Power* (Exeter: Imprint Academic, 2005)

Simms, Brendan, *Unfinest Hour: Britain and the Destruction of Bosnia* (London: Penguin, 2001)

Smith, Geoffrey, *Reagan and Thatcher* (London: Bodley Head, 1990)

Smith, Ian, *The Great Betrayal: The Memoirs of Ian Douglas Smith* (London: Blake, 1997)

Thatcher, Carol, *Below the Parapet: The Biography of Denis Thatcher* (London: HarperCollins, 1997)

Thatcher, Carol, *A Swim-on Part in the Goldfish Bowl: A Memoir* (London: Headline Review, 2008)

Thatcher, Margaret, *The Collected Speeches*, ed. Robin Harris (London: HarperCollins, 1997)

Thatcher, Margaret, *The Downing Street Years* (London: HarperCollins, 1993)

Thatcher, Margaret, *The Path to Power* (London: HarperCollins, 1995)

Thatcher, Margaret, *Statecraft* (London: HarperCollins, 2002)

Urban, George, *Diplomacy and Disillusion at the Court of Margaret Thatcher: An Insider's View* (London: I. B. Tauris, 1996)

Veljanovski, Cento, *Selling the State: Privatisation in Britain* (London: Weidenfeld & Nicolson, 1987)

Veljanovski, Cento, ed., *Privatisation and Competition* (London: Institute of Economic Affairs, 1989)

Walters, Alan, *Britain's Economic Renaissance: Margaret Thatcher's Reforms, 1979–1984* (New York: Oxford University Press, 1986)

Walters, Simon, *Tory Wars* (London: Politico's, 2001)

Watkins, Alan, *A Conservative Coup* (London: Duckworth, 1991)

Weinberger, Caspar, *Fighting for Peace: Seven Critical Years at the Pentagon* (London: Michael Joseph, 1990)

Wheatcroft, Geoffrey, *The Strange Death of Tory England* (London: Penguin, 2005)

Whitelaw, William, *The Whitelaw Memoirs* (London: Headline, 1989)

Wyatt, Woodrow, *The Journals of Woodrow Wyatt*, 3 vols, ed. Sarah Curtis (London: Pan, 2000)

Young, Hugo, *One of Us: A Biography of Margaret Thatcher* (London: Macmillan, 1989)

Young, Lord [David], *The Enterprise Years: A Businessman in the Cabinet* (London: Headline, 1990)

NOTES

Chapter 1: The Impact of Grantham

1 Mrs Thatcher's early life is described in the second volume of her memoirs: Margaret Thatcher, *The Path to Power* (London: HarperCollins, 1995), pp. 3–34.

2 She also showed in these interviews a far greater capacity for self-analysis than that with which she is sometimes credited: see e.g. the interview with Brian Walden of 28 January 1981 (intended, it seems, for an article that in the event was not published), conveniently accessible on the Thatcher Foundation website, www.margaretthatcher.org.

3 Most outrageously, Leo Abse, *Margaret, Daughter of Beatrice* (London: Jonathan Cape, 1989).

4 Cf. John Campbell, *Margaret Thatcher*, vol. 1: *The Grocer's Daughter* (London: Jonathan Cape, 2000), p. 21. Campbell, who in the first volume of the biography he wrote of Mrs Thatcher is usually more judicious than in his second, here gives credence to this view.

5 Ibid., p. 8.

6 'We have always had a sense that work is not only a necessity, it is a duty, and indeed a virtue': speech at the Church of St Lawrence Jewry, City of London, 4 March 1981, published in Margaret Thatcher, *The Collected Speeches*, ed. Robin Harris (London: HarperCollins, 1997), p. 125.

7 This is quite clear also from the fuller context of the remarks: 'I think we've been through a period where too many people have been given to understand that if they have a problem, it's the Government's job to cope with it. "I have a problem, I'll get a grant." "I'm homeless, the Government must house me." They're casting their problem on society. And, you know, there is no such thing as society. There are individual men and women, and there are other families. And no government can do anything except through people, and people must look to themselves first. It's our duty to look after ourselves and then, also, to look after our neighbour. People have got the entitlements too much in mind, without the obligations. There's no such thing as entitlement, unless someone has first met an obligation' (Interview, *Woman's*

459

Own, 31 October 1987).

8 Sir Hector Laing (later Lord Laing of Dunphail) ran United Biscuits and was a major party donor.
9 Thatcher, *The Path to Power*, pp. 12–13.
10 George Gardiner, *Margaret Thatcher: From Childhood to Leadership* (London: William Kimber, 1975), p. 13.
11 I owe this information to Charles Moore – who, I should add, was not the blabber.
12 'I put before the whole House my own views with an appalling frankness . . . Supposing I had gone to the country and said that Germany was rearming, and that we must rearm, does anybody think that this pacific democracy would have rallied to that cry at that moment? I cannot think of anything that would have made the loss of the election from my point of view more certain' (Stanley Baldwin, House of Commons, 12 November 1936). In fact, as his biographers have observed, Baldwin was alluding to the Fulham by-election of 1933, not to the general election two years later. But then and since his 'appalling frankness' has been applied to the whole period – and not unjustly. See Keith Middlemas and John Barnes, *Baldwin: A Biography* (London: Weidenfeld & Nicolson, 1969), pp. 970–2.

Chapter 2: Into Politics
1 See the comments of contemporaries retailed in Campbell, *The Grocer's Daughter*, pp. 49–51.
2 Thatcher, *The Path to Power*, pp. 42–3.
3 Cf. Patricia Murray, *Margaret Thatcher* (London: W. H. Allen, 1980), p. 19.
4 See Thatcher, *The Path to Power*, pp. 73–4, 96.
5 Among the many invaluable documents reproduced on the Margaret Thatcher Foundation website is a manuscript letter from Margaret Roberts to Miss Maxse dated 15 January 1949 providing details of her qualifications for onward transmission to future employers.
6 Gardiner, *Margaret Thatcher*, p. 114. Denis subsequently denied this in discussion with Carol (see Carol Thatcher, *Below the Parapet: The Biography of Denis Thatcher* [London: HarperCollins, 1997], p. 98). But George Gardiner's account rings true, even the tone of DT's irritated exclamation: 'To hell with all this, why not pack it up?' Gardiner's account is also written much closer to the events.
7 Thatcher, *The Path to Power*, p. 266.
8 I never felt that we got to the bottom of what was discussed between them, but see Margaret Thatcher, *The Downing Street Years* (London: HarperCollins, 1993), p. 148.
9 Ibid., p. 846. Her enemies knew that they could rely on Denis to advise her to give up: see p. 329.
10 Thatcher, *The Path to Power*, p. 81.
11 Article in the *Sunday Graphic*, 17 February 1952.
12 'Finding Time', *Onward*, 1 April 1954.
13 See Nigel Lawson, *The View from No. 11: Memoirs of a Tory Radical* (London: Bantam, 1992), pp. 881–7.
14 Thatcher, *The Downing Street Years*, pp. 630–1. Major is not mentioned here by name, but he was the main proponent of this measure, which appealed to families hoping to enjoy two incomes.
15 *Finchley Press*, 8 August 1958.

Chapter 3: The Greasy Pole

1 James Prior, *A Balance of Power* (London: Hamish Hamilton, 1986), p. 42. The less problematical and more dispensable Mervyn Pike was appointed instead.
2 Robert Shepherd, *Iain Macleod* (London: Hutchinson, 1994), p. 429.
3 SET was a complicated measure intended to shift resources from the service sector to manufacturing – then considered more economically 'useful'.
4 Thatcher, *The Path to Power*, p. 144.
5 Ibid., pp. 146–7.
6 Richard Cockett, *Thinking the Unthinkable: Think-Tanks and the Economic Counter-Revolution 1931–1983* (London: HarperCollins, 1994), p. 171.
7 'Consensus or Choice?', *Daily Telegraph*, 17 March 1969.
8 'Participation – In What?', *Daily Telegraph*, 26 April 1969.
9 Interview, 23 October 1969.

Chapter 4: Milk Snatcher

1 Notable among the contributors to the *Black Papers* (and associated pamphlets) were C. B. Cox, John Marks, Rhodes Boyson, Caroline Cox, Ralph Harris, Anthony Flew, Max Beloff, Robert Conquest and Kingsley Amis.
2 See Campbell, *The Grocer's Daughter*, pp. 211–21.
3 Edward Heath, *The Course of My Life* (London: Hodder & Stoughton, 1999), p. 317.
4 *The Sunday Times*, 8 April 1973.
5 Interview with *Liverpool Daily Post*, 7 February 1972.
6 *Evening Standard*, 12 October 1970.
7 Heath, *The Course of My Life*, p. 521.
8 *Finchley Times*, 10 March 1972.
9 *Barnet Press*, 16 February 1973.

Chapter 5: Taking Command

1 Thatcher, *The Path to Power*, p. 246.
2 Interview, *Weekend World*, 29 September 1974.
3 Geoffrey Howe, *Conflict of Loyalty* (London: Macmillan, 1994), p. 87.
4 *Observer*, 13 October 1974.
5 *Evening Standard*, 15 October 1974.
6 Interview, *Sunday Express*, 20 October 1974.
7 Thatcher, *The Path to Power*, p. 267.
8 Interview with the *Daily Mail*, 25 November 1974.
9 Interview with Independent Radio News, 31 January 1975.
10 Hansard, 22 January 1975, col. 1554.
11 'My Kind of Tory Party', *Daily Telegraph*, 30 January 1975.
12 Interview with ITN News, 4 February 1975.
13 William Whitelaw, *The Whitelaw Memoirs* (London: Headline, 1989), p. 185.

Chapter 6: An Uphill Struggle

1 Carol Thatcher, *Below the Parapet*, p. 103.

2 Thatcher, *The Path to Power*, p. 293.
3 Ibid., p. 287; cf. Campbell, *The Grocer's Daughter*, p. 322.
4 Statement launching the Conservative European referendum campaign, 16 April 1975.
5 Article in the *Daily Telegraph*, 4 June 1975.
6 Interview with the *Daily Mail*, 12 June 1975.
7 Interview with Robin Day on BBC television, *Talk-In*, 15 May 1975.
8 Bernard Donoughue, *Downing Street Diary: With Harold Wilson in No. 10* (London: Jonathan Cape, 2005), p. 714.
9 Thatcher, *The Path to Power*, pp. 316–17.
10 Party political broadcast, 5 March 1975.
11 Interview in *Observer*, 7 August 1975.
12 The most important Thatcher speeches are published, with my commentary, in Thatcher, *The Collected Speeches*.
13 Thatcher, *The Path to Power*, pp. 305–7.
14 See Ronald Millar, *A View from the Wings* (London: Weidenfeld & Nicolson, 1993), p. 374.
15 Thatcher, *The Collected Speeches*, p. 34.
16 Ibid., pp. 23–8.
17 Ibid., pp. 39–47.
18 Speech in Finchley, 31 January 1976.
19 Speech in Washington, 19 September 1975.
20 Thatcher, *The Collected Speeches*, pp. 48–57.

Chapter 7: Victory

1 Bernard Donoughue, *Prime Minister: The Conduct of Policy under Harold Wilson and James Callaghan* (London: Jonathan Cape, 1987), p. 191.
2 For example, interview for BBC 1, *Panorama*, with Mary Goldring, Anthony Shrimsley and Peter Jenkins, 11 July 1977; and interview for Tyne Tees TV, *Face the Press*, with Joe Rogaly and Bob Edwards, 25 August 1977.
3 David Butler and Anne Sloman, *British Political Facts 1900–1979* (London: Macmillan, 1980), p. 241.
4 Thatcher, *The Path to Power*, p. 295.
5 e.g. David Dimbleby on *Panorama*, 11 July 1977: 'So that Jim Callaghan . . . you are saying is hell bent on Marxism and the end of Parliamentary democracy?'
6 Howe, *Conflict of Loyalty*, pp. 100–1.
7 Thatcher, *The Path to Power*, p. 404. See also her numerous points of disagreement signalled on the draft document, accessible on the Thatcher Foundation website.
8 Speech to Paddington Conservative Association, 18 December 1978.
9 Thatcher, *The Path to Power*, p. 402.
10 The jurist and constitutional theorist A. V. Dicey (1835–1922), a traditionalist in other respects, was one of the first British supporters of referendums.
11 The essential source on Stepping Stones is John Hoskyns, *Just in Time: Inside the Thatcher Revolution* (London: Aurum, 2000), pp. 39–79.
12 Interview with Granada Television, 30 January 1978.
13 Campbell, *The Grocer's Daughter*, p. 413.
14 Howe, *Conflict of Loyalty*, pp. 98–100.

15 For a more favourable view see Lawson, *The View from No. 11*, p. 17. Lawson concedes that insufficient work had been done on monetary policy, but he extols what had been done on tax reform and public spending.

16 Interview with Brian Walden on ITV, *Weekend World*, 7 January 1979. The interview, planned before Christmas, was brought forward a week to allow Mrs Thatcher a platform for her views.

17 In Scotland the majority in favour did not reach the prescribed 40 per cent minimum of those eligible to vote, and in Wales the vote was lost outright.

18 Had the underlying position of the parties varied during the campaign? It is hard to tell. It would be strange if Labour had not made up ground early on. This is what unpopular governing parties generally do. The Conservative campaign got off to a slow start; indeed, the Labour Party was better at media management throughout. The Tory campaign were right in thinking that it was theirs to lose, and they might have lost it – especially if they had unnerved Mrs Thatcher into making a serious mistake.

19 Campbell, *The Grocer's Daughter*, p. 443.

20 Speech in Aberdeen, 8 September 1975.

21 Party conference speech, 10 October 1975 (Thatcher, *Collected Speeches*, p. 34).

22 Speech in Kensington Town Hall, 19 January 1976 (Thatcher, *Collected Speeches*, p. 40).

23 Speech in London, 6 May 1978.

24 Mrs Thatcher in her memoirs gives a radical slant on the prayer (for peace), but that is only with many years' hindsight (*The Downing Street Years*, p. 19). Ronnie Millar – who provided the text and whose literary judgement in this instance clearly failed him – shows that it was the mawkish, sentimental side of Margaret Thatcher to which the quotation appealed. Astonishingly, she really meant it (*View from the Wings*, p. 266).

Chapter 8: No U-Turns

1 Prior, *A Balance of Power*, pp. 133–4.

2 Howe, *Conflict of Loyalty*, p. 186.

3 Lawson, *The View from No. 11*, p. 128.

4 Hoskyns, *Just in Time*, p. 263.

5 Ibid., p. 401. One should add that this was a retrospective judgement.

6 Ibid., p. 403.

7 It lasted five months and cost £130 million in deferred tax revenue and extra borrowing charges.

8 His memoirs accurately convey the sentiment: see Howe, *Conflict of Loyalty*, p. 128.

9 Both the ending of exchange controls in 1979 and the removal in 1980 of the so-called 'corset' – the Bank of England's supplementary special deposit scheme, used as a means of monetary control – contributed to making the money supply figures much more difficult to read.

10 Thatcher, *The Downing Street Years*, p. 132.

11 Hoskyns, *Just in Time*, pp. 262–85.

12 Hoskyns, ibid., pp. 260–2, gives his contemporary account, which suggests this.

13 The account given by Alan Walters in *Britain's Economic Renaissance: Margaret Thatcher's Reforms, 1979–1984* (New York: Oxford University Press, 1986), pp. 137–50, is authoritative.

14 The letter's peculiarities have been cogently analysed by Professor Geoffrey Wood,

'364 Economists on Economic Policy', in a collection of essays marking the twenty-fifth anniversary of the 1981 budget: Philip Booth, ed., *Were 364 Economists All Wrong?* (London: Institute of Economic Affairs, 2006).

15 Article in *The Times*, 7 April 1981. It is reproduced with the original letter in Booth, ed., *Were 364 Economists All Wrong?*

16 *The Economist*, 29 November 1980. Howe freely admits his mistake: *Conflict of Loyalty*, pp. 193–4.

17 Interview with Robin Day for BBC 1, *Panorama*, 25 February 1980.

18 It is published in Thatcher, *The Downing Street Years*, p. 132; its sombre tone is striking.

19 Ibid., p. 149.

20 Prior, *A Balance of Power*, p. 171.

21 Speech to Conservative party conference, Blackpool, 12 October 1979, in Thatcher, *The Collected Speeches*, pp. 98, 100.

22 Interview with Richard Holmes, BBC 1, *World at One*, 31 December 1979.

23 Interview with Brian Walden, LWT, *Weekend World*, 6 January 1980.

24 Interview, BBC Radio 2, *Jimmy Young Programme*, 9 September 1981.

25 'Mrs Thatcher at Mid Term: Portrait of a Prime Minister at Bay', *The Economist*, 10 October 1981.

Chapter 9: Apprentice Diplomat

1 The Monday Club was formed in reaction to Harold Macmillan's 1960 African 'Winds of Change' speech.

2 Lord Carrington, *Reflect on Things Past: The Memoirs of Lord Carrington* (London: Fontana, 1989), p. 292.

3 Thatcher, *The Downing Street Years*, p. 78.

4 Ian Smith, *The Great Betrayal: The Memoirs of Ian Douglas Smith* (London: Blake, 1997), p. 316.

5 Carrington, *Reflect on Things Past*, p. 287.

Chapter 10: War Leader

1 *Falkland Islands Review: Report of a Committee of Privy Counsellors*, Cmnd 8787 (London: HMSO, January 1983), para. 339.

2 *Falkland Islands Review*, para. 133.

3 Ibid., para. 152.

4 Ibid., para. 153.

5 Thatcher, *The Downing Street Years*, p. 179. Nott's initial view, one must add, was coloured by his lack of faith in the judgement of Leach, the First Sea Lord. He changed his mind the following day (Nott, *Here Today, Gone Tomorrow*, pp. 258–9).

6 Unreferenced quotations in this chapter come from that memorandum. Nott, too, dictated his recollections (see *Here Today, Gone Tomorrow*, p. 250). All concerned knew that they had lived through something unique, and it was natural to wish to capture the memory.

7 Howe, *Conflict of Loyalty*, pp. 246–7.

8 Ridley had been responsible for devising and promoting the 'lease-back' option.

9 This is confirmed by Nott: *Here Today, Gone Tomorrow*, pp. 282–3.

10 Thatcher, *The Downing Street Years*, p. 221. This telephone conversation of 13 May was one of several through which she managed to bring the President into line without creating personal offence – itself a considerable diplomatic achievement.

11 Cecil Parkinson, *Right at the Centre* (London: Weidenfeld & Nicolson, 1992), p. 192. Nott also wanted him in.

12 As revealed by Nicholas Henderson, *Mandarin: The Diaries of an Ambassador 1969–1982* (London: Phoenix, 1994), p. 454.

13 Caspar Weinberger, *Fighting for Peace: Seven Critical Years at the Pentagon* (London: Michael Joseph, 1990), p. 150.

14 Freedman, *Official History*, vol. 2, p. 158.

15 Thatcher, *The Downing Street Years*, p. 205.

16 Freedman, *Official History*, vol. 2, p. 308. This is presumably the occasion referred to by Cecil Parkinson in his memoirs. Though there were other instances of modifications made by the politicians, this was the most important example of political risk assessment overcoming military risk assessment (see Parkinson, *Right at the Centre*, p. 195).

17 Freedman, *Official History*, vol. 2, pp. 298–301.

18 Nott, *Here Today, Gone Tomorrow*, pp. 293–4. Nott gets the date wrong but is more forthcoming than was Mrs Thatcher when she discussed the crucial meeting in her memoirs, doubtless because she knew she had behaved badly. Henderson supports Nott's version (Henderson, *Mandarin*, pp. 460–3).

19 See Nott, *Here Today, Gone Tomorrow*, pp. 263–4, and Bernard Ingham, *Kill the Messenger* (London: HarperCollins, 1991), pp. 294–5.

20 Ibid., p. 84. So did Nott: see *Here Today, Gone Tomorrow*, pp. 75, 247.

21 See Thatcher, *The Downing Street Years*, pp. 259–62, 488–95.

Chapter 11: A Supply-Side Revolution

1 Ian MacGregor with Rodney Tyler, *The Enemies Within: The Story of the Miners' Strike, 1984–5* (London: Collins, 1986), p. 273.

2 Cf. Lawson's comments in *The View from No. 11*, pp. 443–6.

3 It was authoritatively reported that the Queen was dismayed by Mrs Thatcher's handling of the miners' strike (as well as by her lack of attachment to the Commonwealth). Malicious courtiers were doubtless involved in disseminating the story.

4 Mrs Thatcher used the phrase when giving her end-of-term pep talk to Tory MPs, 12 July 1984.

5 Patrick Minford, *Markets not Stakes* (London: Orion, 1998), p. 118.

6 It has been estimated that de-indexing benefits, including pensions, from earnings had by the mid-1990s saved the equivalent of more than 3 per cent of GDP: Nicholas Crafts, *The Conservative Government's Economic Record: An End of Term Report* (Institute of Economic Affairs, 1998), p. 24.

7 For the thinking behind Family Credit, see Norman Fowler, *Ministers Decide: A Personal Memoir of the Thatcher Years* (London: Chapman, 1991), pp. 213, 221; and for Re-start, including the 'hidden agenda', see Young, *The Enterprise Years*, pp. 170ff. On the effect of the Fowler reforms, see also Patrick Minford, *The Supply Side Revolution in Britain* (Cheltenham: Edward Elgar for Institute of Economic Affairs, 1991), pp. 112–31.

8 See Cento Veljanovski, *Selling the State: Privatisation in Britain* (London: Weidenfeld & Nicolson, 1987), p. 7, n. 1.

9 See the important but generally forgotten arguments in Enoch Powell, *Income Tax at 4/3 in the £*, ed. Anthony Lejeune (London: Tom Stacey, 1970).

10 Crafts, *The Conservative Government's Economic Record*, p. 23. For a contrary view, however, see Irwin Stelzer, 'A Review of Privatisation and Regulation Experience in Britain', Beesley Lecture, Institute of Economic Affairs, London, 7 November 2000.

11 See Cento Veljanovski, 'Privatisation: Monopoly Money or Competition?', in id., ed., *Privatisation and Competition* (London: Institute for Economic Affairs, 1989), pp. 26–51.

12 Mrs Thatcher admits as much in her memoirs: see Thatcher, *The Downing Street Years*, pp. 683–5.

13 Nicholas Ridley, *'My Style of Government': The Thatcher Years* (London: Hutchinson, 1991), pp. 63–4.

14 See Nicholas Crafts, *Britain's Relative Economic Decline, 1870–1995: A Quantitative Perspective* (London: Social Market Foundation, 1997).

15 These figures (along with others) are cited by Mrs Thatcher in *The Path to Power*, p. 578. But for an entirely non-partisan view, covering the period up to the end of the Major Government, see the vigorous exchanges between Professor Nicholas Crafts and Old Labour critics in 'Are We All Thatcherites?', *Prospect*, 18 April 1997. Here Crafts argues, for example: 'The mainstream view that long run growth performance has improved is soundly based. Economic growth has improved relative to Britain's peer group of countries, and the current outlook compares well with most of those countries. And it is axiomatic that the growth experienced has been better than would have resulted from carrying on with 1970s policies. This does not imply that Britain has experienced a miracle or that there have not been important errors in economic policy, but simply that economic decline relative to Europe has ceased and that the [Conservative] Government deserves some credit for this.'
    The relative improvement of Britain's performance has also arguably been underrated because conventional comparisons overlook the rise in the real exchange rate of sterling. I am grateful to Professor Tim Congdon for tabular analysis demonstrating this important point.

16 Minford, *Markets not Stakes*, fig. 5.2.

17 The best summary of the arguments and of the changed terms of the debate is to be found in the introduction to Tim Congdon's book *Keynes, the Keynesians and Monetarism* (Cheltenham: Edward Elgar, 2007), which he was good enough to let me read before publication.

18 Minford, *Markets not Stakes*, fig. 5.5.

19 Cf. Francis Fukuyama, *The End of History and the Last Man* (London: Hamish Hamilton, 1992).

Chapter 12: Cold Warrior

1 Thatcher, *The Path to Power*, pp. 367–8.

2 Memorandum from Brzezinski to Carter of 12 May 1979, available on the Thatcher Foundation website.

3 Thatcher, *The Downing Street Years*, p. 68.

4 Henderson, *Mandarin*, pp. 315–20.

5 The second round of Strategic Arms Limitation Talks (1972–9) resulted in agreement to ban new missile programmes. SALT II was not, however, ratified. It

was overtaken by Strategic Arms Reduction Talks on the initiative of the Reagan Administration; these resulted in the 1991 START Treaty, duly signed, ratified and implemented.

6 Scribbled on a memorandum from Brzezinski to Carter of 29 January 1980, accessible on the Thatcher Foundation website. She also refused to freeze Iranian assets.

7 The only time Reagan is known to have lost his temper is when an aide interrupted his speech-writing: Richard Reeves, *President Reagan: The Triumph of Imagination* (New York: Simon & Schuster, 2005), p. xii.

8 O'Sullivan, *The President, the Pope and the Prime Minister*, pp. 27, 60. Reagan's letter of 30 April 1975 is accessible on the Thatcher Foundation website.

9 Geoffrey Smith, *Reagan and Thatcher* (London: Bodley Head, 1990), pp. 43–6; Henderson, *Mandarin*, pp. 388, 390.

10 For a more detailed discussion of these matters, see Robin Harris, *Beyond Friendship: The Future of Anglo-American Relations* (Washington DC: Heritage Foundation, 2006), pp. 18–43.

11 The point is explicitly recognized by Caspar Weinberger: 'Some said later that the British could not have succeeded [in the Falklands campaign] if we had not helped. This is not so' (Weinberger, *Fighting for Peace*, p. 151).

12 Reeves, *President Reagan*, pp. 179–81.

13 See the detailed account of events relating to Lebanon and Grenada in Thatcher, *The Downing Street Years*, pp. 326–35.

14 Weinberger, *Fighting for Peace*, p. 135.

15 The sequence of Soviet leaders after Brezhnev was: Yuri Andropov 1982–4; Konstantin Chernenko 1984–5; Mikhail Gorbachev 1985–1991.

16 Thatcher, *The Downing Street Years*, pp. 322–5. For Gordievsky's message about Soviet fears, see Reeves, *President Reagan*, p. 281. The truth about Soviet perceptions is still murky.

17 Smith, *Reagan and Thatcher*, p. 167.

18 The record of the Reagan–Thatcher discussion at Camp David on 22 December and the (significantly amended) text of the resulting statement are to be found on the Thatcher Foundation website.

19 Thatcher, *The Downing Street Years*, p. 452.

20 In February Mrs Thatcher had paid her first visit as Prime Minister to a Warsaw Pact country, Hungary.

21 See Milovan Djilas, *Conversations with Stalin* (London: Rupert Hart-Davis, 1962).

22 See the documents available on the Margaret Thatcher website. But these official accounts must be viewed in the light of the evidence offered in the authoritative account of Jack Matlock, then US ambassador to Moscow, who was privy to all discussions and to US thinking. His book had not been published when Mrs Thatcher's memoirs were written. This explains the fact that she takes a somewhat more favourable view of Reagan's negotiating stance, notably his refusal to yield on SDI, than the facts seem to warrant. See Jack F. Matlock, *Reagan and Gorbachev: How the Cold War Ended* (New York: Random House, 2004), pp. 232–3, 240–1.

23 The ambiguity was even greater because of a surreal dispute about whether a comma was to be inserted between the words 'programme' and 'which' (see Smith, *Reagan and Thatcher*, p. 222).

24 Handwritten letter of 4 December 1986, available on the Thatcher Foundation website.
25 Even more than Mrs Thatcher, Reagan concentrated on human rights issues and the theme of liberty, particularly in his speech to Moscow State University. Indeed, this speech can be seen as a coda to that which he delivered in 1982 to British Members of Parliament, in which he enunciated the 'Reagan doctrine', according to which the West refused to abandon to communism those oppressed behind the Iron Curtain.
26 George Urban, *Diplomacy and Disillusion at the Court of Margaret Thatcher: An Insider's View* (London: I. B. Tauris, 1996), p. 153.
27 Thatcher, *The Downing Street Years*, p. 824. It was about using available powers to stop Iraqi ships in the Gulf.
28 See the evidence analysed in O'Sullivan, *The President, the Pope and the Prime Minister*, p. 320, and in Vladimir Bukovsky, *Jugement à Moscou* (Paris: Robert Laffont, 1995), p. 514.
29 See Charles de Gaulle, *Mémoires de guerre: l'appel, 1940–1942* (Paris: Plon-Pocket, 1954), p. 7: 'Toute ma vie, je me suis fait une certaine idée de la France.'

Chapter 13: Skies Darken

1 The most accurate account remains Mrs Thatcher's own in *The Downing Street Years* (the apt chapter title is 'Men in Lifeboats'), pp. 829–62. But, naturally, a few details have proved incorrect or uncertain. Kenneth Baker, who adopts a broadly similar interpretation, while stressing how right he was at key junctures, gives his recollections as Party Chairman in *The Turbulent Years: My Life in Politics* (London: Faber & Faber, 1993), pp. 364–421. (Baker's inscription in Mrs Thatcher's copy was nicely ambivalent – 'For Margaret, Without whom there would have been no "Turbulent Years".') Howe's own strangely detached explanation of his behaviour, relying heavily on self-justificatory quotations from others and remaining opaque about his motives, is to be found in *Conflict of Loyalty*, pp. 622–76. Cecil Parkinson provides a well-judged take on events in *Right at the Centre*, pp. 1–50. Another well-informed, though not infallible, study, based heavily on gossip from those involved and written soon after the assassination, is Alan Watkins, *A Conservative Coup* (London: Duckworth, 1991). For light relief, this can be supplemented by Alan Clark, *Diaries* (London: Weidenfeld and Nicolson, 1993), pp. 345–68 – and for sheer chutzpah by Tristan Garel-Jones, 'Thatcher: My Part in her Downfall', *Daily Express*, 17 October 1993. (Garel-Jones's protestations of innocence are not rendered more credible by the fact that he omits to mention that he was asked, with her former political secretary Richard Ryder, to organize the second-round campaign for her – and refused: on which see p. 337 above). The most detailed account published since Mrs Thatcher's memoirs is that of Tim Renton, *Chief Whip: People, Power and Patronage in Westminster* (London: Politico's, 2004), pp. 3–117. I have drawn in this chapter and the next not only on these sources, but also on the recollections of a number of key figures involved, as well, of course, as on my own.
2 Oddly enough, I was also rumoured (wrongly) to be part of such plans: see McAlpine, *Once a Jolly Bagman*, p. 247.
3 Contrary to the suggestion by John Campbell in *Margaret Thatcher*, vol. 2: *The Iron Lady* (London: Pimlico, 2004): cf. 'Of course, Mrs Thatcher's desire to honour her 1974 commitment to abolish domestic rates was undiminished' (p. 503).

4 Simon Jenkins, *Thatcher and Sons: A Revolution in Three Acts* (London: Allen Lane, 2006).
5 *The Downing Street Years* provides a detailed account of the origins, development and implementation of the Community Charge: see pp. 642–67.
6 Even Mrs Thatcher's unsympathetic biographer John Campbell recognizes this (*The Iron Lady*, p. 505). It is, therefore, doubly surprising that the Conservative Party itself still does not.
7 John Major, *The Autobiography* (London: HarperCollins, 1999), p. 173.
8 The speech is reproduced in Thatcher, *The Collected Speeches*, pp. 373–85.
9 Both letters are accessible on the Margaret Thatcher Foundation website.
10 Lawson, *View from No. 11*, p. 789.
11 'Maggie Made Us Scapegoats: Lawson and Howe Hit Back after Thatcher's Bitter Attack', *Daily Mail*, 11 October 1993.
12 Nigel Lawson's review of *The Downing Street Years*, 'The Truth Margaret Can Never Admit', *Evening Standard*, 22 October 1993.
13 Baker, *The Turbulent Years*, p. 296.
14 'Norman Tebbit: You Ask the Questions', *The Independent*, 22 November 2006.
15 Campbell, *The Iron Lady*, p. 693.
16 A full account of the background to the Single European Act is to be found in Thatcher, *The Downing Street Years*, pp. 551–9.
17 'Before the Madrid European Council, where the Delors report on monetary union was to be discussed, the Prime Minister was not planning any discussion with her Chancellor or her Foreign Secretary about the key issues to be tackled . . .': Geoffrey Howe, 'The Triumph and Tragedy of the Thatcher Years', review of *The Downing Street Years* in *Financial Times*, 23 October 1993.
18 This was also Nicholas Ridley's view (Ridley, '*My Style of Government*', p. 230).
19 Thatcher, *The Collected Speeches*, 430–42.

Chapter 14: The Fall

1 In this respect, I believe Kenneth Baker's analysis is correct, though I do not agree with all his judgements of events (see Baker, *The Turbulent Years*, pp. 364–5).
2 Interview, *Daily Mail*, 4 May 2007.
3 Renton gives a full and revealing account. He argued, incredibly, that Tebbit's return would make a leadership election more likely (see Renton, *Chief Whip*, pp. 78–81).
4 Whitelaw was at this stage backing Douglas Hurd (Baker, *The Turbulent Years*, p. 383).
5 Thatcher, *The Downing Street Years*, p. 839.
6 Howe, *Conflict of Loyalty*, p. 676.
7 Keith Joseph, 'Victim of Spite and the Backstabbers', *Evening Standard*, 22 November 1990.
8 See, for all this, Baker, *The Turbulent Years*, pp. 393–7, and Renton, *Chief Whip*, pp. 92–4. My account here is also based on John Whittingdale's notes and diary.
9 Douglas Hurd, *Memoirs* (London: Abacus, 2004), p. 442.
10 See Parkinson's observations and his account of Norman Lamont's role in *Right at the Centre*, pp. 33–4.
11 Major, *The Autobiography*, pp. 182–6.
12 Former Cabinet minister in private discussion with the author.

13　Baker, *The Turbulent Years*, pp. 401–2.

14　Thatcher, *The Downing Street Years*, p. 850.

15　Mrs Thatcher's memoirs are (unwittingly) inaccurate at this point (*The Downing Street Years*, p. 846). MacGregor was seeking information about the views of junior ministers, not directly those of Cabinet ministers.

16　See Thatcher, *The Downing Street Years*, pp. 850–5.

Chapter 15: After the Fall

1　In his memoirs he makes clear that he had more or less given up before the 1997 general election campaign, and the pages describing his departure from office are bathed in a sense of relief. See Major, *The Autobiography*, pp. 692, 729.

2　Ibid., pp. 613–14.

3　*Newsweek*, 17 April 1992.

4　Interview with ITN, 22 November 1991.

5　See Thatcher, *The Collected Speeches*, pp. 571–87.

6　Letter from Margaret Thatcher to the author, 13 December 1990 (emphasis in original).

7　Diary of Judith Chaplin, serialized in the *Sunday Telegraph*, 19 September 1999.

8　Woodrow Wyatt was just one of those who remarked on it: see *The Journals of Woodrow Wyatt*, 3 vols, ed. Sarah Curtis (London: Pan Books, 2000), vol. 2, pp. 445–6.

9　I should add that Mrs Thatcher tried to have me appointed as director of the Centre. This was more than they could take, but they swallowed hard and accepted Griffiths. I stayed on Mrs Thatcher's payroll as speech-writer, memoirs draftsman and adviser on topics that both interested me and affected her.

10　Thatcher, *The Path to Power*, p. 467.

11　Her main American speeches which cover these themes are to be found in *The Collected Speeches*: speech to the Hoover Institution (pp. 459–75), the first Clare Booth Luce Memorial Lecture (pp. 486–99), the John Findley Green Foundation Lecture (pp. 588–604). For her views of America, see Thatcher, *Statecraft*, pp. 19–62.

12　Thatcher, *Statecraft*, pp. 155–60.

13　The speech is contained in Thatcher, *The Collected Speeches*, pp. 617–26. See also Thatcher, *Statecraft*, pp. 170–1. Arguments about the draft went right to the wire. The text from which she spoke shows how the original phrases were softened. Thus the sentence 'There are still many practices – both in China itself and Tibet – which are repugnant to those of us fortunate enough to live in democracies, under a full rule of law' became 'There are still aspects of life in China which are deeply worrying to those of us who live in democracies, under a full rule of law'. But she did not change the passage relating to the world's 'dismay' at the 'recent harsh sentences' on Wei and Wang. On generalities she would be cautious, but not when individual cases were involved.

14　Mark Thatcher was fined by a South African court following his alleged involvement in a coup attempt in Equatorial Guinea.

15　For the debates with Gorbachev about the Cold War that occurred on this visit, see Thatcher, *Statecraft*, pp. 2–9.

16　In *Statecraft* she writes more favourably about him, though not without airing her doubts. The decisive influence on her, though, was the need for Russian support in the 'war against terror' – the book went to print shortly after the 9/11 attack on the United States (see pp. 103–19).

17 Thatcher, *The Collected Speeches*, pp. 556–70.
18 Clark was dismissive of anyone 'ghosting' the book: he planned to 'write' it (Clark, *Diaries*, p. 377).
19 Collins is also the organizing genius behind the indispensable archival material now accessible to researchers on the Thatcher Foundation website.
20 Campbell, *The Iron Lady*, p. 776.

Chapter 16: Three Last Campaigns

1 See Major, *The Autobiography*, pp. 342–5.
2 Carol Thatcher, *Below the Parapet*, p. 284.
3 Robert Blake, *Disraeli* (London: Methuen, 1966), p. 569.
4 Clause A of the treaty contains the aspiration that 'decisions [be] taken as closely as possible to the citizen'. Article 3b declares: 'In areas which do not fall within its exclusive competence, the Community shall take action, in accordance with the principle of subsidiarity, only if and insofar as the objectives of the proposed action cannot be sufficiently achieved by the Member States and can, therefore, by reason of the scale or effects of the proposed action, be better achieved by the Community.'
5 Lamont, *In Office*, pp. 122–3, 133.
6 Speech to the Economic Club of New York, 18 June 1991 (Thatcher, *The Collected Speeches*, pp. 476–85).
7 Thatcher, *The Collected Speeches*, pp. 511–28. John O'Sullivan and Norman Stone were the main draftsmen.
8 Ibid., pp. 540–55.
9 In fact, even now she presented her programme of establishing a new relationship with mainland Europe as part of re-establishing Britain's freedom to trade and act in the new global environment. (The chapter is significantly entitled 'Europe – Time to Re-negotiate': *Statecraft*, pp. 360–411.) The largest specific change compared with a few years earlier was her advice to aspirant EU members to avoid its entanglement and try to negotiate free-trade agreements. But the overall impression is, in any case, not inaccurate: she detested the EU and all its works, and she wanted to have Britain out. On the difficult circumstances of the book's publication, see p. 421 above.
10 She saw him with Fitzroy Maclean, whose own views were very different from hers when the crisis erupted in 1991. For an account of her visit in 1977, see Thatcher, *The Path to Power*, pp. 369–71.
11 Interview with BBC Television, 13 April 1993.
12 In fact, the distinction is of some importance, so the question was not redundant. The retaking of Western Slavonia in 1995 preceded that of the rest of the so-called Krajina area, whereas Eastern Slavonia (around Vukovar) remained longer in Serb hands.
13 'Stop the Excuses. Help Bosnia Now', *New York Times*, 6 August 1992.
14 For a devastating and accurate account of British political and parliamentary opinion, see Brendan Simms, *Unfinest Hour: Britain and the Destruction of Bosnia* (London: Penguin, 2001), pp. 273–313.
15 Speech at the International Free Enterprise Dinner, 20 April 1999. For the political embarrassment surrounding the occasion itself, see pp. 410–11 above.
16 See Campbell, *The Iron Lady*, pp. 794–5.
17 Speech in Santiago, Chile, 21 March 1994. Pinochet had, indeed, restored democracy

and then accepted the outcome of the election, which he lost in 1988, but in which he gained a higher share of the vote than had the Marxist Salvador Allende, whose revolutionary regime he overthrew. Mrs Thatcher was aware of these facts. They prompted her later to assert, with some exaggeration, that Pinochet 'created' Chile's democracy. 'Recreated on a sounder basis' was the phrase urged upon her, but she did not warm to it.

18   This account comes from Peter Schaad, the friend who accompanied and translated for him.

19   Interview with ex-President Patricio Aylwin, *El Mercurio*, 27 March 1999.

20   Sodano had in an earlier incarnation been nuncio in Santiago, so he knew the facts.

Chapter 17: Silence

1   The Nicholas Ridley Memorial Lecture, delivered on 22 November 1996, was intended to stop the gossip that she was an admirer of Tony Blair and accordingly contained a strong attack on New Labour policies (Thatcher, *The Collected Speeches*, pp. 627–43). It did not stop the gossip.

2   These events are described by Simon Walters in *Tory Wars* (London: Politico's, 2001), pp. 181–6. The account was confirmed by Amanda Platell, Conservative Press Director at the time. Walters' narrative omits what was transpiring between Mrs Thatcher and Archie Hamilton.

3   'La vieillesse est un naufrage' (De Gaulle, *Mémoires de guerre*, p. 79. De Gaulle is here writing of Pétain.

4   The statement reads: 'Over recent months Lady Thatcher has suffered a number of small strokes. After thorough investigation involving a number of tests, her doctors have told her that these can neither be predicted nor prevented. They have therefore told her to cut back her programme at once and in particular to avoid the undue strain that public speaking places on her. With great regret, she has decided to abide by this advice and to cancel all her speaking engagements.' Any ambiguity she hoped to retain about the future was effectively and deliberately quashed when it was confirmed by her office to journalists that the decision was final. We had no regrets about doing that.

Chapter 18: Character and its Consequences

1   Thatcher, *The Path to Power*, pp. 73–4.

2   See chapter 11.

3   Report of the National Association of Schoolmasters and Union of Women Teachers conference, *Guardian*, 13 April 2004. The modernizing Tory think tank Policy Exchange also got on to the bandwagon in October 2006 with a report about the problems faced by 'Maggie's Children'.

4   Andrew Roberts, *Salisbury: Victorian Titan* (London: Weidenfeld & Nicolson, 1999).

5   The case is summarized by Clare Beckett in a recent well-balanced assessment. See Clare Beckett, *Thatcher* (London: Haus, 2006), pp. 121–3.

6   See the arguments in Keith Joseph and Jonathan Sumption, *Equality* (London: John Murray, 1979).

7   Cosgrave, *Thatcher: The First Term*, p. 4.

8 Luke 17: 10.

9 O'Sullivan, *The President, the Pope and the Prime Minister*, p. 85.

10 They keep on surfacing because Mrs Thatcher, like most kind people of her generation, preferred to do good by stealth. Some instances are to be found in Iain Dale, ed., *Memories of Maggie: A Portrait of Margaret Thatcher* (London: Politico's, 2000), pp. 128–9 (John Junor), pp. 148–9 (Norman Lamont), p. 150 (Christopher Lawson), p. 294 (Brian Mawhinney).

11 Shirley Robin Letwin, *The Anatomy of Thatcherism* (London: Fontana, 1992), pp. 33–5.

12 See Thatcher, *The Path to Power*, p. 554. Specifically, she read and admired Digby Anderson, ed., *The Loss of Virtue: Moral Confusion and Social Disorder in Britain and America* (London: Social Affairs Unit, 1992) and William J. Bennett, *The Book of the Virtues* (New York: Simon & Schuster, 1996). The term 'cardinal' virtues is not ecclesiastical: it means 'hinge' (Lat. *cardo*). In modern parlance, we would say 'pivotal'.

13 'Father, hear the prayer we offer', by the American poetess Love Maria Willis (1824–1908).

14 Lady Gwendolen Cecil, *Life of Robert Marquis of Salisbury*, 4 vols (London: Hodder and Stoughton, 1921), vol. 4, p. 204.

15 Geoffrey Wheatcroft, *The Strange Death of Tory England* (London: Penguin, 2005), pp. 158–63.

16 Cecil Parkinson would have become Foreign Secretary in 1983 if it had not been for the scandal created by his liaison with Sara Keays. He had to resign as Trade and Industry Secretary, returning to the Cabinet four years later. Margaret Tebbit had been gravely injured in the 1984 bomb attack on the Grand Hotel in Brighton.

PICTURE ACKNOWLEDGEMENTS

In-text illustrations

127   'I don't know what effect she'll have on the enemy . . .', Michael Cummings, *Daily Express*, no date: *Express Newspapers*

162   'Good morning gentlemen!', Nicholas Garland, *Daily Telegraph*, 7 May 1980: courtesy Nicholas Garland

186   'Drip drying', Stanley Franklin, no date: NI Syndication

211   'Take heart, Mrs Thatcher! We're right behind you!', Michael Cummings, *Sunday Express*, 16 May 1982: Express Newspapers

237   'For our next trick . . .', cartoon by Nicholas Garland, *Daily Telegraph*, 16 Feb. 1983: courtesy Nicholas Garland

282   'AIEEEEEEEE!', Nicholas Garland, *Daily Telegraph*, 19 Dec. 1985: courtesy Nicholas Garland

300   No caption (Sir Alan Walters and Nigel Lawson), Nicholas Garland, *Independent*, 21 July 1988: courtesy Nicholas Garland

311   Cover of the *Spectator*, 14 July 1990, Nicholas Garland: courtesy Nicholas Garland

Colour sections

First section

1   MT and family, 1945: Getty Images; MT and her sister, late 1920s: Camera Press Digital; MT's childhood home: Camera Press/Peter Deane

2–3 MT as research chemist, Jan. 1950: Getty Images; MT and Denis on their wedding day, 1951, MT and the twins, Aug. 1953: both Camera Press; MT canvassing in Dartford, 4 Oct. 1951, and MT during Dartford campaign, 4 Oct. 1951: both © 2003 Topham Picturepoint; election poster, Finchley campaign, 1959: Peter Orme/*The Daily Telegraph*; MT, Finchley, 1959: © 2005 Topfoto/PA

4–5 MT in front of the Houses of Parliament, 1961: Popperfoto/Getty Images; MT
with John Boyd-Carpenter, Oct. 1961: Getty Images; MT as Education Secretary, 26
Oct. 1972: *The Daily Telegraph*; MT with schoolchildren, 1970: PA Archive/PA
Photos; MT and Edward Heath, 1970: PA Archive/PA Photos; *Sun* headline, 25 Nov
1971: NI Syndication/*Sun*; MT and Edward Heath, 1974: mirrorpix; MT with
Heath poster, 21 Feb. 1973: Getty Images

6–7 MT at press conference, 4 Feb. 1975: PA Archive/PA Photos; MT with Humphrey
Atkins and Sir Keith Joseph, 1975: Jonathan Player/Rex Features; MT and Willie
Whitelaw, Eastbourne, 1975: © Selwyn Tait/CORBIS SYGMA; MT at Bow Group
reception, 1976: *The Daily Telegraph*; *Sun* headline, 11 Jan. 1979: NI
Syndication/*Sun*; MT at a Britain in Europe rally, 1975: Camera Press

8 MT, Caxton Hall, 1979: PA Archive/PA Photos; MT campaigning, 1979: Ian
Berry/Magnum; MT and calf, 1979: PA Archive/PA Photos; Gordon Reece, 1979:
Camera Press

Second section

1 MT elected leader, 4 May 1979: Getty Images

2–3 MT at 10 Downing St, 1983: Herbie Knott/Rex Features; Cecil Parkinson heckles
MT, 1983: Rex Features; MT at the Conservative Party Conference, 12 Oct. 1979:
PA Archive/PA Photos; MT and Norman Tebbit, 20 April 1987: © John Downing;
MT and Willie Whitelaw, 1984: Peter Brooker/Rex Features; State Opening of
Parliament, 13 Nov. 1986: Rex Features; MT and Cabinet, 13 Oct. 1989: PA
Archive/PA Photos; Sir Charles Powell outside 10 Downing St, 25 March 1991:
Jonathan Player/Rex Features; Sir Alfred Sherman, 23 Oct. 1987: PA Archive/PA
Photos; MT and Bernard Ingham, 1986: Herbie Knott/Rex Features; John Hoskyns,
20 March 1984: PA Archive/PA Photos

4–5 MT dancing with Kenneth Kaunda, 6 Aug. 1979: AP/PA Photos; MT, South
Armagh, 29 Aug. 1979: © PA Photos/Topfoto; *Time* cover, 19 April 1982: Time &
Life Pictures/Getty Images; MT in the Falklands, 10 Jan. 1983: Topham/AP; MT
and Indira Gandhi, April 1981: © John Downing; Orgreave, 1984: Photofusion/
© Julia Martin; MT's hotel bathroom after bombing, Brighton, 14 Oct. 1984:
© Bettmann/CORBIS; Grand Hotel, Brighton, 12 Oct. 1984: Camera Press;
Dennis, MT and Crawfie, 12 Oct. 1984: © John Downing

6–7 MT and Helmut Schmidt, 11 May 1979: © John Downing; MT and Helmut Kohl,
Feb. 1988: Time & Life Pictures/Getty Images; MT with Gorbachev, Dec. 1987:
The Daily Telegraph; MT and Lech Wałęsa, 1988: Topfoto/AP; MT at economic
summit, 6 June 1984: © Bettmann/CORBIS; MT and François Mitterrand, 13 Feb.
1986: PA Archive/PA Photos; MT and Geoffrey Howe, 1983: Camera Press

8 MT and Reagan, 26 Feb. 1981: PA Archive/PA Photos; MT and George H. Bush,
24 Nov. 1989: Time & Life Pictures/Getty Images; MT and Reagan, Washington,
16 Nov. 1988: Sipa Press/Rex Features

Third section

1 Anti-poll tax demonstration, March 1990: © Reuters/CORBIS

2–3 MT and Peter Morrison, 22 Oct. 1990: Tony Harris/PA Archive/PA Photos;

Geoffrey Howe, House of Commons, 13 Nov. 1990: PA Archive/PA Photos; Michael Heseltine, 22 Nov. 1990: Getty Images; MT, House of Commons, 22 Nov. 1990: PA Archive/PA Photos; MT outside 10 Downing St, 28 Nov. 1990: Sean Dempsey/PA Archive/PA Photos

4–5 MT in Zagreb, Sept. 1998: official Croatian government photo, courtesy of Churchill Archive Centre, Cambridge, and the Margaret Thatcher Archive Trust; MT and Vaclav Klaus in Prague, Nov. 1999: Associated Press; MT in front of Pinochet poster, Oct. 1999: Phil Noble/PA Archive/PA Photos; MT and John Major, 16 April 1997: Associated Press; MT and William Hague, Oct. 1998: Camera Press; MT and Tony Blair, June 2007: Ian Jones/*The Daily Telegraph*; MT and Gordon Brown, 13 Sept. 2007: Sang Tan/AP/PA Photos

6-7 MT at the Order of the Garter ceremony, 17 June 2002: Camera Press/Rota; MT at State Opening of Parliament, Nov. 2002: Camera Press; MT at Reagan's state funeral, 9 June 2004: Associated Press; MT at Denis's funeral, 3 July 2003: Brian Smith/*The Daily Telegraph*; MT and family at Denis's memorial service, 30 Oct. 2003: Stephen Lock/*The Daily Telegraph*

8   MT and Chelsea Pensioners, Feb. 2008: Ian Nicholson/PA.

INDEX

Robin Harris worked for the Conservative Party from 1978, and increasingly closely with Margaret Thatcher herself from 1985, writing her speeches and advising on policy. By the close of her premiership, he was probably the most trusted member of her political team at Downing Street, and he left Number Ten with her. As a member of her personal staff, he then drafted the two volumes of her autobiography and a further book on her behalf. After Margaret Thatcher's retirement from public life, Robin continued to see her regularly.